Agile Data Warehousing

Agile Data Warehousing

Delivering World-Class Business Intelligence Systems Using Scrum and XP

Ralph Hughes and the Ceregenics Data Management Team

iUniverse, Inc.
New York Bloomington Shanghai

Agile Data Warehousing
Delivering World-Class Business Intelligence Systems Using Scrum and XP

Copyright © 2008 by Ceregenics, Inc.

All rights reserved. No part of this book may be used or reproduced by any means, graphic, electronic, or mechanical, including photocopying, recording, taping or by any information storage retrieval system without the written permission of the publisher except in the case of brief quotations embodied in critical articles and reviews.

iUniverse books may be ordered through booksellers or by contacting:

iUniverse
1663 Liberty Drive
Bloomington, IN 47403
www.iuniverse.com
1-800-Authors (1-800-288-4677)

Because of the dynamic nature of the Internet, any Web addresses or links contained in this book may have changed since publication and may no longer be valid.

The views expressed in this work are solely those of the author and do not necessarily reflect the views of the publisher, and the publisher hereby disclaims any responsibility for them.

ISBN: 978-0-595-47167-6 (pbk)
ISBN: 978-0-595-91447-0 (ebk)

Printed in the United States of America

Contents

List of Illustrations vii

List of Tables ix

Preface xi

Chapter 1—ADW Motivation and Overview 1

Chapter 2—Generic Scrum in a Nutshell 23

Chapter 3—User Stories for Agile Warehousing 58

Chapter 4—Avoiding Overcommitment with Agile Estimation 92

Chapter 5—Adapting Scrum for Data Warehousing 127

Chapter 6—Starting and Scaling Agile Warehousing Teams 173

Chapter 7—ADW as a Demonstrably Mature Method 216

Chapter 8—Managing Adversity 251

About the Author 285

Acronyms And Initialisms Used 287

References 289

Index 295

List of Illustrations

Figure 1.1:	"Disappointment Cycle" of Many Waterfall Projects	4
Figure 1.2:	Six Stages of ADW Team Development	14
Figure 1.3:	Impact of Agile Data Warehousing upon PMI PMBOK Disciplines	15
Figure 1.4:	Impact of Agile Data Warehousing upon CMMI-DEV Process Areas	16
Figure 1.5:	Components of ADW Assembled into a CMM-Compliant Method	19
Figure 2.1:	Three Cycles of Generic Scrum	26
Figure 2.2:	Simplified Representation of a Scrum Task Board	38
Figure 2.3:	Typical Scrum Burndown Chart	40
Figure 2.4:	Scrum Burndown Chart Adapted to Show Scope Creep	41
Figure 3.1:	Product Owner's Verbalization Cycle	66
Figure 3.2:	Back-End User Epic Decomposition	71
Figure 3.3:	Front-End User Epic Decomposition	71
Figure 3.4:	Decomposing One Epic into Themes and Stories	72
Figure 3.5:	Integrating the Verbalization Cycle with Generic Scrum	74
Figure 4.1:	Distribution of Waterfall Estimates	99
Figure 4.2:	ADW Estimates Are Usable Because They Have Much Less Variation	100
Figure 4.3:	Steps in the Estimation Cycle Overlaid on a Sprint Cycle	102
Figure 4.4:	Tracking Team Progress Using an RLE Burndown Chart	112
Figure 4.5:	Two Possible RLE Trends Indicating Serious Challenges	114
Figure 4.6:	Using Sprint Burndown Chart to Calculate Velocity	117
Figure 4.7:	Extrapolating Team Velocity upon Early Sprint Completion	118
Figure 4.8:	Making Impact of Scope Creep Clearly Discernable	121
Figure 4.9:	Velocity Measurements Must Factor for Scope Creep	122
Figure 5.1:	Schematic Portrayal of an ORDERS Subject Area	129
Figure 5.2:	Tiered Data Model	130

Figure 5.3:	Process Flow Diagram	133
Figure 5.4:	TDM Clarity Suffers When Entities Are Combined for Performance	137
Figure 5.5:	Devising a Strategy to Manage Complex Warehouse Testing	154
Figure 5.6:	Each Scenario Must Iterate through Layers and Tiers	155
Figure 5.7:	Components and Actions of Automated and Continuous Integration Testing	159
Figure 5.8:	With Proper Design, ACIT Can Test Much of a Front-End Application	162
Figure 5.9:	Different Activities Peak at Different Times under Any Method	166
Figure 5.10:	Pipelined Delivery Squads	167
Figure 6.1:	ADW Testing is a Shared Responsibility	186
Figure 6.2:	Partitioning Work between Multiple Teams	200
Figure 6.3:	Data Topology Diagram for a Pharma/Biotech BI Program	202
Figure 6.4:	"Critical Chain" Is the Project's Critical Path after Resource Leveling	205
Figure 6.5:	Critical Chain Shortens Planned Durations by Pooling Variances	206
Figure 6.6:	Managing by Critical Chain Concentrates on Buffer Recovery	209
Figure 6.7:	Scaling Agile Data Warehousing for Large BI Programs	211
Figure 6.8:	Planning Geographic Distribution of an ADW Team	213
Figure 7.1:	Components of the SEI's Capability Maturity Model	219
Figure 7.2:	ADW "Time Multiplexes" the Phases of the Waterfall Approach	229
Figure 7.3:	ADW Can Be Presented as a "CMM Pre-Processor"	247
Figure 8.1:	Standard Risk Exposure Analysis	258
Figure 8.2:	Risk Exposure Analysis Updated for an Agile Approach	260
Figure 8.3:	A Translation Layer Frees ADW Teams to Develop with Speed	277

List of Tables

Table 2.1:	Principles Behind the Agile Manifesto	25
Table 4.1:	Twelve Objectives for Good Estimation	101
Table 5.1:	Typical Back-End (ETL) Patterns for Data Warehousing	141
Table 5.2:	Typical Front-End Patterns for Data Warehousing	142
Table 6.1:	Desired "Abilities" for Good Architectural Designs	176
Table 6.2:	Realistic Timelines by ADW Stage	189
Table 7.1:	Process Areas of CMMI-DEV v1.2	220
Table 7.2:	CMMI-DEV Generic Goals and Practices	222
Table 7.3:	Sample CMM Practices for Planning, Requirements, and Development	226
Table 8.1:	Financial Performance of the Same Project under Contrasting Methods	262
Table 8.2:	Summary of Financial Performance of Two Approaches	262
Table 8.3:	Comparative DPI Values While Development is Underway	264

Preface

This book is special in that it holds over ten years of research by Ceregenics, Inc. into how to make development teams faster and more effective at building data warehouses. We call the results "Agile Data Warehousing." Given that the typical data warehouse can cost several million dollars to build and deploy, if this technique can reduce the required effort by even a third, then it offers the practitioner a large financial return. But perhaps more important are the shorter delivery times and improved application quality that we achieved with our new approach. Business intelligence is the art of transforming enormous amounts of raw data into precisely the information needed to make crucial business decisions. If good decisions allow a company to market more accurately, reduce its production costs, or amplify its ability to fill orders, then a software engineering method leading to faster and better development of data warehouses offers more than cost savings. It could be a pillar to a company's continued survival, and even the key to its competitive success.

We were lucky to be able to refine our Agile Data Warehousing method while building business intelligence systems for Fortune 100 and 500 firms, and we have summarized what we learned in this series of books. In this first volume, we will present how we:

- took two generic Agile approaches which were conceived for building front-end applications rather than data warehouses
- adapted them for business intelligence projects
- groomed the result into a bona fide development method
- demonstrated that the method can pass a formal CMM, SOX, or FDA audit
- avoided or repaired the "political" upheaval radical change often precipitates in a company with a traditional information systems environment

Rarely does a consulting firm roll up all it knows about a subject as valuable as rapid data warehousing and place it into a book. To many, it would make more business sense to hoard the knowledge and trickle it slowly to paying clients. The topic of this book, however, is *Agile* data warehousing. With its many intersections with the Open Source movement, Agile software development revolves around a more broad-minded and inclusive business model. To put it succinctly, Agile development is too big, exciting, and important to keep under wraps.

This notion may be hard to believe at first, but only a first reading of the Agile manifesto and its twelve principles (www.agilemanifesto.org) will convince even cynical readers that this innovative software community has assembled something new and vital: an approach where everyone—consultants, developers, and customers alike—finds more of what he wants by following a simpler way. Agile simply makes software development easier, and because of that, it is growing quickly in popularity. We foresee that someday soon, when Agile reaches a "critical mass" within the business intelligence world, newly-formed project teams will require far less time to get organized and become productive. Developers will instead get to work right away, doing what they love: building software that creates value. Freed by Agile from the mind-numbing, detailed specification documents we used to spend endless meetings reviewing, our teams will instead deliver far more of what our customers love: well-built business intelligence applications.

Some further context will make the appeal of this vision more clear. Since starting in the data warehousing subprofession in the mid 1980s, my associates and I have witnessed many business intelligence efforts that turned out badly and which were absolutely miserable experiences for everyone involved. Post mortem reviews on these projects revealed the same root causes time and time again, such as poorly expressed requirements, unengaged users, false starts, long delivery times that exhausted executive support, excessively detailed procedures paralyzing even those who knew what needed to be built. The only thing that ever seemed to save a troubled project from disaster was a small cadre of dedicated developers who decided to gather in a "war room," roll up their sleeves, and work eye-to-eye with the business experts until they got the application right. When such a fever took hold, paper documents and much of the traditional "waterfall" method that created them were tossed to one side. All that mattered was how much working, bullet-proof code we were able to put online each day. Sure, there were some gaps in the first version to see production, but users got to look through real, integrated and aggregated business data. They would mull over the numbers and then approach us with instructions on how to make them better. As the deadline loomed, three or four versions of software got a turn online, and end users grew increasingly excited about the formerly hidden corners of their business that they could now see, explore, understand, and optimize.

After several such experiences, the natural question was "Why not work like that from the start?" Maybe, if we put the team in a "war room" on day one, we could see the same rapid results without having to go through a mounting crisis. But how does a project manager organize a new effort so that it has on the one hand a sense of urgency, and on the other a sustainable pace? For quality's sake, we need the developers and business experts to stay fully engaged with the project throughout the many months required to build an enterprise data warehouse. Furthermore, what process could a team follow so that it skips the overwhelming portion of traditional methods that produce non-functional artifacts, such as intermediary documents and completed review sheets, rather than working code?

It was in this frame of mind that we began reading the innovative works of the object oriented programming community where they extolled the "lightweight" development methods they had invented. We were thrilled at the notion of "maximizing the work not done," planning to invest all the energy saved into building further data transformation modules and analysis front-ends. There was one problem with all the new approaches we considered, however. As far as database applications go, these "Agile" techniques were primarily focused upon data capture systems rather than reporting and analysis. Since no one seemed to be applying the new paradigm to decision support, executive information, and adaptive analytical systems, we decided to adapt them ourselves.

We quickly found that, where it is easy to sketch an approach in the abstract, a mere approach is still not "ready for prime time." Even the best approach needs to be cultivated and refined into a step-by-step method that teams can follow. So, though we started out hoping to find a complete primer on Agile data warehousing, we had to settle instead for the school of hard knocks. Desiring to repeat as few mistakes as possible, we kept a journal of all we discovered and invented, and this book is the distillation of those notes. It lists the major policy decisions that will allow experienced developers to jump from Agile as a good idea to Agile Data Warehousing, a deployable method. We seek to steer the reader clear of as many ineffective practices of the waterfall approach as possible. Because the amount of material we offer is large, we also provide within this volume a suggested learning path for a new team. Accordingly, our method of Agile Data Warehousing is not an all-or-nothing proposition. Instead this book can be skimmed quickly for a starting point, and then kept close at hand for the moment when the team is ready to take its next step with the method.

As the one who transcribed and organized our collected notes, I was happy to have a multi-faceted background in business intelligence to draw upon. Starting out long ago as an econometrician, I was certainly accustomed to the powerful insights that large data sets can provide those who know how to conjure the spirits within them. During the following decade as a data warehouse developer for both front and back-end applications, I acquired many good litmus tests for practicality, all of which came in handy as we learned and experimented with several Agile methods. In these last ten years, in which I have served as a solutions architect and project manager within our company's business intelligence practice, I developed a more enterprise-wide perspective and an appreciation for how project management techniques must dovetail with program management methods. And finally, the training I acquired for the PMI Project Management Professional and the Certified Scrum Master certifications revealed to me that all technical knowledge acquires value only when it can be communicated to business individuals with little or no technical training. Ultimately, it is these business users who must channel all that data warehousing has to offer into company-wide programs of change.

Though derived from my experience and that of my associates at Ceregenics, this book was certainly larger than a small team could have achieved alone. My deepest gratitude goes to those who augmented our efforts, making this book possible. Sandy Schmidt and Ken Chomic provide invaluable insights from an outside perspective on the technical and management issues involved when adapting and introducing something as radical as Agile into the typical corporate environment. They spent many hours reading initial drafts for content and helped hammer our initially fragmented ideas into a coherent whole. Dave Dubas and Jim Hyatt graciously volunteered an all-essential final proofreading and sanity check of the final draft. And always there to fill any remaining gaps was the tireless Carole Twohey. Together these individuals provided all the missing ingredients that turned a sketchy recipe and a handful of raw ingredients into the nutritious and carefully presented meal we set before the reader now.

Last but not least, I would like to thank all of our many clients who had the vision and courage to try with Ceregenics a new way of building software. They never expressed any doubts, but there had to be times when the chaos within the project room, where a team was learning to "code at the speed of thought," must have caused them to wonder if they should have let some other company blaze the trail. "You can always tell the true pioneers," one customer shared with me during a recent retrospective. "They're the ones with the arrows in their backs." If the material within this volume can help the reader dodge even a few of those arrows, then the long hours it has taken to publish this work will have been worth it.

—Ralph Hughes, MA, PMP, CSM
ralph.hughes@ceregenics.com

Jokes aside, this book details how to deploy Agile Data Warehousing as a fully mature development method

Chapter 1
ADW Motivation and Overview

Cheaper, faster, better. Any book even hinting at a new methodology needs to make a promise such as this to those who would take the time to read it and try its recommendations. The material that we have assembled in this volume presents a novel means of delivering business intelligence solutions, one far more robust than just an Agile approach but yet still not as hermetically sealed from further adaptation as a commercially-purchased, waterfall methodology. We have used it repeatedly to deliver BI solutions that were cheaper, faster, better—to the delight of our customers. Accordingly, we will start our presentation with a value proposition for the Agile Data Warehousing method, a proposition we will strive to deliver upon in the chapters that follow:

> *Agile Data Warehousing (ADW) is the application of two Agile development approaches—Scrum and Extreme Programming—to the specific challenges of data warehousing and business intelligence. By switching to embedded business users for requirements and self-organized teams for development, ADW strips away all but the most essential elements of the development process and thereby realizes a tremendous boost in development speed. From this starting point, ADW then offers five further stages by which a new development team can incrementally refine their work habits, achieving far greater effectiveness in four key areas: requirements definition, level-of-effort estimation, consistent and compliant designs, and error-free deliverables. Though it requires some fundamentally different arrangements in team make-up and the developers' work space, ADW can be "packaged" to fit within the larger notions of program management found in a typical Enterprise Information Systems department, and once fully applied should drive out at least forty percent of the cost out of developing business intelligence systems as well as ninety percent of the risk.*

Admittedly there is a plethora of writings today describing Scrum and XP in general, yet these materials are geared toward developers building software of any type. In contrast, the content in this book and its two companion volumes is specifically designed for data warehousing projects. This focus narrows the context of the development challenge considerably, allowing us to employ BI-specific tools and techniques, enabling us to cut yet more corners and deliver a new release even more quickly than with generic Scrum or XP alone.

Naturally, achieving breakthrough performance in BI development will require some changes, including:

- the physical environment developers work in
- the role of the project manager
- the way we do requirements
- the way we do estimates
- the way we do design
- the way we code and test
- the way we document
- the way we implement the system
- the way we relate to other corporate departments such as Information Systems
- the way we relate to other business stakeholders besides the project's sponsor

This book details how we have successfully applied the Agile methods of Scrum and XP to data warehousing, attending to all the adaptations listed above. The overarching theme throughout the material is how to evolve the paradigms underlying our work so that we can move consistently toward a more "lightweight" approach—investing less labor in to-be documents and procedural ceremony, and more working code for data transformation and presentation, generating business value. This theme is exactly what many Scrum and XP writers have in mind when they describe Agile as "the art of maximizing the work not done."

Though the above objectives may seem to be an ambitious overhaul of development practices, the chapters below lay out a step-by-step means of implementing Agile Data Warehousing in easily digestible increments, the final result being a straight-forward method that is easy for developers to follow and self-police, in contrast to the "process heavy" competitors that have arisen out of the CMMI or PMI traditions. (See the List of Acronyms for any initialisms that may be unfamiliar).

Such a claim is not as brash as it might first appear—waterfall-based methods are, in fact, highly over-engineered, wasting time and money on overly-careful specification-and-review cycles. As we will detail in the next chapter, even a little research quickly reveals that the waterfall approach is based upon entirely the wrong model for software development, to the extent where its inventors in the Department of Defense eventually had to disavow the paradigm entirely. Retrofitting data warehouse methods for "Agile," therefore, is in many ways simply the data management profession recovering its senses after many decades of unfortunately misguided efforts.

Yet depicting Agile data warehousing as a bold, new approach to business intelligence is exactly the wrong way for us to present the method. First, because it is neither bold nor

new in many of its components, and secondly, because brashness
opposition from everyone in the corporate Information Technolo
is not participating in the organization's first Agile project. The
fact, started out as old-school project managers and systems archi
approaches only after a great many hours spent in research and
looking back upon our latest Agile projects, we would describe
data warehousing as still an 80/20 mix of Agile methods with
based development habits.

So let us instead kick off this book with a more balanced introduction than the bold and naked value proposition above would lead readers to expect. First, we will enumerate a few themes we repeatedly find at work in data warehousing projects today, regrettable patterns which led us to look for a better approach to our profession. Secondly, we will provide an outline of the ADW method to give readers a quick notion of the material ahead. Third, we will place that outline into the context of the other two volumes of this series, so that Agile Data Warehousing can be seen as not only a working method, but also as a detailed reference model for a business intelligence program, complete with architectural and engineering elements.

With a better notion of what ADW comprises, we will be able to describe how ADW can be introduced into the organization as an evolution for, rather than as a revolution against, traditional business intelligence development methods—a desirable goal given that we want to keep the peace with all stakeholders and give the method its best chance to succeed in any organization. We will then close this introduction with some caveats we would like kept in mind as the reader considers the material in the chapters ahead.

LAMENTABLE PATTERNS IN WATERFALL BI PROJECTS

To set the context for why Agile data warehousing is both necessary and pragmatic, readers might consider how well their own experiences align with the following dynamics that we find at work in large Information Systems departments pursuing business intelligence projects using traditional methods.

Software development yields notoriously poor ROI

One need spend only a few years in a typical corporation's Information Systems (IS) department to see more than a handful of failed projects. Indeed, the "software development crisis" has been well-documented at a national level by such studies as The Standish Group's series of "Chaos Reports." In a multi-year survey of 365 companies, these studies found that if one defines "success" as a project delivered on time, on budget, and with all the promised features, any project over $1M (1998 dollars) had more than a 50 percent chance to fail.

Yet, project failure is not a simple binary event that one can avoid once forewarned. Our experience with non-Agile data warehousing is that supposedly single-pass waterfall projects often iterate themselves "into the ground." **Figure 1.1** depicts this typical chain of events, which we labeled the "Disappointment Cycle." In this pattern, a sponsor undertakes a business intelligence project with great hopes for high value at reasonable cost. As the development team wades into the realities of the data and often the dysfunctional nature of the company's IS infrastructure, the project experiences a series of crises in which the sponsors must repeatedly revise downward their hopes amid escalating cost estimates. Often this process ends with the sponsors demanding the development team simply "slam whatever you have into production now" so that they can claim at least a partial victory before moving on to another project (or another job). This lamentable pattern appears as

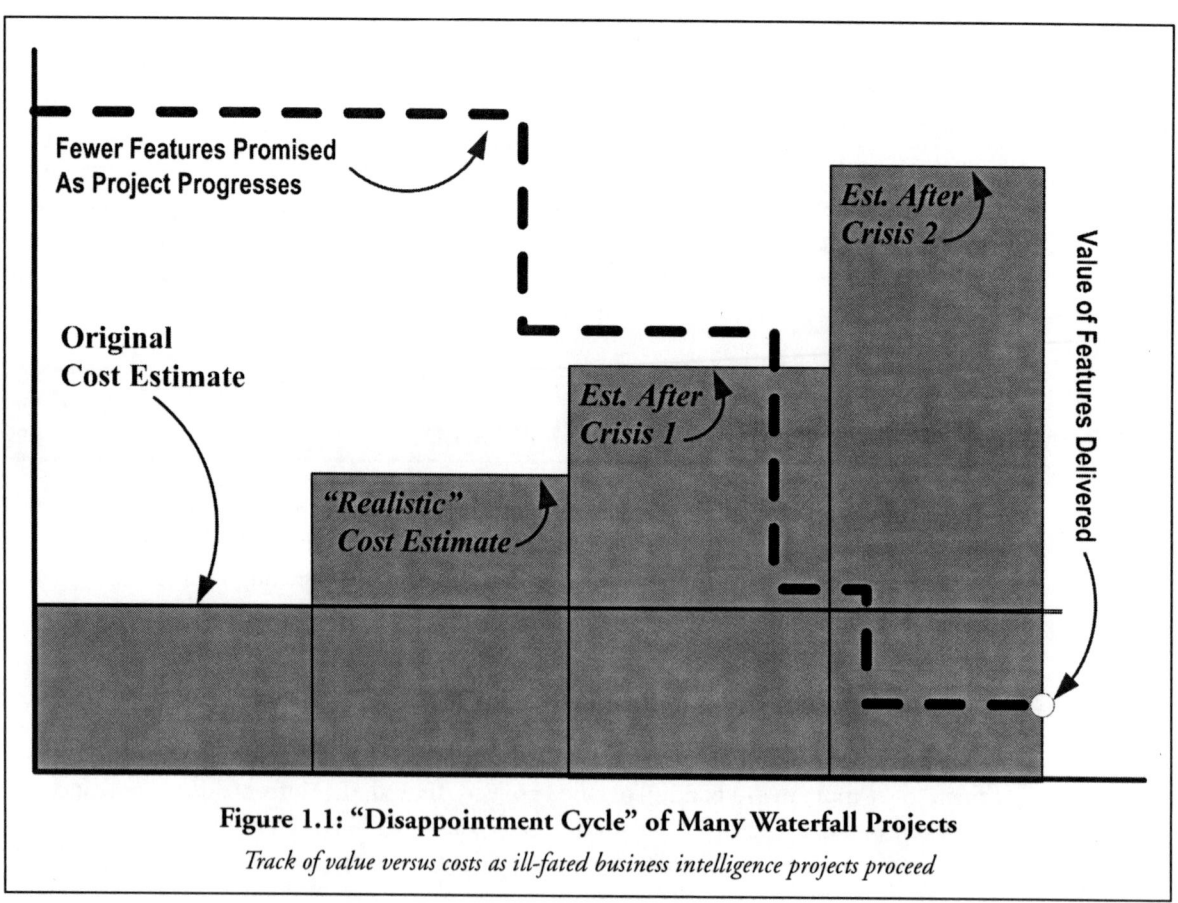

Figure 1.1: "Disappointment Cycle" of Many Waterfall Projects
Track of value versus costs as ill-fated business intelligence projects proceed

a cycle because, often in ignorance of incremental development techniques, the organization decides that it must pursue its waterfall method even more intensively during the next project in order to get satisfactory results.

Customers are increasingly impatient to get BI benefits

Whether because they have seen first hand how problematic software development can be, or simply because of the increasing competitiveness of the global economy, customers today seem far less willing to be patient with protracted BI projects. Whereas some warehousing professionals still subscribe to an Inmon-esqe "big bang" approach where one takes many months to first complete an enterprise data model and then builds out the appropriate subject areas over the ensuing three or four years [Inmon 2001], the majority of customers today see too much risk in this path and want instead tangible results from the project within the first quarter or two. This impatience places a great strain upon a BI team who holds to a waterfall method because the plan-driven approach, even for a moderately-sized project, requires a careful requirements and design specification process that easily exceeds the short timeframe the customer will allow.

BI teams cannot avoid tackling the unknown

Even with a careful requirements process, it is the rare BI project that does not encounter many nasty surprises once the team wades into the customer's dirty data and Byzantine business rules. We have come to accept that warehousing teams are never going to know at the start of a project even half of the detailed characteristics of the software they will eventually build. Though traditional methods allow for some "progressive elaboration," they still guide a team to create work breakdown structures and even budgeting estimates before the project kick off—as if the team members can read the future with even moderate accuracy. Such pretense risks placing the entire project plan on a baseline of very sketchy data, and makes falling into the "disappointment cycle" nearly inevitable.

Infrastructure problems cause problems late in the game

IS infrastructures can be dysfunctional for a wide range of reasons, such as missing test environments, undocumented standards, unaligned database versions, and overstressed messaging layers. When given a choice, BI sponsors would prefer to steer straight into any potentially fatal quirks of the IS platform as soon as detected, so as to risk as little wasted expenditure and elapsed time as possible. However, waterfall methods do not give the customer this choice. Instead they defer implementation toward the end of the project and thus postpone discovering these "land mines" and testing their lethality for as long as possible. As a result, projects that seemed to be on time for the majority of their development window suddenly "go red" as they approach implementation and then run intolerably late as the warehouse team struggles to bridge the chasm that opened before them during integration testing.

Business rules can also appear late in the plan

For several reasons, difficult business rules also tend to emerge only late in the typical warehouse project. To some extent, this tardy appearance stems from the fact that business rules tend to occur deep in the data model that cannot be fully considered until a couple of other strata such as staging and reference tables are implemented first. Most importantly, business users are the experts on these rules, but they rarely get to see warehouse data until the bulk of the transformation code has been written. As with infrastructure problems, the customer would gladly steer the team into these nettlesome rules earlier rather than later in order to minimize the investment placed at risk, so the typical project deprives the sponsor this important choice.

Projects take fatal risks in order to avoid a little rework

Even a well-trained project manager often works at odds to a BI customer's real interests. Project sponsors naturally want coders to hit potential landmines as soon as possible in order to minimize risk, but traditional, waterfall managers believe all requirements and design work should precede development. They accuse teams that start developing without complete requirement and design specs of unwittingly using a strategy of "ready, fire, aim." Yet, because their plans cause the team to defer building transforms and evaluating real results until the latter half of the project, these managers actually increase the possibility that a nasty surprise will appear late in development and require budget-killing amounts of rework to correct.

Specification and review cycles consume excessive effort

Being aware of the projects' fragility in the face of overlooked requirements, the classically-trained project manager demands thorough to-be documentation and extensive reviews. Traditional requirement documents provide three successive levels of detail describing user needs. The users must review this multi-layered list carefully and endorse its accuracy. Architects and developers must document the designs of the systems they would build to meet these requirements, and they must carefully peer review these long documents before a single line of code is written.

Because amassing all this information requires inordinate amounts of time, most waterfall methods advise their practitioners that the "development" phase should actually represent a surprisingly small portion of the overall project. Yet, when the customers funding the project hear such a statement they are tempted to scream in frustration. "Working code is what delivers business value," they would remind us. "Writing working code is what the project should be all about." Only those of us who are too steeped in process-heavy methods, enterprise data models, and thousand-line project plans are too far gone to understand the logic of this point of view.

To-be documents have too short a "shelf life"

Though the bulk of a project's budget can be invested in creating extensive requirements and design documents, simple changes in the business environment can completely obviate large portions of this work. Because business conditions change relentlessly, these documents have in fact a very short "shelf life" and would best be avoided if a way can be found to work accurately without them.

Project management consumes large portions of the budget

Building a warehouse is a complex undertaking, often involving project plans with a thousand tasks or more. Complex efforts like this naturally appear fraught with risk, so detailed progress reporting becomes imperative. Errors and omissions during the requirements and design phases require big changes to the project plan which, when first made and resources re-leveled, result in nearly incomprehensible extensions of timelines. To have any chance of success, the project must take on the expense of one or more project managers. Developers lose copious amounts of time completing time cards categorized by detailed work breakdown structure (WBS) items. They must sit in seemingly interminable status meetings to keep the project manager, who is tracking progress using a 1,000-line work plan, up-to-date. When added up, the management overhead that waterfall methods require is a serious expense to the customer. The money and labor lost to these techniques could shave months off the delivery timeline, if only they could be redirected toward the development of working software components.

Complex methods and elaborate plans rarely perform well

As mentioned above, the natural reaction to the Waterfall BI Disappointment Cycle is often to re-invest even more heavily in the same process, as if it were the lack of fervor that made past projects fail. Many organizations wanting a more thorough process opt for ponderously complex SEI or ISO standards such as CMMI or SPICE, yet rarely do these efforts amount to the cures they are supposed to be. Though enormous expense is sunk into training the organization how to comply with the intricacies of a particular framework or method, many aspects of the process are still glossed over in practice because individuals, including project managers themselves, find these tools high in ceremony and low in advantages, that is, they require more effort than they are worth. Processes concerned more with completing the right forms with the right words than actually getting software built only put the organization father behind in achieving the competitive objectives BI was supposed to help realize.

BI Teams need more time to acclimate to a project

Even if a team of seasoned BI developers is gathered for a warehouse project, its members will invariably admit at the end of the effort that they would be able to build the application far better if they could do it over again. This "learning curve" exists even for BI veterans because when one is placed into a *new* organization, tackling *new* business problems with a *new* combination of tools for extract, transform, and load (ETL) and front-end applications, the last project's "cookie cutter" becomes suddenly inappropriate. Yet traditional methods stipulate that project managers formulate a complete project plan before the project kickoff. Rather than gathering a development team and letting it work for a while in the actual problem space of the project, a traditional method assembles a *representative* team of developers and has it imagine the likely deliverables the project will involve, given some high-level notion of customer requirements. Project managers then estimate budget and timeline based upon this "probable" work breakdown structure, forecasting the resources needed for all phases of the project, including detailed requirements gathering. Unfortunately, planning a project before its requirements are understood in detail cannot avoid producing project plans that incorporate a grievously amount of unknowns, making the customer's next spin on the Disappointment Cycle a near certainty.

Customers need more time to learn about BI

In most project "post mortem" briefings, developers will lament about the quality of the requirements, especially how much was overlooked and misunderstood. Such costly miscues occur despite the fact that the customers sat in lengthy requirement review sessions and signed the requirements spec. Some of these errors arose from the customer being unable to forecast and sufficiently envision all of their data warehousing needs, but a larger percentage is rooted in the fact that many users do not understand what a BI front end looks like and what ETL can do. Customers, too, will emphatically conclude that they would do a far better job if they could do the project over again, because now they know enough about data warehousing to get real value out of BI. Paradoxically, both sides puzzle over how an elaborate waterfall method that took great lengths to prepare a excruciatingly detailed requirements specification still wasted large portions of the effort due to poor requirements.

GOALS FOR A BETTER METHOD

If we were to free our minds for just a moment from the plan-driven, process-heavy waterfall method lamented above, what would be the qualities of a better process that we would search for? In early 2001, representatives of several incremental and iterative development methods gathered at a ski resort in Utah to seek the common ground defining their collective search for alternatives to documentation-driven, heavyweight software engineering. [Agile 2001] The resulting "Agile Manifesto" released an enormous volume of inquiry and discussion among the software and project management professions, and quickly established incremental and iterative techniques as a polar alternative that should always be considered at the start of any project. It achieved this remarkable impact with a set of only four "cornerstones" that provide a consistent theme around which the dozen or so Agile approaches have continued to mature:

- Individuals and interactions over processes and tools
- Working software over comprehensive documentation
- Customer collaboration over contract negotiation
- Responding to change over following a plan

Hopefully, juxtaposing these notions to the unfortunate themes of the waterfall approach we listed earlier will enable the reader to glimpse the beginnings of a better method for building data warehousing applications. The details of translating the four Agile cornerstones into a new, more practical method for business intelligence projects is the focus of this book.

When the members of our BI practice first pondered how the Agile cornerstones could tangibly improve warehousing projects, especially those underway in the heavily regulated industries of pharmaceuticals and defense contracting in which we often serve, several concrete objectives instantly appeared:

- Transform large, risky warehouse projects into a serious of safer smaller deliverables
- Minimize to-be specification documents and committee review steps
- Let the BI team learn about the project and its problem before demanding full designs and detailed level-of-effort estimates from them

- Let the customers learn about BI in a low risk manner, and empower them to steer the team toward the elements of highest value, whether that be simply functionality or risk identification
- Drive each deliverable to near-delivery to "smoke out" both problems with the IT infrastructure and conflicts that a newly updated module might now have with other code units

To these objectives we would add one more that might not immediately suggest itself, but over time has proven to be indispensable: The approach must be able to avoid or mitigate opposition from traditionally-trained IT professionals who may feel threatened or maliciously dismissive of the lightweight methods Agile principles will engender.

Adapting our methods to achieve these objectives was itself an incremental process of trial-and-error, especially as we worked to adapt the new ideas to customer sites requiring a methodological formalism akin to CMM compliance (see Chapter 7). Looking back years later, we now believe we have arrived at a very usable baseline method for building BI in an Agile fashion. We refer to Agile Data Warehousing as a "baseline" because we took pains to keep it easy to adapt by an organization that chooses to deploy it. Though adaptable, the method is still packed with many practical solutions to the challenge of business intelligence, and so it should provide an enormous jumpstart for any team seeking a quick and accurate means of creating BI applications of high value.

A Quick Outline of Agile Data Warehousing

Shortly after reading the Agile Manifesto and its twelve companion principles, we believed we could simply take our favorite Agile approach and implement it wholesale on BI projects. The school of hard knocks quickly taught us that one cannot simply rope a half dozen or so people into a team and have them instantly "go Agile," no matter how highly motivated they may be. There are simply too many old, waterfall ideas to discard and even more new ideas to acquire, making Agile Data Warehousing a method that must be acquired a step at a time. We now believe the method is best presented by following the incremental learning that a new team would need to take in order to master and adapt it successfully. Accordingly, this book presents first an easy-to-grasp, general-purpose Agile starting point, and then progressively layers upon it methodological components in "bite-sized" chunks. Each new layer results in a solution that is more specific to data warehousing and consequently yields better results, as can be seen from the following outline of the learning path new ADW teams will take.

STAGE 0—COLOCATED, SELF-ORGANIZED TEAMS

This stage can be implemented on the first day of a new team because it strives for only three simple objectives:

- Colocating the team members in a shared workspace surrounded by dry erase boards where they can work closely together, relying on lightweight verbal and diagrammatic communication for collaborative designs and coding.
- Embedding the customer into the team as a "Product Owner," so that she can work eye-to-eye with the developers regarding the application the organization needs.
- Asking team members to organize their work in any way they prefer as long as they can transform a significant portion of the Product Owner's requests into "potentially shippable code" every two to four weeks.

As a starting point for the method, ADW in this stage draws upon two of the most streamlined Agile approaches, "Scrum" and "Extreme Programming" (XP). Because the team organizes its own work, a formal project manager is not needed. Instead one of the team members plays "Scrum Master" who can, with a small amount of outside training, keep the team moving forward by relying on only a few, amazingly simple tracking tools.

The team works in this minimalist environment for a few iterations (which Scrum calls "sprints"), with the quality of its work reviewed and approved by the business-based Product Owner at the end of each iteration of development. Though the work product during this preliminary phase can be incomplete and lack polish, the customer does become fully involved, and the team finds ways to meet pressing deadlines without wasting effort on to-be documentation. This achievement provides a solid foundation upon which the Scrum Master can begin to build the rest of the ADW method in five stages.

STAGE 1—USER EPIC DECOMPOSITION AND ESTIMATION SKILLS

This stage introduces the team's guiding Product Owner to several BI-specific architectural notions so that the team begins acquiring a common vocabulary, and so that the many intertwined details of a full BI implementation get addressed in an orderly fashion. The Scrum Master provides the Product Owner a more disciplined way to verbalize her requirements, one that draws upon over a half-dozen dimensions to define the deployable objects typically needed in a warehouse application. These dimensions span both the back end and front end of a warehouse, so that the Product Owner can use them to tightly specify any unit of functionality she might wish to request. It will take the Product Owner a few sprints to get fully comfortable with this framework because it requires her to learn a little about the data warehousing discipline. However, she will get to see the manifestation of her requests every few weeks, allowing her to verbalize requirements with increasing precision and certainty.

With the Product Owner now expressing her requests in precisely-worded descriptions, the developers of the team can begin deriving standard estimates for standard units of functionality. In this stage, the developers learn to estimate their work using the relative "size" of requirements, a technique which they will use to scope each development iteration and double-check the often spurious results of "ideal time" estimation used by waterfall methods. Standard design units and relative sized-based forecasting dramatically increases the team's understanding of how many requirements it can deliver with each sprint of coding.

STAGE 2—RELEASE PLANNING

With the Product Owner and developers now "dialed-in" on both the system they must build and on how fast they can create many of its components, they have learned enough that the Scrum Master can ask them to begin on the project's full release plan. In such a plan, the team sketches the full scope of the desired software release and the number of standard iterations it will take for it to deliver the remainder of the warehouse. ADW doggedly persists in exercising and improving the team's estimation skills to where the release plan acquires the precision required for an accurate funding request and to set a realistic scope for the project.

STAGE 3—REFERENCE MODELS AND TEST-LED DEVELOPMENT

Similar to the way Stage 1 provided greater structure for Product Owner's requirements, this stage elevates to its fullest expression the guidelines by which the developers will engineer their code. While they provide powerful engineering guidance, *reference models* keep the amount of formal, to-be specifications needed to standardize code down to an absolute minimum. *Test-led development* instills a high degree of quality into the code that the reference model shapes, providing a set of re-usable validation objects that will save large amounts of labor throughout the life of the warehouse, yet without wasting a single day on short-lived, to-be specifications.

STAGE 4—PIPELINED DELIVERY SQUADS

By the start of Stage 4, the ADW developers have become quite accustomed to the notion of self-organized teams, but feel the need for some specialization of tasks. They have also adopted such a high standard for their work that they have started feeling that the standard iteration is too short a time span to deliver the requirements with the level of quality desired. In this stage, ADW guides the team to re-organize a bit into semi-formal "squads" that each have a specialization such as "design," "coding," and "integration." By arranging these squads into a progressive pipeline, ADW gives each specialization a full iteration to do its work with full attention to quality and system validation. Yet, by keeping the squad assignments semi-formal, the team retains its overall ability to move labor about so as to keep the most important deliverables on track for a timely delivery.

STAGE 5—CONTINUOUS INTEGRATION TESTING

This final stage completes ADW's quality assurance strategy by establishing an integration environment into which every module is integrated as soon as a developer declares it "done." By continuously running validation routines against a candidate release using pre-defined data sets that should precisely yield the expected results, errors are detected nearly as soon as they are committed by the developer. Moreover, the "nightly builds" of the evolving release give downstream IT Operations and Support teams ample opportunities to verify and steer the evolution of the code they will soon inherit.

TRACKING THE MATURITY OF ADW TEAMS

Maintaining an important feature of the Agile approach upon which it is based, Agile Data Warehousing keeps the intricacies of the method to a minimum, depending as much as possible on the team itself to organize its own work in the most effective way given the project and the IT shop in which it works. Accordingly, each team will wend a unique path through the stages described above. Whereas the customer, wanting some planning information as soon as possible, will typically drive the team quite hard until they complete the release plan of Stage 2, the remaining stages will be completed with the level of thoroughness driven more by software engineering issues, allowing the team to linger too long in each stage of their maturity. Luckily, the stages themselves provide a means of tracking the team's mastery of the method and for choosing the area upon which to concentrate next.

Figure 1.2 depicts a likely level of ADW proficiency we believe a new team can reasonably reach within six months of starting a project. This chart should become progressively "filled out" as the team masters the method, and thus serves as a good review device for Product Owner and Scrum Master to periodically inspect together.

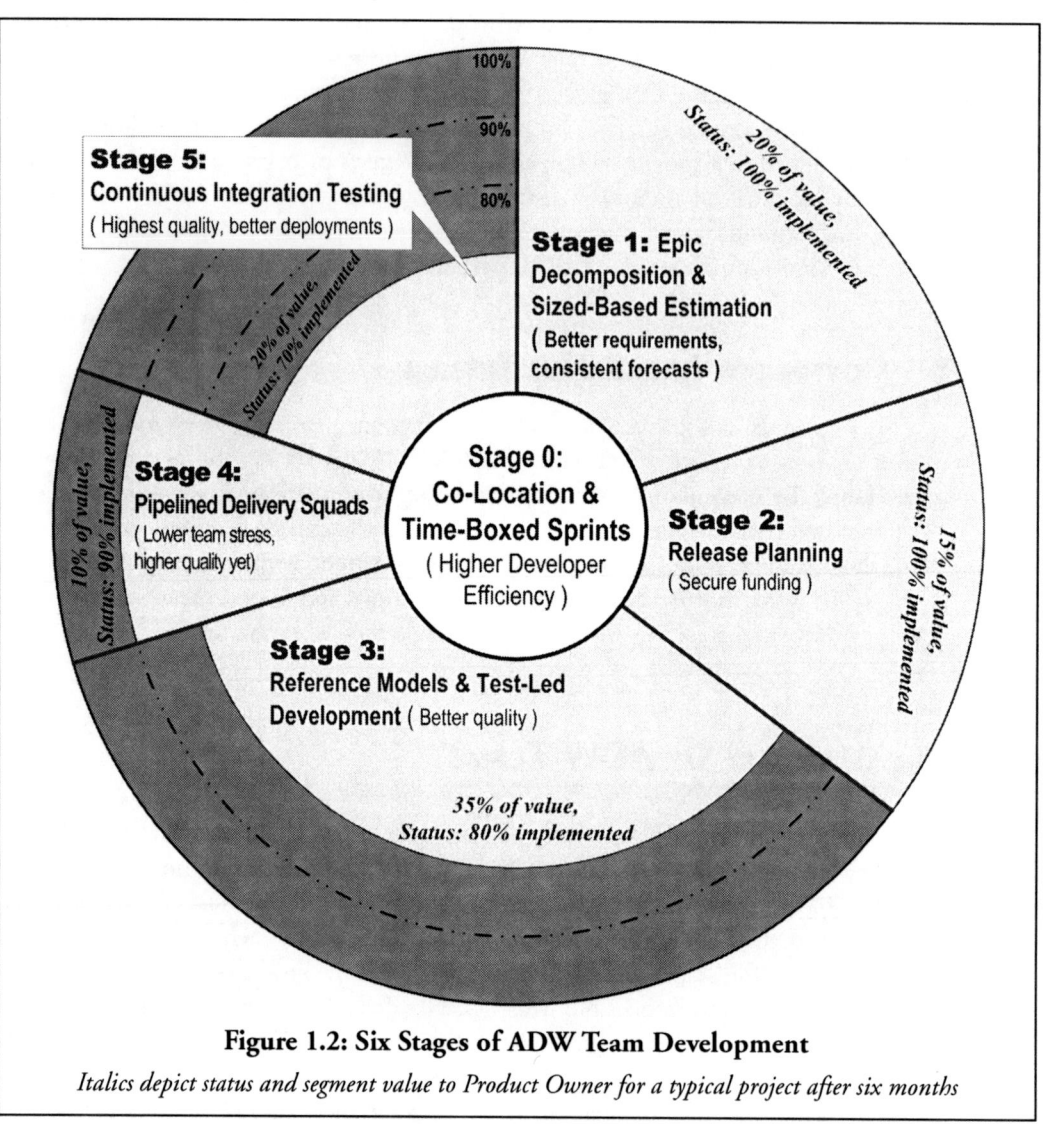

Figure 1.2: Six Stages of ADW Team Development
Italics depict status and segment value to Product Owner for a typical project after six months

Looking first at the full circle that frames the chart, we can see that its has five sections representing the stages described above. Rather than giving these wedges equal widths, however, we drew them so that they are sized according to the value each stage represents, according to the Product Owner, the Scrum Master, or the team as a whole. For the situation depicted in the figure, our hypothetical team used the relative-size estimation technique mentioned above to arrive at relative weightings of 8, 13, 8, 3, and 5 for Stages 1 through 5.

Atop of these framing sections, the figure next places a partial pie slice whose length reflects the team's appraisal of how completely it has achieved the goals of a given stage. In our example, the team rated itself as having acquired after six months all of the requirements and estimating skills needed for Stage 1 and 2, yet they feel less sure of their command of the reference model, test-led development, and pipelined delivery goals, and even less regarding continuous integration testing. Their Scrum Master should be able to inspire them to press on trying and mastering the full breadth of ADW because completing all five stages of ADW will yield them many important benefits, including:

- Far better requirements because the customer is embedded in the team and has a detailed method of translating business needs to well-defined BI work units
- Far better forecasting because the team has added sized-based estimation and draws upon real experience with the project
- Far less risk because it generates a steady stream of potentially shippable code modules
- Far better quality of output due to test-led development and continuous integration testing

Discipline	20%	40%	60%	80%
Communication				
Human Resources				
Integration	■			
Quality	■	■	■	
Scope	■	■	■	■
Risk	■	■	■	
Schedule	■	■		
Risk	■	■		
Cost	■			
Procurement				

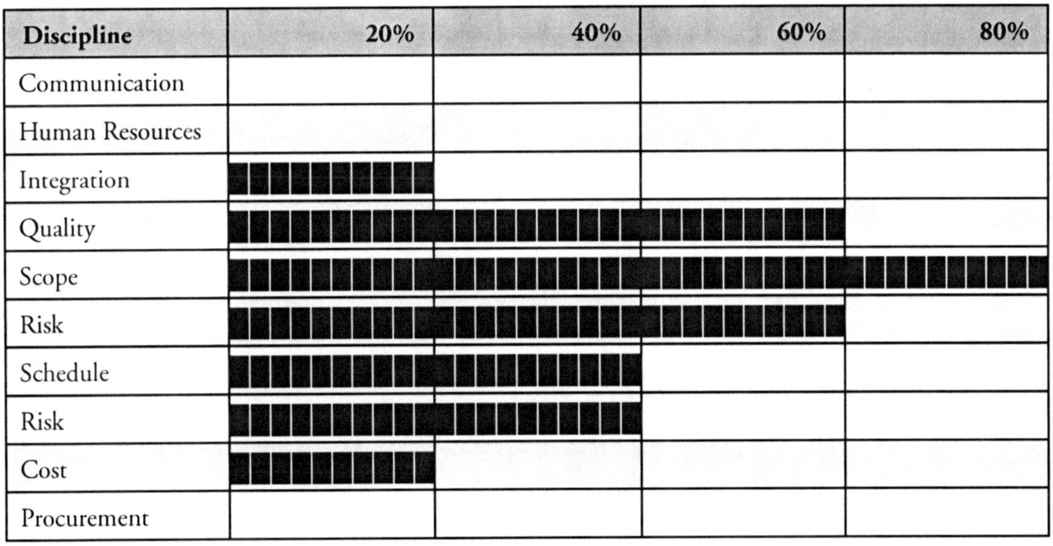

Figure 1.3: Impact of Agile Data Warehousing upon PMI PMBOK Disciplines

NOT A REVOLUTION, JUST AN IMPRESSIVE EVOLUTION

With our quick sketch of Agile Data Warehousing above, the reader might sense what we have seen in practice—Agile Data Warehouse teams quickly begin to deliver value for their BI customers with far greater efficiency of expenditures than traditional methods. But having a large impact—even a positive one—can actually work against a new practice if it is presented as a radical overhaul of an organization's customary work habits.

Luckily, the interface between ADW and the rest of the organization can be buffered so that its contrast with current practices does not appear as "revolutionary." Consider the first panel of **Figure 1.3**, where we have appraised ADW's impact on each of the nine management disciplines defined by the Project Management Institute's *Project Management Body of Knowledge* (PMBOK). The PMBOK applies to projects of all types, but arose from the best practices of the construction industry where the focus is upon creating a physical

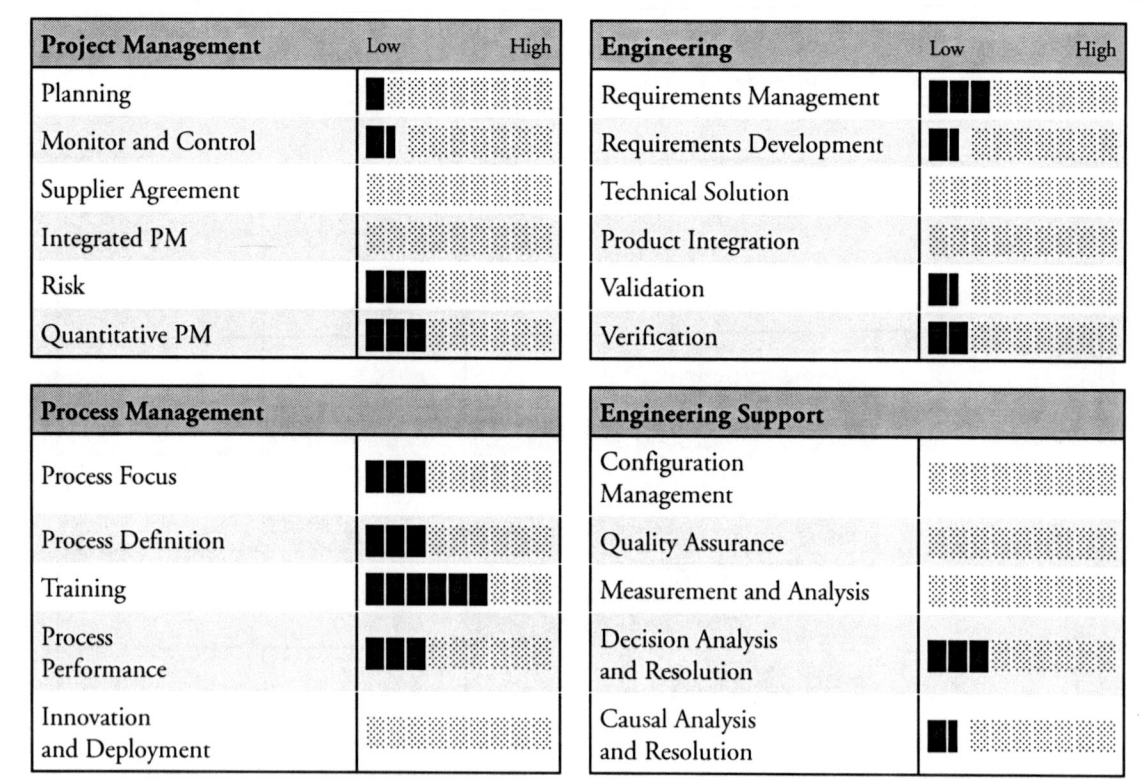

Figure 1.4: Impact of Agile Data Warehousing upon CMMI-DEV Process Areas

structure from a blueprint, and thus it has much in common with software engineering's waterfall approach.

In our experience, ADW—with its embedded Product Owner and self-organized teams—provides a more streamlined means of attending to what PMBOK calls Scope, Integration, and Risk Management. This does not create conflict with the rest of the organization, however, because these three management areas are predominantly inward-looking functions, concerned with organizing the work of the team rather than its interactions with the rest of the enterprise. The remaining PMBOK disciplines are outward-looking, where the ADW team will have to match the non-Agile mindset of the rest of the organization. A modest translation effort will probably be necessary in the areas of Cost and Quality Management because in those realms the two worlds share resources and enterprise compliance initiatives. Very few conflicts exist, however, with the last three standard disciplines of Procurement, Human Resources, and Communications. Thus, ADW can be presented as a focused evolution in development techniques that confines its changes to the project room because it interfaces with the rest of the organization through a standard, PMI-acceptable "wrapper."

Indeed, if ADW was a far-reaching revolution in software project management, it would certainly fail miserably when assessed with internationally formalized process maps such as SEI's *Capability Maturity Model* (CMM). Yet, as we will explore in Chapter 7, a careful review of CMM's twenty-two "process areas" reveals that only one of them, "Organizational Training," will require ADW to make some modest adaptations before it can provide the required and expected practices of a fully mature process. As can be seen in **Figure 1.4**, ADW can support the remainder of the CMM model with little to no reconstruction to the method at all.

SUBSEQUENT VOLUMES FOR ENGINEERING AND AUTOMATION

Agile Data Warehousing is a specific application of two Agile approaches—Scrum and XP—to the business intelligence problem space. Reflecting upon the numerous ways Agile techniques can accelerate BI teams, we have identified three major areas of innovation that we need to eventually present for the reader:

- Organizing how work flows between the development team and the enterprise
- Defining common patterns for the BI objects the team should build once a work package arrives
- Reducing the effort required to build these objects, so that the team has less work to do

This present volume focuses on the first area, that is, translating the customer's often inchoate notions of business needs into actionable work packages for the team, as well as connecting the results back to the sponsoring organization. Our intent will be to show how to combine the Agile approaches of Scrum and XP into a BI-specific manner to achieve worthy goals such as improving project requirements using lightweight *user stories*, preventing over commitment through size-based estimation, raising quality through continuous integration, and scaling up the effort beyond a single project to where it can manage entire data warehousing programs.

Building on the notion of *interfacing* the team to the customer and the rest of the organization, Volume 1 also contains chapters on managing the adversity that Agile often encounters within traditional Enterprise Information Systems (EIS) departments. Because adversaries often claim that Agile is "incomplete" or excessively tactical, we include a chapter detailing ADW's completeness in the eyes of CMMI-DEV, an international standard of methodological maturity.

Whereas Volume 1 will reference several important notions borrowed from XP such as test-led development and continuous integration testing, Volume 2 will provide us the space to "drill down" into these details of software engineering. Topics covered there will include a taxonomy for thorough unit and module testing, automated testing of ETL and report objects across the full breadth of the warehouse problem space, and a means of automatically generating system documentation from the code itself.

ADW combines the issues revolving about Scrum, XP, data warehousing, and method maturity in many intersecting ways. **Figure 1.5** provides a schematic of how these layer upon one another so readers can better orient themselves as they work their way through the coming chapters. Because CMM typifies the most rigorous examination one could make of a new method, we drew this figure to depict how the components of ADW build step-by-step upon generic Scrum and XP until they eventually reach CMM Level 5 compliance.

Because Volume 2 will be so focused upon design, we will also include therein the results of our survey for the most "agile" of the international standards for software architecture and design work. Applying these methods to the challenge of business intelligence, we will derive a baseline architectural description that can serve as a starting point for an enterprise data warehousing platform.

Finally, Volume 3 will look into reducing the work required to create and expand a data warehouse through automated development methods. The foundation for its techniques will include some rarely-discussed data paradigms including *associative* data models and *entity-attribute-value* (EAV) structures. We will explore the prime advantages of these models, especially the fact that their ETL can be code-generated from only a source data schema and a modicum of BI designer-provided metadata. Because providing competing data schemes creates the need to move between them as needed, our last volume will also include discussions of bridging data paradigms by means of *database refactoring* techniques applied to data warehousing.

Taken together, these three volumes communicate a constellation of skills summarized as Agile project management, Agile software engineering, and Agile data architecture for data warehousing, all packaged so that they can "slide" into the standard IS shop with a minimum of disruption while maximizing their effectiveness for an organization's business intelligence program. If the Agile techniques we present in our series can take data warehousing from a practice that only the largest firms can pursue, and transform it into an competitive advantage affordable by Fortune 1000 firms and beyond, we will consider our work successful.

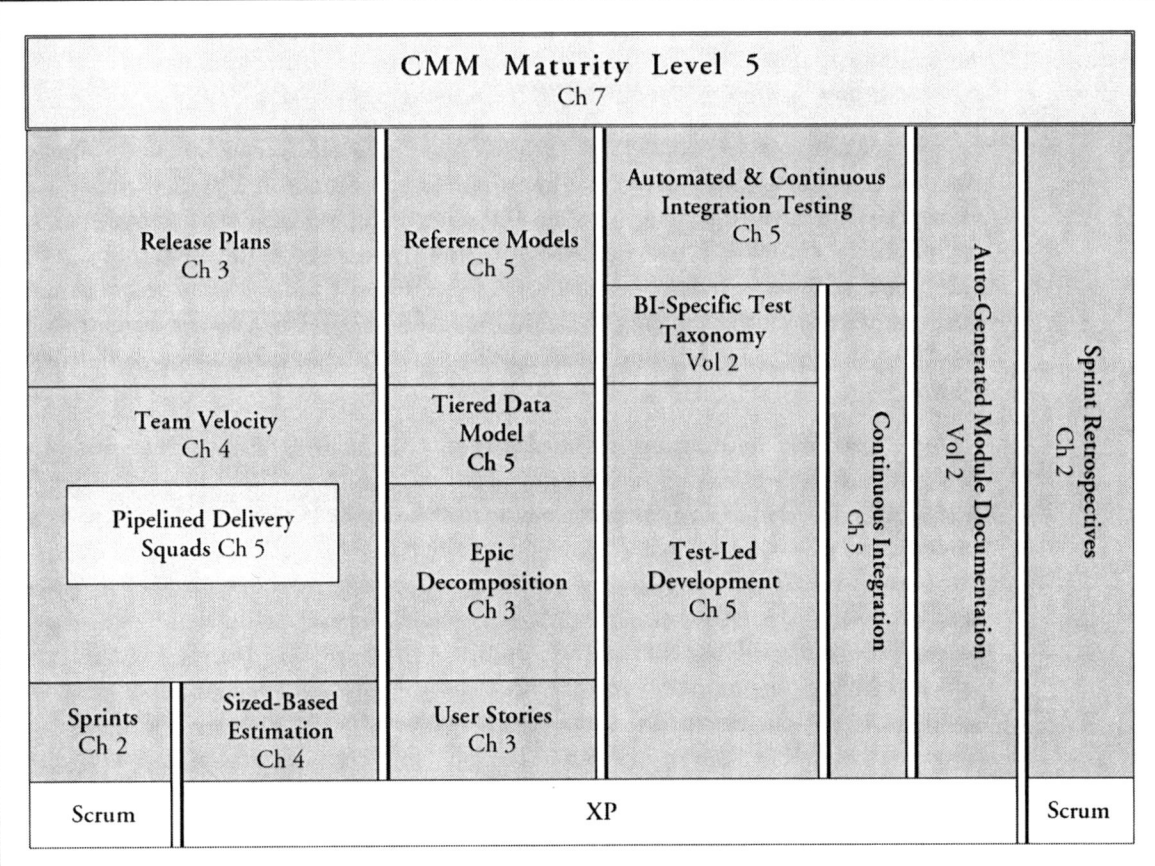

Figure 1.5: Components of ADW Assembled into a CMM-Compliant Method
Listed with coverage by chapter, all Volume 1 unless indicated

Caveat Emptor

Certainly "buyer beware" is not an auspicious way to close an introduction, but tackling such a large subject matter as Agile Data Warehousing naturally requires some small shortcuts that we do not want to employ without giving fair warning to the reader.

First, we should address some terminological matters, chief among them "business intelligence" versus "data warehousing." BI professionals must often re-phrase their statements in order to distinguish between an application of a front-end tool (such as Cognos or Hyperion), from a module built with an extract, transform, and load tool ("ETL," such as Informatica or Microsoft's DTS). For much of our presentation, the distinction between the terms "BI," "data warehousing," and "ETL" will be unnecessary because both worlds have so much overlap when it comes to defining requirements, building executable objects, validation and implementation. Yet, when it is necessary to be clear which realm we are discussing, we will switch our language to the terms "front end" and "back end" to signal end-user facing applications and ETL modules, respectively.

Secondly, we wish to acknowledge the notion of "approach" versus "method." *Approach* is a very broad term, and a particular approach such as Scrum or XP offers only a set of views about the nature of a large problem and some high-level ideas of how to re-tool one's techniques to address it. On the other hand, *methods*—especially those that are commercially purchased—come with such artifacts as precisely defined roles and responsibilities, business processes for channeling the actions of these roles, templates for formatting and validating deliverables, and time tables specifying which tasks should be completed by when.

Agile Data Warehousing, as presented in this series, admittedly falls in between these two extremes. It is clearly an elaboration upon the Scrum and XP *approaches*, defining several roles, key artifacts, and the sequencing of their usage. However, Scrum in particular emphasizes "self-organized work teams," and thereby inherently resists any attempt to transform it into a rigid and unevolving method. Instead, every organization is encouraged to evolve their actual practices toward a unique implementation of the Agile starting points. Due to these dynamics and the confines of space, we have therefore crafted ADW as the start of a method and even the basis for an Agile data warehousing "program," leaving many of the lowest-level details to the reader to derive from the specifics of their situation. Though we refer to ADW as a "method" in order to emphasize the many specifics we have added to the Agile "approaches" it incorporates, we still realize that by leaving much for the practitioner to define, we are using the term loosely.

Third, we understand that our presentation will seem predominantly oriented toward *back-end* issues. This emphasis arises naturally from the fact that data modeling and the ETL modules that load the resulting tables often consume sixty to ninety percent of a project's budget. Front-end tools are so much more nimble than ETL products, often adapting to large changes in end users' requirements with GUI-based modifications requiring little or no change in coded instructions. Shaping front ends can get more involved when the team begins to automate report generation and deploying standard script libraries to make all the GUI front ends appear and behave alike, but at that point precisely the front-end work becomes very much like ETL tasks, making our seeming emphasis on back-end issues all that more appropriate. For ADW, the unmaskable differences between front end and back end arise primarily with the issue of testing, which the reader will find addressed fully in Volume 2 of this series.

Fourth, we want to make clear that often in our practice, we find it as difficult as the next person to simultaneously please all the stakeholders in a complex organization equally. To survive politically, teams must sometimes find ways to be "different things to different people" by selectively emphasizing for a given audience the most pertinent aspects of their work. The Agile warehouse team has the choice, for example, of underlining the fact that every sprint produces potentially shippable code, or alternatively calling the first six iterations of a release "extended prototyping" because its work product will only be implemented during a single release step. Especially in the chapters of Volume 1 regarding method maturity and managing adversity, the reader will see this "slight of hand" called for repeatedly.

Yet, when does "putting your best foot forward" become outright misrepresentation or deceit? We do not have a single, air-tight answer to this important question. In practice, we attempt to give the most honest presentation of our complex work to each party that asks about what we are doing, expressing it in a way that matches the perspective of the person inquiring. We tend to risk the confusion that supplying alternative views can cause only when the project faces a complex hazard that must be understood simultaneously from multiple perspectives.

Keeping with the example above, to the Product Owners of the project, we describe our sprints as resulting in potentially shippable code, because a) it is an honest description, and b) tangible results that minimize project risk are very important to them. To the EIS Operations and Maintenance stakeholders, however, we describe our work as extensive prototyping because a) one can truly see the deliverables as incrementally defining the requirements, and b) their particular interest is having the candidate modules "pool up" in one location where they can perform code verification at a relaxed pace. Now, we could drive home to the EIS Operations and Maintenance (O&M) team that we are delivering every two weeks modules that we consider 95 percent complete and which therefore have many architectural decisions set "in stone," but that would only stir up needless conflict between customers and IT—needless in this case because O&M's interests are already addressed by giving them a place to inspect the code of release candidates as it accumulates.

Our purpose in mentioning this tricky matter here is to make clear that, when we state in the coming chapters that the Agile warehouse team must be "polymorphic" to keep the peace among all the stakeholders of their project, we understand that some ethical dilemmas exist. We realize that our recommendation to selectively present the various aspects of a large warehouse project could be abused, and that in every situation the reader will need to choose the most ethical means of resolving the conflicting interests involved.

Finally, we want to point out the admittedly imperfect solution that we employ for the gender problem confronting anyone writing in contemporary English. Our language does not include a neutral pronoun, yet today men and women make equal contributions to the world of data processing. There are several options for avoiding a verbal bias towards one sex, but unfortunately they all distort the writing in some fashion. As a baseline technique, we chose to refer to people filling singular, highly visible roles as "she," and to transform other references to plurals when possible, speaking of individuals as "he" when some other tactic, such as pluralization, was impractical. We believe that we did not impair the readability of the text with this convention. Where we might have failed in this regard, we hope the reader can keep in mind at least the motivation.

Chapter 2
Generic Scrum in a Nutshell

What is the general outline of the Agile approach called "Scrum"?

Why makes Scrum so much more effective than waterfall methods?

What can we say to convince skeptics to honestly consider trying a Scrum-based method?

Scrum is one of the simplest of the many iterative and incremental development (IID) methods available today, having stripped down the software development process to its core, value-generating activities. It prescribes only enough project management to make progress trackable by and transparent to both development team members and external stakeholders alike. One of its key features is to embed the customer into the development team, doing away with the voluminous specifications and time consuming committee reviews that underlie most waterfall methods. What remains is a process so un-encumbered with work of indirect value that an experienced Scrum Master can explain the method to the uninitiated developer in a half-hour with enough detail to gain almost immediate buy-in.

This chapter provides first a quick walkthrough of the generic Scrum process, much like the presentation that a Scrum Master would give a team of developers. A brief history of the origins of Scrum follows. We finish with an analysis of why Scrum works so well, hopefully giving the reader enough material to convince IT Management to support the first stage of Agile Data Warehousing, namely, a trial implementation of generic Scrum on a BI project.

Because it is light on prescribed tools and techniques, Scrum teams must typically fill in the approach, adapting it to their particular program and organization. In fact, most teams find that, although Scrum describes well how work packages should flow into the project, it says so little about how to build the application that they must immediately supplement it with software engineering techniques from elsewhere. The most common source for these supplemental practices is another Agile development approach called Extreme Programming (XP). Scrum's project management and XP's engineering techniques complement each other so well that many books and training programs actually combine them thoroughly, calling the entire mix "Scrum."

Even with the inclusion of XP engineering techniques, this "generic" version of Scrum is still a high-level approach. Practitioners must bridge for themselves the gap between the approach and the situation at hand. Accordingly, every implementation of Scrum between any two organizations or even two Scrum projects within the same enterprise will be organized differently in their details. Scrum and XP are covered well by many other writers, so our chapter here will provide only an outline of Scrum/XP, so that we can then turn to the details of adapting the generic approach for data warehousing. Readers wanting to research generic Scrum and XP more deeply will find suggested readings at the end of this chapter.

ITERATIONS AND STORIES

A proper presentation of any Agile approach must begin with the two components that the Agile alliance has placed in the public domain to guide its practitioners: 1) The four point Agile Manifesto which we outlined in the introduction, and 2) the more detailed Agile Principles which we list in Table 2.1 below. Though compelling to anyone tired of the process-heavy waterfall paradigm, the twelve Agile Principles are still quite general, making it easy to see how the notion of Agile has blossomed into more than a dozen, differently flavored approaches.

When we began sifting through these Agile variants, our research and experience led us to consider Scrum/XP as the optimal starting point for business intelligence programs because it offers the greatest "power-to-weight ratio" of the collection, in that it:

- Stipulates a minimum of processes and artifacts making it fast to teach.
- Still spans the full life cycle of a software program, not just one project.
- Provides detailed definitions only to a medium depth, allowing customization to particular programs and software genres beyond that.
- Contains provisions for architecture, scaling, and non-standard work.
- Offers an internationally standardized training and certification program.

As certain as we were that an Agile Data Warehousing method could be built upon most of the other Agile approaches, we were pleased how much we were able to accomplish so quickly as we did with Scrum/XP.

Table 2.1: Principles Behind the Agile Manifesto

1. Our highest priority is to satisfy the customer through early and continuous delivery of valuable software.
2. Welcome changing requirements, even late in development. Agile processes harness change for the customer's competitive advantage.
3. Deliver working software frequently, from a couple of weeks to a couple of months, with a preference to the shorter timescale.
4. Business people and developers must work together daily throughout the project.
5. Build projects around motivated individuals. Give them the environment and support they need, and trust them to get the job done.
6. The most efficient and effective method of conveying information to and within a development team is face-to-face conversation.
7. Working software is the primary measure of progress.
8. Agile processes promote sustainable development. The sponsors, developers, and users should be able to maintain a constant pace indefinitely.
9. Continuous attention to technical excellence and good design enhances agility.
10. Simplicity—the art of maximizing the amount of work not done—is essential.
11. The best architectures, requirements, and designs emerge from self-organizing teams.
12. At regular intervals, the team reflects on how to become more effective, then tunes and adjusts its behavior accordingly.

Source: http://www.agilemanifesto.org/principles.html

The bare outline of the approach states that one needs only to:

a) colocate a team of six to nine developers in a shared workplace,
b) embed into that team and that workspace a representative of the customer organization who will direct what the team works on next,

c) derive from this customer representative a set of lightweight "user stories" regarding the functionality the application must provide,

d) instruct developers to deliver "potentially shippable code" at the end of repeating time boxes of fixed length (usually two to four weeks), and

e) validate programming and design by letting the customer representative operate the new code during a semi-formal half-day demonstration.

Scrum makes its process *iterative and incremental* by orchestrating the development work to occur by means of three nested cycles, as depicted in **Figure 2.1**. Large business intelligence projects will involve multiple "releases," each of which is created by a turn of the Release Cycle. The code for a given release accumulates from the modules produced by repeated "sprints" which are turns of the multi-week development cycle. Team members review and fine-tune the current sprint's activities through short meetings known as "scrums" that represent turns of the daily cycle. Let us give each of these three cycles a bit more of an introduction before we examine the project management techniques at work within them.

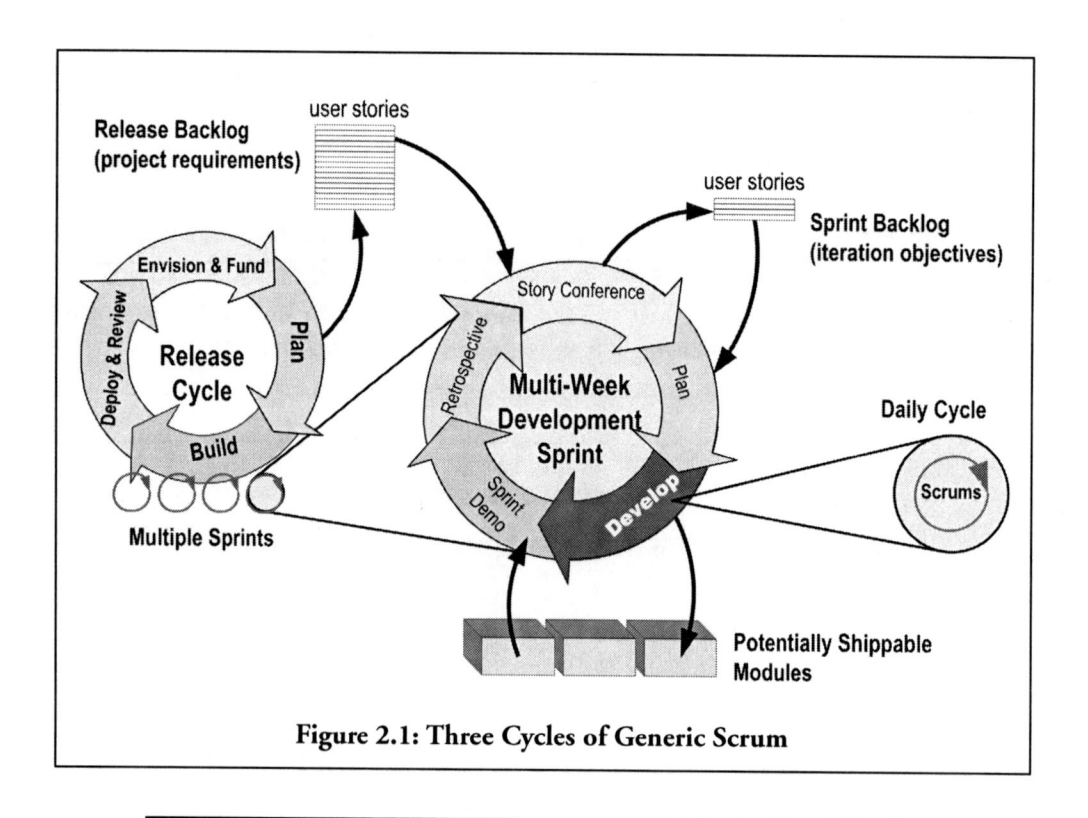

Figure 2.1: Three Cycles of Generic Scrum

The Release Cycle

The Release Cycle is mainly a wrapper process for scoping and funding a large increment of development. The first segment of the cycle shown in our figure is the Envision and Fund phase, in which stakeholders working with very high-level information:

- Define the rough outlines of the project,
- Describe the major enhancements of functionality they seek as a solution to an important business need,
- Estimate the costs for the development required to deliver this large increment, and
- Set assumptions and constraints within which the lower cycles will operate.

For a new initiative, this portion of the Release Cycle ends with the formation of a Scrum team. For a continuing effort, the existing team is simply re-chartered to move on to building the next version of the application in question.

During the Plan phase, stakeholder representatives and the team work through a list of business needs that might be addressed through new software development, and agree upon which of them will be within the scope of the next release of the application. Those requirements falling within scope are expressed in a very lightweight format called "user stories," described in more detail by our next chapter. Those stories making the list are known as the "release backlog," and the developers strive to work this backlog down to zero by the projected day of the next deployment.

For new initiatives, the Plan phase must proceed with sketchy information, much of it deriving from the envisioning and funding conversations completed during the previous phase of the cycle. For ongoing efforts, however, the lower Development Cycle will have returned some valuable information concerning requirements, design, and level-of-effort estimates. This input will allow the release planning team to be more specific concerning the scope and cost of the next release.

The Build phase of the Release Cycle involves many iterations of an even shorter cycle, the multi-week development "sprint," in which the real coding work of the project will be done. Each of these sprints will strive to generate as much "potentially shippable code" as can be created by programmers working at a sustainable pace. The modules produced during each sprint are added to the deliverables of prior sprints until the team feels the entire collection represents an acceptable release, which it then deploys. The Release Cycle concludes with a review process where "lessons learned" can be identified and used to improve the effectiveness of the next turn of the cycle.

Chapter 2—Generic Scrum in a Nutshell

The Development Cycle

The Build phase of the Release Cycle consists of multiple, development iterations called "sprints." These sprints are lightly structured "time boxes" of uniform length—usually two to four weeks—during which the team designs and codes the software modules needed. Throughout the Build phase, the stakeholders invest their desires and authority into a single representative of the business community, called the "Product Owner." During the sprints, this Product Owner works with the developers on a daily, eye-to-eye basis, directly providing them statements of system requirements.

Each sprint begins with a "story conference" in which the Product Owner presents the user stories from the top of the release backlog. She presents these stores to her teammates in priority order, answering their questions regarding requirements, until they have identified the largest set of the most important stories that can be transformed into working code by the end of the sprint. This subset of stories becomes the "sprint backlog," that is, the list of expected deliverables which the team will strive to develop and validate during the time box they are about to begin.

The sprint proceeds next to a half-day, "task planning session" where the team translates each story into the series of programming tasks necessary to deliver it. When all of the sprint backlog has been planned out, developers estimate the level-of-effort for the tasks in order to double check that their total labor required will truly fit within the time and resources they have for that sprint.

From there until the last day of the sprint, the developers are free to self-organize and get the slated work done in the way they deem most effective. The goal is simply to translate the sprint backlog into "potentially shippable" code that the Product Owner can operate herself.

The sprint ends with a half-day "user demo," where the team steps through the newly working code with the Product Owner, who validates that it operates as desired. After the demo, the sprint concludes with a half-day "retrospective" during which the team members discusses how they might improve their work process and make the next sprint more effective.

During this retrospective, the team quantifies its "velocity"—the amount of work it successfully delivered within the time box of the sprint just completed. After a few sprints, the team's velocity stabilizes into a predictable range, allowing project stakeholders to group the stories in the release backlog using sprint-sized brackets, and thereby forecast how many time boxes it will take to deliver the entire release.

Scrum emphasizes that the Product Owner works directly and extensively with the developers during the sprints. It trusts that direct and frequent communication between the business and technical worlds is superior to most written specifications. Scrum sees detailed "to-be" documentation and work planning as largely unneeded once daily, eye-to-eye collaboration has been established, because the higher level of communication with the Product Owner (as the "business representative") provides the guidance developers need at precisely the moments they need it.

Scrum does involve some fine-grained planning and control, but unlike waterfall methods, its detailed management does not span the entire project. It is restricted instead to the "near planning horizon," where there are the fewest unknowns involved, staying focused almost entirely upon the sprint backlog that will shape the next few weeks of work. Scrum embodies the belief that the details of the distant future are unknowable because creating an application that has never existed essentially requires inventing and learning as you go. Demanding a detailed plan at the project outset is to ask the team to "out-drive its headlights." Any forecast beyond the current iteration or two will fall prey to the surprises that the next few tasks will be sure to uncover.

Instead, Scrum has the team forecast and optimize within a near planning horizon where its vision is going to be accurate. Of course, this forces all stakeholders to drop the illusion of certainty found in the early months of many traditionally-managed projects. In compensation, Scrum reveals the team's true pace of sustainable development. By combining this team velocity with the release backlog, everyone derives as accurate a notion of the project's delivery schedule as is humanly possible. To insist on any further planning or design would only waste resources that the team should spend instead on developing working code and providing business value.

THE DAILY SCRUM

Nestled within the Development Cycle is a simple, daily process for keeping the team on track. The team convenes at the same time each day for a fifteen minute, stand-up meeting—the "scrums" for which the approach was named. In these daily scrums each member quickly announces the work they have completed since the last scrum, the work they will finish by the next, and any situations impeding their progress.

DETAILS REGARDING THE GENERIC SPRINT

We kept the outline above brief by glossing over many important details, especially regarding the iterative sprints that make up the Development cycle. Since the sprint is the essence of Scrum, let us now consider more carefully the five phases that generic Scrum/XP defined for it.

STORY CONFERENCE

The first day of a sprint is divided evenly between first a team "story conference" and then a "task planning" session. The objective of the story conference is to identify a candidate list of requirements that the team believes it can deliver within the time allowed by the sprint. The Product Owner provides these requirements in the form of user stories—one or two line statements of business need—listed in priority order on the release backlog.

Scrum wants the team to always deliver the most important requirements first, so it encourages the Product Owner to reshuffle and update her release backlog whenever business conditions change. Accordingly, the top of the release backlog in one story conference can look very different than it did during the last. With this possibility of change, the story conference must begin with the Product Owner walking the team down the current incarnation of the release backlog in priority order until the collection of stories reviewed is clearly larger than a single sprint can address. This set of stories is the candidate sprint backlog. The team now needs to decide carefully how far down this list to draw the actual "commit line," that is, the line designating the portion of the candidate sprint backlog they can promise to deliver while working at a effective and sustainable pace.

In all but the earliest sprints, the team comes to most story conferences having measured its "velocity," the rate with which it converts stories into potentially shippable code. The bulk of each story conference consists of the developers discussing the candidate stories in detail with the Product Owner, estimating their size, and proceeding until the stories accepted onto the sprint backlog equals the velocity of the team.

Each story accepted onto the actual sprint backlog receives a capsule summary of one or two sentences, placed upon a small, paper "story card." These story cards do not need more verbiage than that, for according to generic Scrum/XP, they are only "a reminder to have a conversation" about the functionality they describe. When it comes time to actually develop the feature suggested by the card, the short description will be enough to get the conversation between the developer and the Product Owner started. Keeping the story cards short avoids investing time into to-be specs that might soon be obviated by other developments.

Though the story cards are kept short, the developers make sure during the story conference they really understand what each represents so that they can estimate their level-of-effort. They might jot a few notes down on a card when there are crucial details that everyone will need to recall. During the story conference, each story's level-of-effort is estimated in "story points." Story points are simply measures of a requirement's "size" relative to some previously delivered stories that the team remembers well. Scrum/XP settled on the story point mechanism in response to research showing that programmers are notoriously bad at forecasting how many work hours a particular unit of code will take, but fairly good at estimating when one task is bigger than another.

Story points express relative size and therefore have no base unit of measure such as "hours," making them awkward for the team to use at first. Many teammates will try to drag the team back into estimating in labor hours, so team leaders must insist on story points during the story conference, reassuring everyone that they will be estimating in hours during the next phase of the sprint. The team must get good at estimating in story point because not only do they allow them to estimate a proper sprint backlog very quickly, but they also enable them to eventually estimate an entire release cycle's worth of work.

One brilliance to Scrum is that it requires developers to estimate with every iteration, so they get proficient at forecasting, and then stay in practice. After a few sprints, the team members will have come to understand its reference stories well, feel more comfortable comparing new stories to this reference set, and see their story point estimates converge into a tight range around actuals. Estimating accurately by size is so crucial in enabling the team to avoid overcommitment and to forecast milestone dates, that we dedicate a full chapter to this practice later in this book, making it specific to data warehousing.

The story conference ends when the team has identified the portion from the top of the Product Owner's release backlog that adds up to the number of story points it knows it can deliver in one sprint. The team uses size-based estimation and its velocity measure to reach this goal quickly. Because its velocity figure usually varies within a small range, the team often draws a second limit on the release backlog somewhere below the commit line to represent "stretch goals" for the sprint—items its members will work upon should they complete the formal sprint backlog faster than expected.

Task Planning

The task planning stage occupies the second half of the sprint's first day. The objective is to confirm that the candidate sprint backlog emerging from the story conference is indeed no more work than the team can deliver in one sprint. The developers work toward this conclusion by enumerating for each story the development tasks that will be required and estimating the level-of-effort that each task will take. They then add up the projected labor hours to ensure they fit within their bandwidth of available work hours for the iteration.

For each task identified for a candidate story, the developers create a short "task card" with a one or two sentence description of the work it will involve. This card gives them a place to jot down the considerations that should guide their level-of-effort estimate for the task, and will later give them an easily-moved pointer by which they can track progress on that work assignment. Because these tasks can include analysis, design, development, testing, and documentation work, Scrum can actually pursue a mini-waterfall method for each story if that is the best way to proceed, although the team expects to complete all those steps for a given module within the given time box.

Because task planning discussions revolve around technical activities, the Product Owner is far less central during this stage, but she needs to remain in the room to answer the many detailed questions concerning requirements that will arise as the team begins to picture the deliverables each story calls for.

Usually teams take a first pass at defining all the tasks required for the stories of the candidate sprint backlog, and then returns to estimate each one. Estimates made during the task planning stage can be called "Original Labor Estimate" (OLE, deliberately pronounced "oily" to remind everyone to take them skeptically). The OLE is defined in terms of person-hours needed to complete a given task card. Once all the task cards are estimated, the teammates total the OLEs and perform a second "reality check." They compare the projected total to the OLEs they successfully completed during the last sprint, adjusting for any significant changes in teammate availability due to upcoming vacations and the like. If the total OLEs exceeds the limits for the time box, then developers and Product Owner will reconsider where they have drawn the commit line, discussing what stories can be reprioritized or deferred in order to make the sprint backlog feasible.

The task planning session concludes when a consensus has been reached that the team has targeted a realistic set of deliverables that the Product Owner can expect to test-drive at the next user demo. Scrum is truly efficient because, by the end of this first day of the sprint, Product Owner and developers alike have arrived at a solid and fairly detailed understanding of exactly what they have promised to deliver, what they must do in the next few weeks to succeed, and two measures showing that their work plan is indeed doable.

DEVELOPMENT PHASE

On day two of the sprint, the team begins the iteration's Development phase which consumes the rest of the time box except for the last day. In generic Scrum, the team "self-organizes" its work during this phase in whatever way necessary to complete the stories in the sprint backlog, although the emphasis will always be on delivering the most important stories first.

Self-Organization

Self-organizing implies a few different notions. Foremost, it means that the team decides sprint by sprint, or even day by day, how its members get assigned to tasks. Some teams prefer to follow a strict division of labor based upon their differing technical specialties. Other teams have a greater need to crosstrain and let people self-assign depending upon current interests. The later approach has an advantage that, once everyone is cross trained, the members can fluidly assign themselves to whatever tasks have the greatest need at a given moment, accelerating the group to its maximum possible velocity.

Self-organization also implies that teams will provide their own definition of "done." Ultimately, the code must work when the Product Owner attempts to use it during the upcoming demo, but most projects involve many engineering and technical documentation objectives that the Product Owner cannot realistically validate. We will address the entire topic of quality assurance in much greater detail in later chapters, but for now we can simply point out that there will always be a large component of self-policing by the team so that everyone programs to the same level of completeness. New teams have the mental bandwidth to achieve only a modest amount of technical polish as they adjust to the demanding deadlines imposed by Scrum's short time boxes. However, as the team matures, self-organization will foster among the developers increasingly sophisticated definitions of done—whether it be templates or a particular intensity of testing

Self-organization also means that the team is free to invent or adapt tools and techniques as needed, even adopt them from waterfall methodologies. Teams should be encouraged to consider whatever innovations increase their velocity without hurting their work quality. In practice, this criteria will rule out almost every form-based or electronic mechanism for planning, tracking, and reporting because very few tools can meet the blazing efficiency of working eye-to-eye with informal artifacts to deliver a small increment of new code. Most teams do eventually adopt some non-Scrum devices, especially if they must integrate smoothly with other projects and IT service groups. Self-organizing can thus imply an eclectic mix of tools and their usage, and is a big reason why each team's implementation of the Scrum turns out to be unique.

Daily Scrums

Scrum leaves most of the structure of the Development phase to be determined by self-organization. One notable exception is the daily scrum—a fifteen minute, standup meeting in which each team member takes a turn stating three things: "What I did yesterday, what I will do today, and what is holding me up." All other detail is relegated for discussion after the scrum. Because generic Scrum colocates all team members including the Product

Owner within a contiguous workspace, this follow-on communication takes place easily and spontaneously as needed.

The team holds these daily stand-up meetings in its shared workplace, gathered around a large bulletin board upon which it tracks progress on tasks. This task board will also have a printed summary of the team's overall progress in working off the sprint backlog, the "burndown" chart. We discuss both of these tools shortly below and mention them here to show that daily scrums feel very "real" for developers because the Product Owner is part of the team and everyone can see these two, very tangible measures of progress.

2-to-1 Design and Test Led Development

XP's greatest contribution to the Scrum/XP amalgam appears in its two main quality assurance practices. First, generic XP contains the notion of 2-to-1 programming—two programmers to one keyboard, so that one codes and the other watches for errors in thinking or syntax. In our practice we find this notion slightly too extreme because many of the ETL and BI tools rein in a developer's keystrokes, making errors less likely once the basic layout is established. Instead, we have achieved higher productivity with "two developers to one design" where one programmer builds out the envisioned component once two of them have produced a good sketch of its basic structure.

Accordingly, in our use of Scrum/XP, any developer wanting to begin work on a module proposes a design to one or two other teammates. They use a dry erase board for their diagramming and snap a digital picture of the final consensus for storage in the project archive, thus keeping the cost of design to a minimum. Only when they find themselves working through particularly thorny business rules are they encouraged to slow down and do a careful to-be mini-spec which will also be preserved in their document repository.

By focusing just two or three developers on one module at a time, the team ensures that designs are well-validated before they become code. Yet the number of people working on each design is still small, so that the project saves the expense of the extensive design walkthroughs that some waterfall methods require, sessions that seem in contrast to be taxingly detailed reviews of enormous documents that consume sizable blocks of many people's time and often exhaust their ability to concentrate and be effective.

Secondly, generic XP also stipulates that once a design has been sketched, the developer who would translate it into code must first write a thorough test package that will reveal any conceivable flaw in the programming. As we will see in a later chapter, Agile Data Warehousing goes further by prescribing that the Product Owner and team architects participate in drafting these tests, because each brings a unique perspective on the requirements that a given module must meet. Only when such a test package has been planned, created, and run against the system's current programming (usually resulting in a large number of errors), can the developer then dive into coding the module. By coding to pre-existing tests, the team guarantees the Product Owner that its work is both well-built and correct.

Architectural Compliance and "Tech Debt"

During the Development Phase, the team will naturally encounter tasks or design points that were not thought of during the sprint planning. These can either be added to the current sprint by creating additional task cards (and estimating their OLEs), or placed in a parking lot list called "tech debt" which contains mostly non-functional requirements that need to be addressed sometime before promoting the release to production.

Scrum sees software development as a discovery process, so that the application architecture grows as the team learns more. When teams uncover an engineering feature that should be standardized between modules, they typically add it to tech debt, and address the necessary rework during the next sprint. Whereas any rework may sound like an inefficiency to waterfall method fans, each team should include one or two senior developers who have built an application of the focal type before. Self-organization will include letting these senior members work with the rest of the team in a way that inculcates good architecture from the start, and in this way minimizes rework.

Architectural compliance is an important part of Scrum's intent when it focuses the team on delivering "potentially shippable code." Because architectural aspects are somewhat invisible to the Product Owner, Scrum teams typically hold back during the story conference ten or twenty percent of their story point velocity, so that they can use that bandwidth to attend to such architectural issues. Agile advocates assert that many overarching design notions only get "surfaced" by the real work of development. Because Scrum gets development underway early, it naturally uncovers important architectural issues sooner, and therefore results in better overall design. In contrast, waterfall approaches tend to leave coding conundrums buried all the way through requirements, analysis, and even design, so that they become prohibitively expensive to fix when they are finally discovered during development, late in the project.

USER DEMO

During the first half of the sprint's final day, the Product Owner validates that the stories the team claims to have delivered actually resulted in the additional functionality requested. The Product Owner searches for the presence of those stories by operating for herself the latest build of the application, which should have resulted from integrating the newly delivered code into the instance reviewed during the prior demo. Acceptance is typically a binary "done" or "not done" on a story by story basis, with gaps often noted on the back of the story card for later reference.

Working through the stories of the demo, the Product Owner validates that the release candidate achieves the functionality of not only the short verbiage on the story card, but also all the conversations she had with developers as they engineered a given module during the preceding weeks of the sprint. Because each iteration takes on only a half-dozen cards or so, the tight focus makes it possible for the team to conduct an entire review working solely from the story cards and memory.

Those stories which the Product Owner accepts as complete are removed from the sprint and release backlogs. These cards had to pass through a status called "Ready to Validate" before arriving at "Ready to Demo," a step meant to guarantee that the code behind the new functions meets the team's current quality standards. An astute Product Owner will also ask the developers to acknowledge any task cards they had relegated to the team's collection of "tech debt."

Stories found to be still "not done" will remain in the release backlog. They will be re-prioritized as the Product Owner re-visits the backlog in preparation for the next story conference and may very well re-appear in the next sprint backlog.

SPRINT RETROSPECTIVE

The final half-day of the sprint comprises the "sprint retrospective" in which the team does some self-reflection and fine tunes its use of Scrum so that the next sprint will proceed even better. Each retrospective starts with a reading of a short "Retrospective Prime Directive" (see Sidebar) to establish the open, non-defensive mindset within the team that will allow an honest self-appraisal. Each teammate then completes a few sticky notes concerning "what went well" during the sprint just completed, and then a few more regarding "what could have gone better."

Sidebar: Sprint Retrospective's "Prime Directive"

Regardless of what we discover here today, we understand and truly believe that everyone did the best job they could, given

- what they knew at the time,
- their skills and abilities,
- the resources available, and
- the situation at hand.

Next the team brainstorms how to organize the "could have gone better" items into a handful of themes. Themes are discussed until the team has generated a good list of action items and members have volunteered to shepherd implementation of those action items during the next sprint. This aspect of the retrospective instills continuous improvement into Scrum, an important consideration for teams wishing to assert that their method is "mature" when viewed by such international standards as CMMI.

Finally, and perhaps most importantly, the team revisits its velocity. For the stories the Product Owner considered "done," the team simply totals the story points to each story card and the original labor estimates of their task cards, all assigned on the first day of the sprint. Optionally, the team can credit a percentage of the story points and OLEs for stories that the Product Owner deemed not yet done, but still substantially complete. These totals reflect the true speed that the team is actually working through the release backlog, a crucial metric for planning the next iteration. The team should then conclude the retrospective by looking ahead on the calendar and projecting each member's availability during the next sprint, so that it can further prorate the new velocity number and enable itself to make an accurate commitment during the next story conference.

GENERIC TRACKING TOOLS AND PROJECT VISIBILITY

Generic Scrum provides only a few, easy-to-use tools for tracking progress during a sprint—the task board and the burndown chart. Though simplistic in their format, they both offer a high level of visibility of project progress to stakeholders within and outside the team and are therefore essential to display in the project room.

THE SPRINT TASK BOARD

The task board is a very large surface (even 12' x 8' would not be too big) onto which the story cards and task cards can be pinned. The story cards are placed in priority order in a column running down the left side of the task board, as shown in **Figure 2.2**. To the right of this column are several columns dedicated to tracking the progress of tasks as the team works upon them: *Tasks Waiting, Tests Written, Under Development, Waiting Validation,* and *Ready to Demo.* A swim lane is drawn horizontally across the board for each story so that one can see the task cards associated with each story.

When a team member needs work to do, he can assign himself the next task card of highest priority waiting in the To Do column. He then authors tests for the deliverables he is about to create and moves the task card to the *Tests Written* column. Developers can begin developing for units waiting in this column, moving the appropriate cards to Now

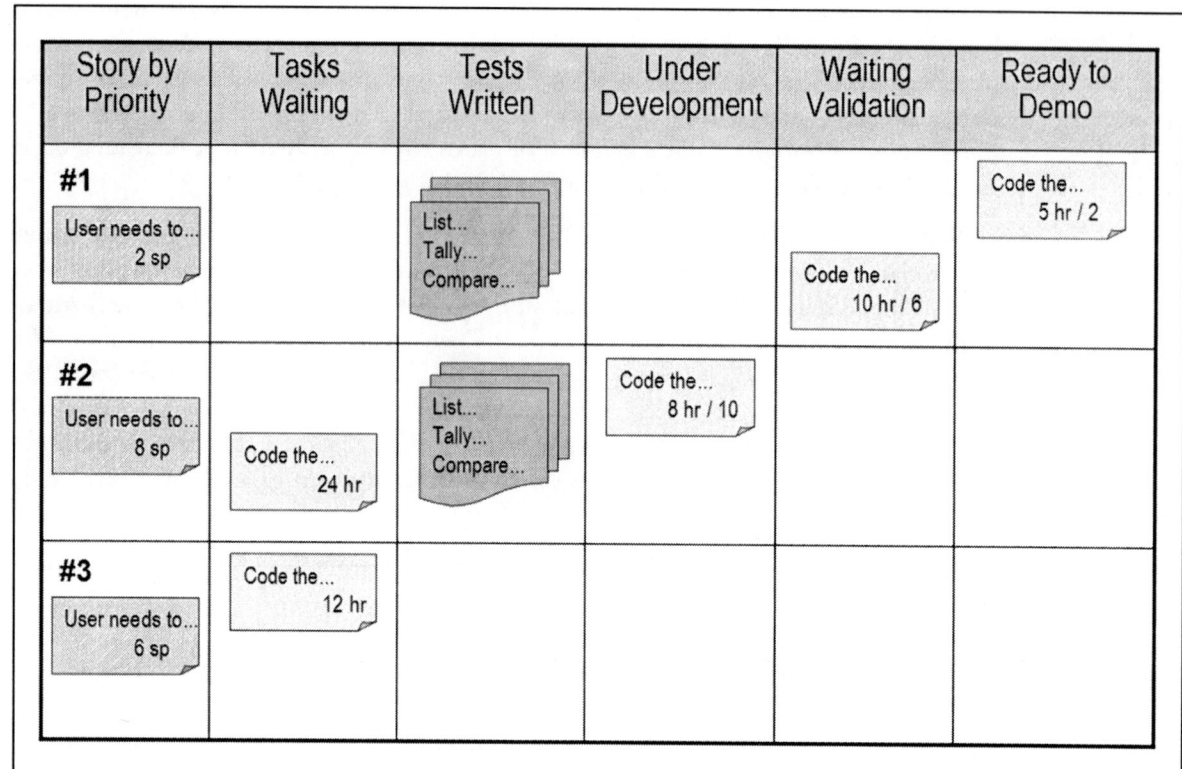

Story by Priority	Tasks Waiting	Tests Written	Under Development	Waiting Validation	Ready to Demo
#1 User needs to... 2 sp		List... Tally... Compare...		Code the... 10 hr / 6	Code the... 5 hr / 2
#2 User needs to... 8 sp	Code the... 24 hr	List... Tally... Compare...	Code the... 8 hr / 10		
#3 User needs to... 6 sp	Code the... 12 hr				

Figure 2.2: Simplified Representation of a Scrum Task Board

Coding, and moving them later to Needs Validation when the work product passes unit testing. Finally, other team members validate that all units pass an independent application of the tests written for them, both individually and as an integrated system. When tested successfully, the task card is moved to Ready to Demo. During the sprint demo, the Product Owner will only attempt to validate those stories that have all task cards waiting in this last column.

Scrum is often criticized for incorporating too little validation, yet we can see from this brief outline that there are indeed three separate validation points for both functional and technical qualities: 1) the developer must code a unit to pass previously written tests, 2) another team member later repeats these tests for units and integrated system, and 3) the Product Owner ensures each unit meets business needs. Scrum is a marvel of efficiency in that units passing all three of these validations reach a high level of quality without the team having to create an expensive requirements document or trace each requirement through an elaborate validation matrix as required by many waterfall methods.

The task board provides a natural focus for each developer during the daily scrum, allowing him to make his check-in even more specific:

- Here are the cards I moved since yesterday.
- These are the cards that I will work on today.
- Those are the cards I'm working where the remaining labor estimate has gone up or can't be decreased, and let me quickly list the reasons why....
- Let me mention some other roadblocks in my way....
- I need to meet with the following people after this scrum....

Stakeholders who need detailed knowledge of team progress are invited to attend the daily scrums to hear these listings of achievements and roadblocks. However, they are asked to simply observe and not participate, so that the scrum can stick to its fifteen minute, stand-up format. Stakeholders can always meet with the Product Owner or developer(s) of their choice after the scrum to further explore items mentioned during the standup.

THE BURNDOWN CHART

The task board with its swim lanes and its moving task cards make it very easy for any stakeholder to glean a task-by-task notion of the developers' progress throughout the sprint. However, it is still a bit difficult to project on any given day by looking only at the task board whether the team is still on track overall to complete all the sprint backlog by the time of the user demo.

Scrum provides a second, lightweight tool for this purpose, namely the "burndown chart," which supplies an instant notion of whether the sprint will complete in time. Before each daily scrum, developers mark on all the cards that they are working a current "remaining labor estimate" (RLE, pronounced "early" to remind developers which way everyone hopes these forecasts will trend). RLEs are expressed in person-hours and can be totaled for the day, so that a line chart of RLEs by sprint day is easy to print and pin to the task board. **Figure 2.3** depicts a typical sprint burndown chart for a point about three quarters through an iteration. If the line of total RLEs is trending to zero by demo day, the sprint is on track. If the line is straying off to somewhere above the desired trend line, the team can instantly see that something has gone awry and investigate.

The burndown chart is displayed on the task board in the team's shared workspace, which is open to all stakeholders. This arrangement makes a Scrum project extremely transparent to developers, customers, and IT management alike, and contributes significantly toward getting long-term endorsement as an acceptable development methodology for the organization.

Figure 2.3: Typical Scrum Burndown Chart

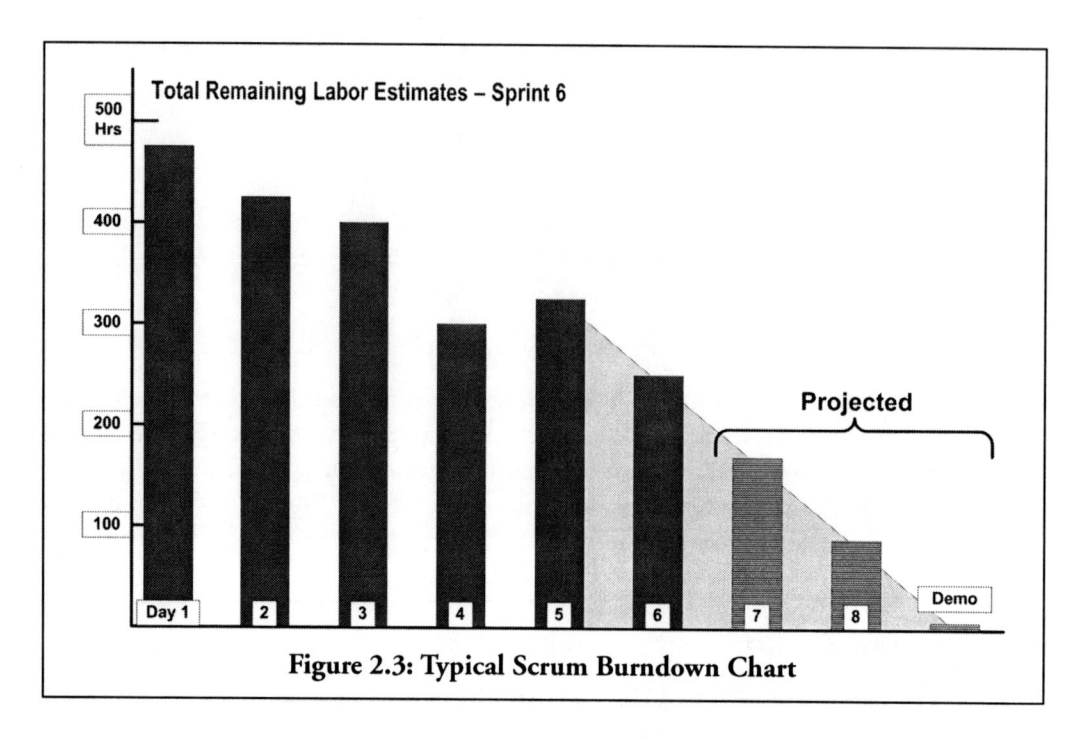

Over the long run, the burndown chart is key to fostering a first-class team of Agile developers. Its presence at the daily stand-up meeting places a good deal of pressure on the team to keep the remaining labor estimate line on track. Yet there are only two ways to do so: a) either work harder, in the case that the line is not dropping as fast as needed, or b) estimate better during the next sprint planning so the team does not end up with an impossible amount of work to complete. By creating this direct connection between the quality of estimation and the amount of stress developers experience, the burndown chart provides a daily motivation for developers to become good estimators, making Scrum self-optimizing and reducing much of the need for detailed project management.

Seeing Scope Creep

Burndown charts also provide a good way to clearly depict the effect of scope creep on a team and its current sprint. Product Owners are supposed to redirect the team's efforts only during a story conference and not within the Development phase of a sprint. Though much diminished by this policy, scope creep still occurs during some iterations due to oversights during sprint planning and business contingencies that the Product Owner decides must be addressed before the upcoming user demo.

Team members should treat scope creep items like any other requested deliverable—they should create a story card for it and estimate its size in story points. They should then create the necessary task cards and estimate their OLEs. If the total of these scope creep OLEs ("SCOLEs?") are displayed beneath the burndown chart's X-axis, as depicted in **Figure 2.4**, not only can everyone track the scope creep separately, but they are also able to see its impact on the team's ability to complete the sprint by demo day.

Seeing Progress for an Entire Release

Scrum can provide the Product Owner a burndown chart for not only a single sprint, but entire release as well. To build a release burndown chart, the Product Owner must provide a full release backlog of user stories, and the team must take the time to estimate the story points for this long list of features. As each sprint delivers working code, the reduction in story points still waiting for development can be measured and displayed on

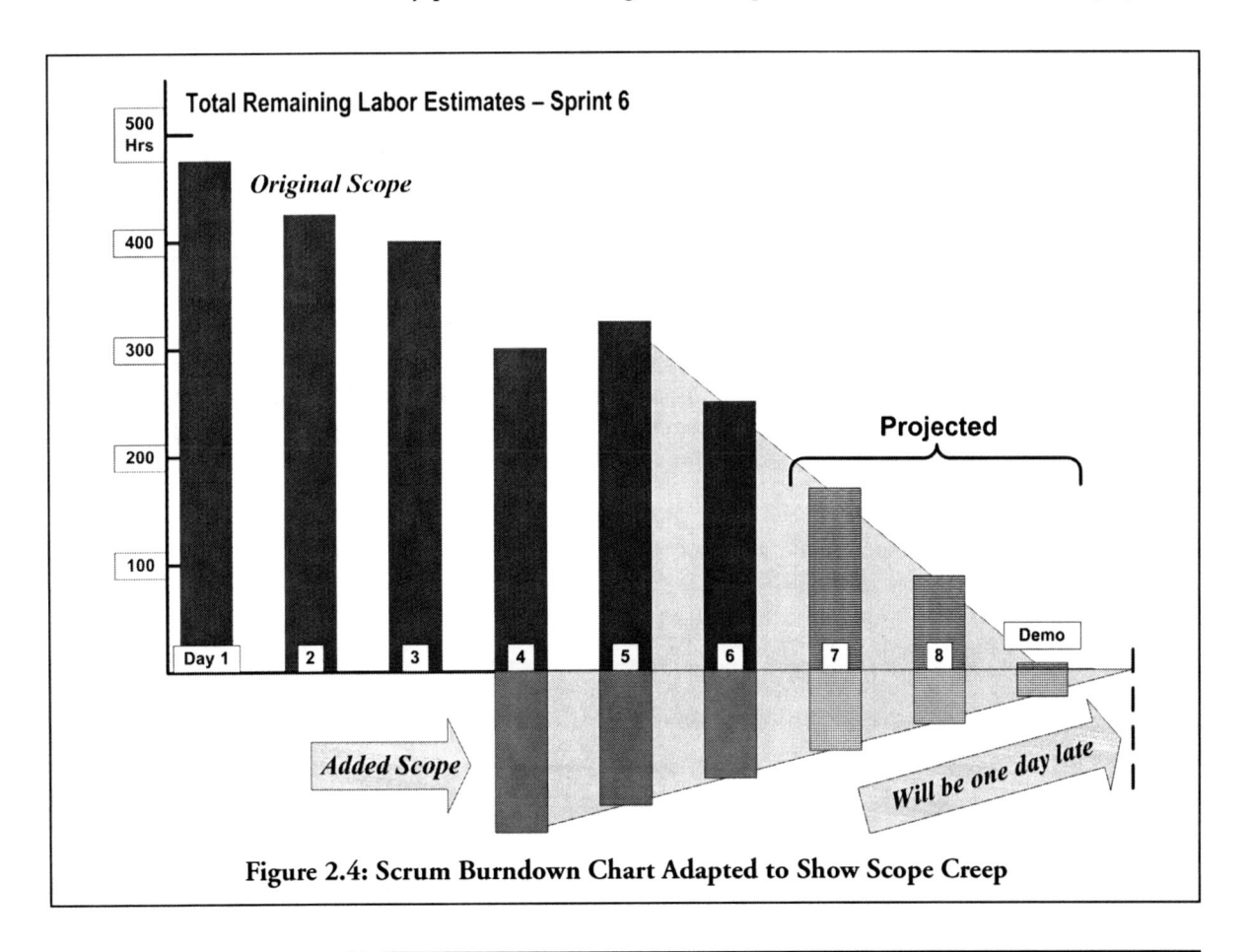

Figure 2.4: Scrum Burndown Chart Adapted to Show Scope Creep

the multi-sprint, release burndown chart. The team's velocity, in story points completed per iteration, can provide a trend line that will suggest how many more sprints it will need to finish the release backlog.

New teams will be unable to provide accurate release planning or start a release burndown chart right away, of course, because they must first learn about stories, size-based estimation, and their average velocity. They should allow themselves five or six sprints to hone the ability to verbalize stories effectively, identify appropriate reference stories for estimation, and derive a clear notion of their velocity. Only at that point would it make sense to hold a "release planning meeting" to hammer out story cards for the remainder of the project, estimate their relative sizes, and start a release burndown chart. Although the Envision and Funding Phase of the release cycle typically provides project sponsors with some concrete notions of what the release will deliver, Scrum practitioners should neither confirm nor deny that vision until this release planning session occurs. In exchange for waiting this short while, the external stakeholders will receive better planning information, all the more accurate because it will be based upon actually building a small portion of the envisioned system.

Often the release planning effort results in the Product Owner discovering that she has asked for more than the team can deliver within the allotted number of sprints. Three aspects of Scrum keep this realization from becoming a disaster as so often happens on waterfall-managed projects. First, the Product Owner learns of this fact early on in a Scrum project rather than towards the end, so that she can take corrective action and minimize the overall impact of the shortfall. Secondly, with each iteration the team delivers "potentially shippable code," so whatever the Product Owner reviewed during the last user demo can be implemented despite the undelivered components. Third, because the team worked the highest priority stories first, whatever is delivered by a given date will be the most important portion of the desired functionality. In this way, Scrum can be described as "minimizing the impact of what does not get done."

Taken together, task boards, burndown charts, separately tracked scope creep, and release planning sessions make a project's progress extremely visible to the entire organization. More importantly, Scrum achieves this visibility with a bare minimum of tools, so that it diverts very little effort from the main purpose of the team—creating working code.

THE SCRUM MASTER

Given Scrum's emphasis on the efficiency of "self-organizing teams," it is not surprising that projects using this Agile approach need far less project management than we find under waterfall methods. Scrum does define a special team member called a "Scrum

Master," but unlike a "Project Manager," this role is subtle by design so as not to impede the self-directed and collaborative way Scrum teams work together. In Scrum, the Product Owner is the keeper of the backlog lists, and the Scrum Master is the keeper of the process that turns that list into working code. The Scrum Master's focus is to keep everything about the process as lightweight as possible, so that the maximum possible effort goes into creating high-quality deliverables rather than being absorbed by "the method" used to organize the work.

Because the team itself continually derives and adapts its work methods, the Scrum Master role is minimized. In fact, Scrum suggests that the person in this role need only dedicate half of her time to shepherding the process, and invest the rest of her hours to collaborating with developers in building deliverables. The time she does devote to the process will include at a minimum reminding her teammates to attend to the following:

- Move your active task cards to the right columns on the task board.
- Update those cards daily with new RLEs.
- Arrive on time for the scrum each day.
- Ensure that all validation steps were truly completed for all tasks landing in the "Ready to Demo" column of the task board.

To help everyone visualize progress, the Scrum Master should be posting an updated burndown chart on the task board before each scrum. During the daily stand-up meeting, her influence will be crucial in keeping each team member's mini-summary restricted to answering the few questions identified above—what cards did you move, what cards will you move tomorrow, and what's holding you up? The Scrum Master reminds them to relegate any further discussions to break-out meetings after the scrum is over.

Beyond the daily work, the Scrum Master's most important role is guardian of the estimation technique and "keeper of the velocity metric." As was evident in our discussion earlier, the team must develop and maintain a high degree of estimating accuracy and a clear notion of what it can accomplish within a standard sprint. Size-based estimation is the key to both of these goals, but programmers seem to gravitate toward their old habits of spurious labor-hour forecasts if not occasionally nudged back into the flock.

The Scrum Master has also several crucial but sometimes invisible duties that include:

- Training Product Owners in both Scrum and in formulating a prioritized release backlog using a language that developers can understand and estimate.
- Negotiating and properly managing scope creep occurring within a sprint.
- Keeping the peace with the rest of the organization, and building strong support for Scrum from IT management and service groups such as enterprise architects and data base administrators (DBAs).

- Training the team in the Scrum method, as adapted for the project at hand, including new team members who will invariably join once the project is underway.
- Facilitating story conferences, sprint planning sessions, demo days, and perhaps most importantly the sprint retrospectives that allow the team to consistently increase its effectiveness.

Agile literature often describes Scrum Masters as the "owners" of the process, but we believe this is an overstatement of their role. If Scrum Masters were free to improvise or adapt the process single-handedly, there would be little use for the sprint retrospective and Scrum's notion of self-organized teams would be gravely undermined. It is probably more precise to think of the Scrum Master as the "compliance officer" for the team, one who ensures developers follow the group's current adaptation of the generic method. In this perspective, the sprint retrospective becomes the "change control board" that actually owns the process and the only entity that can adjust the actual method the team should follow.

Non-Standard Sprints

Sometime soon after their introduction to Scrum, seasoned IT professionals will inevitably ask "How does this process provide for good architectural planning?" Even before they fully understand the approach, they may criticize Scrum as being "too tactical" or even condemn it as "institutionalized scope creep." Though it is indeed an incremental, iterative approach, Scrum has two vehicles for establishing the infrastructure of a project and for setting bounds upon the types of problems the project can be asked to address at any given time. These devices are known as "Sprint 0" and "spikes," and they not only extend good design throughout the application and but they also keep the enterprise from expanding the project's scope without giving the team the necessary "time outs" required to retool its platform.

Sprint 0

As we saw above, Scrum suggests that a team reserve a small percentage of its velocity, say 20 percent, for cross-iteration design and integration efforts, as well as for working off accumulated tech debt. To address architecture on a more systematic basis, however, Scrum teams often add a "Sprint 0" to the beginning of a release. During Sprint 0 the team reviews the Product Owner's release backlog, sketches the architectural components that will be required, and gets a head start on building the necessary infrastructure, including its quality management aspects. With an overarching architectural plan in place, the remaining details of the infrastructure can be addressed within the regular sprints as they become necessary.

Because Sprint 0 does not aim to deliver any of the user stories, it is a good way for a new team to learn the daily rhythms of the Scrum/XP approach before adding the Product Owner, user stories, and sized-based estimation to the mix. More importantly, Sprint 0 establishes a clear limit on the type of features the developers will consider including in the project. Because the Product Owner hails from a business background, she can inadvertently request features that are far beyond what the existing code library can support. During a Sprint 0, the developers prepare to deliver an entire class of requirements quickly, and thus arrive at a clear notion of what their standard library can and cannot easily support. When the Product Owner later makes an non-standard request, the developers can draw upon this understanding to quickly realize that the request is "out of scope" for the current architecture, and thus keep themselves from committing to an impossible task.

Spikes

Fortunately, whenever the team is faced with a technical or functional "show stopper," Scrum allows it to resort to a "spike" (another rugby term). A spike is a second type of non-standard iteration, in which the team takes a few days out of the current release's Build phase to deeply research a topic and return with a framework or sample implementation that will guide the rest of the project. Spikes are typically utilized to solve a very focused technical question with wide implications, such as "what approach to encrypted data transfers should we use for this application?" Despite the best efforts of developers, these detailed "show stoppers" can arise in mid-release under any methodology through the natural process of discovery.

Spikes are the best solution to suggest when the team must tell a Product Owner that her latest request is "out of scope" for the current architecture. Instead of refusing to deliver upon the request, they ask instead for a few days to explore and resolve the technical issues which are currently unsupportable. Often it will be enough for the team to simply sketch a solution to be implemented later using the bandwidth reserved for Tech Debt. Resorting to spikes lets the team not only solve the problem, but also communicates to the Product Owner that extraordinary requests have their costs and cannot be simply "slipped in" among the other stories of the release.

Where Did Scrum Come From?

The presentation of generic Scrum sketched above gives us a starting notion that we can now adapt for business intelligence projects, as we will begin to do with the next chapter. We would like to conclude here with a notion of the rich intellectual history behind Scrum as well as an outline regarding why it works so well, two topics that will allow Agile data warehousing advocates to portray it as a mature and proven method, ready for enterprise information systems projects today. Our discussion here will be a general treatment of the topic, and those readers looking for greater detail can turn to Chapter 7 where we do a detailed consideration of ADW's potential for CMM Level 5 compliance.

Distant History

Like many good ideas, Scrum arose from the intersection of multiple innovative threads, in this case three from the late twentieth century: 1) Japanese advancements in Operations Research; 2) growing incremental, iterative development research in the U.S., and 3) the rise of Object Oriented (OO) technologies in software. At its deepest level, Scrum draws upon the lean manufacturing movement and quality circles originating in Japanese manufacturing during its economic boom years during the 1980s. The word "scrum" as a project method was in fact first employed as a metaphor for better management in product manufacturing companies in a 1986 *Harvard Business Review* article "The New, New Product Development Game" by two Japanese business academicians Hirotaka Takeuchi (Dean of the Graduate School of International Corporate Strategy, Hirotsubashi University), and Ikujiro Nonaka (professor in the School of Knowledge Science at the Japan Advanced Institute of Science and Technology). [Takeuchi 1986]

During this same time frame, innovative thinkers in the U.S. software industry were exploring project management using iterative and incremental methods. Important milestones in this effort include IBM's NASA Space Shuttle software project that involved 17 iterations over 31 months ending in 1980, and a widely read 1988 paper, "A Spiral Model of Software Development and Enhancement." by a researcher at TRW. [Boehm 1988]

The third thread materialized in the mid-1990s as software managers realized that their object-oriented developers had yet to realize the breakthrough productivity that OO coding technologies seemed to promise. Believing that qualities such as inheritance and polymorphism made OO components far more flexible than modules built with traditional procedural code, they began stripping the procedural aspects out of the current IID techniques in an effort to make them as nimble as their style of coding. Important moments in this effort included Microsoft's book *Dynamics of Software Development* [McCarthy 2006 (latest edition)], and Kent Beck's first XP project at Chrysler in 1997. [C3 Team 1998]

Perhaps the clearest melding of IID and OO surfaced with a series of books on the Rational Unified Development Process that aligned a well-described development method with Rational's object-oriented software development tools. [Jacobson 1999] In 1995 the Standish Group published its seminal "Chaos" study detailing the software industry's abysmal track record in delivering large systems through traditional methods. Their 1999 follow-up revealed that those companies experimenting with shorter time frames and incremental delivery seemed to be turning the situation around, creating some important momentum behind those approaches that utilize quick time boxes and tighter incremental scoping. [Standish Group 1995 and 1999]

SCRUM EMERGES

The three threads described above merged into the major approaches behind this book when two eventual signers of the Agile Manifesto, Dr. Jeff Sutherland and Ken Schwaber, adapted the notions in Takeuchi and Nonaka's paper using their own work in iterative methods for OO development and further studies of process theory performed at the DuPont's Advanced Research Facility. [Control Chaos 2007]

1994 saw the first Scrum development project at Easel Corporation, a maker of a fourth generation language for mainframe data integration. Sutherland and Schwaber formalized their project management approach in a 1995 presentation before the Object Management Group's "Object-Oriented Programming, Systems, Languages, and Applications" conference [ADM 1995], after which they began offering Scrum-specific training and innovation conferences. In the intervening years since OOPSLA'95, Scrum has gained greater depth and formalization as it cross pollinated with XP and incorporated research on the Theory of Constraints [Goldratt 1990], spawning many books, and eventually evolving into a certified Scrum Master training program for project managers. [Schwaber 2004]

For its first fourteen years in existence, most Scrum implementations were bottom up, but as it achieved increasingly more successful projects, we have recently seen many top-down implementations sponsored by corporate EIS departments. Today Scrum is practiced by many global, name-brand companies such as Microsoft, Yahoo, Ariba, Cadence, Adobe, GE Healthcare, Borland, Google, Primavera, Sun, Siemens, State Farm, Philips, IBM, U.S. Federal Reserve Bank, HP, Motorola, SAP, Bose, CapitalOne, and Xerox. [Behrens 2005]

WATERFALL METHODS—A MISTAKE FROM THE START

The vast majority of corporate IT departments today still utilize methods based upon the waterfall method. How can we foster the right frame of mind among IT managers that they will give Scrum/XP a honest try? We will draw upon two stratagems. First, point out that the predominance of the waterfall method is due to a tremendous error on the part of the U.S. military when it was codifying software development methods, and second, provide a long list as to why Scrum is many times more effective than a traditional approach. We deal with the military's SNAFU here, and leave the advantages of Scrum for the next section.

The standard waterfall approach became the standard paradigm only through a series of mistakes. In 1970, W.W. Royce first identified the classic waterfall categories as only "essential steps common to all computer program developments, regardless of size or complexity." In the second half of that same paper he clearly advocated an iterative path for progressing through these steps. To pursue the waterfall steps sequentially from analysis through coding in a single pass, he cautioned, "is risky and invites failure." The single-pass waterfall method is only the simplest possibility for organizing a development project, and he suggested that "it only works for the most uncomplicated projects." [Royce 1970]

Undaunted by these warnings from Royce, the Department of Defense proceeded to make the single-pass waterfall method its standard approach for systems development with its official specs MIL-STD-1521B and MIL-STD-2167. One can only speculate that they read just the first half of Royce's paper and missed the later sections that contained his recommendations. The MIL-STD-2167 spec was particularly influential and soon propagated into many further standards both within the U.S. and internationally. Yet, when interviewed in the mid 1990s, the author of MIL-STD-2167 admitted that he had been unaware of the notion of time boxes when he drafted his recommendations, and with hindsight he would have strongly advocated iterative and incremental development methods instead. [Larman 2004 and Oestereich 2006]

In 1994, DOD replaced MIL-STD-2167 with an IID-promoting standard. Unfortunately, the other governments and standards bodies that based their methods on the earlier spec did not update their policies to match, so the single-pass waterfall approach sadly remains the basis of many methodological standards today. However, one can argue that to cling to a non-iterative, incremental approach is to persist in making a known, fundamental error in software engineering.

Chapter 2—Generic Scrum in a Nutshell

WHY DOES SCRUM WORK SO WELL?

With that important bit of history uncovered, we can now focus on the many positive reasons to advocate Agile methods. As we commented in the introduction, the approach advocated by this book is an adaptation of two Agile methods, Scrum for project management and Extreme Programming for systems engineering. Rather than relentlessly hammering for the remainder of this book on why Scrum and XP are good choices for data warehousing projects, we will gather most of that thinking here, giving readers only one place to search if they are ever challenged to defend their choice of Scrum/XP and even Agile methods in general. The disadvantage will be that we will have to anticipate the material explored more fully in the second volume of this series which will focus upon the engineering practices XP can offer data warehousing.

Scrum/XP works well for system development for a host of reasons, most importantly because it:

AVOIDS OVER-INVESTMENT IN FRAGILE ARTIFACTS

Waterfall methods spawn large requirement and design documents that are frequently an exercise in time-consuming futility. These write-ups have very short "shelf lives" because even small changes in the business can obviate large portions of the material contained within them. Of course, in the spirit of self-organization, Scrum teams will create to-be documents when they see that such a careful treatment will result in greater speed overall, such as in the area of complex business rules. But Scrum teams never experience creating documents for documents' sake, which is a common complaint heard regarding waterfall methods that can seem more concerned with shifting blame for possible errors onto end users, who verbalized the requirements, rather than with getting a new application built. By focusing documentation efforts exclusively upon the bare minimum needed, Scrum eliminates a large, expensive, and unproductive portion of the work included in standard methods.

CONNECTS DEVELOPERS WITH REAL USER REQUIREMENTS

Users gain important insights into the true nature of their requirements once they see a working application with real data—insights that can sometimes reverse their understanding of business needs, destroying the value of any to-be documents prepared earlier. By embedding a customer representative into the team as the Product Owner, the developers have a fully-engaged subject matter expert from whom they can acquire on an eye-to-eye basis the detailed knowledge necessary to create good designs. Developers are no longer stuck working with incomplete and imprecisely expressed "requirements" recorded months earlier which no longer reflect the true needs of the enterprise. Instead, they have an authoritative resource to answer nettlesome questions that arise as they code. With this level of support, unit designs can be sketched on whiteboards and coded. Errors in interpretation are caught the moment they are made, greatly reducing the risk of rework by increasing the accuracy of the code.

Eliminates Many Ineffective Meetings

Not only does Scrum eliminate needless documentation effort in a project, it does away with many, expensive peer-review meetings. Once the project enters the Development phase of the Release Cycle, eye-to-eye collaboration and 2-to-1 design techniques places a reviewer inside every creative effort. Test-led development quickly brings modules with problems to the surface. Validation becomes more effective because it is spread evenly throughout the Development phase rather than being segregated in a separate step occurring many months after the team was last actively focused on the code.

In contrast, waterfall methods include many committee reviews of abstract to-be documents or dense as-built presentations. Any one of them can consume two or more hours of a dozen senior professionals' time, and those attending will inevitably spend much of that time thinking about other things unless being directly addressed by the presenter. In this way, traditional approaches squander a tremendous amount of resources that could be better directed to developing working code.

Increases Effective Planning

As we saw above, Scrum teams spend two full days of every iteration planning their work and tuning their method. This practice brings the amount of time spent planning to between 10 and 20 percent, depending upon whether the team uses two or four week sprints. This range represents one out of every five to ten weeks dedicated to thinking through one's work and techniques. Very few teams following a traditional method can claim anything close to this level of reflection and preparation. Moreover, Scrum spreads this planning evenly throughout the project, keeping the forecast horizon very close in, so that the team minimizes the risk of basing important decisions on unknown conditions. Scrum planning includes a business-based Product Owner as an integral part of the team, further improving the quality of information used. With such extensive, quality planning, it should be no surprise when Scrum teams outperform traditional waterfall efforts, especially in quality.

INCREASES THE ACCURACY OF ESTIMATES

Quality planning requires accurate estimates, and Scrum teams conduct two separate estimating sessions during each iteration. As we saw above, each session employs its own technique—first size-based and then labor hours—so that both forecast cross-checks the other. With these considerations in mind, one can easily argue that the Scrum teaches teams to estimate better and then keeps them in practice throughout the project, whereas waterfall estimates are formally performed only one or two times at the very beginning of a project.

TRANSPARENT TO THE CUSTOMER AND MANAGEMENT

Scrum incorporates three key features that make a project's progress and challenges highly visible: the task board, the burndown charts, and the daily scrums observable by all stakeholders. Because these are the tools that the team itself uses to monitor progress, it is very rare that important issues can adversely affect the sprint without being visible to the project stakeholders.

ELIMINATES 1,000 LINE PROJECT PLANS....

With such transparency, stakeholders need little additional reassurance that the project is on track. Once the team has a documented velocity, stakeholders will be able to view the stories of the release backlog organized by the probable delivery sprint. Knowing that a business-based Product Owner is directing the team, the Stakeholders will no longer see the need for a Project Manager to micromanage team activities, and the traditional 30-page project plan with its inscrutable task names will not be missed.

... MAKING PROJECT LESS EXPENSIVE TO MANAGE

By switching to Scrum's implicit "Program Management Lite," the project can save the expense of a formal project manager. The project can eliminate not only the micro-level project planning efforts but also the time wasted on detailed progress reporting. These resources can be invested instead in more development and strategic-level planning, which will greatly improve any project's overall performance.

ELEVATES QUALITY TO A DAILY ISSUE FOR DEVELOPERS

The particular combination of Scrum/XP that we sketched above includes continuous and automated testing for data warehouse objects. In such an environment, developers who submit a faulty unit for the daily build will discover in the morning that their unit has made the nightly batch fail. Because a batch crash affects the entire team, the poorly coded unit will clearly emerge as a "roadblock" during the team's daily scrum—in other words, there is no hiding low quality work on a Scrum team.

INCORPORATES CONTINUAL IMPROVEMENT

Scrum not only leads the organization to a highly productive means of creating software, but its retrospectives and velocity metrics spur innovation in techniques and quickly institutionalize improvements in the team's working methods. Thus, Scrum inherently includes the notion of "continual improvement" as advocated by the most highly regarded EIS process models such as CMM. [SEI 2006] With this positive feedback in place, it is no surprise that an enterprise implementing Scrum will see initial *and* ongoing improvements in productivity, improvements that are self-reinforcing rather than requiring additional resources to monitor and maintain.

ADAPTS TOOLS FROM OTHER METHODS AS APPROPRIATE

Self-organization plus continual improvement make Scrum extremely "open minded" to the other tools and techniques the organization might already have in place. Any potential contribution from outside Scrum needs only to pass one crucial test: does it help developers meet the demanding delivery deadline imposed by each short sprint more than it distracts them from that goal?

LEAVES MOST EIS "BEST-PRACTICES" IN PLACE

Scrum is tightly scoped to a subset of the overall EIS domain because it is a *development* approach. Its focus is only how a project's code is created. Functions such as approving, deploying, and supporting the resulting application can remain as already stipulated by the EIS department's existing policies. Whatever wisdom is built into those practices remains in place, unaffected by the adoption of Scrum.

Allows Customers to Change Their Minds

By keeping the prioritized release backlog up to date, the customer representative can steer the development team in new directions at the beginning of each iteration. A sensible Product Owner will not use this capability capriciously, but for those organizations in highly competitive industries, this feature of Scrum may well be a life saver. Not only can the team be redirected in the short term if the competitive landscape suddenly changes, but, because of the prioritized feature list, the team will instantly begin delivering the most competitive response first.

Quick to Teach

A solid presentation of Scrum for the project leader requires less than 150 pages or a two day class. A four-hour orientation for developers will more than suffice to get the team moving. Given a choice between a traditional method that includes many binders of process descriptions and detailed templates to follow, versus an Agile method that takes less than a day to communicate, one could reasonably prefer Scrum even if its many other advantages did not exist.

Surfaces the Problems Early On ...

Traditional methodologies, with their massive up-front planning and protracted delivery schedules, can allow projects to seem "on track" until the delivery date looms. Then even a small mistake can make the project suddenly go "red" on VP-level status reports and stay red till the system is eventually coerced into operation. In contrast, Scrum requires potentially shippable code at the end of every iteration, bringing problems to the surface quickly. The user demo built into every sprint typically does not run smoothly at first because every little error in architecture, standards compliance, and handshakes with external systems seem to prevent the application from working as planned. By repeatedly punishing developers with embarrassing demos until they get all the details right, Scrum forces issues to be resolved early in the project when there is still a relatively small amount of code that needs to be fixed.

... So There Are Fewer Surprises Upon Implementation

With problems in requirements and design uncovered earlier in the project, Scrum teams will display the reverse pattern of traditionally managed projects: early sprints may well turn "red" on status reports, but as the challenges get systematically resolved, later sprints will stay green. IT management will have fewer nasty surprises to manage as the code accumulating in the release pool approaches a critical mass worthy of implementation.

Results In Fewer Support Costs When Deployed

Because these aspects of Scrum firmly push teammates toward high-quality development and keeps them there, "meltdowns" in deployed applications become rare. With Agile Data Warehousing in particular, ETL and BI modules undergo automated integration testing on a daily basis, letting very few flaws sneak into production code. This result lowers the program's support costs and allows resources to be redirected to enhancements rather than repairs.

Makes Cost Overruns Far More Manageable

No method can change the fact that creating software involves engaging an expensive team that must work through a large number of unknowns. Though delivery and cost overruns will always be possible, Scrum allows organizations to manage such challenges sooner rather than later and achieve far better results. Working from the Product Owner's prioritized wish list for the application, the features with the greatest ROI are implemented first, and because the method yields "potentially shippable code" with each sprint, the delivered modules include the necessary integration and architectural features to be successfully deployed. If the money does run out before the coding is fully complete, customers will have received much that can be used, and in fact the most valuable aspects of their requests will be online.

Scrum Addresses Stakeholders' Fears

The above list of advantages might be summarized by observing that Scrum/XP's addresses a wide swath of organizational fears—fears held by IT management, customers, and warehouse development staff alike. (For a more extensive discussion of this topic, see Chapter 2 of [Beck 2001].)

Customer Fears

Customers fear the big requirements specification process, knowing that a large development effort will be based upon this one snapshot of what they *think* they need. From their perspective, the large requirements document seems more like a contract, and one that will largely transfer to them the blame for any failure that occurs.

Once the monolithic requirements specification is formalized, customers fear that the development team will promptly disappear from sight for nine months or longer. The project sponsors increasingly fear that the project is going off track with every intervening month that the team spends mysteriously typing away at their keyboards.

They also fear the implementation phase of the large system that emerges at the end of a protracted development effort because it is difficult to dedicate the time needed for acceptance testing, especially when the delivery gets repeatedly delayed due to coding gaps that seem to sprout like weeds late in the project when system integration testing starts. They fear all project delays because they know they could lose control of the overall cost of the system, that they may have to invest far more than they want, and that they can easily be left with nothing usable at the end.

Developer Fears

On the other side of the table, developers on traditionally-managed projects have fears, too. They fear being asked to code from incomplete specs and being given too little time to program the system properly. Because architecture and integration problems can hide until integration testing begins, they fear crucial flaws will surface only after a massive amount of code accumulates that must be re-worked in the eleventh hour before implementation. They fear having to support the application after implementation because they know they did not have enough time to make the system "bullet proof."

Developers also dread the 1,000 line project plans that they cannot understand but which represents an impossible deadline they will be expected to meet. Quite often, they realized that the plan became unrealistic the week after it was forged, but there is too much organizational investment in the plan to challenge its dictates, so they remain silent and fear what will happen when milestones are missed toward the project's end. They dread sitting through endless status meetings where "group think" takes over, painting a rosy picture of progress because the project manager is over-stressed and desperately wants to report their project status as still "green."

IT Management Fears

IT management fears having dozens or hundreds of these projects "in flight" with the inherent methodological problems of the waterfall approach constantly eroding away the value of the deliverables to be received. Because multiple systems are typically required to deliver even the most simple C-Level business initiatives, IT managers fear they will be held accountable for the failure of an entire mission critical program should any one of the component projects experience delays or implode altogether. They know such a disaster is probably already festering somewhere, but they do not have the means to find it in time to take corrective action or mitigate its impact.

Why Live With All This Fear?

Inventing new applications involves a plethora of unknowns—questions that get resolved only when working code is delivered. If so much is riding upon conquering these unknowns, should project teams not deliver "early and often," continuously proving that projects are on track? By adapting Scrum/XP for business intelligence, Agile Data Warehousing achieves this goal.

As will be seen in the remainder of this book, the project management methods, system engineering, and architectural frameworks for data warehousing we recommend take some work to put in place. Sometimes this effort is hard to defend until the entire organization has been convinced of the merits offered by Scrum and XP. But because an Agile approach delivers frequently and makes the intervening process transparent to all, these practices allay the fears of customers and IT managers that they will not be allowed to change their minds after a project starts, that no progress is being made, or that disastrous problems are going undetected.

ADW releases developers from having to guard the value of outdated specs and maintain the pretense that their project is the picture of health. Instead, all they are asked to do is to work steadily on requirements and tasks that are accurately described, well understood, and recently confirmed to be still relevant. In that context, despite the effort Agile data warehousing may require to initiate, it becomes their preferred method simply because it is self-corrective, stays "real," and is clearly the most effective means by which large systems can be built.

Hopefully the analysis above will be enough to convince readers and their corporate comrades that the Agile techniques lying at the core of this book's recommendations are a win-win for customers, IT management, and developers alike. If so, then perhaps all parties will give an open-minded appraisal of the remainder of this book's proposal—Agile techniques and tools specifically devised for business intelligence projects.

SUGGESTED READING BY TOPIC

Full references to the materials cited can be found in the References list at the end of this book.

Selecting an agile method	Larman 2004
Adapting standard IT for Agile approaches	Augustine 2005
	Boehm 2003
Generic Scrum	Schwaber 2004
Generic Extreme Programming	Beck 2004
Agile quality assurance	Crispin 2003

Chapter 2—Generic Scrum in a Nutshell

Chapter 3
User Stories for Agile Warehousing

What are "user stories," and how can they be organized into a comprehensive requirements package?

How should Product Owners move from vaguely understood business needs to well-expressed user stories?

How can the team break down large requirements into small and consistent statements that they can quickly estimate and begin developing?

The embedded Product Owner is the "secret weapon" in the Scrum/XP framework, enabling developers to accurately create software without reams of requirements specifications and lengthy review sessions. However, Scrum is a general approach adaptable to building many types of systems. We can further accelerate our BI teams by leveraging the fact that they are building data warehouses. For requirements processing in particular, the Product Owner can decompose large statements of need using a system of BI categories that parallel the design components developers will later employ to architect the necessary data transforms and repository. By sharing with the Product Owner a business-intelligible version of these architectural concepts, a Scrum Master can move the entire team to where the Product Owner expresses requirements in bite-sized, BI-specific work bundles that developers can immediately begin developing. Furthermore, these work bundles provide a set of consistently-defined labor assignments that the team can learn to estimate quickly and accurately. Because good, BI-specific user stories organize the work and sharpen labor forecasting, they are, more than any other technique, the linchpin of Agile Data Warehousing.

Traditional Requirements And Its Discontents

The formal requirements specifications produced by traditional methodologies are complex documents, so involved that organizations are wise to employ specialized, commercial software applications such as Caliber or ReqPro to manage them. The assumption behind the waterfall notion of requirements is that somehow the customer's subject matter experts (SMEs) can specify hundreds of detailed statements of need during one or more interviews before development begins. Waterfall projects are wise to assign well-trained "user analysts" or "systems engineers" as they attempt this task, for there are many subtleties inherent in the process, any one of which can undermine the success of the project if overlooked:

- Requirements are complex, each one capable of having an extensive tree of sub-requirements beneath it that must be followed as far as it leads.
- SMEs tend to describe only the requirements of their division of the enterprise, and no one person may fully understand both sides of an important interface between two particular departments.
- Without some prompting, stakeholders typically speak of their requirements as of the day of the interview, and may be entirely unaware of changes that will emerge over the 12 to 24 months it will take to implement the application envisioned.
- Users express requirements imprecisely in terminology only the business community understands and which means very little to the technical team who must bring them to life through coded programs.
- Even a slight change in wording or interpretation could lead developers into writing thousands of hours of code that will have to be essentially thrown away when the misunderstanding is finally detected.

This last consideration actually represents a pivotal concept in traditional computer systems training courses which warn practitioners that there is a 100-to-1 ratio between the cost of fixing a mistake after it is coded compared to catching it during requirement gathering. Because so much rides upon the accuracy of output from this traditional single-pass requirements phase, user analysts typically build a careful hierarchy of requirements that drill down through increasingly detailed A, B, and C levels. The requirements in these trees are also carefully organized horizontally between a dozen or more categories such as "user interfaces," "data formats," "processing business rules."

Given all that it contains, the traditional requirement specification easily becomes a sizable document that is difficult to understand and manage for anything larger than a small business application. So difficult, in fact, that analysts often reformat its contents into a Requirements Traceability Matrix (RTM) to ensure nothing was overlooked during the many months it takes to build the system so described. As implementation draws near, a team of users and technical reviewers must wade through the RTM, validating line by line that all requirements have been met. Unfortunately, given the months that have passed since the interviews with the subject matter experts, the people who verbalized and understand the requirements may no longer be with the organization.

With all this effort and thoroughness that careful requirements specifications entail, teams should have few complaints regarding the resulting documents. Yet, in our experience "we should have done better at gathering requirements" is the number one lament made during the lessons-learned sessions at the end of projects. Despite the elaborate hierarchies and traceability matrices, something always seems to undermine the value of the traditional requirements spec, including:

- User analysts were not actually given enough time to do a thorough gathering because project sponsors demanded to know early on "why isn't somebody coding yet?!" (WISCY)
- Developers were unable to understand the unwieldy document delivered by the user analysts, and, under the same WISCY pressure as the requirements team, proceeded into design with an incomplete understanding of the task ahead.
- The users who actually verbalized the requirements were unclear what they truly needed because they had never seen software of the type being considered. This is especially common with data warehousing projects.
- Due to business pressures, these "subject matter experts" cannot always dedicate the time needed to carefully express their requirements.
- Perhaps most importantly, the business changed in fundamental ways after the requirements were gathered, making much of the resulting code unusable.

It is easy to see that these factors make the "shelf life" of the traditional requirements specifications document too short to be the proper foundation for months of expensive software development.

One of the early Agile methods called the Unified Process (UP) attempted to address this deficiency through "use cases" which embody the two-fold strategy of a) focusing requirements gathering only on the most important human-machine interactions and b) capturing those needs in a more streamlined format. Use cases are often completed iteratively through their own style of "drill down," often starting with a simple diagram connecting named business roles to high-level features of the user interface. As designers repeatedly interview the subject matter experts, the use cases incrementally accumulate larger sections of prose. Depending upon the particular template used, the first pass may capture for each use case only paragraphs labeled Actors, Triggers, and Flow of Events.

The second pass might result in paragraphs titled Pre-conditions, Post-conditions, and Variations. [Cockburn 2001]

From a Scrum perspective, the use case is a step in the right direction, but still falls short. First, the process aims to collect all information before development, resulting in long documents that must be reviewed. Second, the focus on only the most important interactions risks overlooking important requirements. Third, use case templates became increasingly complicated as UP matured, and many business users consider them even harder to understand than a traditional RDS. Perhaps most importantly, the process still takes too long, and thus is subject to expiring "on the shelf" before the application's code is written.

These realizations led the creators of Scrum and XP to look for something even more lightweight, asking in essence "Is it possible to reduce to zero the lag between requirements gathering and coding?"

THE GENERIC SCRUM USER STORY

In their simplest format, the user stories of generic Scrum/XP are simply a 3x5 index card with one or two, hand-written sentences that frame in a simple way an important business need. They are no more than labels without content, working titles for an individual unit of value the developers could build for the users. They need no further content because in Scrum requirements are expressed in person by the Product Owner just in time for developers to design and code. Thus, Agile practitioners often describe user stories as nothing more than "a reminder to have a conversation with the Product Owner," when the time is right to build the concept captured on the index card.

One beauty of these user stories are that they can be created, moved, edited, or discarded almost as fast as the speed of thought by the Product Owner. With next-to-zero cost, a few dozen story cards can track the entirety of what a Product Owner is thinking as she iteratively discusses with the developers what she needs versus what is possible to build.

User story cards are the focus of the story conference that begins each sprint. The Product Owner pins a dozen of the most important user stories to the task board and moves them around to reflect changing priorities as the entire team reviews them together. The team works its way down through the Product Owner's highest priority cards until it has identified a set that can be delivered during the current iteration. During the story conference, developers often jot down a note or two on a card, so they can remember important points to discuss with the Product Owner when they start working on that requirement. Finally, during sprint planning, the team members will estimate the size of each story in "story points" (discussed in the next chapter), which will help them decide whether they have the bandwidth to deliver upon all the requests during the sprint they are starting.

As long as the working title contained on the user story card is properly expressed, there is no need for the Product Owner or developers to overly invest in details, that is, until they are ready to build out the story described. For this reason, we refer to user stories as "just in time" requirements. Because they are communicated eye-to-eye, no expensive to-be documentation is required, and because the team moves from expression of requirements immediately into design and coding, there is no impairingly short "shelf life" to threaten the team's accuracy.

While story card accuracy can be deferred, the Scrum Master still needs to listen carefully during the story conference for the quality of the stories being transferred to cards, and in Scrum, quality stories means "INVEST":

- **I = Independent:** The team can develop the story without having to start or substantially revisit the work done on another story.
- **N = Not-Too-Specific:** Keep the description short—just enough to propel the team into brainstorming the problem and inventing solutions. Long, specific stories have the unfortunate tendency of miring teams in trying to reconstruct old thinking, often done in haste weeks earlier.
- **V = Valuable:** The story, once implemented, should yield a discrete unit of business value for the customer.
- **E = Estimable:** The concept represented is specific enough to be estimated (more on this in the next chapter).
- **S = Small:** The story, once estimated, will require only a minor portion of the labor available in a sprint, say 20 percent or less.
- **T = Testable:** The story describes a unit of functionality that is small and distinct enough to be testable, especially via XP's continuous testing techniques (introduced in Chapter 5).

We often include "demonstrable" as an objective as well, meaning that a story should result in a tangible unit of working code that can be touched and reviewed by the Product Owner at the end of the sprint.

The above criteria cause the scope of each story to be fairly tight, which is good because each sprint allows only a short time frame in which to move from requirements to working code. Yet, focusing story cards at a very detailed level will result in too many stories. As a rule of thumb, there should be only a half dozen story cards or so per sprint backlog for a team of 7 to 10 working in two- to three-week sprints.

Once committed to paper, formal requirements from a waterfall method are prescriptive and feel "non-negotiable." Scrum's user stories, on the other hand, are descriptive and purposefully vague, so that the discussion they spark during the development phase of a sprint will be collaborative and unrestrained. Scrum wants developers and Product Owners free to be creative, cross-disciplinary, and innovative when they work through a story, believing that the more engaged the parties are in the discussion, the better they will think through all pertinent factors, the better they will detect errors of thought as they occur, and the better the resulting application will be.

Because the Product Owner is typically a single person, she is only a representative of the many types of users that will benefit from the application under development. Scrum suggests that before Product Owners start drafting stories, they first identify the different "roles" that exist in the user community. With those roles (or "personas") in mind, the Product Owner can then verbalize the stories following a simple template: "As a <user role>, I can <action>, so that <benefit>."

In the business intelligence sub-industry of data processing, a typical user story following this template might be: "As a marketing manager, I can obtain a bar chart that shows me how many electronic mailings to existing customers we have sent out by business day over the last three calendar months, so that I can quickly spot a lapse in our marketing efforts."

GENERIC STORIES, EPICS, AND THEMES

For a new team, the Product Owner may often try to pack too much into a story. Product Owners typically go through one or two stretches of high inspiration where they can envision a plethora of valuable services that a BI application might provide, and they can barely write stories big enough or fast enough to capture their excitement. Luckily, Scrum provides an easy device for user stories that lets Product Owners think big at first and refine their notions later.

A draft user story can be too big, as defined by INVEST, either because of the number of details it actually has or because of the number of details it implies. Either way, the team cannot discuss them, let alone code them, as a single, independent effort. So, sticking with the story metaphor, Scrum labels an impossibly large expression of requirements as an "epic" and not a "story." Epics may well need an entire release cycle for the developers to write enough code to bring them to life. In order to make this development incrementally deliverable, they must be broken down before the team proceeds with them.

Somewhere in between an epic and an INVEST-quality story is a "theme." It is still too big to fit on one story card—maybe requiring a full sprint or more to implement—but it definitely has enough specificity that the developers can begin asking questions that will lead to properly-sized stories when answered. Here is a hypothetical interaction between Product Owner and developers that should help Scrum Masters define these three terms more clearly to their teams:

Product Owner: As a manager, I want to use the warehouse to improve our company profits.

Developers: OK, but that's a really big "epic," not yet a story. Can you break that thought down to smaller ideas that each pertain to, say, one type of manager in the company?

Product Owner: All right. As a fulfillment manager, I want a reporting module that shows me where the problems occur in our custom-manufactured product lines.

Developers: That requirement is sure a lot smaller than the epic you first described, but a reporting module can still include many different bar charts, line graphs, pivot tables, and spreadsheets—so we would call what you just described as an important "theme." Can you zero in on one device that you would like to see in a BI tool's display screen and describe what it would tell you?

Product Owner: OK, as a fulfillment manager, I want to start with a summary bar graph that shows me shipments for each custom-manufactured product type versus orders for a given month, so I can see which products we're faltering on.

Developers: Now that request is very specific—we can certainly put that one on a story card. Once you have this summary bar graph and spotted a problem, what would you do next?

Product Owner: I want to double click upon a bar where deliveries are significantly below orders, and then see that gap broken out for each workflow status code.

Developers: Great! That request is also very specific. Let's write that one down on a second story card of its own. Go on....

Developers will be surprised at how quickly most Product Owners will adopt this epic-theme-story hierarchy. Product Owners will assiduously strive to express themselves in story-sized units when they see how well it lets the programmers focus their efforts. Once up to speed, Product Owners should be encouraged to draft user stories on their own, using all three levels of this hierarchy as needed, so that they can walk the team through the project's requirements starting with named epics, drilling down to component themes, and finally to INVEST-quality stories. Such a presentation will make the overall organization of the users' needs much easier for the developers to remember and internalize.

We can also see now a crucial difference between a traditional requirements specification and the requirements that Scrum provides: A highly-trained user analyst builds the hierarchy seen in a waterfall requirements document. In Scrum, the user representative herself generates the inventory of needs, and maintains them in a format and language that the users can readily understand.

As they prepare for the start of a new sprint, Product Owners need only to review the most important stories from their prioritized list and select enough to keep the team occupied during the coming iteration. While still a large task, this assignment is far less onerous than sitting through a seemingly interminable series of interviews with user analysts, struggling to accurately describe everything they could possibly want from the system.

STILL A SEEMINGLY ENORMOUS UNDERTAKING

Generating user stories will be a major undertaking for the Product Owner. She must break down the complex business needs of the enterprise into a prioritized series of bite-sized assignments that the team can use to estimate, track, and control its development work. Because Product Owners come to the team from a business background, not information systems, they are going to be overwhelmed by this responsibility in two ways. First, there is the starting point: the business problem itself will seem enormous and intractable, especially since the solution has been expressed only in enough detail to get the project funded. Second, developers want their assignments in manageable chunks, but how small does a story have to be before it is considered "workable"?

To many Product Owners, defining user stories for a warehouse project can seem like trying to eat an elephant in the dark with nothing but a spoon. The Scrum Master needs to provide the Product Owners with a process and a tool. The process is the easier half: we call it the user story "Verbalization Cycle," and it is a standard Plan-Do-Check-Adapt technique. We have tuned it, however, to dovetail nicely with Scrum's notion of coding sprints and made it specific to business intelligence projects by adding a tool called "User Epic Decomposition." Agile Data Warehousing derived this analysis tool from the target architectures one sees repeatedly in BI projects. Let us look first at the user story Verbalization Cycle and then turn to the User Epic Decomposition tool upon which it relies.

VERBALIZING USER STORIES

Generic Scrum heavily leverages the prioritized list of user stories by employing it to frame the requirements backlog for both a given sprint and an entire release. But where do these stories come from? How does a Product Owner go about verbalizing the needs of her organization into INVEST-quality stories? One approach to this large undertaking is the six step "Verbalization Cycle" as depicted in **Figure 3.1**. We have rendered it as a cycle because Scrum embraces the "progressive elaboration" of requirements in which the team members revisit each requirement with increasing scrutiny as it approaches the top of the priority list. We also portray this cycle as repeating in synchronicity with the team's development sprints to reflect that Product Owners work eye-to-eye with developers, supplying requirements at exactly the breadth and depth needed for each development iteration.

The Product Owner starts with the top half of this cycle, in which she describes and analyzes the as-is situation in business terms. Upon entering the bottom half of this cycle,

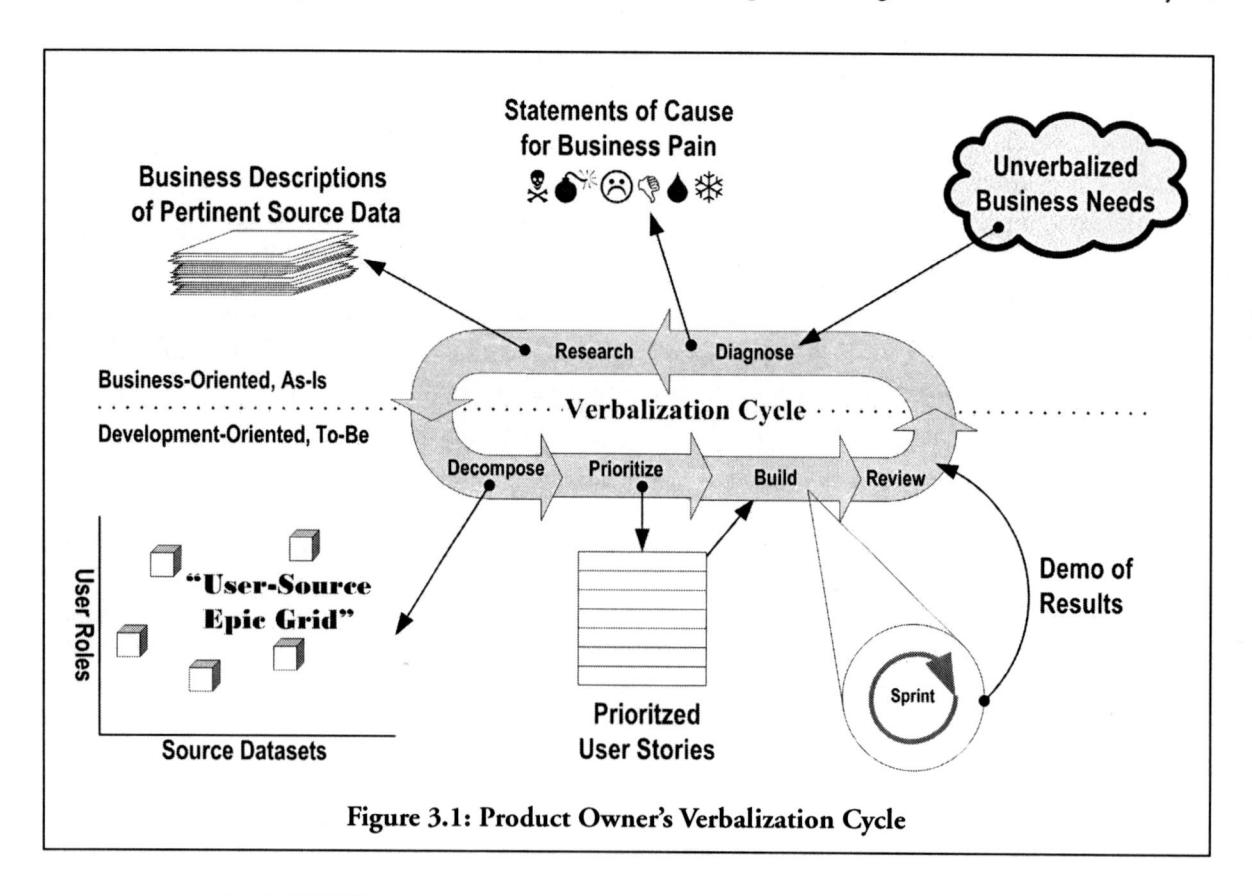

Figure 3.1: Product Owner's Verbalization Cycle

she redirects her focus to the to-be situation desired, adapting her thinking and terminology a bit to meet the developers "half-way" between the business and technical worlds. Her objective throughout the entire cycle is to produce quality users stories so well scoped that developers can use them to both schedule work bundles and guide their daily coding activity.

Although the figure shows what might be tangible artifacts around the perimeter of this cycle, ADW does not require these to be even semi-formal documents. Instead, they should be kept as lightweight as possible. The user story cards will be of course tangible objects, and the business descriptions of source data will probably be data dictionary listings from the line-of-business systems. However, the rest of the artifacts shown on the figure can be nothing more than the Product Owner's well-informed opinion of what the company needs and some hand-written notes that she uses as she guides the team. By and large, it is Scrum's penchant of passing to developers only a small part of the requirements at any one time that allows the team to work with informal documentation and conversation alone. Let us now take a closer look at each step of the Verbalization Cycle, in the order it occurs during a sprint, to see how "lightweight" we can keep the artifacts of each phase and still be effective.

DIAGNOSIS PHASE

In this step of the cycle, the Product Owner confronts the broadly painted goals and objectives set forth by the stakeholders when they proposed and funded the warehousing project. These notions are typically so broad that the Product Owner might as well consider them still unverbalized for the purposes of her team. Accordingly, her goal in this phase is two-fold: put words to the exact business "pain" and identify who is feeling it. These notions map to two of the three segments in the generic Scrum user story template, and should result in a statement along these lines: "As <user role> I want some kind of application so that I can <business benefit sought>."

Let us take a revenue assurance project for a telecommunications vendor as an example. For such an application, the Product Owner might verbalize the business pain as "The billing director knows that we are losing revenue because in some instances customers have ordered services that we have not provisioned, and elsewhere we have provisioned services that we do not bill for." While this statement is not yet a user story because it contains no indication of how to improve the situation, it does identify a purpose and beneficiary for the project well enough to allow the Product Owner to move on to the next phase of verbalization.

BI projects that skip this step of identifying "pain and victim" suffer greatly later in their life cycle. Typically these projects do not achieve any precision in expressing the business benefits underlying their effort. Their user stories tend to repeat the same handful of tired notions of general value and are thus far less than compelling. Benefits are key to "reselling" the project to stakeholders who are new or going stale on the project. Without a substantial list of business pains and those who are suffering each one, the project's value proposition will seem weak, and funding can evaporate. A small increment of extra effort in this step will pay off by not only maintaining sponsor interest but also by kick-starting detailed discussions of requirements when each story drops into a sprint backlog.

RESEARCH PHASE

Given a working notion of current business pain, the Product Owner next maps these issues to broadly defined data sets, identifying groups within the organization that can provide the information needed to solve the problems. This exercise requires an understanding of the organization's line-of-business systems, the general scope of their function, and their data at a business level. Most directors and many managers already have this type of understanding. Using the example we started above, the Product Owner would evolve the statement of business pain into something akin to: "To make sure we collect all the revenue we could potentially earn, the billing director needs to compare the order entry system to the provisioning work orders and both of them to the invoiced services in the billing system to make sure there are no discrepancies between any two of them."

The Product Owner can catch many nuances at this point in the analysis, all of which are still business-level concepts, including:

a) whether the systems owners can be persuaded to provide data extracts, either by pushing exports to the warehouse or by letting the warehouse connect and pull data out.

b) whether the granularity and timing of extracts match (e.g., "Can all source systems provide transaction histories by customer and service code by 2 a.m. every day?")

c) whether the data contained in these sources is complete and/or free of errors from data entry or prior system data conversions.

The extreme data normalization of many commercial line-of-business applications places detailed understanding of data structures beyond the reach of most business users, so the Product Owner will rarely refer to actual data tables in expressing her findings from this phase. Instead logical, working titles for the data sets will have to suffice for guiding the team. For example, the Product Owner might refer to simply "customers," leaving it to the developers to discover later that the extract will have to join the Party and Party Role tables.

With this high-level list of the source data sets required, the Product Owner can now devise a notion of how these data sets should combine in order to address each point of business pain identified in the Diagnosis phase. Of course, many data sets such as "customer" can be found in multiple source systems. We mentioned above that the Product Owners should inquire as to the completeness and quality of source data. This information will allow her to guide the team on choosing and combining this overlapping data.

We can imagine that all the probable data sources for a warehouse will line up side-by-side to form a reference axis, and that the user roles can be ordered similarly to form another such axis. These two axes, then, define a plane of users and sources upon which we can record the results of our Research phase where each point identifies an intersection of source data with key user roles. This is the "User-Source Epic Grid" depicted in Figure 3.1, so named because, as Product Owners articulate solutions they want in Scrum-style epics, we can conceptually locate each one somewhere on this plane.

Such placement has a very important value in terms of constraining the work assignments verbalized by the Product Owner so that they are actionable work assignments. By insisting that the Product Owner clearly specify the one user and the one combination of source data for every work assignment, the team goes a long way toward ensuring that all assignments are small and independent. The remaining constraints needed to achieve INVEST-level quality will be instilled into the user stories by the next phase, Decomposition.

As a final note, let us mention that the team will buy itself some extra speed if it considers during this phase whether all data extracts will be accessible using the team's existing tools and in usable formats. One developer will need to play "systems analyst" for this effort, because some IT applications knowledge will be needed. Yet, even a cursory look at source data formats may require the Product Owner to adjust her notion of the work packages the project will require. For example, developers working entirely in Unix might be vexed that a particular data extract is available only through IBM mainframe tools, because it will be encoded in a difficult character set (EBCDIC). Negotiating and developing an alternate ASCII-based extract transferred via FTP will probably require significant labor, enough that the Product Owner should create a story card for this effort so that it will be visible and properly managed throughout the release cycle.

DECOMPOSITION PHASE

At this point in the Verbalization Cycle, the Product Owner is very clear on the business problems to be addressed and the combination of existing source data that can solve them. In the Decomposition phase, the Product Owner begins articulating BI modules she wants built. At first these work requests are expressed at user epic level, but the Scrum Master and developers will help break down these notions into more granular and actionable user stories.

In this step, the Product Owner will take each epic and begin decomposing it using a set of categories that mesh well with BI applications. The team needs to have identified these categories ahead of time and communicated them to the Product Owner. This framework is easily defined because the categories match the architectural elements one finds in most enterprise warehouses, such as front end versus back end, as well as data layers, and refresh types. We provide a full sample set in the next section.

In deriving a usable set of architectural categories by which to guide a BI development program, teams need to achieve several objectives:

- Moving a single step within any category represents an increment in value that a business person working with the data warehouse can understand.
- The elements in these categories have been arranged in approximately the order in which they must be developed. For example, one must populate a staging layer before loading data into the rest of the warehouse.
- These elements are mostly independent of one another, so that the team can enhance one through programming without having to work on any of the rest.

Naturally, there will be a separate set of architectural categories for the front-end and back-end portions of the warehouse. **Figure 3.2** depicts a suggested set for the back end, and **Figure 3.3** portrays a similar set for the front end. As can be seen in these figures, each set organizes the categories into four axes, with two of them being common to both front and back ends: transformation type and refresh frequency. However, the difference between data transformation and presentation force us to define the remaining two axes uniquely: The back-end set involves target layer and refresh type, whereas the front end requires user friendliness and automation level.

For both front and back end, these architectural categories will allow the Product Owner to describe a desired end state as a location within the "space" created by the four axes. Once this end state has been identified, the Product Owner can decompose it using the categories comprising each axis into a specific path they want the team to take in solving the focal business problem. As portrayed in **Figure 3.4**, these axes allow this path to be described as a series of incremental steps, each one involving a change along only one

Figure 3.2: Back-End User Epic Decomposition

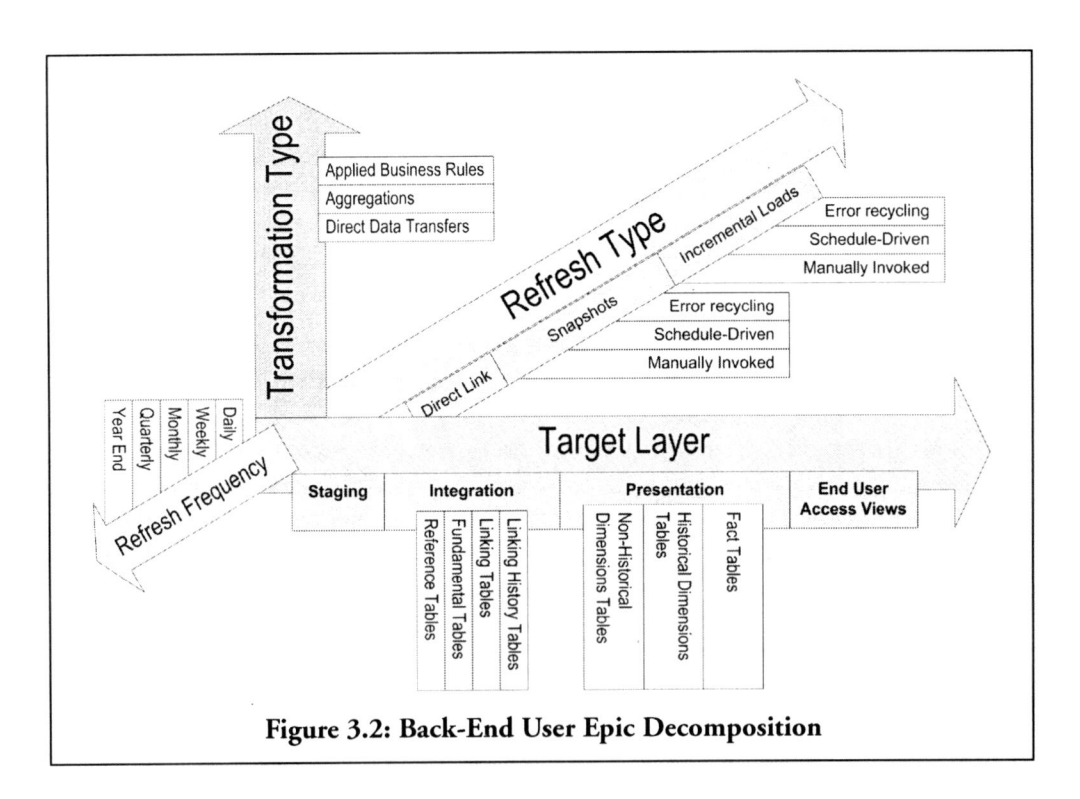

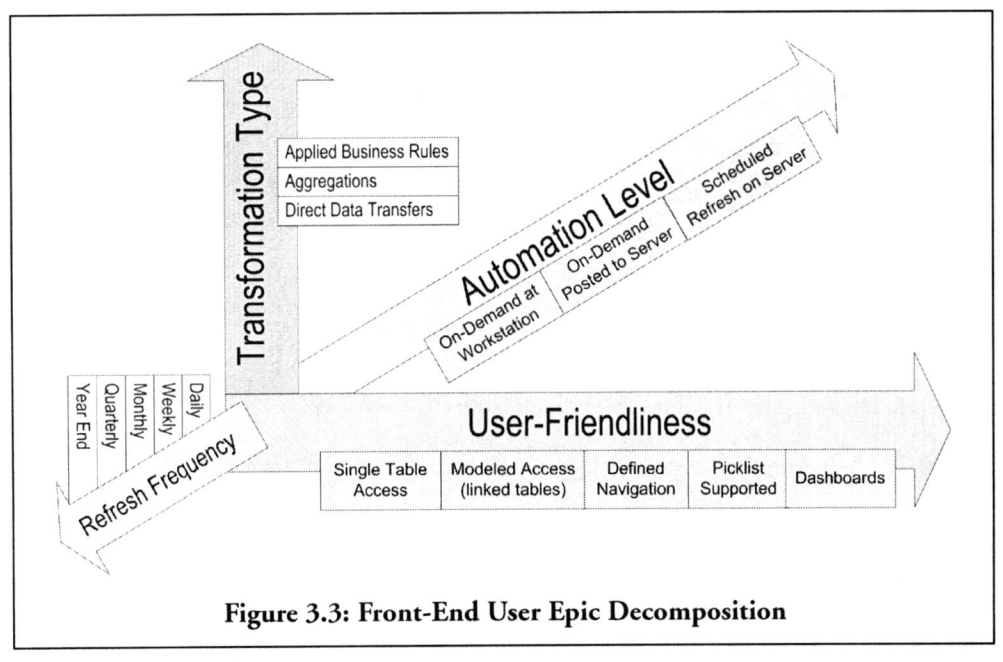

Figure 3.3: Front-End User Epic Decomposition

Chapter 3—User Stories for Agile Warehousing

axis at a time. (For clarity, the figure depicts progress on the plane defined by only two of the back-end dimensions, Refresh Type and Target Layer.)

Such a progression is perfect for Agile warehousing because each of these steps represents a small, independent, valuable increment of business value, in other words, a user story. Themes become visible as well as two or more single-category movements. When all themes have been achieved, the parent epic can be considered complete.

Though this process might seem complicated at first glace, the dimensional approach provides a strong measure of badly needed organization to a warehousing project, and in practice Product Owners seem to embrace the approach quickly. As we will see in the next chapter, it also streamlines estimation for our Agile Data Warehousing method because the stories it generates are tightly scoped using terms that match the way the team prefers to build its BI applications. Every story is verbalized as a simple choice of four coordinates, each taken from a small domain that is very familiar to the developers. So familiar, in fact, that any such combination is instantly understood to the point where they can forecast the effort needed to build it quickly and accurately.

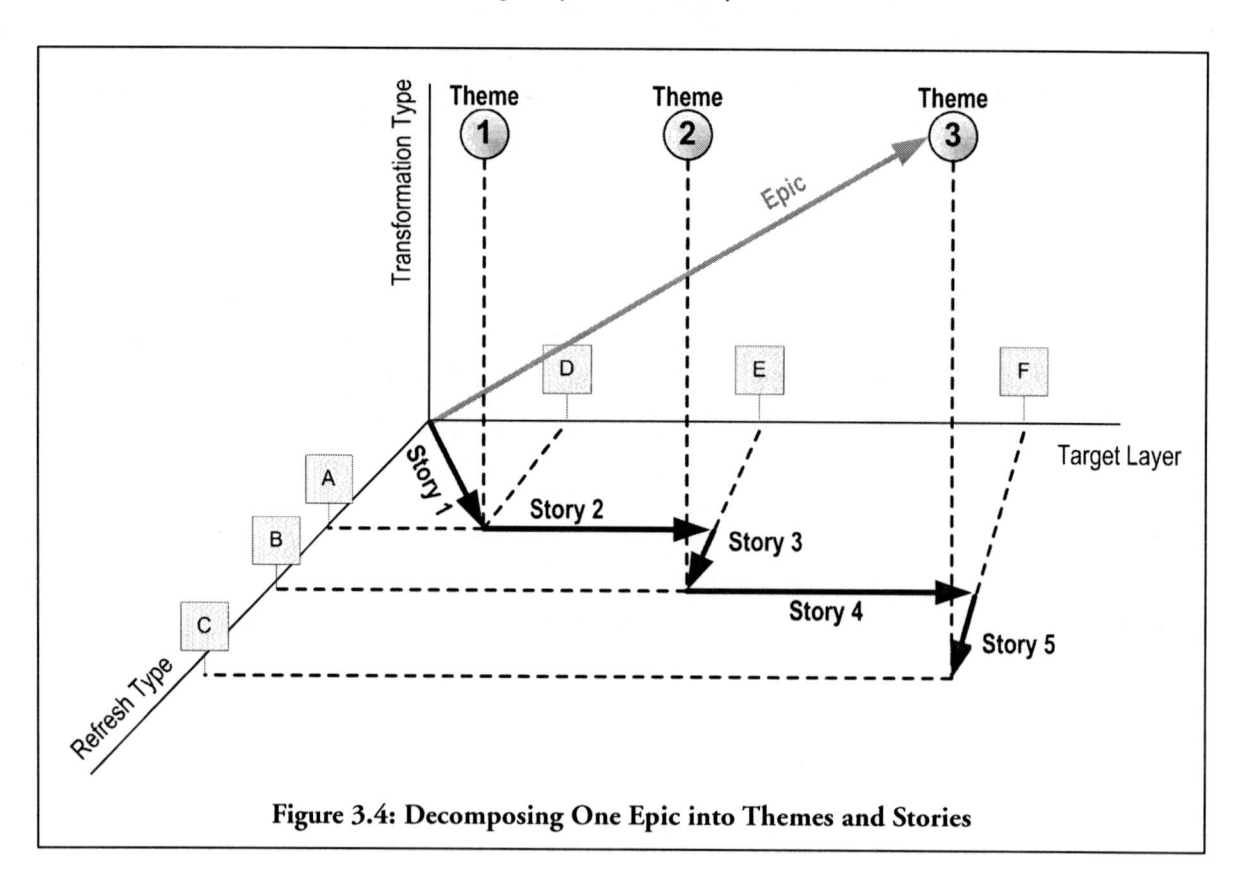

Figure 3.4: Decomposing One Epic into Themes and Stories

PRIORITIZE PHASE

While the Decomposition step may require some thinking to get started, it quickly yields well-scoped stories and thereby places Product Owners in a position to prioritize their needs into sprint backlogs, and eventually release backlogs when need arises. When working with a large number of stories, grouping them by the themes from which they were derived is a good way to start off sorting them. Luckily, the Product Owner needs to arrive at a precise ordering only for stories that will be considered for the next sprint. If there are a few themes where the Product Owner is ambivalent as to priority, the developers will often have an opinion as to which order will be easiest based upon the technical issues involved. Once prioritization is completed, the Product Owner is ready for the next story conference, armed with a set of tightly scoped, high quality user stories that the team can immediately understand, flesh out, estimate, and build.

BUILD PHASE

The Build phase of the Verbalization Cycle is simply a full Scrum development sprint, including story conference, development, and user demo. We re-cast the sprint here as a discrete step of the Verbalization Cycle because the story conference and discoveries during development often prompt the Product Owner to re-express stories in greater detail. Although the descriptions produced during this step can be quite wordy, Product Owners find the verbalization of the Build phase straightforward because the preceding Decomposition step suggested a particular solution for a well defined business problem faced by a specific user.

REVIEW PHASE

The Review phase of the Verbalization Cycle begins with the sprint's user demo because at that point the Product Owner not only inspects the working application for operational flaws, but also evaluates how well the code answers the need expressed by the user story it addresses. For the most part, the Product Owner reflects privately upon how well she has worded the user stories. However, the developers will naturally mention during the sprint retrospective the quality of the story wording if it impeded the speed of their coding. Whichever the case, the Review step ends with a sprint retrospective. The inclusion of this review step makes the Verbalization Cycle a continually optimizing process, which, as we will see in Chapter 8, is important in preparing ADW for CMM Level 5 maturity.

SPRINT/VERBALIZATION INTEGRATION

Figure 3.5 includes the linkages between ADW's Verbalization process and generic Scrum process, as highlighted in the step descriptions above. True to the spirit of Agile, none of the artifacts depicted in this figure, including the prioritized list of user stories, require formal documentation or review. The lightweight nature of all these artifacts cause many Product Owners, when they are first introduced to Scrum, to think the project will not require much of their time. Yet as we have seen, the full cycle actually implies a good deal of work for them, starting early in the project and continuing for at least two thirds of the release cycle. Even then, integration and testing activities will have grown to absorb the Product Owners attention, so at no time during the project should the Product Owner find herself idle.

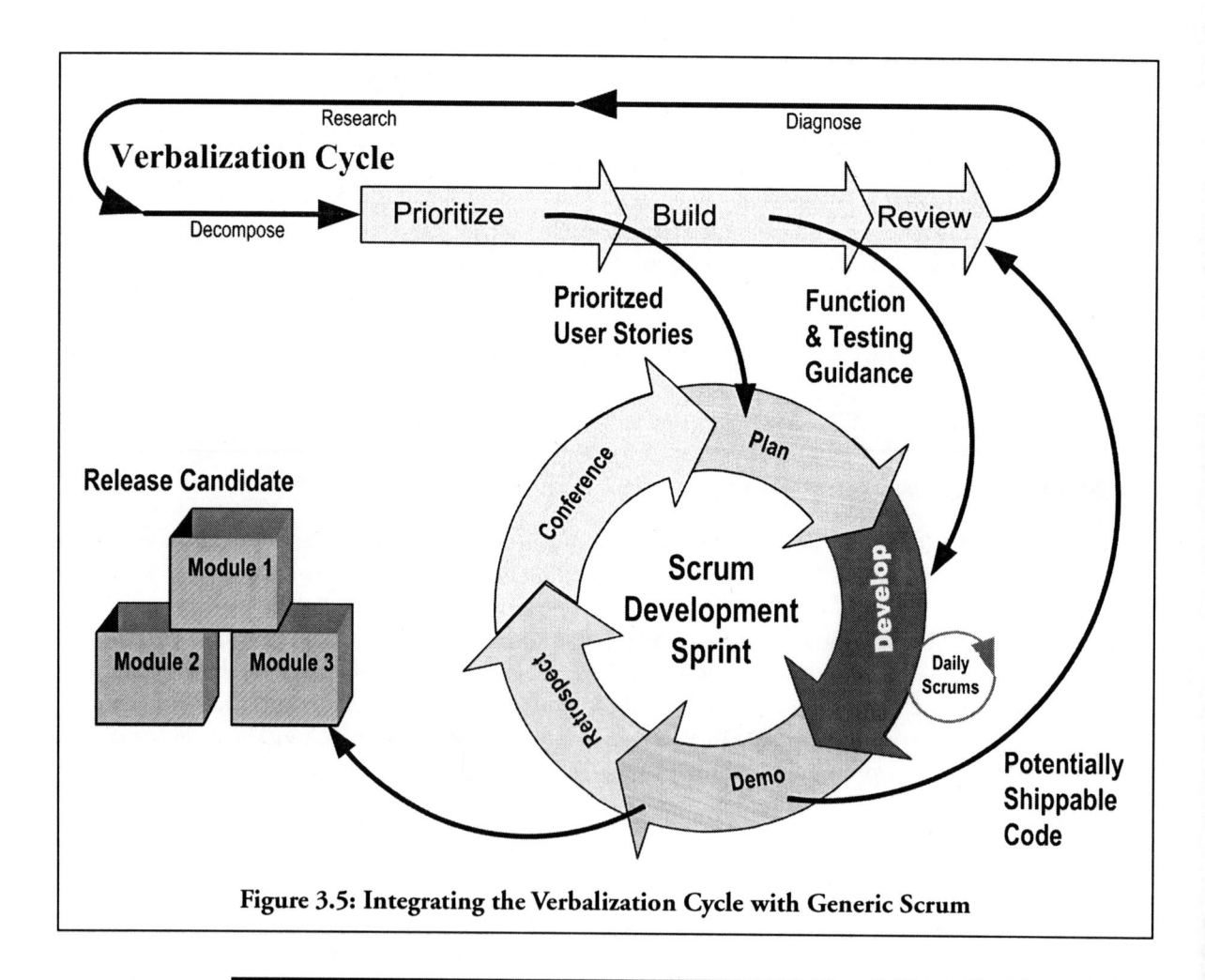

Figure 3.5: Integrating the Verbalization Cycle with Generic Scrum

Decomposition For Back-end Epics

While examining the Decomposition phase, we saw that the proper breakdown of user epics is the key to both generating quality user stories and enabling the developers to estimate the level of effort coding will require. Although the coordinates suggested for our front and back-end decompositions are derived from the developers' desired data warehouse architecture, they must still be labeled and described in such a way that they make business sense to the Product Owner as she employs them for her analysis work.

Every warehousing program will have a different preferred architecture, and even that will change over time, so we cannot put forth in this book a single set of coordinates that will cover all of business intelligence across all organizations. We can, however, provide a starter set of coordinates, giving readers a good place from which to craft a decomposition scheme of their own.

Returning to Figure 3.2, we can see it includes the dimensions required for the back-end epics of a fairly typical enterprise data warehousing program. The epic "cubes" that would fill the four-dimensional space defined by the axes displayed can represent any user stories pertaining to the data repository and its load processes the project will require.

Not all of a Product Owner's requested epics will be equally ambitious. Many will occupy only a portion of this space whereas others will seem to span it completely. Because we have arranged the coordinates along each axis to match the sequence in which code typically evolves, we can think of this space as being filled in an orderly fashion from the origin outward as the code for a given epic matures. Simple epics can be pictured as smaller cubes resting against the origin rather than having many disjointed segments in this space with gaps of unimplemented features between them. The collected stories of a completely functional back-end module will typically fill all the space defined.

In the remainder of this section we will look at the coordinates along the four axes utilized in this figure for the back end. To make analysis immediately useful to the reader, we describe these coordinates in terms that a business person working with data warehouses will understand. We will address them in order, considering the incremental benefit gained by moving from one coordinate to the next.

Seeing the benefit of many of the steps along these story axes will be easier if the reader keeps in mind that, for the Product Owner, guiding a development team across the multiple iterations of a release will often seem like herding cats. Yes, developers want to deliver what the Product Owner requests, but they often propose what seems to be wild detours, and use many technical terms when describing why each is needed. Furthermore, Product Owners quickly learn even seasoned developers are challenged to align all at once the many business rules, data structures, and ETL modules required. Accordingly, the primary benefit the Product Owner obtains from many of the steps described below will be only proof that the team understands the source data and has truly mastered its ETL environment.

TARGET LAYER DECOMPOSITION

A typical data warehouse involves several structural layers in the target database that taken together form the facility's "data repository." These layers can be named in the order they appear as data moves from source to end users, as depicted in the Figure 3.2: staging, integration, presentation, and finally "end user access views." What follows below are descriptions of these component layers and, for most of them, the types of tables found in each. Moreover, we describe the benefit the Product Owner will see when the team finishes loading data into each layer or table type, benefits she can use as the verbiage for her user stories.

STAGING LAYER

Description: A place to "land" source data so that ETL applications can begin working with it. Usually contains one staging table for each source table or view drawn upon.

Benefit: Populated staging tables prove that the warehouse team has finished the technical setup and business negotiations required to actually connect with the source systems. Source data can be now easily accessed for inspection regarding completeness and quality. Join patterns between tables can be validated, proving that data integrates, at least using "natural keys" of the source.

INTEGRATION LAYER

Description: A layer of the warehouse that end users typically cannot access. Facilitates splitting, re-assembly, and historical layering of source data in a way that the front end can eventually use. Commonly modeled in third normal form or higher, with tables linked together using synthetic keys. One staging table often supports the load of several integration layer tables.

Benefit: Where the target tables contain records derived from multiple sources, loading this layer proves that the team can manipulate the data and still have it tie together despite its new, synthetic keys. This layer also allows the ETL to detect and reconcile between contradicting values in cases where sources have overlapping information.

Component Tables

Reference Tables
- **Description:** Independent tables in the integration layer providing standard encodings for text and numeric values. Often the Product Owner and other business representatives specify the codes to be employed. Frequently these are the first warehouse tables to be loaded because they contain standalone records with no values in "parent" tables that they must match.
- **Benefit:** Gets the integration layer started and ready for business—Proves that the developers and the DBAs have physically created the storage space in the database.

Fundamental Tables
- **Description:** Contain business data needing no parent tables in the data model. More dynamic than reference tables because they derive from values in the source system.
- **Benefit:** Begins adding business data to the integration layer, laying the ground work for later loading of the all-crucial linking tables that integrates the warehouse data.

Linking Tables
- **Description:** Tables with records that tie to one or more "parent" tables. Many will require fundamental business data to be previously loaded.
- **Benefit:** Can now review how complex hierarchal data and transactions will be stored in the warehouse. Proves developers understand how each source table should be distributed across multiple target tables. Proves the team can successfully manage synthetic keys which will later enable them to depict the histories of business entities.

Linking History Tables
- **Description:** Tables recording how the relationships between records in parent tables change over time. Team may have created these objects as simple linking tables and included history features later by adding columns such as "Valid From" and "Valid Till" dates.
- **Benefit:** Can now review how the warehouse will portray changes in source systems as seen through successive data extracts. Proves that developers have mastered closing out the old image of an item before adding its new image.

PRESENTATION LAYER

Description: Holds the "data marts" which are departmentally-oriented subsets of the enterprise data warehouse. Often they are based upon a dimensional model rather than the relational, third normal form. Typically, the tables in this layer are wrapped with database views that provide some last minute formatting and expansion of data, as well as controlling who can access the information.

Benefit: Data is now ready for the front-end tools to access and present to the end users, or at least to the reporting tools. Many of the tables in this layer can be accessed directly by "power users" who have some skills with the reporting tools and are accustomed to building their own reports.

Component Tables

Non-Historical Dimension Tables

- **Description:** Tables holding the attributes of major business elements, organized in a series of progressively finer categorical subdivisions. These "analytical dimensions" allow users to tightly focus the reports they will request from the warehouse, and often allow users to "drill down" through the data retrieved to focus on ever smaller corners of the business. Portrays business elements in their current state, not how they have changed over time.
- **Benefit:** Can now try out the filtering capabilities end users will some day employ. Demonstrates that the team can successfully express each hierarchy in a business-intelligible fashion. For complex data dimensions involving two or more hierarchies, proves that the hierarchies were planned so that their intersections were clear and usable.

Historical Dimension Tables

- **Description:** Dimension tables with records that change over time. Teams often start by loading only current values for dimensions with hierarchies, and then add historical layering once the latest values are modeled accurately.
- **Benefit:** Can now review how end users will restrict reporting to a particular point in time or time range. For those situation where a related fact table exists, the Product Owner can now see how the BI application will depict historical trends in business activity.

> *Fact Tables*
> - **Description:** Tables holding the "metrics" or numeric values describing the business. When these tables are linked to the dimension tables built earlier, users can disaggregate these numbers down to the lowest components of the business elements modeled. Fact tables can only be loaded after their related dimension tables have been populated.
> - **Benefit:** Can now see the numbers behind business events. Can drill down to break out the numbers across a wide range of business elements. Proves that the team can successfully distribute the numbers of the organization to the business elements involved. Can also demonstrate that the numbers will "roll up" properly as one moves from a very detailed examination to a higher level of summarization.
>
> *End User Access Layer*
> - **Description:** A set of "wrapper" views around the tables of the Presentation Layer. Defines join paths between tables so that users cannot build inefficient queries. Gives team an inexpensive way to add additional features such as final formatting or simple calculations. Allows the team to mask out maintenance changes made to the base tables.
> - **Benefit:** Proves that warehouse has a working means to prevent many long-running queries. Demonstrates team's ability to reformat or extend data quickly without having to involve more labor-intensive changes to the database or ETL.

REFRESH TYPE DECOMPOSITION

The Refresh Type dimension of our back-end decomposition scheme speaks to how data actually accumulates in the tables enumerated above, whether appearing there via a direct link to another database, a "kill-and-fill" snapshot (total refresh), or an incremental load. We provide some details each type of refresh and the benefits accruing to the Product Owner as the ETL developers successively achieve the increments along this dimension listed in Figure 3.2.

Direct Link

Description: A direct connection to the table as stored in the source system. Direct links are employed in the staging layer only and for source tables that can be utilized as-is. For line-of-business sources, direct links are temporary measures, allowing the team to postpone physically staging data while investigating issues such as data quality that bear upon whether a table will be used at all. They can be utilized as a permanent measure for accessing tables already warehoused in another subject area or warehouse.

Benefit: Like those of the staging target layer—quick data access, proof of data usability.

Snapshots

Description: "Kill and fill" loads of a table where all existing data is expunged and the target table is refilled with all of the source data or the particular portion that is needed.

Benefit: Can be used to get any target layer of Figure 3.2 started and ready for business. Provides motivation for a new team to get their ETL tool up and running. Provides a low-effort means of quickly loading some "real" data that will let front-end teammates begin developing reports.

Snapshot Refresh Sub-Types

Manually Invoked

- **Description:** Only occurs when the developers directly trigger the ETL code to run. The first invocation against an empty table simulates an initial load. Subsequent invocations are needed to simulate incremental loads.
- **Benefit:** Can prove that a new ETL module works. Allows validating the implementation of business rules. When applied against a source subset, supplies benchmark ETL durations for projecting the likely run times of full initial loads.

Schedule-Driven

- **Description:** ETL is invoked by the scheduling software.
- **Benefit:** Proves team can configure jobs in the scheduler. Allows ETL to run hands-free, proving that long chains of transforms will run without manual intervention.

> *Error Recycling*
> - **Description:** Records that cannot be loaded are sent to a "suspense" table. Records are later removed from the suspense table when a subsequent ETL run succeeds in loading them.
> - **Benefit:** Can trace the processing of all records in the staging table. Provides details as to what cannot be loaded so records can be repaired in the source systems. Empty suspense tables indicate that the team has finally aligned all warehouse components including source descriptions, ETL, and target structures for a given data set.

> **INCREMENTAL LOADS**
>
> **Description:** Only the records that have changed are added or updated. Can require retiring old images of a record before adding its new incarnation. Detecting and loading delete transactions can require some additional staging and ETL support. For staging, may require maintenance of "high watermarks," (e.g., the last transaction date seen in the previous data set loaded).
>
> **Benefit:** Reduces load times for the warehouse. Proves that warehouse can synchronize with the source data in an efficient manner without duplicating or dropping records.
>
> **Incremental Load Refresh Sub-Types**
>
> *Same as "Snapshot Refresh Sub-Types" above.*

REFRESH FREQUENCY DECOMPOSITION

This decomposition dimension describes how often the data loads occur. Figure 3.2 lists only a few of the possibilities, ranging from daily to year end. Any step along this dimension can represent a large increment in value to the Product Owner because, especially with financial data, some of the most important metrics arise only during month-end and year-end processing.

Each step along this dimension can involve a unique set of business rules, so the Product Owner will probably want to use each increment as the basis of a separate story to make the effort manageable for the team. This dimension is also highly visible to the larger stakeholder community because, as the team delivers on each of its increments, end users can begin reviewing a large, new set of key performance metrics. These financial period-based metrics are often so important that they might easily have been the primary reason the warehouse project was chartered, so this Refresh dimension becomes an major consideration in most ADW release plans.

TRANSFORMATION TYPE DECOMPOSITION

This architectural dimension speaks to the processing that occurs among the columns of any given record, and is a consideration for both front-end and back-end systems.

> **DIRECT DATA TRANSFER**
>
> **Description:** No processing of the columns taken from source—they are written as-is to targets.
>
> **Benefit:** An uncluttered starting point that confirms basic ETL capabilities and which makes the data at least accessible to the Product Owner.

> **AGGREGATIONS**
>
> **Description**: Application of group functions such as sums and averages. Often creates the actual metrics that users want to see. Required to decrease record volumes along the path to the presentation layer and thus speeds up later data operations.
>
> **Benefit:** Product Owner can begin validating many of the figures the warehouse was intended to provide. Reduces load windows. Speeds performance of front-end apps.

> **APPLIED BUSINESS RULES**
>
> **Description:** Application of inter-column and inter-table logic. Provides columns of the derived metrics that users frequently need to assess progress along high-level business initiatives.
>
> **Benefit:** Product Owner can begin providing her customer with the metrics only advanced data transforms and integration can supply.

DECOMPOSITION FOR FRONT-END EPICS

Front-end reports are objects that can be not only generated when needed, but also automatically scheduled and distributed among stakeholders. Thus we can speak in terms of automation and refresh frequency for the warehouse's front-end application. Like the back end, front-end epics also decompose into actionable stories using four dimensions. In fact, front-end epics borrow two axes from the back-end decomposition framework—Transformation Type and Refresh Frequency. However, as portrayed in Figure 3.3, the back-end dimension of Refresh Type has been simplified into "Automation Level," and the Target Layer has been replaced outright with "User Friendliness."

We provide in this section a suggested categorization for the two axes unique to the warehouse's front end, listing for each coordinate along them the benefits each step offers the Product Owner. Again, in crafting one's own set that a Product Owner can readily use, the key is to express the categories for each axis in business terms rather than technical terms, and then to place them in the order that they will naturally occur as the warehouse evolves.

One fortunate characteristic of business intelligence systems is that front-end and back-end objects can be largely un-coupled. One can deliver a very elegant front-end module, say, by drawing upon only the simplest back-end repository, such as staging tables. This assists the Product Owner's efforts to define INVEST-quality stories because it permits front-end stories to be largely independent from back-end enhancements. The Product Owner can in fact focus mostly on one side of the warehouse, front or back, leaving the the other face unchanged during one or more iterations.

User-Friendliness Decomposition

This axis of our front-end decomposition scheme sequences the complexity of the user interface from the most simple data access to the most polished and functional forms of BI application displays. Here we describe each point along this continuum and list the major benefits the Product Owner should expect from each one.

Single-Table Access

Description: Simplest possible BI module that presents an individual table (or pre-defined view) of the warehouse.

Benefit: Allows quick access to a variety of tables for validation purposes.

Modeled Access

Description: Still utilizing the default interface the BI tool provides, this approach now pulls data from multiple tables. Joins between tables are pre-configured by developers. The BI tool then uses these joins to generate at run time the query language needed to yield the desired output.

Benefit: Validates the relational integrity of the underlying back-end data repository. Provides the groundwork upon which more complicated BI objects can be built.

DEFINED NAVIGATION

Description: Users can move between multiple analytical objects packaged within one BI module. Optionally, users can double click on some displays to either travel to another analytical object or to drill down into a subset of the data originally shown.

Benefit: The team can begin validating usability of the front end. Can move quickly between objects because users no longer need to open a separate module per item displayed. Can traverse and validate the hierarchies stored within data mart dimension tables.

PICK LIST SUPPORTED

Description: Eliminates much of the work of defining a "report" by giving users a data entry form to define the query limits using pull-down lists of appropriate values. The choices for many fields can be selected from a pre-populated set, and the entry form often dynamically removes choices from later lists given the values entered earlier.

Benefit: The team can begin validating potentially shippable BI modules. Reports take much less effort to define. Furthermore, if these pick lists are based upon a fetch of distinct values from the database at the time the reports are run, they will eliminate much maintenance programming later when the business creates new values in the source with which they will want to incorporate in their report definitions.

DASHBOARDS

Description: Several analytical features of multiple types (e.g., listings, graphs, and pivot tables) placed together in a single display.

Benefit: End users cannot only quickly view the current situation facing the organization, but also click on display elements that appear out-of-the-norm, in order to drill down and research underlying causes.

AUTOMATION LEVELS DECOMPOSITION

Once a front-end module is defined, it can be accessed by the end users in more than one way, each of which can serve as a increment of development around which the Product Owner can organize her user stories.

> **ON-DEMAND OPERATING ON USER WORKSTATIONS**
>
> **Description:** BI modules transferred from the designer's workstation directly to that of the end users. Users will have to invoke the module as an executable loaded on their personal workstations or a shared network drives. No data will be displayed until the module is executed by the user.
>
> **Benefit:** Quick, low-cost way to distribute BI modules to a few users such as the acceptance reviewers. Creates the groundwork for automated data refresh.

> **ON-DEMAND, POSTED TO SERVER**
>
> **Description:** BI module placed on server so that users with the proper privileges can retrieve the most current version.
>
> **Benefit:** Distributing changes becomes quick and easy because all users access a single instance posted on the server. Query execution times can shrink if the application server has a high speed connection to the database server.

> **SCHEDULED REFRESH ON SERVER**
>
> **Description:** A front-end module posted to the server, then run on a scheduled basis with results stored as a shared object on the BI host.
>
> **Benefit:** Avoids the contention caused by many front-end queries invoked at peak times. Processing can be scheduled to occur during slack times when the servers have processing power to spare. Results are available to end users the moment they open the report.

VALUE CHAINS PRODUCT OWNERS CAN UNDERSTAND

We have now built a detailed framework for decomposing user epics into warehousing-specific user stories. Let us now use it to build a couple of sample story sequences and see if it indeed produces a chain of deliverables, each providing incremental value that a Product Owner can appreciate.

Sticking with the revenue assurance example we started above, let us say that the team has already placed the billing data in the warehouse. The Product Owner now wants to see the services installed for customers versus those being invoiced. Indeed we are starting from a well defined point on the User Role-Source Data Set grid: the user feeling the pain is the billing director, and the next data set we need to solve the problem is work orders.

Given our framework, the Product Owner might express the goal for a given sprint as "add the work order data to the back end's integration layer and give it a daily refresh." For the front end, she might ask the team to provide "a report screen where I can define a given billing cycle and then get a report showing any discrepancies between the list price of a service and what was actually billed." The team would quickly respond that those requests are both epics—much bigger than a story that one developer could accomplish within a half-day/half-sprint time frame. They must be decomposed into stories that are independent, estimable, and small.

A Sample Back-end Value Chain

With the help of the team and the decomposition framework established above, our Product Owner might break down the back-end epic into a series of user stories that would read as follows:

1) Build and manually invoke a staging job for the work order data, so that we confirm our access to the data which the Provisioning System's owner promised. (Start at "Snapshot, Staging, Direct Data Transfer" coordinates on Figure 3.2.)

2) Build and manually invoke a snapshot of work order data in the integration layer, so that we can see whether it links to billing data like our analysis suggests it will. (Move to the "Integration" coordinate of Target Layer axis.)

3) Now that we have seen that manual, kill-and-fill work order snapshots take three hours, convert the ETL into an incremental load so we can be sure the whole set of warehouse transforms will complete within the four hour load window we have been allowed. (Move to "Manually Invoked Incremental Load" coordinate.)

4) Schedule that incremental load so that work orders will run each morning without a hiccup or manual intervention. (Move the to "Scheduled-Driven Incremental Load.")

5) Add some business rules to filter out open work orders from the integration layer and prorate the list price for the number of days in a billing cycle. (Move to "Applied Business Rules" on the Transformation Type dimension.)

6) Load the work order dimension tables one time by hand so that we can confirm the drill down paths created for the Work Order Types. (Move to "Presentation Layer, Non-Historical Dimension Tables" on the Target Layer axis.)

7) Load the work order fact table one time by hand, so that we can prove that the complex dimensional model our design recommends actually gives results that reconcile to our billing system reports. (Move to "Fact Tables.")

8) Schedule the incremental loads for the work order dimension and fact tables so that we can begin tracking these discrepancies across the cycles of the billing system. (Bring the Presentation Layer transform up to "Schedule-Driven.")

Each of the above requests required movement to the next category along a single axis of the back-end decomposition space. Stories in such a sequence will be very close to small, independent, and estimable. Verbalizing each step required only a cursory knowledge of how the envisioned warehouse would be built, but no more than a good developer could explain and a computer-literate Product Owner could understand. Finally, each step moved the team perceptibly closer to the Product Owner's goal of placing a second data set along side of another in the data mart, and thus had real value in the eyes of the Product Owner.

A Sample Front-end Value Chain

A similar chain of stories offering incremental value can be crafted from the framework we sketched above for decomposing front-end requirements. We'll focus in this example on the two axes that are unique to the front-end decomposition plan. Some steps will imply a companion step in the back-end system, but most of those were listed in our list of user stories above, and are assumed to occur as needed. Let us note also that all changes are made on a development platform, so that stories regarding promotion of code into production are out of scope. The Product Owner's front-end stories, then, would read similar to what follows:

1) Build a default listing of Work Order Type, which we just added to the data mart, so we can validate that we are creating a usable hierarchy. (Start at "Single Table Access.")

2) Add the work order fact table to this model and build a default listing for the work order table, so we can validate the new entities just loaded into data mart join correctly. (Move to "Modeled Access.")

3) Add a link to the billing data and then add a screen where we can easily specify the billing cycle, work order types, and date range the application will report on. (Move to "Pick List Support").

4) Now that this module works on my desktop, post it to the BI server so that others in my department can validate its information. (Move to "On-Demand, Posted to Server.")

5) Schedule this module for automatic refresh and email distribution so that we will not have everybody running the same query first thing in the morning. (Move to "Scheduled Refresh.")

As with the back-end module, each of these user stories required movement by only one category along a single axis of our four dimensional decomposition space, and thus is small, independent, and estimable. None of them required the Product Owner adopt extensively technical language, but instead only high-level ideas of what goes where in a data warehouse and how it arrives.

A Utility For Managing User Stories

As we have seen, Scrum Masters can devise a framework to guide the Product Owner in crafting user stories to lead the team. However straightforward such a framework might seem, it will still generate a large number of stories with several classifying elements. From this large collection the Product Owner will soon wish to filter, sort, and print select stories for the next story conference.

IT professionals coming out of large, waterfall-oriented shops might suggest a requirements management package, but in our experience the leading packages are too involved to be deployed quickly, plus all their features make maintenance of the stories difficult to sustain. Luckily, managing the user stories created using this chapter's framework involves only one table and a few filtering elements. We will close this chapter with a high-level design of just such a "story management utility," so that readers will have a jump start on supporting their Product Owners when they become overwhelmed by the large number of stories this method can generate. These stories need to be well-managed because they are the input stream for our next chapter—estimating the user's stories accurately now that they are well defined.

A Single Table Data Model

A perfectly usable story management utility (SMU) can be constructed using only one table—"user_story." The hierarchy between epic, theme, and story is simply modeled as a self-referential link that relates one story record in the table to its parent. A "story type" column, which can take the values "STORY", "THEME", or "EPIC" creates levels for the records involved in a particular hierarchy, and a simple constraint requires that STORY records be linked only to THEME or EPIC parent records, and that EPIC records be linked only to "EPIC" parents. Thus the records within the user_story table can be assembled and queried as a "bill of materials" structure, which provides the Product Owner the ability to drill down from epic to component stories.

Columns For The User_Story Table

The following list identifies some columns that the user_story table will require and some thoughts on the contents and constraints affecting them. Understanding that the Product Owner may wish to enter a candidate set of stories, and then polish them later during conversations with the developers, all columns suggested will take a null value unless otherwise marked.

Label: A short name by which a story can be quickly referenced during a sprint's story conference. Non-nullable.

Priority: The all-important column for the Product Owner, allowing the SMU to print an ordered wish list for the team to discuss. Should be nullable so that stories can be added without forcing the Product Owner to prioritize before they are ready. We suggest making this a rational number with at least two decimal digits so that new stories can be easily placed in between existing ones. In order to keep the Product Owner from having to wallow in increasingly smaller numerical increments between priorities, the application will need a "re-set priority numbers" function that will bump all the decimal priorities to whole numbers while maintaining the order already set by the Product Owner.

Story Class: Non-nullable, either "FRONT_END" or "BACK_END."

Story Type: Each record can be designated as either an EPIC, THEME, or STORY. The value set here will constrain which type of parent and child links the record can have, as mentioned above.

Value Class: Either USER (default), ARCHITECTURE, or TECH_DEBT. Most records entered by the Product Owner will be categorized as "USER," meaning they describe a increment of value some end user is seeking. Developers must work upon long term architectural issues and to close off any "tech debt" accumulated during previous sprints. This attribute allows the team to track both these two categories of "stories" using the SMU.

Subject Area: A field for recording the major division of the target warehouse to which the story pertains. Sample values can be MARKETING, FULLFILLMENT, CUSTOMER_CARE. Non-nullable but the last value entered should become the default for the session since a particular Product Owner will generally stay focused on one subject area at a time. Large projects can have multiple Scrum teams focusing on separate subject areas, so this field will allow candidate work lists for individual teams.

User Role: This field and the next capture the high-level scoping of the story in terms of its location on the User Story/Source Data set grid. This non-nullable field captures the business party needing the solution expressed by the story.

Source Data set: The Product Owner's best guess at what constellation of sources will be necessary to implement a given story. Nullable because defining a source data set may require assistance from a systems analyst on the team.

Function: This field and the next complete the Scrum story template of "As <user role>, I can <function>, so that <benefit>." Its data type should be a very long string, perhaps even a "memo" column.

Business Value: Another "memo" field where the Product Owner can enter the "benefit" portion of the Scrum user story template. In our experience, this field needs to be left nullable because in practice Product Owners prefer to focus upon the who and what and later "backfill" the reasons why.

Framework Coordinates: Supported by a pull-down list showing the dimension-coordinate pairs shown on Figures 3.2 and 3.3 (or the modifications upon this set that the team has chosen to use instead.)

Product Owner: A short, non-nullable column for recording the initials of the product owner who verbalized the story. Very useful for situations where there are either multiple parties creating user stories (each responsible for drafting stories for a different user community) or where the lead Product Owner has changed over time (common in lengthy warehouse programs).

PO Comments: A memo-type column where the Product Owner can record any further insights into the story.

Record ID: A serial number uniquely identifying a story record.

Parent ID: The ID of the parent story record, which must be of the proper story type to be assigned, as discussed above.

Previous Story ID: For those stories comprising a step-by-step chain of incremental value, a pointer to the story upon which the current record builds, allowing reports to list a beginning state that a particular iteration improves upon.

Last Definition Update: The last date any of the fields above were modified for a given record.

Inclusion Status: A non-nullable field taking values such as "DEFINED", "QUEUED", "REJECTED", or "ACCEPTED," which match the life cycle of a story. Allows the Product Owner to alternatively focus upon stories that are completed, underway, or waiting for implementation. For records of "USER" category, the value of rejected and accepted is determined by the Product Owner based upon what they see during a sprint demo. The development team must set the status for architectural and tech debt categories.

INCLUSION DATE: An automated field recording the date the field above was last updated.

ACCEPTANCE DATE: Date the story was accepted as "done" by Product Owner during a sprint user demo session.

DEVELOPER COMMENTS: Like the Product Owner Comments field, this column gives developers a place to record the answers to questions they posed to the Product Owner during the story conference and which might help them estimate the level-of-effort later. Such notes will be mostly added by hand to the cards that this utility prints, but having this field provides a notes field for a Product Owner and team member who might be entering an initial set of stories as preparation for the next story conference.

Chapter 4
Avoiding Overcommitment with Agile Estimation

Why is overcommitment so common and how does Scrum's sized-based estimation avoid this trap?

How can we use the burndown chart to spot and correct problems with our estimation?

Can a solid measure of a team's Agile velocity be the only metric we need to guide the team?

The Standish Group's *Chaos 1999* report revealed that less than one third of IT projects over $750K are implemented within budget and with all the features promised. They cited "underestimating project complexity and ignoring changing requirements" as basic reasons why projects fail. [Standish 1999] Our presentation of Scrum and user stories for data warehousing in the preceding chapter offer a means for revealing project requirements more accurately and for responding constructively to change, but it still leaves the problem of estimation unaddressed. Put bluntly, developers rarely estimate accurately, leading project sponsors into expecting too much and budgeting too little for the undertaking to succeed. Despite the growing sophistication of our industry, inaccurate estimates continue to vex information systems groups, as it has since software engineering began, leading one long-time observer to sadly ask "How can experts know so much and predict so badly?" [Camerer 1991]

Given the pivotal role accurate estimation plays in any project's success, Agile Data Warehousing has focused carefully on the practice to devise a clear-cut path toward better level-of-effort forecasting. ADW begins with an innovative "triangulation" approach offered by Scrum and XP, adding to it the User Epic Decomposition framework we presented in the previous chapter. The resulting approach reformulates the practice of estimation from a pressure-laden contract with IT management into simple, historical reporting. ADW focuses estimation upon standardized parts, and embeds it into a repeating cycle with a vital feedback loop so that developers learn to forecast accurately and then continue to stay in top form.

The result benefits all parties. Managers receive low-cost and dependable planning information. Developers discover new and powerful ways to prevent management and themselves from overloading their team. Moreover, by removing unrealistic deadlines, developers stay focused on writing shippable code, so that system quality improves, and everything else in the project seems to progress far more smoothly. Good estimation becomes so integral to project success that Agile warehouse developers sometimes half-jest that accurate estimation is their real job and the only true metric of success—notions we will explore at the end of this chapter.

THE DAMAGE DONE BY BAD ESTIMATES

To understand our motivation for focusing so intently on re-tooling level-of-effort (LOE) estimation, one only has to consider the incredible swath of destruction a significant under-estimate can cause for waterfall-based BI projects. There is considerable empirical evidence that developers forecast only half the effort their tasks will take, with a large amount of skew in the distribution above this mean. [Demarco 1982, Little 2004]. If management funds and schedules the project based upon only one half the effort required, then somewhere near the expected delivery date, the project is going to appear for all intents and purposes undoable as defined.

Suddenly, developers will be making heroic efforts requiring large amounts of overtime to deliver something of value, but because they are missing 50 percent of the time and resources they need, these efforts will soon prove futile. Quality, which became moderately neglected as soon as overtime started, will fall precipitously as developer morale begins to sink. The extra costs of overtime will exceed the project budget long before the first release sees production, resulting in unhappy sponsors. Scope will be cut in order to restore some measure of feasibility, creating unhappy customers. Downstream teams that had taken the project's forecasted delivery date and feature set only with a single grain of salt will find that an important prerequisite to their projects will not be delivered.

As the logistical, financial, and political strains of the situation reverberate between departments and executive offices, the organization enters, crisis by crisis, the "disappointment cycle" sketched in Chapter 1, so that eventually final costs far exceed the value delivered. At the project postmortem, tempers will flare before the team arrives at the crux of the problem, one that many of them have seen before: "Why did we promise *again* to fit 10 pounds of sand into a 5 pound sack?"

Two Estimating Approaches

Estimating software development requires a good deal of thought because we are trying to mentally anticipate all contingencies in a complex set of tasks for an application we have never built before. The profession has taken two main approaches in forecasting level-of-effort: formal estimation models and expert judgment.

Formal estimation models are parameter-driven formulas that will, when provided sufficient metrics describing the software envisioned, yield both a mean and a variance for the level-of-effort required to build it. Expert judgment, on the other hand, involves providing a system description to experienced systems professionals, then relying upon their largely intuitive processes to provide a probable level-of-effort and a range of uncertainty.

Formal models are appealing because they seem to encapsulate years of lessons-learned into formulas that one can inspect, if interested. In practice, however, such models have been expensive to build and disappointing in results for the simple reason that, for all their cost, they are no more accurate than expert judgment. One survey of a hundred IEEE papers regarding software effort estimation methods indicated that "… estimation models are very inaccurate when evaluated on historical software projects different from the project on which [they] were derived." [Jorgensen 2000] Data warehouses constantly change due to technological innovation and their application to new business areas of the enterprise. This novelty frequently amounts to a new type of project and undermine the value formal estimation models might provide.

A second reason that formal models often disappoint their sponsors is that, as they incorporate steadily more lessons learned and internal formulas, these tools become "over-engineered"—incomprehensible and mistrusted by the estimators using them. We have seen systems engineers working with 3,000 cell estimating spreadsheets who have actually overwritten the output cells with values of their own judgment because they did not believe the figures provided. They had neither the time nor the interest to trace the doubted output's derivation across the fifteen sub-sheets involved.

Third, formal models require time and effort to create and maintain, effort that might have been better spent bringing the desired warehouse online and yielding value. Expert judgment, on the other hand can be deployed in very short order and "… seems to be more accurate when there [is] important domain knowledge not included in the estimation models, [or] when the estimation uncertainty is high as a result of environmental changes.…" [Jorgensen 2004] For this reason, we will focus exclusively upon expert judgment for the remainder of this chapter.

The project management profession suggests several methods for both gathering the input and then collating it into an expert judgment forecast, such as "wide-band Delphi."

[PMI 2004 and NASA 2004] The least disciplined approach to LOE forecast is unfortunately the most common: the *planning forum*. In this "technique," representative experts gather into a protracted, face-to-face meeting where they simultaneously draft or refine the project's WBS and forecast task-by-task the LOE estimates any way they see fit.

Many organizations claim to utilize formal expert judgment methods that instill discipline into their approach, but we have witnessed the "single pass" planning approach of waterfall methods combine with normal business time pressures to repeatedly overwhelm the best of intentions. Too often teams abandon the formal method, gather into a single conference room, and "hammer out" an estimate for management as fast as possible. Time and time again, a company's prescribed estimating approach dissolves into a harried planning forum.

Because the combination of a waterfall approach and a planning forum is such a common context for estimation, we will use it as a baseline to examine several systemic forces that make typical LOE forecasts not only inaccurate, but heavily biased toward underestimation. Once we have those shortcomings in mind, we can then consider an Agile approach that will lead us to a faster and more accurate technique for data warehousing estimates.

Why Waterfall Teams Underestimate

A recent study of 120 projects at a world-leading firm in the oil industry confirmed what studies twenty years earlier had first documented: Information Systems teams display an inability to forecast LOE accurately. The average forecast was only one-half of the actual labor required, the distribution of estimates was so wide that no usable confidence interval could be discerned. [DeMarco 1986, Little 2004]. What are the dynamics at work within IS groups that causes them to underestimate so relentlessly? The bulk of the answer lies in the lamentable nature of the waterfall approach to software development that makes estimation an unrewarding task, performed as a one-pass effort, typically in a suppressive climate for developers who would otherwise estimate more carefully.

A Single-Pass Effort

According to the PMI's outline of the standard project management practice, company management works through a series of cost estimates as they envision, fund, and later plan the project in detail. Supposedly, project managers should work with the project team or a group closely resembling it to derive forecasts that range from order of magnitude (-25% to +75% accuracy) down to a definitive estimates (-5% to +10%). [PMI 2004] In the waterfall approach, this last estimate is married to an elaborate work breakdown structure, at which point the team can begin analysis, design, and development, making the detailed estimation effort essentially a single pass effort, though cost and schedule may be "re-baselined" as needed throughout the project.

In this common approach to development projects, LOE estimation is something developers are asked to do only once in a while. It is tedious work and many months pass before the estimators discover how well their forecasts match actual results. With these three factors in place, developers view accurate estimation as only a low priority requirement for their job, no where near as important as technical skills and even political acumen.

Management also subconsciously discounts estimation because of this single-pass approach. Obtaining an estimate from the development team is simply a milestone that must be achieved before managers can finish their project proposals or hold a project kickoff. They approach the developers with a detectable emphasis on getting the estimate done quickly so it can be presented at the next steering committee meeting, often giving the team insufficient time to make a proper assessment. Furthermore, estimation is a cost, and once a (supposedly accurate) estimate is in hand, there seems little sense in continuing to invest in an effort that has already delivered its payload. Like developers, management sees estimation as something done rarely—an occasional, necessary evil.

FEW IMMEDIATE CONSEQUENCES AND FEEDBACK

In the single-pass approach the reward for estimating well is remote and indirect. Accuracy in overall LOE estimates is measurable only many months later as the system approaches implementation. Because the actual work eventually involves a mix of tasks very different than those foreseen, the quality of the many small estimates that went into the overall forecast is difficult to ascertain. Tallies of actual labor hours eventually arrive, but they are usually aggregated across WBS components, so that the root cause for forecasting errors end up hidden in averages and standard deviations. Furthermore, troubled projects often get cut in scope, making it impossible for developers to match their earlier level-of-effort forecasts to the project actuals. In this context, little natural learning occurs that would make the developers better at estimating.

Moreover, the slow and muddy feedback on the quality of their LOE forecasts means that the developers are not subject to forces encouraging accuracy in estimation. Developers, working line-by-line through a tedious WBS in a planning forum must conscientiously envision in detail the steps required to complete each task and how long that work will take. Yet as mental fatigue sets in, what immediate consequence keeps them from estimating each subsequent task a little less carefully? Whereas making both a bottom-up and a top-down pass through the WBS would provide a good cross check on their overall tally of labor hours, as teams tire half-way through their first pass on a large project, the urge to finish up eventually overtakes their initial thoroughness. They rush through the rest of the first pass and can omit the second pass altogether, so no cross-checking takes place.

OVER-OPTIMISM REWARDED

Compounding the inaccuracies introduced by a single pass context with little effective feedback, developers feel pressure to pare their estimates for several reasons. Whether projects are proposed to internal boards or external customers, everyone involved with the estimate realizes that too high a tally will cause the proposal to be rejected. Accordingly, a "price-to-win" mentality takes over where each developer begins quoting each task at the smallest possible estimate that the team or higher-ups will accept. This approach has the added advantage of avoiding many micro-conflicts with the Project Manager, who often has an opinion on how long the effort should take and can have autocratic powers to override the estimates provided by developers. Even worse, research has documented that managers view high estimates as a signal that a developer is less qualified than he should be, and do not correct this bias when the lower estimates turn out be wrong. [Jorgensen 2006] Over the years, developers learn of this bias and become reluctant to send the wrong signals with pessimistic estimates.

NO GUARD RAILS AGAINST ERRORS

The factors above combine to give pre-eminence to overly confident estimators within the group. There may be several bright developers on the estimating team who can see both the ineffectiveness of the planning forum approach and the enormous harm that bad estimates can cause, but there are some powerful forces keeping them from correcting the situation.

As recent research has shown, the problem with incompetent people is that they lack the ability to recognize their own incompetence, a blindness that allows over-competent developers to thrust hasty guestimates for each task upon the group. [Goode 2000] Unfortunately, groups engaged in a shared effort such as estimating often fail to properly push back upon improper impulses due to *group think*, defined as a "mode of thinking that people engage in when they are deeply involved in a cohesive in-group, when the members' strivings for unanimity override their motivation to realistically appraise alternative courses of action." [Janis 1972] Whereas many would expect a Project Manager to guard the team against this unfortunate pack mentality, the same research defining group think revealed that "directive leadership" actually exacerbates the problem.

Conscientious members of the estimation team may wish to correct the error-prone process unfolding within the planning forum, but have no alternative to propose because many organizations do not teach a standard estimation process or at least one robust enough to undercut dynamics as pernicious as overconfidence and group think.

THE ADW ESTIMATION TECHNIQUE

Clearly, estimation using the planning forum has many obvious flaws. Over the years, waterfall methods worked at improving the practice, but only by incorporating Agile's iterative planning will we escape the limits of the single-pass approach. As a further step, Agile Data Warehousing adds to Agile estimation such assets as the user epic decomposition framework, reference models, and basis-of-estimate cards yielding a new method altogether for estimating business intelligence projects. The components of the resulting process involve many components, which we will detail in this section, namely:

- Sized-based estimation to give the team greater speed, accuracy, and validation of its labor hour forecasts
- Frequent estimating sessions so that teams keep their estimation skills honed
- Standardized reference stories and task lists to minimize unknowns
- Thorough feedback so that teams can steadily improve their accuracy
- Re-footing of the estimation process to remove conflicting goals
- Cross-checking of estimates through top-down and bottom-up comparisons

Before looking at the ADW estimation process, we should be clear that there are three, key objectives for level-of-effort estimation. First, when teams estimate the upcoming work at the beginning of a sprint, they seek to avoid overcommitment. Second, when they estimate work remaining during a sprint, they wish to assure everyone that development tasks have not grown to where they threaten the success of the current iteration. Third, when teams estimate an entire project's worth of stories, they seek to confirm for management that the project is indeed as doable as everyone believed when it was originally proposed and funded.

For all of these purposes, we need reliable level-of-effort forecasts, and this need moves the emphasis on estimation in an unexpected direction. In the previous section, we described how Demarco's and Little's research showed that the average team underestimates development effort by one half. One might think this revelation means we need only to double a team's estimate in order to achieve the reliable forecasts, but unfortunately such an adjustment would only give us estimates that are accurate *on average*. Because cost and schedule overruns have such adverse impacts on an organization and careers, stakeholders are actually far more interested in estimates that have a 10 or even 5 percent chance of being too low, rather than simply accurate on average.

In practice, developers must nearly guarantee that actual expenditures will not exceed their forecasts, yet 90 to 95 percent accuracy would require enormous estimates. **Figure 4.1** shows the distribution of estimates versus actuals as revealed by research. [Little 2004] The long tail to the right indicates there are many projects that run far in excess of their original effort forecasts. With such a wide distribution, one would have to actually forecast costs at *quadruple* the average in order to achieve a 90 percent confidence level. Quadrupling our estimates might make our estimates dependable in that they are rarely exceeded, but the resulting quotes will be so high that sponsors will refuse to fund most projects.

Consequently, the hallmark of a good forecasting approach is not that its level-of-effort estimates average to a value close to actual expenditures. Instead we would rather have the estimates cluster tightly together at the same distance from the actual values observed later, even if that discrepancy between forecast and actual expenditures is quite large. In other words, a small *variance* is far more important than the location of the *mean*. As shown **Figure 4.2**, a forecasting method that has the distribution depicted by Line A may hover around a average that is too low, but because the estimates cluster tightly around the mean,

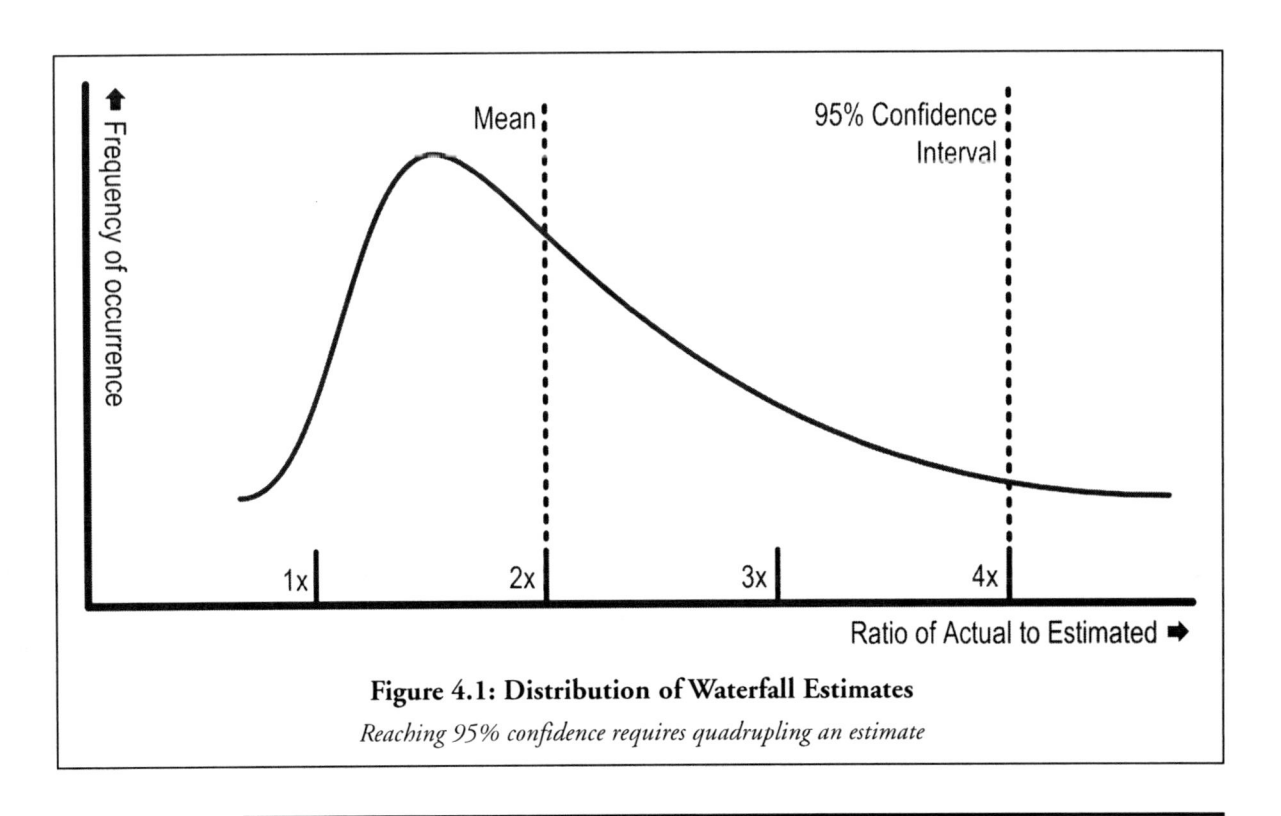

Figure 4.1: Distribution of Waterfall Estimates
Reaching 95% confidence requires quadrupling an estimate

Chapter 4—Avoiding Overcommitment with Agile Estimation

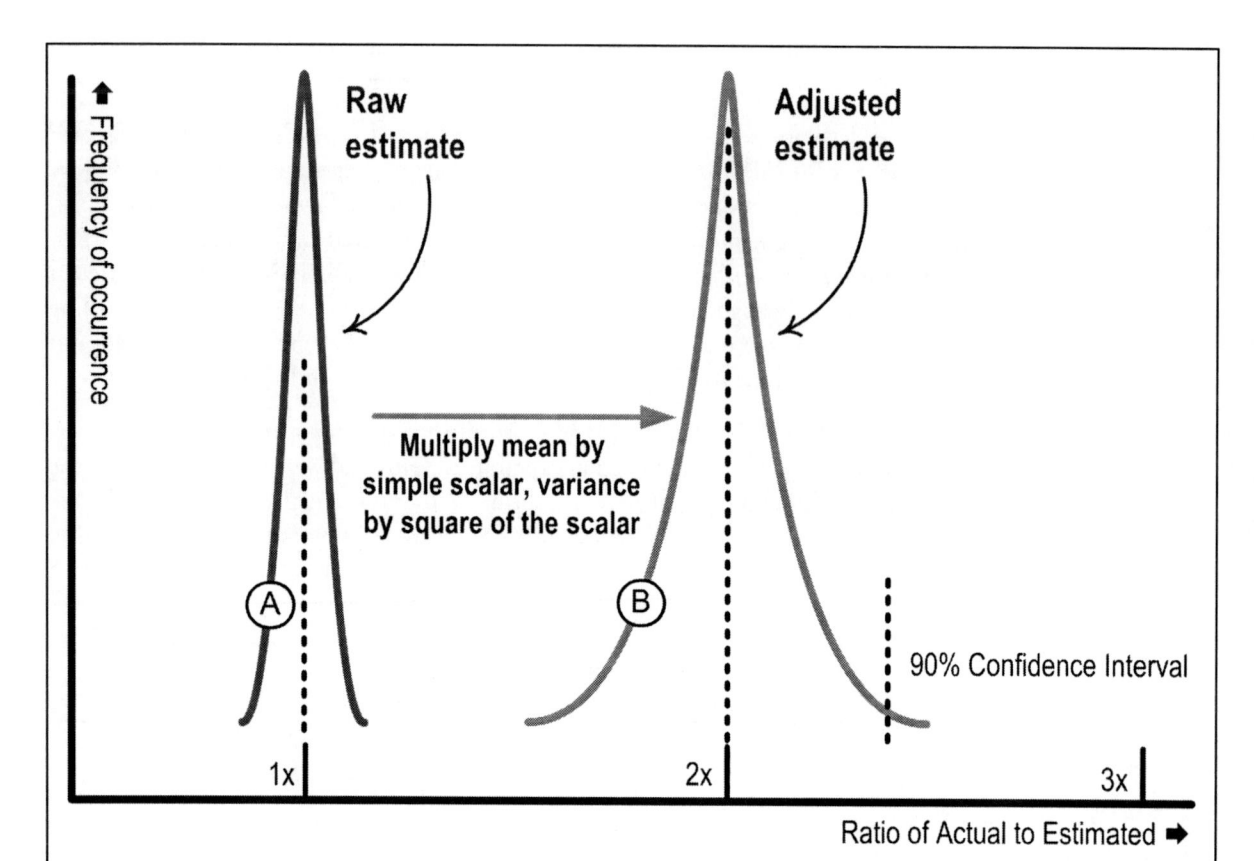

Figure 4.2: ADW Estimates Are Usable Because They Have Much Less Variation
The small variation allows planners to correct underestimation by simple multiplication

its predictions are still quite usable after a simple adjustment. The adjusted estimates will retain the small variance, so that the 90 percent confidence levels will be only slightly to the right of the forecast made by Line B, and projects can be safely funded without drastically inflating the estimates.

Given the pivot role that forecasting effort plays in setting stakeholder expectations, it is not surprising that the IS profession has studied effort estimation in great depth. Over the years, research has amassed more than a hundred possible objectives for the practice, although recently one researcher was kind enough to consolidate them into twelve key recommendations, which we have listed in **Table 4.1**. [Jorgensen 2004] In our work with data warehousing, we were able to blend the User Epic Decomposition framework presented in the last chapter with the common estimating techniques of generic Scrum/XP.

Table 4.1: Twelve Objectives for Good Estimation

Listed with how they are incorporated into the ADW method (adapted from Jorgensen 2004)

Topic/Objective	How in ADW
REDUCED SITUATIONAL AND HUMAN BIASES.	
1. Evaluate estimation accuracy, but avoid high evaluation pressure.	Evaluation by group performance only
2. Avoid conflicting estimation goals.	Consistency as the only goal
3. Ask estimators to justify and criticize their estimates.	Estimating Poker & Sprint Retrospective
4. Avoid irrelevant and unreliable estimation information.	Scrum Master monitoring
5. Use documented data from previous development tasks.	Reference stories and BOE cards
6. Find estimation experts with proper background and experience.	Developers are the experts
SUPPORT THE ESTIMATION PROCESS.	
7. Estimate top-down and bottom-up, independently of each other.	Story points v. OLEs
8. Use estimation checklists.	Reference stories and BOE cards
9. Combine estimates from different experts and estimation strategies.	Story points & OLEs
10. Assess the uncertainty of the estimate.	Sprint Retrospective
PROVIDE FEEDBACK AND TRAINING OPPORTUNITIES.	
11. Provide feedback on estimation accuracy and task relations.	Burndown Charts
12. Provide estimation training [learning] opportunities.	Practiced in every sprint

This combination yields a streamlined method that is easy to follow but also rich enough to achieve the key objectives for effort estimation.

THE ESTIMATION CYCLE

Generic Scrum/XP revolutionizes effort estimation by turning the central question on its head. Rather than asking the development team "How long will it take to build the whole system?", the Agile approach asks instead, "How much can you build in a set time frame, namely, one sprint?" If the team can provide an accurate and consistent answer to that question, management can and should use that figure to calculate project cost and duration for themselves, leaving the developers in peace to actually write the code.

The answer to the question is, in fact, the team's *velocity*, as introduced in our chapter on generic Scrum. Tracing how the team's velocity evolves and interacts with the User Epic Decomposition framework across the iterations of a project, one can easily sketch a four-step ADW Estimation Cycle that runs concurrent with the multiple development sprints that make up the Release Cycle's Build Phase. This cycle is depicted schematically with the major features of each step in **Figure 4.3**.

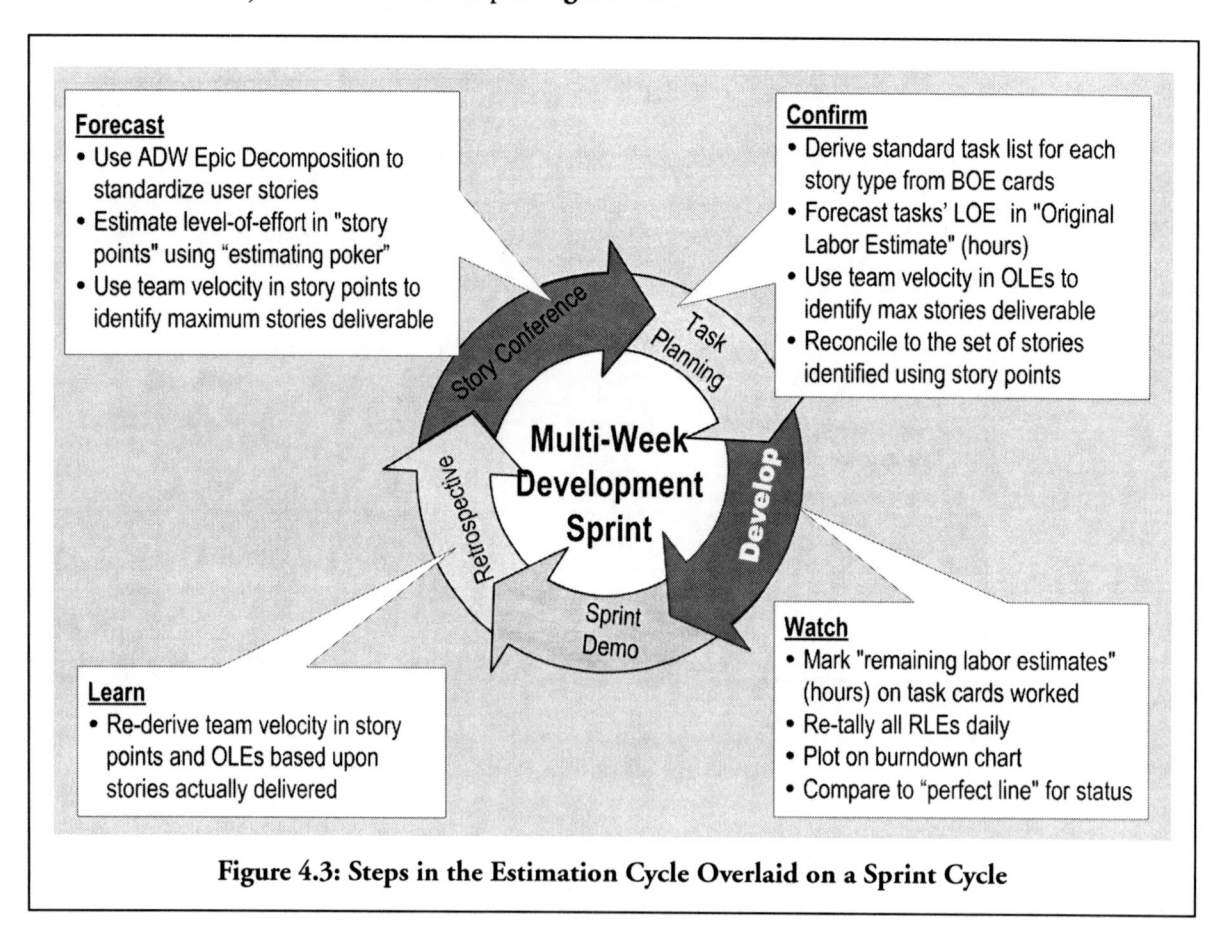

Forecast
- Use ADW Epic Decomposition to standardize user stories
- Estimate level-of-effort in "story points" using "estimating poker"
- Use team velocity in story points to identify maximum stories deliverable

Confirm
- Derive standard task list for each story type from BOE cards
- Forecast tasks' LOE in "Original Labor Estimate" (hours)
- Use team velocity in OLEs to identify max stories deliverable
- Reconcile to the set of stories identified using story points

Watch
- Mark "remaining labor estimates" (hours) on task cards worked
- Re-tally all RLEs daily
- Plot on burndown chart
- Compare to "perfect line" for status

Learn
- Re-derive team velocity in story points and OLEs based upon stories actually delivered

Multi-Week Development Sprint (Story Conference, Task Planning, Develop, Sprint Demo, Retrospective)

Figure 4.3: Steps in the Estimation Cycle Overlaid on a Sprint Cycle

Forecast Step

Occurs during the sprint's story conference. The team uses its current velocity in story points to identify how much of the top of the Product Owner's release backlog it can deliver. Because it considers the work ahead in terms of modules, which are considerably larger than programming tasks, this selection of sprint objectives represents the team's "top-down" estimation pass.

Confirmation Step

Occurs during the sprint's task planning step once developers have identified the programming tasks the candidate set of stories will require. The team members estimate an Original Labor Estimate (OLE) for each task and then use their current velocity in terms of OLEs to confirm that the stories currently in the sprint backlog do not exceed the team's capability in terms of labor hours. The User Epic Decomposition framework breaks building a warehouse into an incremental series of features, most of which require the same type of programming to deliver. With this standardization of stories, the team should be able to document a set of tasks needed for each story type and their customary OLEs on what we call a "basis-of-estimate" (BOE) card, which we will discuss a bit later.

Because tasks are typically so much more granular that user stories, these OLE forecasts are considered the team's "bottom-up" estimation pass. By checking the feasibility at a separate granularity and in different units, this step provides a double-check that the sprint backlog selected during the story conference is indeed achievable.

Watch Step

Monitoring the accuracy of the estimates occurs during the Development portion of a sprint. The team updates task cards with Remaining Labor Hours (RLEs), allowing the Scrum Master to re-tally the total RLEs for the sprint and update the burndown chart. Team members are therefore watching on a daily basis whether or not the estimates they made for the sprint are realistic. Tasks with stubborn RLE values can be revisited individually or grouped by task type.

As factors affecting estimation are uncovered, they can be included on the BOE cards, making the next iteration's estimation all the more accurate. With such daily feedback on the accuracy of forecasts and the evolving BOE cards, the Estimation Cycle is a self-policing process, and the team is constantly focused upon improving its estimation skills.

Learn Step

Learning occurs during the sprint retrospective. Given that the estimate for the sprint was phrased in terms of how much can be done in one iteration, the team can tally the work actually delivered to arrive at an updated answer to this question. By tallying story and task cards, the team's velocity can be measured both in terms of story points and original labor hours.

Teams, including their Product Owner, discuss during the story conference the overarching forces affecting estimates. They can update their policies, their particular adaptation of the User Epic Decomposition Framework, and the BOE cards alike with what they learn, thus making the Estimation Cycle a self-optimizing process.

DEFER RELEASE PLANNING FOR NEW TEAMS

The team's Product Owner will naturally have a strong interest in planning the overall release, which will take multiple sprints to deliver. Often Product Owners will insist upon developer estimates during or even before the first sprint so that they can forecast for their management the features the new application will have by a certain set of calendar dates. Such a request derives from a legitimate business need, however catering to it should be deferred as long as possible when working with a new ADW team. As we will see below, the developers' ability to estimate improves greatly during the first few sprints, and it would be dangerous for parties outside the team to base any important decisions upon the forecasting skills of Agile beginners. If an early release plan is absolutely necessary, then it should be honestly labeled "preliminary" and definitely be revisited after the team has completed four to six sprints.

STORY POINTS VERSUS IDEAL TIME

An interesting transition takes place between the Forecast and Confirm Steps in the cycle sketched above. Whereas in the first step, the team compares the cost of each story to its total labor resources in "story points," in the next step it performs this analysis in labor hours. Looking only at the unit of measure employed, this change moves the team from *size-based* estimation to one expressed in *ideal time*. Many developers find it puzzling that sprint planning involves two different units of measures, so we should look closer at them to ensure we alternate between them effectively.

Story Points Defined

As described in Chapter 2, story points are a measure of size. Saying that delivering a certain feature will take "five story points" is analogous to saying it will fit in a five pound sack. When developers are new to Scrum, they can only make an educated guess at what a single story represents. After a few sprints, however, they will have an acute, intuitive notion of its size. If on Sprint 2 the team managed to deliver new modules that added up to 20 story points, then no matter how those points were defined a single story point is about five percent of its effective labor capacity per sprint.

Especially when coupled with *relative* estimation, this notion of size becomes very effectve. Say this same team has two tasks that they understand very well to which it arbitrarily assigns three and eight story points. When it estimates a third requirement as "five story points," this is a very lightweight way of saying that the level-of-effort the task requires will be about halfway between the two reference stories, probably a bit closer to the first rather than the second. By gauging these three development tasks in story points relative to each other, this team immediately uncovers that altogether the tasks will consume 80 percent of the next iteration, leaving only a smidgen of capacity for anything more. Even though the units employed were completely arbitrary, the team came to this insight without having to draft a long list of work steps and carefully appraise the hours each would require to complete. Using story points, the team can speedily review the Product Owner's proposed backlog for the next sprint or the entire release, economically avoiding overcommitment.

Ideal Time Defined

The alternative to story points is "ideal time," which requires much more effort to employ and thus should be used judiciously. It is the only paradigm that most IS professionals use for their estimates, especially during the expert judgment "planning forums" we considered earlier. Estimating the third story of our example above in ideal time might result in a statement such as "Story C will require 140 labor hours." At first this sounds far more precise than an estimate in those new-fangled story points, but given the inaccuracy of developer estimates we considered above, we need to take a more careful look at this type of statement with all its seeming certainty.

Let us ask the team a few questions about its estimate: Do you mean 140 hours *elapsed* time as in time finished minus time began, as shown by the clock on the wall? Do you mean 140 hours for Terry, who typically codes "twice as fast" as everyone else? Last month Sam coded a story using the very same target table … would she not take far less time to complete the task compared to someone who is new to the data? Does the 140 hours assume the developer is left alone to code, or can he be interrupted to support the year-end close?

Questions like these quickly reveal how teams begin "out-driving their headlights" when they estimate in ideal time. There are simply too many picky details that must be clearly settled before we know what "140 hours" really means. More crucially, we want effort estimates to be additive, so that we can a) provide the funding and planning information management needs to get the project approved, and b) accurately draw a line on the release backlog so that developers do not have to work eighty hours per week to meet the coming sprint's deliverables.

The Big Advantage To Story Points

Research has shown what many of us realize intuitively, that the human mind is good at comparing the relative size of two complex objects, but does poorly at identifying their absolute magnitudes if there are more than a few abstract factors involved. This result arises from the difference between developing an intuitive feel for the major attributes that makes X different from Y, as opposed to maintaining a running total of a dozen or more debits and credits of widely ranging magnitudes. Investigators have found that estimating the relative size of a task via pairwise comparisons is decisively more accurate than forecasting a magnitude for the task's actual level of effort. [Miranda 2000, Lum 2002, Hihn 2002]

A further advantage of using story points is that they automatically include and "net out" the hundreds of minute details that must be separately listed and appraised for each task estimated using labor hours. Speaking practically, one cannot accurately say "Story C will take 140 hours" because there is simply too much uncontrolled variation in the work of creating software. Story points, on the other hand, actually operate in terms of percentage of team bandwidth observed over the past few cycles, and thus tacitly incorporate notions such as "Developers are more effective from one day to the next." Some days involve more interruptions than others, and some designs require more thought than anticipated. With so much built-in to the very unit of measure, story points save the developers a great deal of effort, makes them more consistent, and accelerates their estimation work tremendously. They are a major step toward Agile's desire to "maximize the work not done."

Quick Story Points Via "Estimation Poker"

Given that the objective of a story conference is to identify a workable sprint backlog so that everyone can move on to planning development tasks, the team will want to put no more effort into estimating stories than is necessary to be accurate. Luckily, the Scrum/XP community has developed a particularly streamlined means of uncovering the proper story point estimate for each user story, a technique called "estimating poker." (See Cohn 2005 for a longer treatment of this topic).

Before estimating begins, the Scrum Master gives each team member a small deck of cards. Each card has a different number printed on it, so that for any story being considered, a member can express how many points he thinks it should get by simply selecting the appropriate card from his deck.

To estimate a story, the team discusses it with the Product Owner and then takes a moment in which each member selects the card representing the points he thinks the story represents. Everyone shows their card to the group at once, and the team then discusses the range of estimates seen among the cards, focusing especially upon the outliers. Often they will pose questions to the Product Owner in order to resolve the different interpretations of the story that arise during the discussion, but soon they will feel ready to re-estimate the story, at which point they repeat this voting cycle. The team iterates in this way until the cards selected converge upon a consensus story point value for the story in question.

In order to steer the group quickly to consensus, the estimating decks typically have only a short sequence of rapidly diverging values, such as powers of two. The important quality is that the numbers are far enough apart that one can easily distinguish between any two of them. The following series, which begins with the Fibonacci sequence, works well: 1, 2, 3, 5, 8, 13, 20, 40, 80. Guided by this sequence, most stories will end up with a value among the first half dozen of these values. Stories receiving 20 and above should be quickly labeled "themes" by the group, at which point the Product Owner probably should disaggregate it into a set of smaller stories. Scrum Masters often include in the decks cards with 0 and one-half on them, so that members can vote that a story has somehow already been accomplished or will require very little effort to address.

During the story conference, developers begin estimating stories at the top of the Product Owner's prioritized release backlog, and continue until the story points identified add up to a bit more work than they think they can deliver in one sprint. Estimating poker may start slowly as the team warms up, but soon proceeds quickly because it is highly interactive and develops a rhythm. In order to manage the length of the story conference and know when the team is getting hung up on a particular story, the Scrum Master should learn their team's average estimation pace. In our practice, the pace has been typically around five minutes per story.

Estimation poker is accurate because it focuses upon the "size" of a story relative to a reference story, a comparison which developers learn to judge well. It avoids mistakes because it focuses on outliers—the team endeavors to understand the high and low estimates before re-voting, so that crucial nuances are not overlooked. Outlier votes should disappear as team members discuss a story and revote, but sometimes they will become strongly split between two values with no consensus emerging. In this case, the Scrum Master can simply pick a reasonable value somewhere between the two, so that the team can move on.

One or two such compromises will not drastically affect the team's objective of identifying the collection of highest priority stories they should include in the next sprint.

Labor-Hour Estimates Still Valuable

Despite the advantages of relative sized-based estimation, Scrum/XP does not advocate abandoning labor hour forecasts, but instead guides teams to apply each technique where it is most appropriate. They can then use the two sets of forecasts to check each other, thus "triangulating" towards as accurate a forecast as possible.

As we have seen, sized-based estimation is top down and faster, making it ideal for the first estimation pass required by the story conference because a) the team must process a large number of user stories simply to identify a candidate scope for the upcoming sprint, and b) the Product Owner will be present and must be kept actively engaged during this particular step.

Once story planning has identified an approximate scope for the iteration, the team moves on to detailed task planning. Here ideal time estimation becomes more appropriate because a) the team can slow down to consider carefully the component tasks for only the candidate stories, b) the Product Owner's role is minimal as long as she remains available to revisit a story if needed, and c) the team can break into smaller groups based upon work specialty, each processing in parallel tasks it knows well.

For each task, the team's Original Lab Estimate should anticipate all work required to move the card from the "Tasks Defined" column of the task board to the "Ready to Demo" column. It should factor in work often overlooked in less disciplined settings such as defining tests, design conferences, and the effort required to include the resulting module into the build and validate it via the Automated and Continuous Testing Facility. OLEs for tasks requiring more than one person's contribution should reflect the cumulative labor time of everyone who will participate rather than just the elapsed time in which they will work together. In this way, the forecast will reflect the percentage of the team's total resources the work will consume.

Ensuring Consistency Of Estimates

Earlier, with Figure 4.1, we discussed the importance of driving as much of the standard deviation out of our estimates as possible in order to facilitate management's interpretation of the results. ADW's estimating technique has several qualities that yield a high level of consistency. First, we use the two very different estimation approaches to double check our forecasts. The top-down story conference step identifies a candidate scope using top-down, size-based Story Points. The task planning step then confirms the appropriateness of that scope employing bottom-up, ideal time-based Original Labor Estimates. Using two methods with completely different frames of reference, Scrum teams arrive at far more realistic scope for their sprints than they could by using either method alone.

Secondly, in the story conference, the team uses a set of "reference tasks" against which to compare all the stories it needs to estimate. Through the User Epic Decomposition framework of Chapter 2, we could potentially generate hundreds of different categories for the stories. In practice the team will need to execute only a handful of these categories for any given iteration. Even new ADW teams will need to execute only a few sprints to settle upon a couple of well-understood reference stories for each type of user story. By encouraging the teams to employ the same reference stories for the story conferences as much as possible, Scrum Masters can ensure a great deal of consistency in the estimates.

Third, as the team members begin estimating task labor time during task planning, ADW asks that they utilize and update for each major task type a "basis-of-estimate" card. As the sprints proceed over time, they should collect upon the BOE card for each task type a list the major steps required to complete it and an observed range of labor hours each typically takes. This range should be expressed in terms of a 50 and 90 percent confidence level in order to facilitate critical chain program management (discussed in Chapter 6). These BOE cards make labor hour estimation faster and less tiring by allowing teammates to quickly reload into their minds the many activities involved in a given type of task. This fast reload is essential to warding off "estimation fatigue," letting the developers focus mostly on how the upcoming effort will differ from the last time they performed such a task and how the labor requirements of this occurrence will fall in the range recorded on the BOE card. In a sense, BOE cards allow teammates to boil OLE estimation down to the pairwise comparison process which people seem to perform well. This time they are comparing the envisioned work with short and long instances of the same work delivered at least once before.

Fourth, once all tasks of a particular type have been estimated, the teammates should place all the tasks of a particular type together so that they can spot and reconsider any tasks with OLE estimates diverging wildly from the other estimates for the same work type.

Fifth, at the end of the task planning session, ADW asks the developers to compare the tally of task OLEs for each candidate story to the Story Points estimated for it earlier. If the team has been careful and consistent, there should be tight agreement between the total OLEs for all stories of a similar size. Some discrepancies in this regard can be tolerated, but developers may discover an important oversight as they discuss why, for example, the tasks for one four-point story adds up to 16 labor hours and those for another four-point story tally to 40 hours. In particular, this comparison often helps teams move toward more accurate story points ranges for their usual types of stories, for example ETL or front-end reporting.

In ADW, the Scrum Master ensures that the team re-visits the accuracy of both the reference stories utilized for the story conference and the BOE cards during the sprint retrospective step at the end of the iteration. In this way reference stories, BOE cards, and standard OLE ranges become increasingly accurate as the team gains more experience. They soon impart a good deal of consistency to the team's estimation, achieving the narrow distribution of actuals versus forecast.

Finally, the team calculates a total of estimated labor for all the candidate stories of the sprint and considers whether that tally still represents a doable amount of work given the bandwidth the team will have during the upcoming sprint.

At the end of the task planning step, the team will have checked and re-checked in two separate units of measure not only the estimates for the individual components to be built, but also the total amount of work it is committing to complete during the upcoming development iteration. Yet, how exactly does a team know whether a particular total of story points or original labor estimates is "doable" within one sprint? The magic device making such an insight possible is called the team's "velocity," a notion which we will discuss in detail in a moment.

RE-ESTIMATING STORIES AFTER A RELEASE PLANNING

Although teams get better at estimating as sprints progress, the degree of this improvement across the full range of data warehousing story types is often uneven. Especially with the large differences between back-end ETL and front-end BI applications, teams will realize that they need to significantly re-calibrate the estimates for a whole class of stories and/or tasks. Evolving the standard estimates for tasks is straight-forward given the BOE cards, but revising the story points for stories already incorporated into a "firm" release plan can cause some problems.

Unfortunately, the team can do little to avoid the uproar that "re-estimating" the components of a release plan will probably create—the Product Owner and other stakeholders deserve to be kept up-to-date regarding the likely future progress of the team. Sometimes the underlying cause is entirely outside the team's control—a new tool makes certain stories faster to deliver or a new security requirement makes other stories harder to complete—making re-estimation an inescapable hazard.

We can only point out here two devices to make the actual process of re-estimation a bit easier. First, the team should try to identify the class of items to be re-estimated by using coordinates from the user-source epic grid that the Product Owner developed for verbalizing user stories. Using these coordinates, the developers should be able to identify the specific combination of specific user role, source data set, and/or load type defining the group of stories with estimates that have consistently troubled them. By aligning with this breakdown scheme, the team makes it as easy as possible for the Product Owner to understand the reach of the re-estimation and envision its impact on the current sprint and release plans.

Second, the team should strive to derive a single multiplier by which to adjust all the estimates in the class of stories identified. The three dimensions employed already make the adjustment fairly specific. In our experience, anything more detailed offers too little additional accuracy and steals too much time from the development work that still needs to be done.

Tracking Progress & Measuring Velocity

Triangulating estimates with story points and labor hours allows a team to be doubly confident in their labor forecasts on a story by story basis, but how does it know how many stories it should promise to deliver within a single sprint? Scrum uses the same burndown chart that keeps the team on track for a given sprint regarding how much it has accomplished. Once the developers can consistently estimate stories and tasks, they can begin to use the burndown chart to measure their team "velocity" per sprint by simply calculating story points promised less those not delivered. The same difference can be performed with Original Labor Estimates to double check the figure derived. The Scrum Master ensures that the team takes stock of its velocity at the end of each sprint, so that even with a new team, the observed delivery quantities soon provide a predictable range of what the given team working in the given situation can reasonable expect to accomplish in future iterations.

Discovering the team's velocity range as soon as possible and publicizing it to all stakeholders is the single most effective means of avoiding overcommitment throughout the remainder of the project. Developers and project sponsors will always wish that software development would proceed more quickly, so the natural tendency will be for the team to commit to too much with each sprint. Because the velocity measure is based upon observed team performance and tuned with each sprint, Scrum adroitly prevents the team's forecasts from becoming distorted by these emotional desires. However, interpreting actual results on a burndown chart and then setting the velocity right for the next sprint takes some skills, as discussed in this section.

Burndown Charts

The longest segment of a sprint is the development phase, which occupies all but the first and last days of an iteration. At a regular time during each day of the development phase, the developers gather for their fifteen-minute, stand-up "scrum" meeting where they cover the past day's progress, objectives for the coming day, and the items holding them up. Before each daily scrum, the developers should have scanned the task board for the cards they are working, and for those that are underway, they should update them with the hours needed to complete the task, that is, the "remaining labor estimate" (RLE).

Just before the scrum, the Scrum Master can make a quick tally of all the RLEs. The RLE for a card still in the "Tasks Defined" column of the task board is simply its original labor estimate (OLE). If the total RLEs for an experienced team are plotted against time, they will most often reveal a line that heads toward zero, as depicted in **Figure 4.4**. This plot is, of course, a sprint "burndown chart," which shows how the team is working off day by day the total RLEs for the iteration.

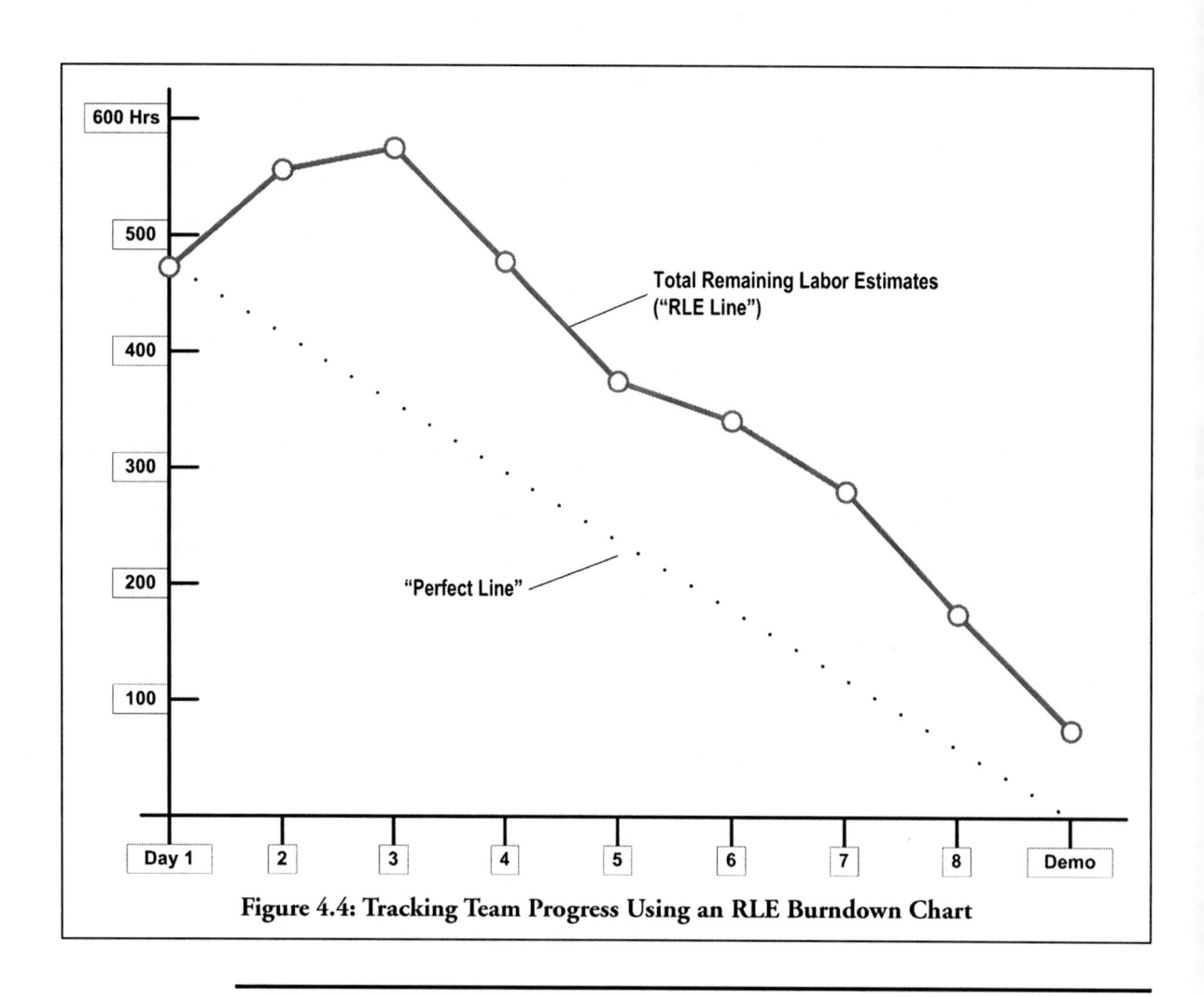

Figure 4.4: Tracking Team Progress Using an RLE Burndown Chart

Since the sprint planning did everything possible to assure that the team took on only what it could reasonably finish within one sprint, this total RLE line should hit zero by the day of the demo. The straight line drawn between the beginning OLE total and zero at the end of the sprint is called the "perfect line" because, theoretically, if the developers estimated and executed the sprint without a flaw, the daily RLE total should follow this line exactly.

Typical Patterns and Their Causes

As one might expect, burndown tracks do not always trend toward zero, especially during the first few days, and sometimes they stray persistently above the perfect line. When these situations occur, the burndown chart is serving as a powerful tool for detecting problems within a team and its work habits. Let us look at the most common patterns encountered.

An Early Hill To Climb

Figure 4.4 shows perhaps the most common burndown chart experienced by Scrum teams—the team's total remaining labor estimate increases during the first few days rather than trending steadily downward. A common cause for this pattern is the team did not consider the tasks required to deliver the stories carefully enough during the task planning. When they actually started working on the task cards, the developers suddenly discovered several other tasks that the stories would require. They dutifully wrote these additional tasks along with a reasonable range of OLEs on the BOE cards for the given task type. Then they increased the remaining labor estimates on the appropriate cards pinned to the task board, driving up the next day's total RLE.

Overlooking tasks is understandable for a team during the early sprints of a project. However, the team vision should get steadily better with each sprint, not only because of the BOE cards, but also because a properly guided Product Owner will soon express user stories in terms that increasingly align with the major components that each new feature requires. A minimum early hill will persist, however, because developers naturally mull things after the task planning day and always add a task card or two the next morning and nudge up a couple of their estimates here and there. Fortunately, by committing to an OLE load below the actual total labor hours available in a sprint, the team automatically accounts for these residual early hills.

Another possible cause of a big "early hill" is simply a surprise somewhere in the work. For example, the source for the billing data proved to be encoded in an old mainframe standard, and a new task card had to be added for pre-processing the extract into ASCII. The Product Owner can sometimes be the source of a large early hill if she guides the team into a story that turns out to involve tougher business rules than anticipated. Teams will benefit from discovering such problems as early in the sprint as possible so they will have enough time to get the errant RLE line back on track. Accordingly, Scrum Masters should encourage developers and Product Owners to start on tasks that have any hint of serious risk a tad earlier in the iteration than scheduled.

Persistent Under-Delivery

Whereas the "early hill" pattern is common and easy to address, the two patterns shown next in **Figure 4.5** portray a sprint where more serious challenges are at work. Both the burndown patterns in this diagram represent a persistent inability of the team to deliver as much as it planned. Because there is no one "bump" that suddenly put the RLE Line

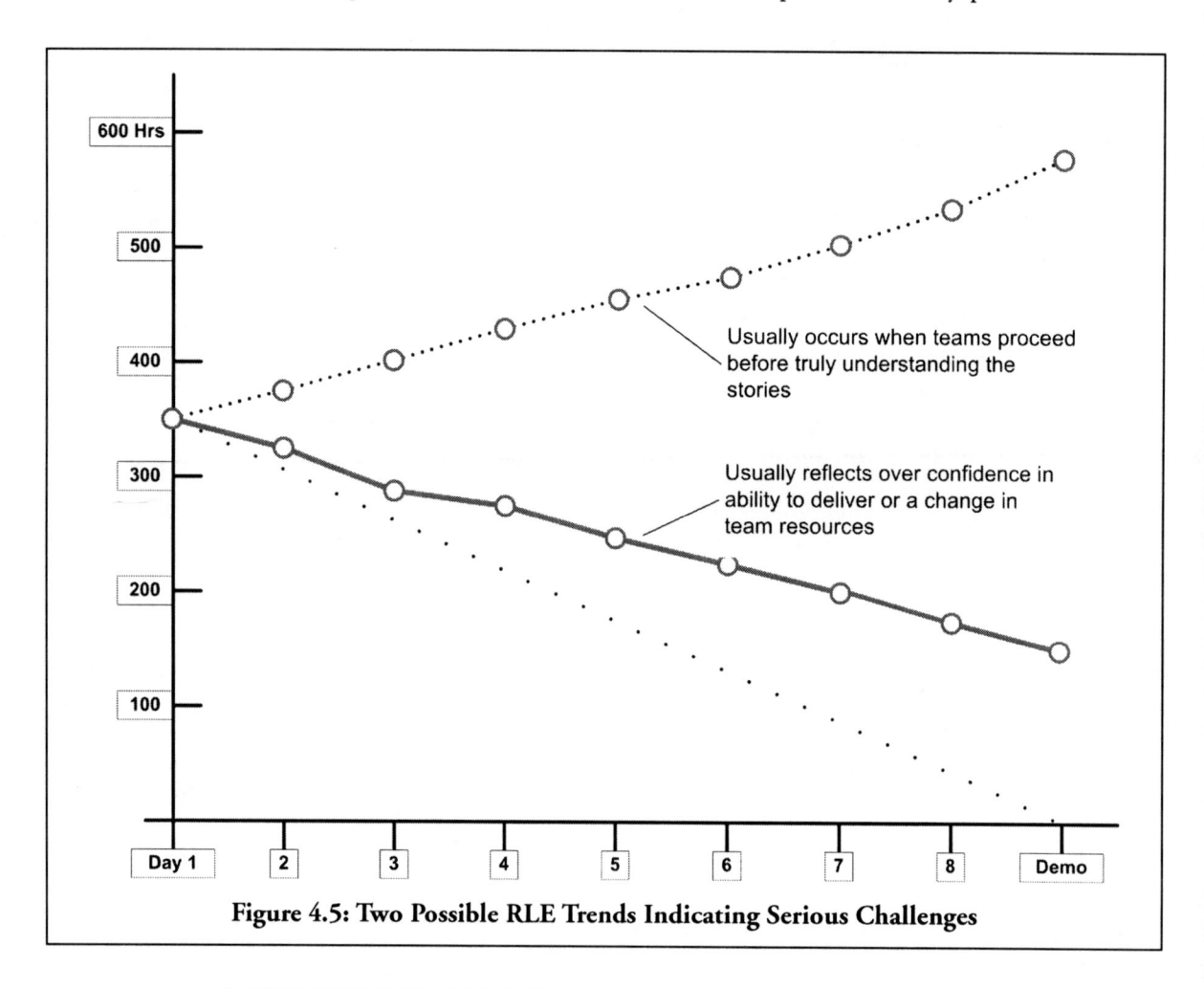

Figure 4.5: Two Possible RLE Trends Indicating Serious Challenges

above the Perfect Line, it is hard to see how either of the patterns could be caused by a single surprise.

The solid track is the more common of the two possibilities considered here, and it is more frequently seen in the ETL portion of the development work than in the business intelligence front-end tasks. It demonstrates steady progress in burning down the RLE, but just not at the rate the team projected.

Several reasons can underlie this phenomenon. For new teams, such a path can reflect a lack of appreciation of how much work even the simplest ETL modules require. Another common cause of persistent under-delivery is "organizational friction," where the team members are getting push-back from some of the other IT teams with whom they must coordinate, such as database administrators or quality assurance. Given such challenges, the developers have essentially placed too many stories in their team inbox for the sprint. Their under-delivery will teach them a valuable lesson when the team velocity is measured during the sprint retrospective. Large under-deliveries should disappear within a few sprints, because the developers will take such actions as recalibrating their story points for certain types of work, revisiting the steps listed on their basis-of-estimate cards for common tasks, and revising upward the hours they should allow for each step.

For established teams whose burndown charts have been tracking the perfect line during past sprints, however, the solid track in Figure 4.5 usually represents a change in team bandwidth, and the most common cause is resource contention—for example, one or more of the team members may have been pulled aside to perform maintenance programming on another system.

The even more dire, dotted track in the diagram, where the RLEs rise steadily above the sprint's total OLE, is luckily a rare occurrence once ADW teams get established. When it does appear, it usually represents that neither the Product Owner nor the developers really understood the stories accepted during the story conference. Once development began, they found themselves investing large amounts of unanticipated time in analysis and design. The problems encountered led to the creation of many more task cards being created than being worked off.

If a project encounters one or two tracks such as this, it is a sign that the total chain of work stretching from analysis to design through coding is too long to fit within the standard time box length chosen for the project's sprints. Rather than changing the duration of a sprint, the team might seriously consider "pipelining" itself into semi-formal squads—a strategy explored in the next chapter. With pipelining, each sprint can have a squad focused upon development prep work such as story analysis and high-level design. By adding a "pre-processing" squad, the development squad will then start each sprint with a set of tasks that are predominately coding rather than high-level design and investigation, and thus the RLE Line should once again track the Perfect Line.

Fine-Tuning Daily Stand-Up Questions

With the sprint burndown chart displayed so prominently at the daily scrums, teams naturally begin to elaborate upon the third question of the standard stand-up format. In addition to simply asking "what's holding you up?", Scrum Masters should prompt each teammate with "Do you think this sprint is still on track?" In response, each developer should affirm that the OLEs he estimated are still accurate, or explain why the completeness of the deliverables on demo day is now suddenly problematic.

From an even larger perspective, once a team establishes a quality release plan, Scrum Masters should prompt all the members with a similar question during the sprint retrospective, namely, "Are we still on track with the release plan, or are there reasons to think it is now at risk?"

DERIVING VELOCITY IN ORIGINAL LABOR ESTIMATES

At the end of each sprint, the burndown chart give us a means of graphically measuring the team's velocity, thus revealing how much it can realistically expect to complete during future iterations. **Figure 4.6** updates a previous figure (Figure 4.4) in which the developers were surprised in the first two days of the sprint and was then unable to complete all their programming tasks because of that early setback. Whereas our earlier figure displayed only a line for the Remaining Labor Estimates, the new graph adds a second line for the iteration's total Original Labor Estimate hours for tasks still not complete.

The RLE line allows the team to see whether it will be done by demo day. In the new diagram, for example, three days before the Demo, the Scrum Master could extend a line from the peak of Day 3 through the RLE of Day 6 and see that the team was going to be a day or two short of the time need to complete all the tasks. Scrum strongly urges the team to keep the demo day as scheduled and present whatever was completed by that time. Keeping the length of the sprint time box unchanged is indeed the right choice, but how should the team adjust their level of commitment for the next iteration?

Considering first the story points used during the story conference, if the team committed to, say, 24 story points for the sprint and has stories with six story point undelivered at iteration's end, then a reasonable estimate of the team's "velocity" in story points would be 18 per sprint, all other things remaining equal.

What about in terms of labor hours? It is important here not to mix OLEs of Day 1 and RLEs from other days. We seek the amount of work as envisioned on Day 1 that the team will dependably deliver by the end of the sprint. Whereas some Scrum practitioners simply

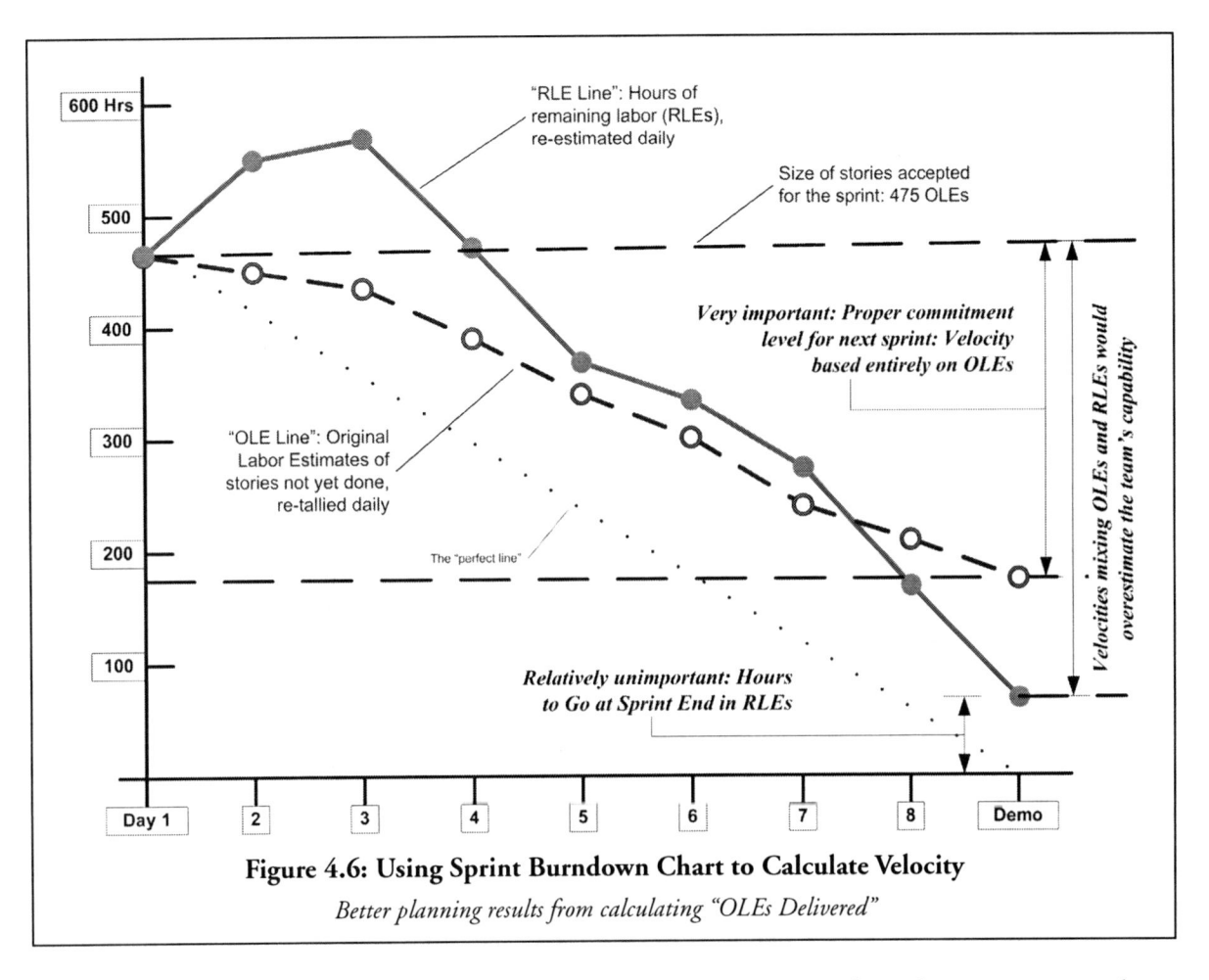

Figure 4.6: Using Sprint Burndown Chart to Calculate Velocity
Better planning results from calculating "OLEs Delivered"

subtract the Remaining Labor Estimates on Demo Day from the OLEs estimated on Planning Day, we feel such a calculation mixes apples and oranges. Quoting a velocity based upon Day 5 or Day 8 RLEs has no value during planning day, because Day 5 and 8 are many days off when we are setting the commitment level on Day 1. We need a measure of team velocity in Original Labor Estimates alone.

Accordingly, the team should measure its velocity in labor hours by subtracting the OLEs of tasks undone at sprint's end from the OLEs quoted during task planning. As can be seen in Figure 4.6, working with the OLEs declared during the planning day can yield a very different bandwidth than if the team had subtracted out the RLEs on demo day.

Chapter 4—Avoiding Overcommitment with Agile Estimation

MICRO-ADJUSTING VELOCITY FOR THE NEXT SPRINT

Sprints that finish early can calculate a velocity with a small amount of extrapolation, even though the effective time box was shortened. **Figure 4.7** depicts a team that completed all of an iteration's stories and demonstrated the results two days ahead of schedule. It still needs to base its working velocity for the next sprint upon a standard length time box, so in this case, the Scrum Master simply draws a line between the OLEs of Day 1 through the zero remaining OLE of Day 7 to uncover how many OLEs the team could burn off if it had found some more stories and kept working till the scheduled demo day.

Even after a full length sprint, there are a few considerations the team members should consider carefully when selecting the velocity for their next iteration. First, should they simply use the velocity measured for the sprint just finished, average the velocities of the last three, or commit to only the minimum seen during the life of the current project? As suggested earlier, the sprint retrospective is the setting in which the teammates should discuss this question. They would do well to set the planning velocity for the next sprint equal to the mean or median of those measured for only the past handful of sprints, so that their next

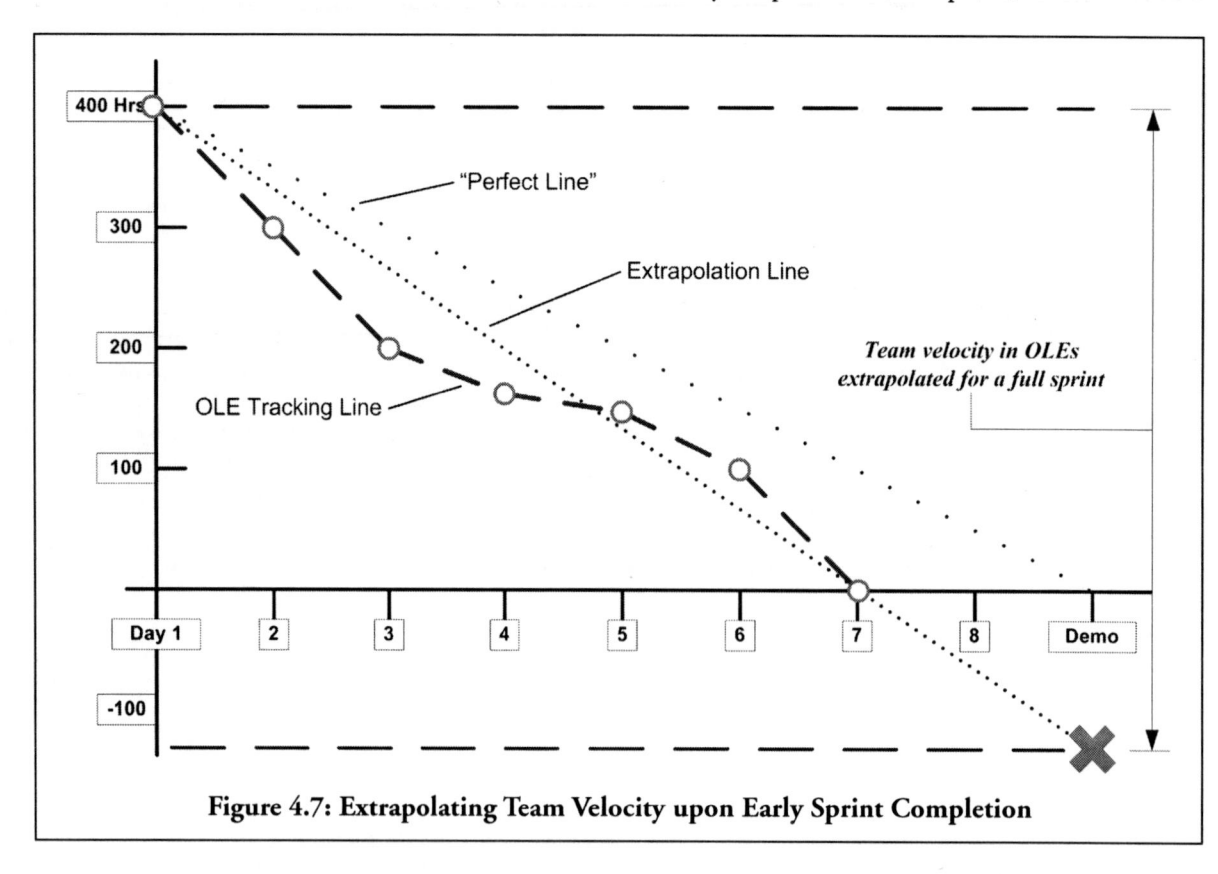

Figure 4.7: Extrapolating Team Velocity upon Early Sprint Completion

commitment is based on their most recent experience. They can always utilize the max over the same period to identify an appropriate few "stretch goals" for the upcoming iteration.

Furthermore, the team will need to adjust its working velocity measure for the next sprint by the expected availability of its teammates because upcoming vacations or legacy maintenance work might make one or more of them less than fully available. The relative skill levels of the members that will be absent may have to be considered also.

SETTING A WORKING VELOCITY FOR A NEW TEAM

Choosing a velocity figure for upcoming sprints will be particularly difficult for new teams, because they will not have any actual experience with which to calculate an average delivery speed. Instead, the developers will have to interpolate a starter velocity by picking a handful of the most important stories from the release backlog. They should assign these stories whatever amount of point values the team deems reasonable, making sure that the points awarded are truly proportionate to the size of each story. A spread including three, five, eight, and thirteen points makes for a handy reference set. The development tasks required by the reference set should be thoroughly analyzed and their Original Labor Estimates carefully derived. With this small set well understood, the developers can then return to estimating additional requirements by means of relative sizing.

As they employ story point estimation to continue adding stories to their first sprint backlog, the developers should also track how many OLEs the backlog has acquired. When the total OLEs exceed their labor resources for the upcoming sprint, they should stop adding stories. Whatever total story points the backlog now holds will be their velocity for the first iteration. The key to drawing this line is understanding how many hours of original labor estimates they can deliver in one time box. They have to be careful here not to over-appraise their capabilities. In practice, new teams believe they can complete far more stories than they will actually achieve. An effectiveness of thirty-three percent, or one hour of original labor estimate burned off for every three hours actually worked, is quite typical during the first few sprints as the team works through hidden issues of infrastructure, architecture, and team dynamics. In identifying a candidate velocity, we suggest that the developers assume no more than one-third effectiveness and use fifty percent effectiveness to set their stretch goals.

The developers should carefully nurture the reference stories we mentioned above not only during the first few sprints but throughout the remainder of the project. During every sprint retrospective, they should take a moment to update the list of tasks that each requires and the reasonable range of OLE hours for the story. Keeping themselves very familiar with these reference points will allow them to not only estimate more fluidly but greatly improve the accuracy of their forecasts.

DEALING WITH MID-ITERATION SCOPE CREEP

One big advantage to Agile's iterative approach is that it largely shelters teams from the ravages of "scope creep." Scrum does encourage the Product Owner to respond to changing business needs by pointing the team toward whatever objectives are most pressing during any given story conference. Sprints are kept purposely short, so one would expect that there is rarely the need to redirect the team before the next story conference occurs. Unfortunately, few projects seem to finish without having at least one major, must-do-it-now contingency thrust upon the team while in mid-sprint. Given that a tightly scoped set of stories and detailed task planning underlies the solid velocity metric upon which the accuracy of future estimation rests, how should a team incorporate scope creep during mid-iteration without becoming completely derailed?

At first the alternatives seem very unattractive. The team could simply cancel the sprint and jump upon delivering the new demand. Yet it risks being too accommodating, for if successful, many Product Owners would make this deviation from the method a common practice. With frequent, mid-sprint course changes, ADW's well-planned time box of activity will lose its coherence, leaving the supposedly Agile team with no method to work whatsoever.

Another unattractive option would be for the team to estimate how much additional time it needs to deliver the incremental requirements and add it to the sprint. Yet a mix of iteration lengths will make the team's story points and original labor estimates meaningless, destroying its firewall against overcommitment, and soon thereafter its ability to deliver quality enhancements. For this reason, generic Scrum and XP mentors caution very strongly against tactically adjusting the length of a team's standard iteration.

A far better approach to accommodating a mandatory mid-sprint demand is too add it as another story in the iteration currently underway without changing the sprint's duration. The Scrum Master should track and openly display its impact, so that the insistent stakeholders who forced it upon the team cannot hide from the disruption it causes. A simple modification to the burndown chart provides the perfect tool for tracking and demonstrating this impact.

Figure 4.8 depicts a sprint suffering from iteration scope creep. A mandatory story was added on Day 4, but here the additional work is not depicted as a jump in the RLE line, as happened in Figure 4.4 when the team discovered they would have to complete some unanticipated tasks for one of the stories. Instead, for scope creep, the team took time out to perform a mini-planning session for the new story, estimating its story points and OLE. On the burndown chart, the Scrum Master drew a line for the additional labor hours

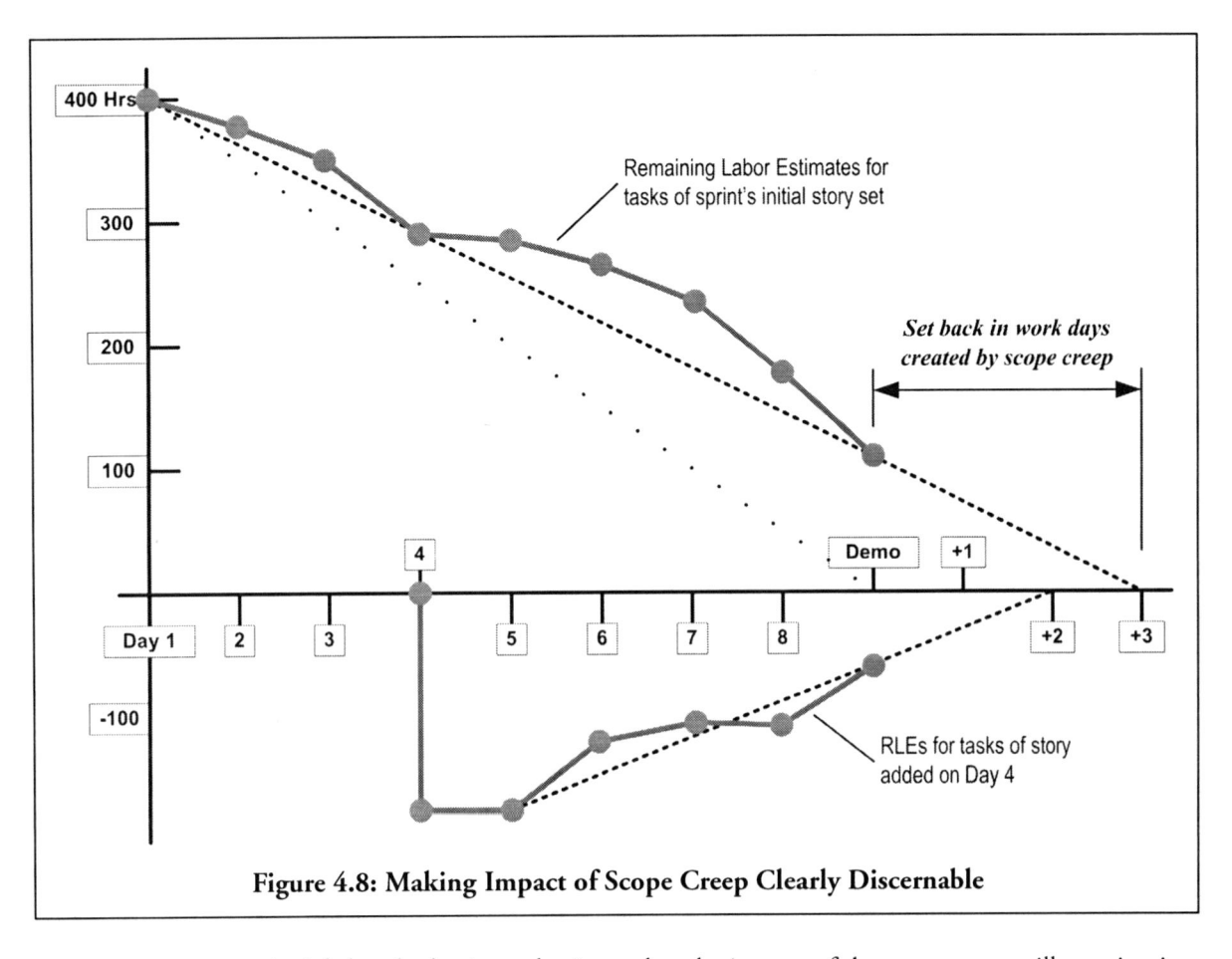

Figure 4.8: Making Impact of Scope Creep Clearly Discernable

required *below* the horizontal axis, so that the impact of the scope creep will remain visually distinct as the current sprint's work days pass.

Typically, such scope creep will keep the team from delivering all of the original stories slated for the sprint, and often it will be unable to fulfill all of the scope creep story. As depicted in the figure for the day of the sprint demo, it is easy for customers and IT management alike to see the impact of the added requirements. Progress against the original stories almost stopped during the first few days after the emergency requirement was added—and then resumed at a delayed rate after that—due to the disruption and the diversion of resources. By projecting where the RLE lines would hit the horizontal axis if the sprint had been extended in fact indicates to the stakeholders how large a setback the emergency requirement created in terms of work days.

Velocity calculations for sprints suffering from scope creep becomes a bit more involved as well. Naturally, the team should credit itself for progress made against not only the initial story set but the scope creep stories as well. As depicted by the OLE tracks in **Figure 4.9**, the Scrum Master will need to calculate the true velocity of the team as the sum of these two components.

On the release level, scope creep is a slightly broader concept, encompassing any stories added after the original story planning conference. Accordingly, the burndown chart for the entire release—which depicts story points still to be delivered—should have the story points for scope creep items displayed below the horizontal axis as was done for the sprint RLEs in the last two figures.

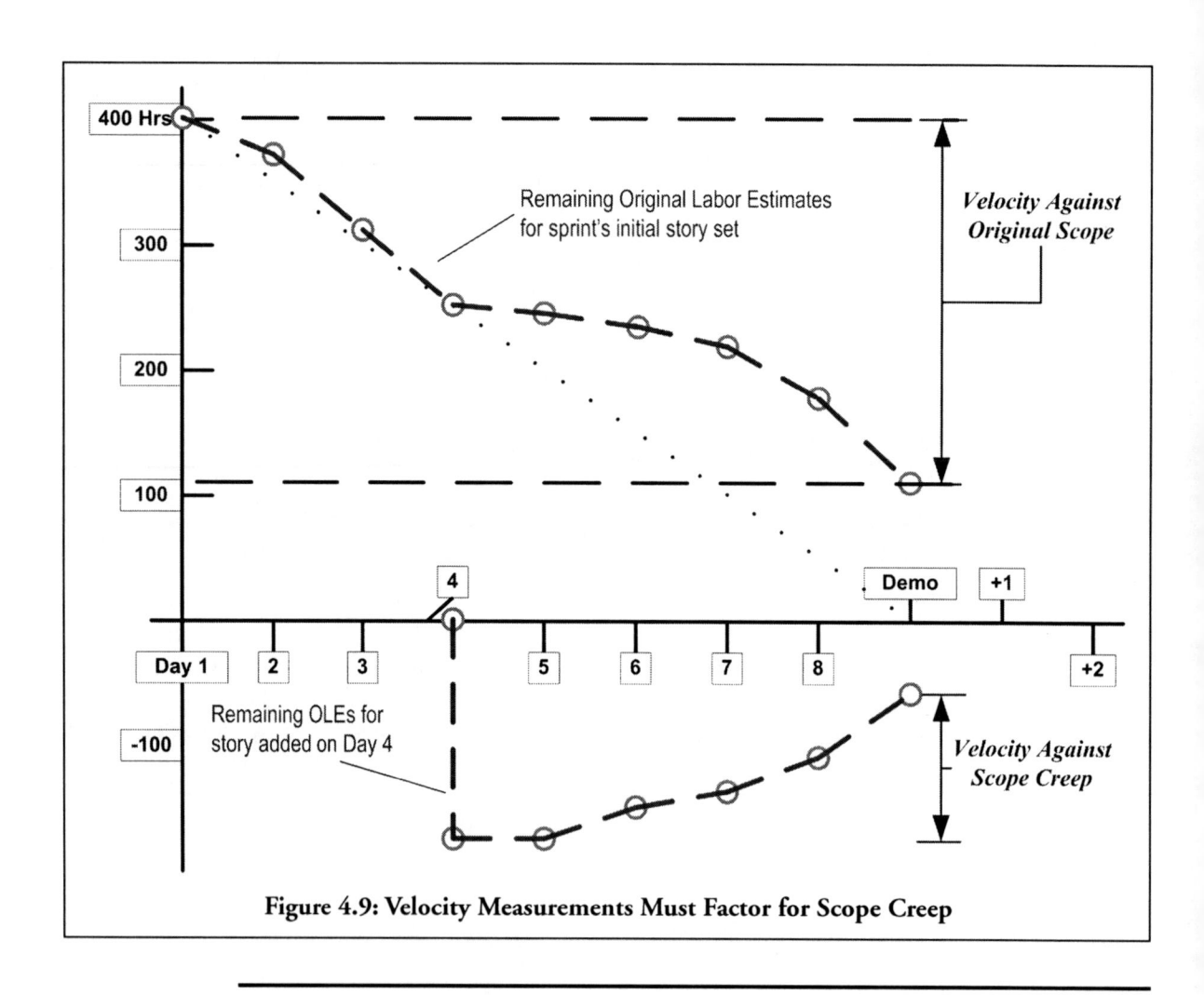

Figure 4.9: Velocity Measurements Must Factor for Scope Creep

Velocity As The One True Metric

As we have seen, establishing a velocity number requires not only some careful thinking by all the team, but an investment in standardizing of time frames and work patterns. So extensive is the effort required, in fact, that Scrum Masters should anticipate some grief from developers, Product Owners, and IT management alike as they steadily guide their teams toward an accurate measurement of this crucial planning value. Developers, who love to code, will want to gloss over the nuances of making their velocity a dependable number and just get started with the next sprint. On the other hand, Product Owners and IT management will be more interested in delivery schedules and will want the Scrum Master to cite a velocity value long before their teams have acquired enough experience to measure it accurately.

As "keepers of the velocity metric," Scrum Masters must resist pulls from both ends of the spectrum. The team's velocity number is too valuable to allow anything to muddy its magnitude or meaning. In fact, it may well be the only number that the team needs to defend and utilize.

With one simple measurement—expressed in both story points and original labor hour estimates—the velocity figure takes into account a large host of considerations that teams repeatedly overlook while forecasting effort. After a half dozen sprints, a velocity of X means the developers can deliver very close to X amount of new features *despite* the usual mix of chaotic "background" factors that are always chipping away at its efficiency, such as:

- Illnesses or other personal time off among team members
- Resolving confusion underlying the Product Owner's stories
- Extra collaboration between developers to derive quality unit designs
- Being pulled away for short periods to perform maintenance programming on other implemented systems
- Hiccups on some tasks and unforeseen delays due to dependencies between others, both of which cause developers to "thrash" back and forth between assignments
- Underestimating coding effort on a few tasks
- A background level of rework caused by belated discoveries and changes in general designs
- Inefficient meetings and interfacing with external parties
- Hundreds of little tasks that individually were too small to even mention during the planning session, but when added together represent a significant drag upon the developers' time

Given this list, we can see that the single notion of "velocity" actually smoothes over a large host of items that make traditional estimates in labor hours extremely inaccurate. In fact, developers and project managers both will be pleased to hear that working with a team's "velocity" eliminates the need to estimate *accurately* altogether. As discussed in the opening of this chapter, teams need only to be able to estimate *consistently*, not accurately. If a team says these ten stories are 40 "story points," or that their required labor will be 400 hours, it does not matter what a "point" is, nor whether the tasks really take 400 hours. As long as the team consistently delivers at least 40 story points and 400 OLEs per iteration, it is safe for everyone to plan on this performance for the next sprint (with reasonable adjustments for anticipated changes in developer availability).

Furthermore, we have seen above that delivering X story points of potentially shippable code each and every iteration requires that developers standardize and internalize a wide range of good practices including estimating properly, consistent designs, test-led development with daily builds, and automated cycling through a full set of testing scenarios. If any of these mandatory corners are cut, the substandard module will either fail during the daily test suite, be rejected by the Product Owner, or be singled out during the sprint retrospective. Modules must be truly "done" before they contribute to the team's velocity.

Seeing that one number can automatically incorporate so many diverse considerations while simultaneously keeping the team from over committing, Scrum Master and Product Owner alike would be wise to ask the developers to make establishing an accurate team velocity "job one." In other words, being able to review a list of user requests and consistently quantify how much can be delivered per cycle at a high level of quality is far more valuable to the organization than the developer's willingness to pull all-nighters and heroically deliver code on a hit-and-miss basis.

Assuming consistent estimating skills and a clear definition of what it means to "deliver" coded modules, a team's velocity becomes its "one true metric" needed to reveal its true performance and whether it has improved. Given the central role this measure can play, Scrum Masters are well advised to get a team's velocity established as soon as possible, and then to protect it from all forces that might lower its level or make it difficult to interpret from one sprint to the next. In fact, as one of the highest priorities for the sprint retrospective, the team should not only accurately set their velocity figure for the next iteration, but also find ways to deepen the meaning of "done" upon which it is based.

MAINTAINING A MEANINGFUL VELOCITY

During the build phase of a release cycle, teams need to adhere faithfully to practices that can keep a team's velocity firm. Number one among these practices is keeping a consistent team roster if at all possible. A group of seven to ten individuals must master hundreds of technical concepts and dynamics between themselves as they learn to collaborate effectively on modules meeting a high level of quality and completeness. Changing the members every few sprints will force the team to repeat much of this learning and can easily undermine the team's current velocity value or its meaning.

Scrum Masters must also watch for practices during development that can make velocity difficult to measure once the sprint reaches its retrospective. A couple of examples can be valuable to explain to teammates. First, a team can fall into the practice of leaving RLEs on many task cards at one or two hours because they are not quite "done." A couple such cards can be tolerated, but finding many stalled cards on the task board signals that either developers are uncertain what completing a card entails, or they are being held up by a shared obstacle that they have yet to address. How can a team definitively measure its velocity during the retrospective if a dozen tasks or more still read "one hour remaining," even after the modules have been demonstrated?

If coders are holding these cards open because one or two things *might* still be needed, the Scrum Master should have them go ahead and close off such cards. Scrum Masters can explain that the contingencies that actually do occur after their cards are closed will be accounted for by slightly lowering the team's velocity, which will be accurate. The team does not have to "sweat the small stuff" because the method's velocity number already allows for a background level of revisiting tasks once done.

A second example involves tasks cards on high priority stories that never advance while developers begin working off cards of lower priority stories. This practice can reflect the coders' unwillingness to state that they do not consider these "orphaned" tasks as truly necessary. Somehow the team's thinking during sprint planning was different from when the work was due to be done. Such a disconnect strongly suggests that the team has tacitly fallen into a dysfunctional divide between "planners" who write out the task cards and "coders" who fulfill them.

Any distance between the sprint's work plan as displayed on the task board and this plan's execution threatens the quality of the estimate and thereby the usability of the team's velocity number. Scrum Masters need to insist that the basis-of-estimate cards be kept up to date with the team's true consensus on the tasks required for each type of story. At the next stand-up meeting, they can force the disconnect into the open by asking "how can a team that fundamentally disagrees over what must be done provide consistent estimates and hence a reliable velocity?"

As a final means of galvanizing the team behind deriving a quality velocity metric, Scrum Masters can explain that it gives them the ability to avoid pressure from management to deliver impossibly large increments of system functionality in short time frames. Before switching to Scrum, when estimates were done infrequently and everyone knew they were numbers mostly "pulled out of the air," management felt free to disagree with them and insist that the work be done in far less time than quoted. With Scrum, estimates are done frequently and their accuracy constantly measured and tuned. The team can state unequivocally that "we can deliver X amount of deliverables each iteration." By basing estimates upon velocities which are observed, and *historical facts* rather than speculation, the team eliminates the gamesmanship between developers and management regarding forecasts, and makes it management's burden to demonstrate why the team should be magically able to deliver more, when all the evidence points to the contrary.

Resources For Further Learning

This chapter is the last of this book's presentations containing generic Scrum and XP topics. From here we focus exclusively on applying these Agile approaches to starting, scaling, polishing, and defending Agile Data Warehousing as a development method for systems involving ETL back ends and business intelligence front-end applications.

This observation does not suggest, however, that we feel we have provided more than a simple introduction to topics of Agile estimation, nor other aspects of Scrum and XP. Whereas previous chapters suggested further reading regarding these two Agile approaches in general, here we provide references to several resources for readers wanting more details on the particular topics of Agile estimation, velocity, and managing scope creep.

Inaccuracy of Traditional Methods	Little 2004
	DeMarco 1986
Surveys of Various Methods	Jorgensen 2004
Accuracy Through Combining Methods	Hoest 1998
Sized-Based v. Ideal Time Estimates	Cohn 2005
Pairwise Estimation	Miranda 2000
	Hihn 2002
	Lum 2002
Learning Through Feedback	Jorgensen 2006

Chapter 5
Adapting Scrum for Data Warehousing

How can we further streamline Scrum/XP given the specifics of data warehousing?

How should we evolve our work habits to achieve higher quality assurance?

What if our team needs more than a single sprint to develop and deliver a full ETL module from scratch?

As set forth in the introduction, this volume of *Agile Data Warehousing* focuses on adapting a generic Scrum/XP approach for organizing the work that flows from BI project sponsors toward a warehouse development team. Up to now, we have examined two highly complementary notions: how user stories can decompose business intelligence requirements into actionable work packages, and how the Agile team can derive quality level-of-effort estimates. In this chapter, we will take the practice of decomposition to its logical conclusion, going deeper than the user story "surface" that customers perceive, to the point where stories become a set of standardized tasks developers can complete in the shortest time possible.

Taking advantage of the business intelligence context of our work, this decomposition process for development work will go well beyond the general guidance that generic Scrum gives us in three ways. First, we will consider a "tiered data model," which is a simple way to decompose the target warehouse schema. This breakdown will enable designers to immediately identify the processing modules ETL will require and the order in which they must occur.

Secondly, we will take an initial look at quality management. Our adaptation of the quality management techniques found in XP offers a data warehousing team both a reference model and an *automated testing and continuous integration* facility. Both are crucial to the communication between the customer and the team because they define when tasks are truly complete.

Finally, we will explore a "pipelined delivery model" that employs the distinct types of design and build activities involved in ETL construction, further decomposing development so that it can span multiple sprints if necessary without violating Scrum's time-boxed approach. The pipelined delivery model allows us to discuss developer specialization and organize coordinated "squads" within the development team.

Once these techniques have been applied, the team will have at last translated its enormous undertaking into realistic work assignments that will fit reasonably within the tight iterations of Scrum. The decomposition approach we outline also provides a high level of standardization for the work of the team, thereby maximizing its ability to estimate, plan, and manage commitment.

TIERED DATA MODEL

The tiered data model is a simple re-formatting of a typical entity relationship diagram (ERD) that provides an Agile warehouse developers with a half-dozen angles for quickly translating a user story into task cards which they can use to plan and track their work.

Figure 5.1 depicts a summarization of a small ERD, the type warehouse developers typically receive from their data modeler. This model portrays the integration layer of an Orders subject area. In this example, the data modeler has done his best to keep the diagram readable and even organized the tables by the target "topic areas" that Orders typically breaks into, namely Party (customer), Product, and Transactions. ERDs are not easy to read—even this summary takes a few minutes of study before one can answer anything more than the most trivial data questions, such as:

- The next user story says "build a load for Order Role"—what upstream tables must we have loaded to support this enhancement?
- The third wave of loads failed during the last batch run—what tables do we need to reset before we restart it?
- The initial load of Order Items left the table empty—what parent tables do we need to examine for clues as to why?
- Party has too many records—which upstream tables should we look at for the duplicates that probably caused this to happen?

Keep in mind that Figure 5.1 is a schematic of a real Orders data model which would be even harder to read given its far larger number of entities connected by a host of squirrelly lines depicting multiple relationships between many pairs of tables. In our practice,

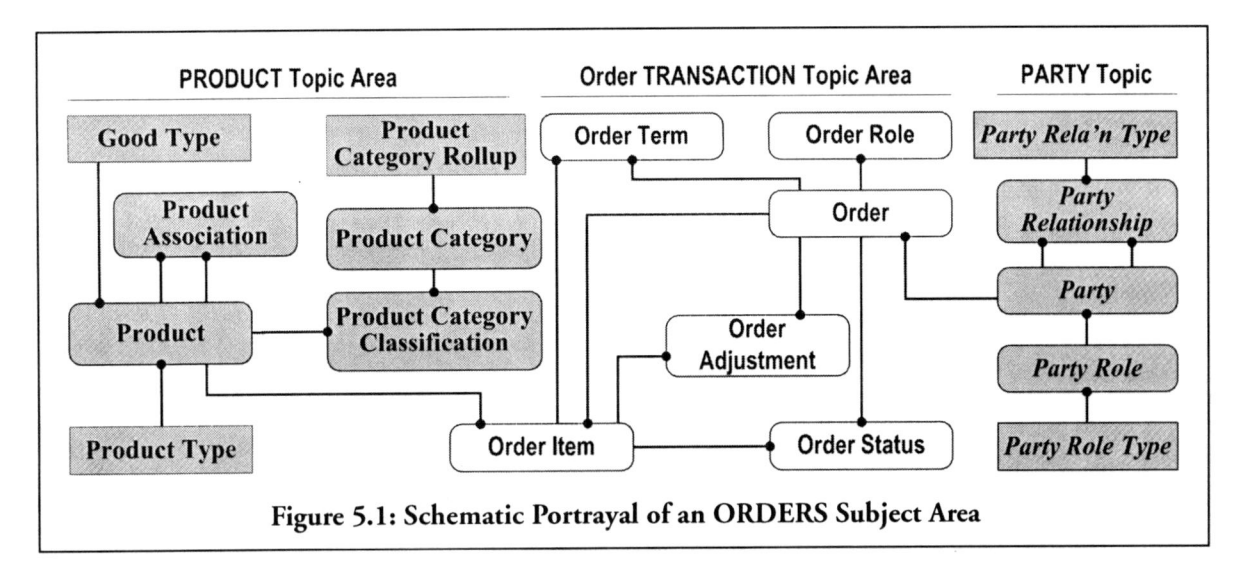

Figure 5.1: Schematic Portrayal of an ORDERS Subject Area

we have regularly encountered warehouse data models portrayed by a six- by four-foot plot of hundreds tables and their relationships—diagrams seeming more fitting for microprocessor circuit boards than a human-comprehendible business intelligence application.

When handed a user story to deliver by the end of an amazingly short iteration, the Agile warehouse developer needs to be able to go right to the challenge and begin design. The next diagram demonstrates how the ERD of Figure 5.1 can be re-drawn in tiers to facilitate the ETL design work. In its small format, **Figure 5.2** is very close to how a *tiered data model* (TDM) would appear. It displays the entities without attributes because its goal is to communicate only presence and hierarchy. We have the DM's original "can of worms" format and other table listings to find columns and data types when we need them.

Indeed, the TDM does little more than arrange table names so that every child entity is placed at least one level lower than any of its parents. A few of these child tables, such as Party Relationship, lie more than one layer away from a parent because another branch of their ancestry involves a multi-layer structure. To enhance intelligibility further, the TDM provides horizontal grouping for the target topic areas, making it simultaneously easy to focus on the particular subset of tables needed to implement a story. Furthermore, like many standard ERDs, the TDM gathers *reference tables* into a corner called "Tier 0" rather than cluttering the diagram with hundreds of lines connecting them to the entities they support.

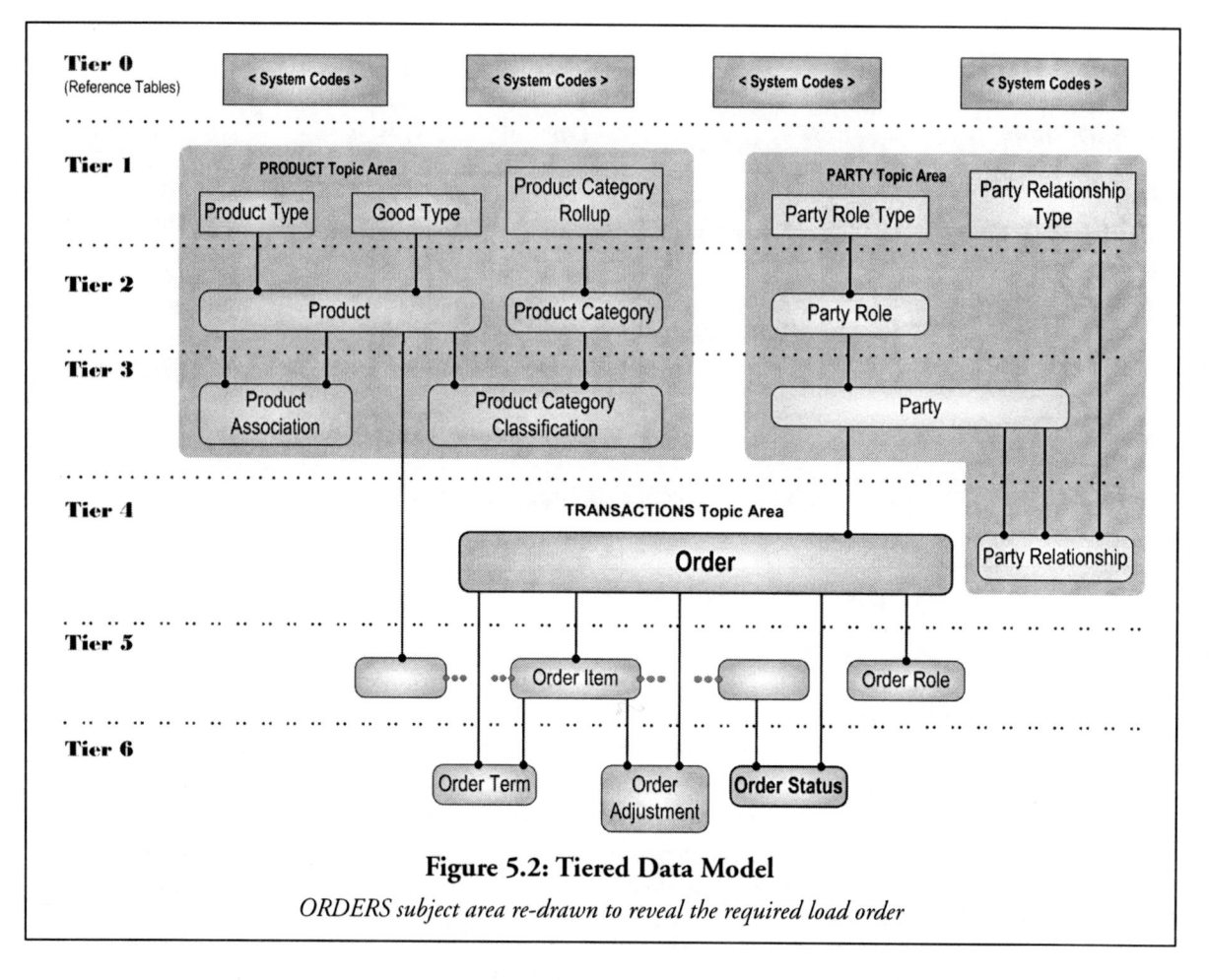

Figure 5.2: Tiered Data Model
ORDERS subject area re-drawn to reveal the required load order

In some particularly complex areas of a data model, a few tables will have to be segmented and spread horizontally so that relationship lines can remain simply vertical. For this reason, Order Item was so "vivisected" in our example.

EASIER SCOPING DECISIONS FOR UNITS & MODULES

As we will discuss in detail in Volume 2, many architectural methods set as their goal the decomposition of complex development goals down to the named module, at which point detailed design and development can begin. With its uncluttered portrayal of tables, tiers, and topic areas, the tiered data model allows the warehouse process designer to easily identify units and the modules that should be considered together, thus accelerating the high-level design work for the project.

As a baseline approach, the architect can define ETL *units* so that they correspond on a one-for-one basis with the table objects portrayed in the TDM. A set of baseline modules would be the collection of such units by tier and topic area. With this first-pass approach in mind, the team can look at the TDM and quickly see that Figure 5.2 suggests 10 modules that approach the granularity needed for development tasks:

- Tier 0 Reference Tables
- Tier 1 Product, Tier 2 Product, and Tier 3 Product
- Tier 0 Party, Tier 1 Party, Tier 2 Party, and Tier 3 Party
- Tier 3 Transaction, Tier 4 Transaction, Tier 5 Transaction

Seeing The ETL Units Needed

This simple example makes it easy to see the support that the TDM gives developers during the task planning of a sprint. Recall that Product Owners, using the user stories decomposition described in Chapter 2, have already expressed requirements so that they align to a large extent with the high-level organization that developers will design into the warehouse and its ETL. Continuing with our example, developers planning a mid-release sprint might find that the next story in the sprint backlog is "Add the order header data currently in staging to the integration layer, so that we can report on purchase volumes by order status per customer per period." Developers faced with this story can turn to the TDM in Figure 5.2 to see that this story splits immediately into two task cards:

- **Add Order Table:** If the Party table exists and ETL is already loading it, then the developers can begin developing an Order table and its load routines right away.
- **Add Order Status Table:** Developers cannot start upon this task card until the Add Order Table task is complete because the Order Status entity is a tier below Order.

This example may seem somewhat trivial, but we must keep in mind that during the planning and design activities of a sprint, developers must answer scores of questions such as these, many of which span a half dozen tiers or more. Having the target ERD laid out hierarchically as shown in the figure lets developers find modeling and sequencing answers far more quickly than tracing relationships through a standard, can-of-worms formatted ERD.

As the developers gather experience with the tiered data model for the warehouse, they will discover that their data management routines involve the repeated application of a relatively small number of ETL processing patterns, and that the proper transform type for a given table is determined by the target table's role in the TDM. For example, tables with no parents are reference entities and will require a relatively simple load routine, whereas a table with two or more parents on the tier above is linking associative tables and needs a complicated transform that retires and recreates history records as the source data changes. By making the role each table plays in a model as clear as possible, the tiered data model facilitates this ETL pattern recognition, thus accelerating the team's design work.

Seeing The ETL Modules Needed

Beyond suggesting the proper type of ETL unit for each table in the warehouse, the TDM also facilitates organizing multiple ETL units into cohesive transformation modules. In designing these modules, one wants to gather together the load routines for tables that are not only part of the same topic area, but also those tables that can be loaded in parallel because a) there is no dependency between them and b) when they execute, records in all the required parent tables will have been populated. Referring again to Figure 5.2, we can see not only that Product, Party, and Transaction can be treated as separate topic areas corresponding to the large divisions in the data model, but also that the ETL units for Product and Product Category can be loaded in parallel by a single "Tier 2" job because all their parent tables will have been updated by Tier 1.

The tiered data model provides an easy way to discern good processing patterns. This is not to say that the processing plan should be drawn as a TDM. Instead, the team should transfer the modules identified using the TDM onto a separate *Process Flow Diagram* (PFD), which is better thought of as a re-projection of the knowledge contained in a TDM rather than an independently insightful artifact. Aside from keeping the TDM uncluttered, the PFD has the additional advantage of giving the team a vehicle for analyzing and documenting important design considerations for warehouse operations: inter-process triggering and restartability.

The PFD for our example TDM can be found in **Figure 5.3**, which depicts the daily batch processing for the Orders subject area. Architects would draft similarly prepared PFDs for the weekly, monthly, and year end processing modules as well.

Process Flow Diagrams are simplified dataflow diagrams, and like those ancestors, they can be drawn at a high level first, with each object on the summary diagram detailed by a separate diagram. Our sample PFD for the daily batch processing portrays the process flow implied by the TDM of Figure 5.2 at both high and detailed levels. In the Level 0 diagram, we can see that the three topic areas have been organized into separate sub-batches with sequential dependencies noted. One can easily see that Product and Party modules can be started separately, but that the Order Transactions ETL must wait for the first two to complete.

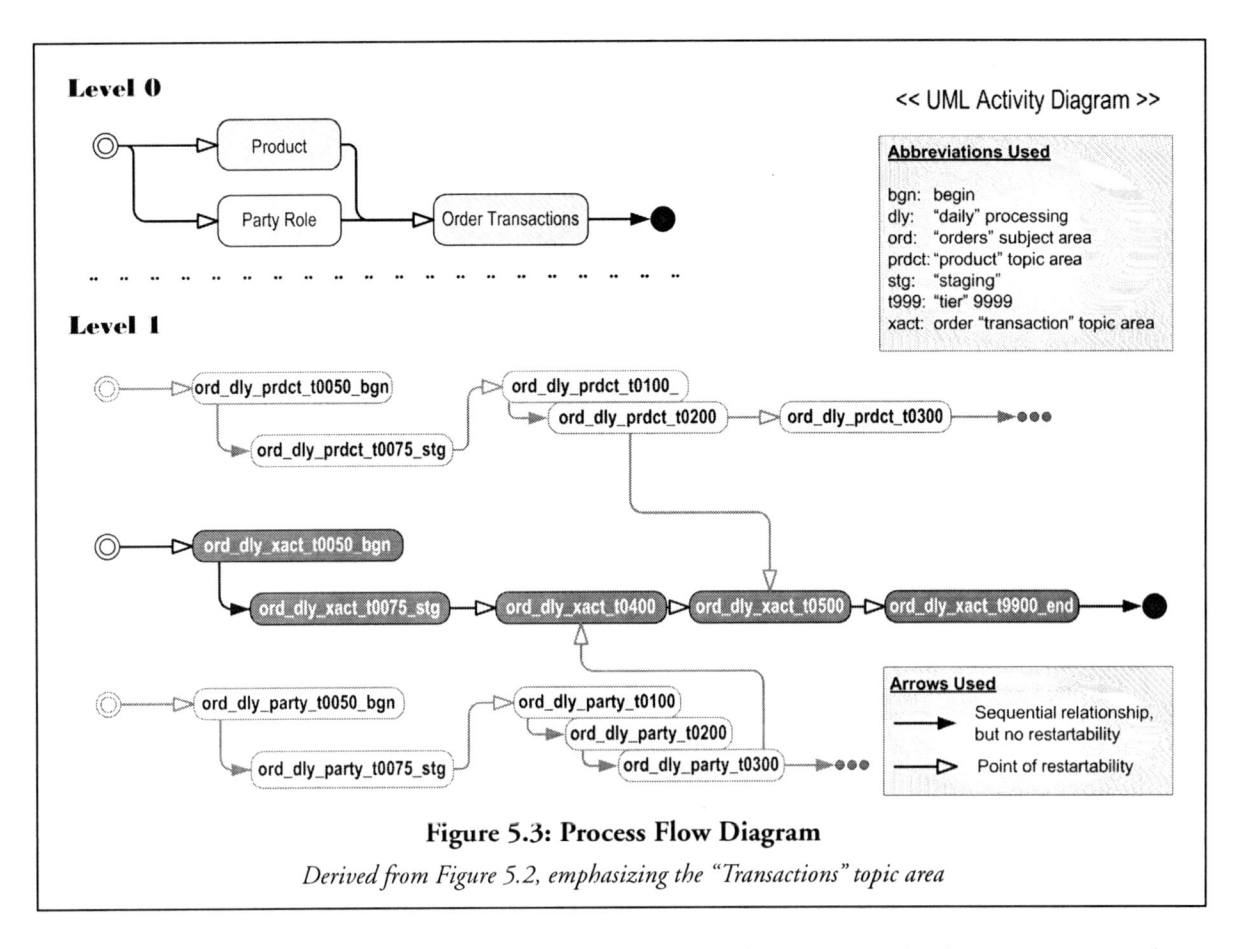

Figure 5.3: Process Flow Diagram
Derived from Figure 5.2, emphasizing the "Transactions" topic area

More can be read when we drill down into the PFD's Level 1 depiction. For simplicity of presentation, we have streamlined our figure to focus upon the Transactions sub-batch and how the other two sub-batches support it. The names have been standardized to begin with the subject area, time frame, and topic so that related modules appear together when sorted on the Operations console. We have converted the tier numbers into process numbers by appending two zeros after the tier number, allowing each processing bubble to be easily traced back to the corresponding level in the TDM. For example, one can instantly discern that "order_daily_product_t0200" contains the daily load routines for the Order subject area's load of "product" tables found in Tier 2 of the TDM. We gave the tier numbers the extra zeroes so that we can add additional modules at a later time by inserting them into the sequence, rather than renumbering the modules.

Chapter 5—Adapting Scrum for Data Warehousing

We have added bubbles at both ends of each topic area's process flow to indicate where the scheduler will call standard auxiliary processes. "t0050" modules might contain routines for archiving the log files of previous runs, for example. "t0075" invokes the staging routines, so that source data is available when the first tier's processing kicks off. "t9900" performs some wrap-up duties such as archiving source flat files and invoking some load validation scripts.

The PFD gives us a handy place to document process restartability as well. In our example, solid arrowheads indicate simple sequencing between processes, whereas a hollow arrow indicates a point where the operator could safely restart an ETL batch after a crash without fear of duplicating or otherwise corrupting the warehouse data. Of course, to make a module restartable, developers must have a) designed its units to check that a record does not already exist before writing it to the database, or b) included a lead-off unit that resets the target tables for a load. We will examine patterns for both approaches in Volume 2. The point of illustration here is to indicate that drawing the PFDs with the restart points highlighted increases the likelihood that Operators can keep a batch moving forward without needing developers to intercede.

Easier Progress Tracking

Because it is so quick to find one's work on a well-drawn tiered data model and its sibling process flow diagram, either the TDM or PFD can serve as a convenient tracking mechanism for the team. These diagrams nicely complement the task board, and makes progress many times more understandable to the Product Owner.

As we have seen, the task board contains details regarding developer work bundles. It is displayed in the project room so that the method is visible to Product Owner and other stakeholders. However, "visible" is not always "understandable" to non-technical stakeholders due to the complex nature of many BI tasks. Each box on the Tiered Data Model provides a summary of several work assignments from the task boards—insert, update, and retirement ETL units may all need to be finished before a developer can call a unit on the TDM "complete." Similarly, the Process Flow Diagram often summarizes several ETL units into named modules.

As they work the task cards that make up a unit, the team can use colored push-pins on the TDM to display the overall progress of work supporting a given warehouse table. As the team begins to complete the units contained on the TDM, they can use the same colored pins to summarize the status of an entire module on the PFD. One color scheme that works well with push-pins widely available today is as follows:

- **Clear:** Team found enough definition, now starting work on object
- **White:** Tests written, development underway
- **Yellow:** Development done, now waiting integration and validation
- **Green:** Passed validation, now schedule-driven and ready to demo
- **Blue:** Wrap-up activities completed, ready to promote
- **Red:** Held up by something—let's discuss during the next scrum

Product Owners may have trouble understanding all of the team's task cards, but they readily understand the units of the Tiered Data Model and modules on the Process Flow Diagram, because they all map back to one or more user stories. Furthermore, while the task board is scoped only to work belonging to the current sprint, the status depicted by colored pins on the TDM/PFD can provide a status snapshot for the release as a whole. Front-end developers can also use the pins on the TDM/PFD to discover, without asking the ETL members which tables are now supported by schedule-driven ETL and thus contain data for them to begin developing against. Using this simple color scheme for pins on these diagrams instills into the Agile data warehouse project a very high degree of transparency.

Sidebar: Benefits of the TDM/PFD Diagrams

Tiered Data Model Diagram

- See dependencies and necessary load orders quickly.
- See required load types quickly.
- See where simultaneous table loads are possible.
- See what ETL units can be combined into a shared ETL module.
- Derive module names easily.
- Derive corrective action after abnormal ETL termination (ABENDS).
- Augments the task board by allowing team to depict development progress of ETL units easily with colored pins.

Process Flow Diagram

- See process dependency and necessary sequencing.
- Document restart points.
- Track development progress of ETL modules easily with colored pins.

Balancing Design Clarity & ETL Performance

Given the many benefits listed above, warehouse designers might advocate architecting a warehouse precisely as the TDM and PFD dictate, but there is a downside. ETL performance is maximized by picking the data up off the disk as few times as possible, and this consideration usually dictates that each ETL unit writes to as many targets as possible. ETL designers intent on maximum performance might suggest that the TDM provides a good "first pass" at identifying ETL units, but that on the second pass many of the resulting units should be combined in order to minimize disk I/Os.

In actuality, a good design balances the two notions. Clear, hierarchical organization of any code is a strategic asset to the organization in that it makes software faster and less expensive to understand, enhance, and maintain. On the other hand, fast data loads are also a strategic asset in that they allow organization knowledge to be created and distributed in a timely basis. The dangers of combining units or modules that the TDM suggests to keep separate are:

- Each such combination will be yet another exception to the rule that teammates will have to remember when they work with the diagram.
- These exceptions will keep developers from easily seeing the boundaries of their development or maintenance work.
- Such exceptions will no longer correspond to the patterns supported by the reference model, and will thus require non-trivial efforts to design, validate, and support.
- Teams cannot provide accurate estimates for non-standard units.
- Non-standard units require custom execution planning, restart analysis, and documentation, thus incurring the cost of "reinventing several wheels."
- Tracking progress with Product Owners by simply placing a colored pin on the TDM will no longer be sufficient.

ETL code that effectively combines the units indicated by the TDM will require the team to draw dotted lines on the diagram to remind everyone where the non-standard designs can be found. **Figure 5.4** suggests one way our sample ERD might be adapted should the team decide to combine the population of the order Term, Adjustment, and Status tables with that of Order Item. One or two of these combinations will not prove fatal, but a significant number can cause the value of the TDM and the overall intelligibility of the warehouse data model to die "a death by a thousand cuts."

Clear designs and performance are often at odds, thus the best compromise policy might be to keep the design as streamlined as possible by following the dictates of the TDM, except where the team must solve known performance problems. In Volume 2, we

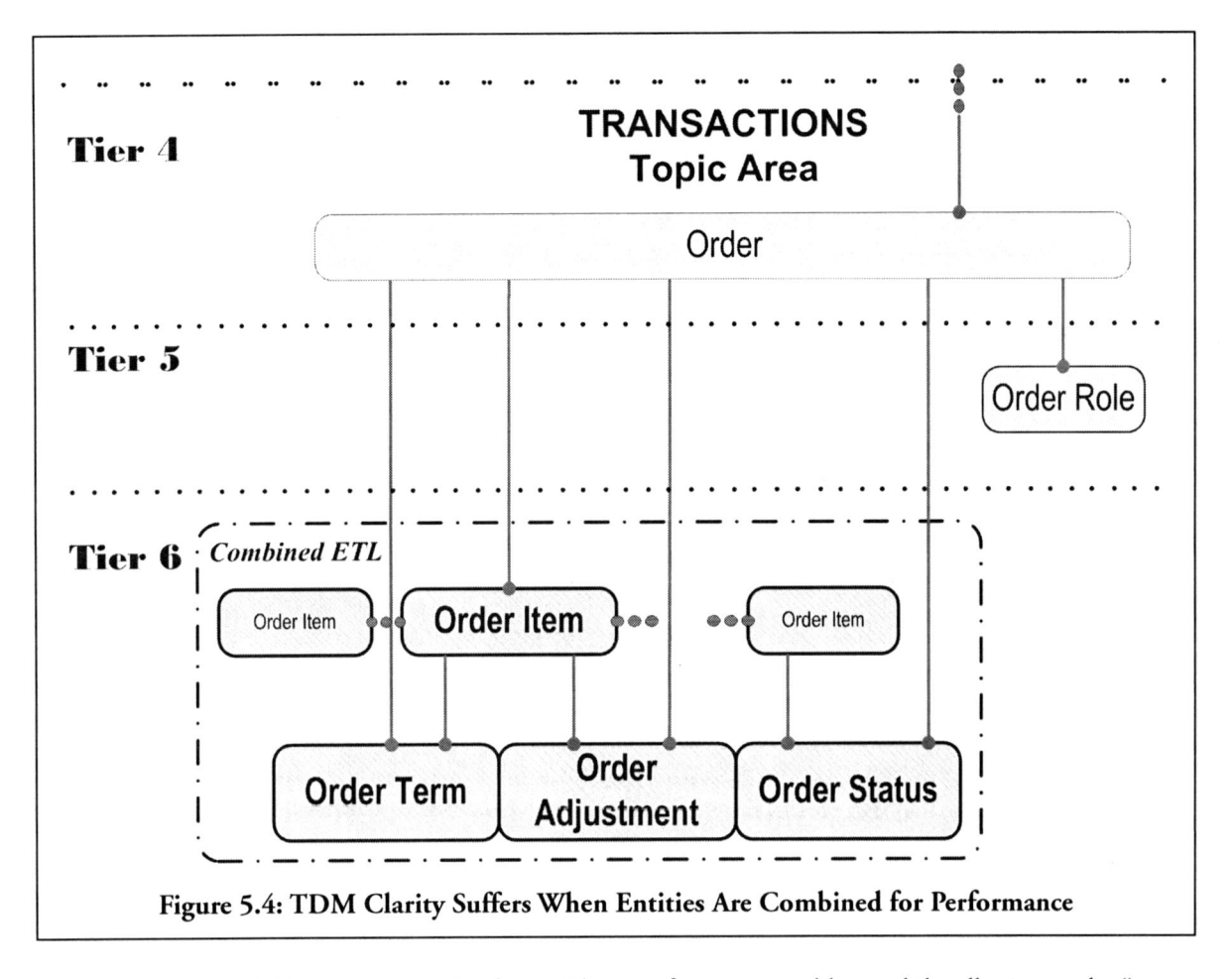

Figure 5.4: TDM Clarity Suffers When Entities Are Combined for Performance

will discuss some tactics for avoiding performance problems while adhering to the "atomist" design suggested by the TDM, such as volatile tables and chaining ETL units through host memory rather than disk.

Where it becomes absolutely necessary to combine ETL units, certain diagrammatic conventions can keep the diagram as easy to manage as possible. Sibling tables loaded in the same unit can be placed touching side by side. For combining the processing for a parent and child, the diagrammer will have to push the parent table down to the next tier down—its processing cannot start, after all, till ETL has loaded all the parent entities a given child table requires. Figure 5.4 displays both of these conventions.

AGILE QUALITY ASSURANCE OVERVIEW

A generic Scrum iteration theoretically aims to demonstrate "potentially shippable" code to the Product Owner at the end of a sprint. Teams that over commit for an iteration, however, often neglect the more technical features that a Product Owner would never think to validate. These omissions lower the standard of the deliverables to only "demonstrable" rather than "shippable." This possibility raises a very important question for which Scrum Masters must have a solid answer: What does an Agile warehouse developer mean when they say they are "done" with a unit of work?

It is easy to see that one developer might quickly assemble some code that is just good enough to demo, while another might strive for a long while to write "bullet proof" code. How can these two developers working on similar tasks mean the same thing by the deceptively simple word "done"? Can differing contexts make them both correct? And if a single definition could be agreed upon, would it need to change throughout the life cycle of a release? How should the team set objectives for quality of work and determine if a given unit truly meets its standards?

The definition of "done" brings the Agile team knee-deep into the notion of software quality management (QM). The QM field is so complex that if the team were to take the time to survey, summarizing, and incorporate ideas of "done" from the existing literature, the effort would quickly consume all its labor resources, making it anything but Agile. If we are indeed going to maximize the "work not done," we will need an approach to QM as effective and economical as the other tools that Scrum utilizes, such as user stories and the tiered data model.

Generic Scrum suggests that "done" is whatever developers, Scrum Master, and Product Owner working in concert define it to mean—as long as they do define it and include the extra effort it will require into their task cards and estimates. Scrum borrows many of its QM approach from XP. Agile Data Warehousing has elaborated upon the elements of that approach to make them specific to data warehousing. Though we will discuss in detail the ADW implementation of these techniques in Volume 2, we can introduce several of them here, so that Product Owners and Scrum Masters can share with their teams that a unit is not "done" until they have completed at least the following for it:

- Association with a comparable unit in the reference model
- Writing of tests prior to coding
- Planning the structure of it during 2-to-1 design sessions
- Coding the module to pass the pre-written tests

- Observing its executions under multiple scenarios as part of the daily build
- Adding lessons learned to basis-of-estimate cards and units in the reference model

We will be able to sketch all these practices in the remainder of this section by presenting a) patterns and references models, b) test-led development, and c) automated and continuous integration testing.

QUALITY FROM PATTERNS AND REFERENCE MODELS

Speaking loosely, "patterns" in software development are design ideas that have proven useful frequently in the past and are sufficiently adaptable to be useful in the future. A sampling of patterns utilized for the analysis and design of user-interface-based data capture applications reveals that good patterns are crafted to be fairly abstract in order to enhance their re-usability between unrelated software applications. As an example of typical patterns and how they assemble into functional systems, we can note that pattern books offer creational notions such as *builder* which can be called by *facade* and *decorator*, which provide the stage for action patterns such as *command, interpreter, iterator,* and *state*, which in turn support larger behavioral patterns such as *quote, transaction,* and *post.* [Gamma 1995, Fowler 1997]

Patterns prove to be highly reusable because a) most applications must provide general system services such as user accounts and logins, and b) their particular functions often consist of only a handful of specialized services, such as "update account balance," applied in many different ways across the contexts managed by the software. Because software components based upon patterns detect and adapt to the contexts in which they are invoked at run time, they allow teams to build large portions of big systems by assembling multiple instances of only a relatively few, well-programmed components.

Reusable design components clearly offer great benefits to data warehousing as well. On the back end, for example, the function "incrementally load a linking table of the integration layer" follows a largely predictable set of major steps, no matter what a particular instance's particular sources or targets might be. On the front end, a majority of reporting modules require pre-populated pull down lists whose values must be fed into a query before a pivot table is produced. Conceivably, these functions could require only calls to a handful of robust BI patterns. Such a set of such "Lego blocks" would greatly help teams in meeting Scrum's never-ending series of stiff deadlines by reducing the effort required to design, development, and document the application.

Unfortunately, the bulk of documented patterns seen in the past decade have been in object-oriented front-end applications. A single, open-source repository of patterns for data warehousing does not yet exist. Agile data warehousing teams will need to gather one of their own. We will discuss several means of doing so in a moment, but we must mention first one further task required to make this effort successful. Before they can use them effectively, developers will need to learn not only the pattern in its abstract but also see a sample implementation. Accordingly, ADW teams should build their pattern library in the context of an organizationally-specific *reference model*.

Much of the art to employing a pattern is working through a myriad of micro-decisions concerning how the code will recognize its context and in each situation choose the most appropriate variant of its primary function. Much of this behavior is constrained by the basics of the Information Systems environment in question, that is, the specific line-of-business applications that serve as source, the particular database management system (DBMS) the line of business and warehouse applications utilize, and the data communication resources that interconnect them. Having a good pattern may give ADW developers a good conceptual orientation, but they will not be productively coding until they know the syntax and parameter values for interfacing with the organization's source applications, target DBMS, and the middleware.

As far as patterns go, the reference model is the ADW team's "implemented pattern repository." The reference model does not have to be a big, expensive undertaking—it can be nothing more than a list of the most archetypical of the existing modules that are currently doing real work within the warehouse. The key quality for the reference model is that the code units on this list a) clearly demonstrate the details of implementing the team's design patterns in the actual environment of the warehouse in question, and b) they have superb as-built documentation so that a new developer can understand any one of them in depth after a small bit of study.

In the reference model, developers can find an example of how a generic idea such as "loading a fully-refreshed reference table," should be configured when the source is the company's SAP installation on Oracle as opposed to its legacy Siebel system running on DB2. A well-organized reference model becomes a menu of proven solutions which will accelerate the ADW team's efforts to match a particular need to a detailed design solution, thus greatly improving team velocity. To provide a warehouse-specific notion of what patterns an ADW reference model might contain, we have provided a starter set to consider for BI back ends and front ends in **Table 5.1 and 5.2**.

Table 5.1: Typical Back-End (ETL) Patterns for Data Warehousing

- Kill and fill staging
- Staging data above a "high water mark" (max date seen)
- Incremental load of a relational
    - Reference or fundamental table
    - Associative table
    - Associative history table
- Incremental load (from integration layer source) of a dimensional
    - Fact table
    - Type 1 Dimension table
    - Type 2 dimensions table
- Kill and fill load of an aggregation table
- Incremental load of an aggregation table

Amassing Patterns for the Reference Model

With patterns understood as reusable, micro-architectural building blocks, and the reference model seen as the guide to how they should be implemented, the team needs only to begin finding the patterns and placing them carefully in the reference model.

After familiarizing themselves with the non-BI patterns found in a couple of OO design books, the first place for the team to start collecting its own pattern library is the User Epic Decomposition framework which the Product Owner has been hopefully refining since the project's kickoff in order to express her requirements to the team. As we saw earlier, this framework comprises a surprisingly small set of essential business intelligence services, as seen from the predominantly business-oriented perspective of the Product Owner. The Product Owner has been encouraged to use as tight and consistent a set of concepts such as "kill and fill (fully refreshed) reference tables" or "incremental loads of history tracking dimensions" to express their needs. A tight and consistent set of requirements translates to a relatively finite set of patterns required to deliver upon it, thus placing tangible boundaries on the number, type, and variety of BI patterns the ADW team will need to collect for any particular project.

Table 5.2: Typical Front-End Patterns for Data Warehousing

- Line chart: single line, multiple line, stacked line
- Bar chart: vertical, vertical stacked, vertical cluster
- Pie chart
- Query definition screen with
    - Fill-in text limits
    - Pull-down limits
    - Radio button
    - Record count governors
- On-demand refresh
- Pre-populated results
- Single table
    - result set only
    - variable limits
- Dashboard (switchboard):
    - To sections within current reporting module
    - To sections of other reporting modules
- Multiple queries based upon a master data model
- Pivot table
    - plain, sub and grand totals
    - drill down and drill through

Once the content of the reference model has been scoped, the team should take the next step of polling its ETL, BI, and DBMS vendors for patterns. These vendors offer a plethora of books, web pages, whitepapers, sales engineers, and technical support staff all readily providing opinions on how applications are best built using their tools. Helping customers with these materials makes sense for these vendors because customers who sharpen their skills with the tools frequently require less support in the long run and provide vendors with further success stories they can point to. Filtering these design ideas through the User Epic Decomposition framework will take some effort, but will make the torrent more manageable and is thus a good use of the 20 percent of velocity that we encourage ADW teams to reserve for architectural work.

A third resource for patterns is user groups supporting the IS tools in question. Because the members are often data warehousing professionals applying tools to solve the challenges of one company rather than hundreds of customers, user groups provide advice that is far more implementation specific than vendors. Often one can find a peer who has applied the same tool to the same source and target applications for purposes closely matching ones confronting the ADW team. Suggestions from practitioners go far beyond patterns. They are nearly reference units that can be placed with little adaptation into the ADW reference model, and which will save enormous amounts of design time.

Moreover, one should continue to survey the commercial IS books because they are becoming increasingly fruitful resources for discerning important data warehouse patterns. The market now offers books that touch upon many core activities involved in growing, adapting, and reworking BI applications. For example, there are now books on "database refactoring" [Ambler 2006], "federating warehouses" [Adelman 2002], and "common warehouse metamodel" [Poole 2003]. The astute ADW team will be able to discern in these works many long-term warehouse design requirements. Whereas the data management tasks these books describe are needed only infrequently, they are inescapable once they arise, such as changing the structure of an existing table that already contains large volumes of data, combining the data of two or more overly-focused warehouses so that one can answer enterprise-level questions, and exchanging information between old and new warehouses once a new design comes online. An ADW team would be wise to prepare for such contingencies arising in the future by seeking robust designs now. Evolving one's BI pattern repository so that it anticipates these needs is a highly effective means of institutionalizing the advanced design details throughout the warehouse components long before most developers would realize they need them.

Once the team has begun to acquire patterns and reference units from external sources such as vendors and user groups, it can profitably start to mine internal sources as well. Having intimate knowledge of even a handful of patterns will sharpen their eyes to where they can discern many potential patterns in the existing source code of their own previous BI development work. Furthermore, many large companies have Enterprise Architecture teams that may have staff members already at work identifying patterns within the organizations. Patterns that the architects have found in the company's non-warehouse reporting systems may actually be an important data transformation technique that the warehouse team can adapt quite handily.

Finally, after scouring all the above sources outside the team, the developers will reach a point where they become their own best source of patterns. Drawing still on the architectural reserve built into their velocity planning, the team must make a steady effort to actively identify every programming task that could be profitably standardized. Once abstracting and polishing each candidate to provide an appropriate amount of "polymorphism" in foreseeable situations, the team needs only to add an extra dose of as-built documentation to transform a particular deliverable into a reusable team asset, easily located within the reference model.

Getting The Most Out Of A Reference Model

If the reference model merely provided a repository for project-specific implementation of design patterns, it would be worth building for the acceleration that such a resource would infuse into the ADW team's 2-to-1 design sessions alone. Fortunately, a good reference model provides several further advantages that are so valuable that they make the reference model a must-have strategic asset for any BI program. In particular, a well-built reference model will provide the ADW team:

- Better level-of-effort estimates
- A detailed "definition of done" for its developers
- Faster as-built documentation
- More effective code promotion procedures
- A superior means of testing upgrades to any BI tool
- The bulk of a thorough training program for new developers

Better level-of-effort estimates

The reference model will accelerate the ADW developers' 2-to-1 design sessions because for any given functional requirement they should be able to scan the reference model's list of implemented patterns to find one that closely matches the module that needs to be built. The discussion should proceed something akin to "The Product Owner wants us to load the part list into the integration layer. Why isn't that just like *load the customer list into the integration layer* we've already placed into the reference model?"

Resources for polishing working modules to the status of reference units for the reference model should come from the 20 percent of velocity ADW teams should reserve for architectural work, making them part of the sprints. In ADW sprints, we make it a point to discuss during retrospectives how to make our basis-of-estimate cards more accurate. By tying these BOE cards to reference modules in the reference model whenever possible, the reference model will gradually become the primary reference for developers judging story points and original labor estimates during sprint planning sessions.

With such a resource, the conversation sketched becomes "OK, so we're going to build it like Reference Unit #4. That means our story point estimate should be somewhere around 8 and our OLE around 32. Does that sound right?" Being able to draw upon a well-organized reference will greatly accelerate a team's estimation in both relative size and ideal time, while making these estimates far more consistent across sprints.

A detailed "definition of done" for its developers

The reference model also becomes a key component of ADW's quality management mechanism, for any one of its modules establishes a high level of completeness for modules built to emulate it. A developer might demo an ETL module to the Product Owner by displaying only the resulting data, arguing that its particular story is "done" because the data appears as it should once loaded into the warehouse. But the simple statement of "this module is based upon reference model unit #21" allows the developer's peers on the team to walk through the write-up on that unit, checking for many qualities of well-written code that the business-oriented Product Owner will probably overlook. A typical question might be phrased as "reference model Unit #21 makes an entry into the error table for every source record that fails to join to a related table. Is that true with your code as well?" Given that reference model-empowered walkthroughs will greatly increase the quality of coding provided by all developers, ADW teams are wise to structure the as-built documentation of reference units to make such point-by-point comparison as easy as possible.

Faster as-built documentation

Once accepted as "done," every module, even those not destined for the reference model, should receive some as-built documentation to support operations as well as future enhancement and maintenance programming. Such as-built documentation will be far faster for teams to generate if they can simply state that a particular module is based upon a particular reference model unit with a list of exceptions.

The resulting prose might read "The *stage electronic purchase order* module is based upon reference model Unit #17 and is therefore called with the same parameters, except for the addition of an *xml_schema* parameter because our order entry application allows customers to submit POs referencing either ANSI- or EEC-standards."

Just as the reference model tended to modularize to-be design discussions, it can also modularize as-built documentation—once again maximizing the "work not done" and greatly accelerating the team's development velocity.

Better-crafted code promotion procedures

Promoting code from an integration environment to either user acceptance or into production is always a thought-intensive and labor-consuming process. Such promotions are usually accomplished by first preparing a thorough list of steps and validation points, and then following them carefully under time-constrained conditions. Because errors and omissions in these procedures become very frustrating and costly, these guiding lists must be prepared carefully, often at considerable expense.

If the team has invested in a reference model, however, the documentation of each unit includes a section on "Typical Promotion Activities." This allows the team to borrow a large percentage of each new module's promotion process directly from the appropriate reference model unit. Being able to "cut and paste" promotional steps from a "canonical" reference not only reduces the time and expense of compiling these procedures, it also increases the accuracy of the resulting process, enhancing the team's effectiveness in this crucial aspect of bringing data warehouse enhancements online.

A Superior Tool For Testing Upgrades To BI Tools

Given that BI tool vendors are constantly upgrading their products with desirable enhancements, every warehouse team must frequently take time out to upgrade major pieces of its technical infrastructure. Upgrade efforts are often more demanding and expensive than even promoting new BI releases to production, because one flaw in a tool can disable the entire warehouse, rather than just a particular module.

With a reference model in place that includes at least one implementation of every feature of a given tool that the team utilizes in its code, testing new tool versions need not be so demanding. One must test new tool versions carefully because the enhancements can introduce serious flaws in previous functionality, such as the time we examined a major new DBMS release to discover it had lost its ability to provide correct results to queries utilizing a star transform based upon views rather than base tables. Certainly, putting that new DBMS version into production with such a flaw would have spelled disaster for the warehouse team and its customers, yet the real question is why should the ADW team risk the time and expense of upgrading and testing the entire warehouse application when testing a comparatively small reference module would have quickly uncovered this flaw with far less effort and cost?

A Better Training Program for New Developers

Finally, if the reference model contains, as we suggest, a detailed implementation of every pattern and tool component the warehouse facility utilizes, the reference model becomes the perfect training vehicle for new team members. A non-ADW team might take on new developers and put them to work after assessing their general skills through interviews, only to watch them flounder given the many things they still must learn about how BI applications have been built to date within the organization's particular IS environment.

An Agile Data Warehousing team equipped with a reference model, however, can match candidates to its staffing needs far more accurately by giving them a few, key reference model modules to review and explain. Those that pass this far more pointed evaluation process can then be trained quickly in all the specifics on "how enterprise warehousing is done here" by having them read the remainder of the reference model, giving them the background they need to begin working effectively. Furthermore, reading a reference model is far faster for the recruit and far less expensive for the team than providing new members on-the-job training through one-on-one sessions from veteran developers who would otherwise be building new code for the warehouse.

QUALITY THROUGH TEST-LED DEVELOPMENT

Coding units to match the outlines of well-implemented objects in the reference model suggests that the programmer is essentially "done" with a task, but does it prove that a given module has actually achieved the level of "potentially shippable" code that Scrum takes as its goal for every sprint? As mentioned briefly in earlier chapters, Scrum teams typically borrow two features from XP in order to ensure that every module has been coded without flaws: *test-led development* (TLD) and *automated and continuous integration testing* (ACIT). Although we will examine these techniques in detail in Volume 2 of this series, we present them in this section and the next so that the crucial contributions they make to Agile Data Warehousing's overall quality assurance plan will be clear.

Whereas waterfall methods often designate a separate phase of the software lifecycle as "testing" which occurs after development is complete, in Scrum/XP we utilize test-led development which integrates testing into the work of the development team and actually places test planning and preparation ahead of writing code. This order of precedence was seen on the layout of the task board presented in Chapter 2 in which the column for "Writing Tests" came before "Under Development."

Test-led development increases a team's quality over waterfall methods because a good test plan will thoroughly reflect a module's requirements of all types including user functional, system integration, and error management. Crafting a thorough test plan and coding a unit to pass all the tests included therein demonstrates in no uncertain terms that all requirements have been met. So, as long as the test script is properly commented, it can serve as a detailed technical requirements document. When combined with user stories, which verbalize business requirements, an ADW test plan eliminates the need for detailed, to-be requirements documentation altogether, making a big leap in "maximizing the work not done." As to quality assurance, establishing a rigorous testing regimen as the first-line evaluation of whether a module has been properly developed will instill far higher quality into the team's coding practice than waterfall's post-hoc testing, which often seems a hit-or-miss afterthought even when pursued as an independent phase of the software development life cycle.

The full gambit of tests needed for proper warehouse test-led development is extensive. When well written, a given test module will cover the full solution space addressed by a module, both horizontally and vertically. By *horizontal*, we mean that it must test the full width of features that the unit supposedly provides. The Product Owner should be highly involved with drafting these horizontal tests so that the resulting warehouse will support by design all the elements of user acceptance testing that reviewers will throw at the fully assembled release candidate. By *vertical* we mean that the test module demonstrates the code's ability to properly respond to errors occurring in every layer of its design—at all points from initialization, database connectivity, transformation logic, through finishing with an appropriate status code.

When the team becomes adept at test-led development, the practice of planning tests should take on a rhythm much like developing code, complete with a 2-to-1 design approach and a heavy reliance upon patterns. In fact, if the developers make a modest effort to include validation procedures in the documentation of the units in their reference model, they will find that planning even rigorous testing soon acquires a good deal of speed and consistency.

Working With Test-Led Development

At first test-led development will seem backward to the team, but the work patterns it fosters are actually very easy to understand. Once testing for an envisioned unit of code is designed, the team constructs the appropriate testing object and executes it, even though the code changes it will attempt to validate do not yet exist. Accordingly on this first run, the cases in the new test module will all fail. After witnessing the test unit comprehensively fail, the team can move the task card to "Under Development" and begin coding the desired new unit. When they believe they are "done" they run the new code unit, immediately re-run the test module, and review the test results. They repeat this code-test-review cycle until the unit passes all tests devised for the unit.

Only when all failures disappear can the task card be moved to "Waiting Validation." To validate, another team member reviews the code and test designs, executes the code and examines the results. Because this second developer often tests the module under slightly different assumptions using different data, this validation step catches oversights both in the code and the testing units. Once these flaws have been remedied, the team can at last move the task card to "Ready to Demo," assured that the unit is functional and robust.

At this point, it would be natural to discuss in greater depth the many types of testing an ADW team should incorporate into its test modules. As long as the notion of test-led development is understood, however, these details are better presented in the next section on automated testing, so that wide variety of test types can be seen in the context of the driver that will invoke them. Readers wishing to look into the actual coding of test units in terms of such notions as calling parameters and return codes are invited to turn to Volume 2 of this series or pursue some of the references we suggest at the end of this chapter.

QUALITY THROUGH AUTOMATED TESTING

For all of its strengths, test-led development cannot guarantee quality on its own because its focus is upon *units* of code. In a data warehouse environment, end users only see results at the end of a long chain of processing steps and tools. Developers working under the steady time pressures of a sprint might claim a particular package of code is now "done." Yet, what guarantees do we have that, once integrated with the other modules, this unit will not encounter interference from upstream processes, create problems for downstream units, or slow to a crawl under realistic data volumes and processor loads? Clearly unit testing will not suffice.

Full integration testing has long been a practice of system developers, but most waterfall-based initiatives schedule testing after the bulk of development is completed. Such an arrangement would not work for Agile projects because the developers commit to delivering "potentially shippable" code with every short sprint. They cannot afford to lose several days locating a programming flaw. They need to detect errors as soon as they are introduced when the culprit is still easy to identify.

For this reason XP urges developers to assemble and test a fully integrated system daily. Because daily testing greatly increases the total testing conducted, XP also recommends automating the testing so that this strenuous validation does not consume too much human effort. However, we must remember that XP is a development approach forged for user-interactive or "online transaction processing" (OLTP) systems, not for business intelligence's "online analytical processing" (OLAP) needs. Considerable details needed to be added to XP's approach to make its testing recommendations work for data warehousing.

The Agile Data Warehousing method starts with XP's notion of "daily build and test" and evolves it into **Automated and Continuous Integration Testing** (ACIT), which includes an extensive Test Data Repository (TDR). Implementing ACIT requires a non-trivial investment of team resources, yet it rewards that investment by driving the developers to such a high level of quality that all stakeholders can feel confident that their warehouse project is receiving "bullet proof" code despite the barely controlled chaos they might see during mid-sprint in the Scrum team's project room.

ADW Testing Requirements

The value of the extensive testing that the ACIT provides will make no sense to warehousing teams that do not appreciate either how high a level of quality a warehouse should reach or how complex a system a business intelligence application truly is. Let us start the discussion with a quick look at both issues.

Regarding Quality

Regarding quality, teams should be aiming for something very close to 100 percent accuracy. In warehouses belonging to decision support systems the information provided must be correct ... period. The organization will make crucial tactical and strategic choices based upon the information found therein. If the warehouse is proven wrong even a few times, decision makers will find another source that they can trust, and the warehouse will be left without customers or sponsors. BI applications in regulated industries face an even higher quality requirement given that errors in their information can lead to product recalls, extensive external audits, tort actions, and, in this age of SOX, criminal investigation of company officers.

For these reasons, a team might first set its quality objectives to the gold standard of the data processing: "provably correct," which would require that their validation efforts demonstrate that a) every feature requested is present in the deliverable, and b) all such features function without error. Realizing that no programming or testing effort can ever be perfect, the team might adjust its goals slightly to "essentially correct and fault tolerant," which asserts that a) the code is complete with no known bugs *as far as their validation efforts can demonstrate*, and b) when an unanticipated problem does arise, the application follows a planned and constructive response. Given the pattern of dependencies between entities in the warehouse and the differing values of the topic areas, this planned, constructive responses may well differ on a table-by-table basis. Most will involve some combination of the following tactics:

- Load what is possible of the remaining source data, so that users still receive some value.
- Write details of the fault occurring to an error log.
- Write unloadable source records to a "error suspense" table.

- Attempt to reload suspended records on subsequent runs, when they might have been corrected by users on the source system.
- Roll back the target table to a previous state.
- Terminate the current load process.
- Selectively suspend triggers for downstream processes so that modules dependent upon the faulted module do not attempt to run.
- Allow the batch to be restarted midstream without duplicating records or otherwise corrupting the data loaded into the warehouse tables.

For most BI projects, essentially correct, fault tolerant code will be the only quality standard that project sponsors and other stakeholders will accept. Indeed, if the BI team were to ask them to accept less, it is doubtful that many warehouse projects would be funded. Yet, warehouse teams have one large obstacle to surmount before they can deliver upon this high quality standard—the complexity of their application.

Regarding Complexity

Let us consider the ETL side of a warehouse first, since it is usually more involved than front-end applications. The typical ETL application is complex because it:

Integrates data from many sources.

- Does not control the quality of data from those sources
- Transforms data using many modules
- Includes modules that make many decisions
- Encounters many kinds of errors

Multiplying together the component counts for the categories above will reveal that the number of validation points required to *thoroughly* test a BI application is astronomical. Consider, for example, the many types of errors that a single ETL module might experience during its execution:

- Extract data set incomplete or corrupt
- Source system extracts run too slow or are intermittently available
- Data out of expected range
- Missing reference values
- Imperfect relational integrity between source data (foreign keys do not link)
- Upstream ETL process ABENDs (crashes) or never completes

- Target storage system runs out of space
- Programming syntax error or unsupported logical case

The responses to these contingencies are almost as varied as the types of errors. For some kinds of error, such as source unavailability, the problem might be corrected at the network level, allowing the batch to be simply resumed at an appropriate place. Others will require that records be updated in the source system, and so will take a day or more to correct. Still others are going to require that coding flaws be diagnosed, repaired, and the batch re-executed, perhaps days after the fault occurred.

Regarding number of components, we can note first that a warehouse has several subject areas, each of which might require a different error strategy that the team will have to prove through testing. For example, if the Customer Master Data module ABENDs in mid-batch, the Sales subject area probably should not load, but Manufacturing, which references customer information less extensively, might be able to proceed.

Subject areas themselves are not monolithic. ETL loads their data by progressing through five architectural layers: extraction, staging, integrating, presentation, and user access. The boundaries between these layers are useful places where the ETL can be restarted after many types of ABENDs, but each restart point chosen must be tested to prove that it does not duplicate or otherwise corrupt the target data. Subject areas themselves contain many "topic areas" such as Geography (addresses) and Organizational Unit. These in turn have varying levels of dependencies between them that the ETL will have to navigate accurately in choosing its response to a processing error.

Finally, ETL applies business rules—logic that generates values based upon what is already stored in other columns and other rows, often implemented by chaining together dozens of logical units. These rules often depend upon the input values to be non-null and fall within certain ranges, yet these qualities are determined by the source systems, many of which can have their own foibles.

With all these considerations, the complexity of warehouse testing is daunting. Teams must prepare validation plans that demonstrate fault tolerance by testing for conflicts occurring between subject areas, architectural layers, restart points within those layers, and even between the columns of data spanned by the application's business rules.

Moreover, proving that a module of code is essentially correct and fault tolerant once does not free a team from having to retest it many times later. The high level of dependency between the numerous objects in an ETL application requires that development teams perform extensive "regression testing"—proving that what used to work still functions properly now that changes have been made. Even a small error introduced in an unrelated module can spawn serious challenges for other modules downstream or the loading of other subject areas. Accordingly, developers must demonstrate the quality of not only their updated units, but also that of all "collateral" modules in the ETL application.

If we take just a moment to multiply the various types of errors we must consider and the number of function points in the ETL we should validate, we can easily see that demonstrating that code is correct and fault-tolerant will require an extensive testing process. We can omit from this calculation the number of subject areas and architectural layers because they are implicit in the topic areas and restart points, respectively. Even with this simplification, confirming the application's response to eight types of errors listed above for a warehouse containing 25 topic areas, five restart points per topic area, and 50 business rules each will involve something on the order of 50,000 required test points that must be executed every time a new or updated module is integrated into the application—straining the rational person's willingness to believe that this level of testing is feasible or even humanly possible.

Automated Test And Complex Validation

Having now examined why thorough integration testing is both necessary and difficult, we can now begin to strategize a practical means to achieve it. Obviously, we need to make the effort economical, so that this avenue of quality assurance and the BI project itself will be funded. Given the large number of test points required, the solution must involve a good deal of automation to make it doable. Because in an Agile data warehousing effort, developers can deliver new module code at almost any time, integration testing will also need to run repeatedly, perhaps more than once a day, so that errors are caught as soon as they are introduced. Taken altogether, these considerations can only be fulfilled by a testing mechanism that is a small development effort in its own right—a sub-application of the BI project which ADW calls the *automated and continuous integration* facility or ACIT.

Using our host machine's job scheduler, we can make the ACIT "continuous" by configuring it to run every six hours or so. Keeping it simple, the ACIT master schedule simply calls a set of scripts each time it runs, and these scripts in turn execute the tests. Planning the scripts is relatively straight-forward if one aligns them with the large divisions we have seen in the required testing described above, such as subject area. We present the thinking behind the ACIT organization employed in our practice in **Figure 5.5**, where we first examined the various components of testing in terms of their number. Subject areas have a low count and are a major, user-visible division in the warehouse, so we address them each with an ACIT script of its own. Next, there are eight or more classes of errors we want to consider, so we organize those as "scenarios" within a given subject area's test plan. Each scenario calls a "setup" subscript that will properly configure major environmental factors such as source and target data connectors, as well as the set of test data that will be fed to the ETL process during its run.

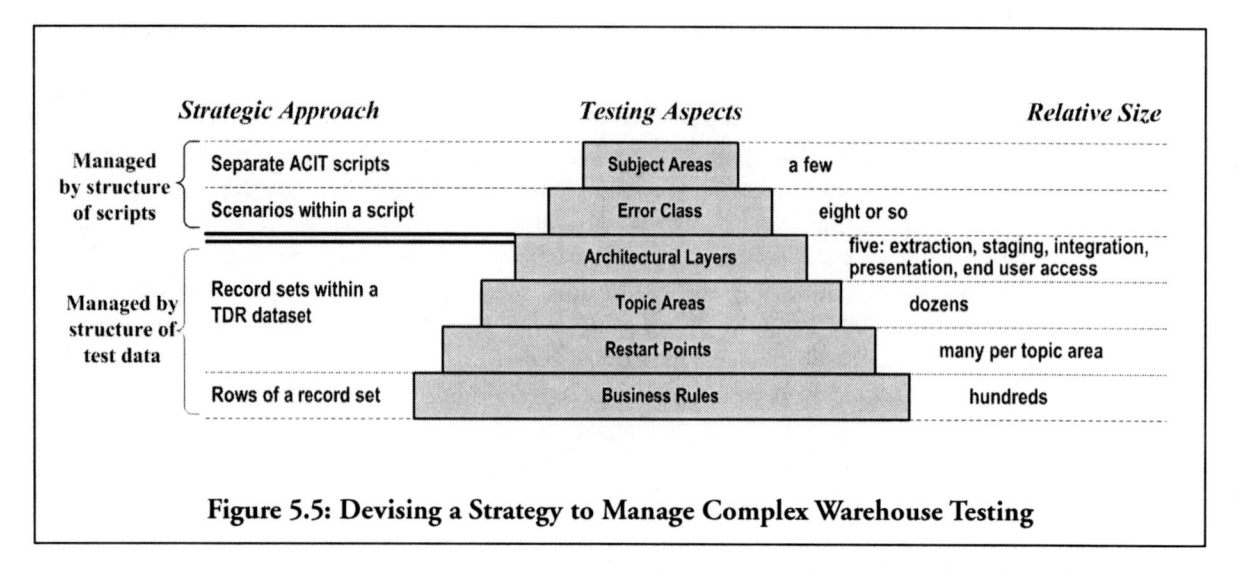

Strategic Approach		Testing Aspects	Relative Size
Managed by structure of scripts	Separate ACIT scripts	Subject Areas	a few
	Scenarios within a script	Error Class	eight or so
Managed by structure of test data	Record sets within a TDR dataset	Architectural Layers	five: extraction, staging, integration, presentation, end user access
		Topic Areas	dozens
		Restart Points	many per topic area
	Rows of a record set	Business Rules	hundreds

Figure 5.5: Devising a Strategy to Manage Complex Warehouse Testing

The next three strata of our testing requirements stack—architectural layers, topic areas, and restart points—require not only the specific set-up of a given testing scenario, but also a specific set of extracts and other data objects that will challenge the ETL when it runs. To test just the staging layer, for example, we feed the ETL a data set where a particular table is missing, and another where the decryption of a vendor's extract used the wrong key.

Once past the staging architectural layer, the ETL jobs will begin working through the many topic areas of the Tiered Data Model, and passing the many restart points found on the Process Flow Diagram. Errors that test the handling of interdependencies among these notions can be caused by placing "landmines" in the records themselves—flaws in data values, nullability, or referential integrity that will make normal processing impossible for the ETL.

We addressed all three of these layers by organizing the record sets within the test data to have hierarchical grouping by architectural layer, topic area, and restart point. Thus, for a given subject area and class of errors to be tested, the ACIT repeatedly invokes the warehouse loads to work through a series of record sets, each one "drilling down" a bit further into the code before it feeds the ETL a record that is known to cause an error.

Figure 5.6. depicts this progressive drill down for one subject area, displaying the process for only a few error class scenarios. When the ACIT is first called for the given subject area, it runs a "nominal" scenario, that is, it feeds the ETL a data set that should load normally. Results from this scenario can be examined to prove that all transports and transformations work as expected when the data is complete and clean. On the next call, ACIT employs a script that tests how the ETL will respond when the data is incomplete. This script will first utilize a data set that simulates a flawed staging run, so that one can prove the ETL loaded no more than it should for each possible omission of source extracts. After testing the staging layer in this way, ACIT begins back at the top, this time testing how ETL responds when given data that will cause problems in the integration layer. ACIT continues iterating through the architectural level using carefully prepared data sets, until errors of the given type have been forced to occur at all architectural layers. At this point the incomplete data scenario has been exhausted, so the ACIT moves on to the next error class, dirty data.

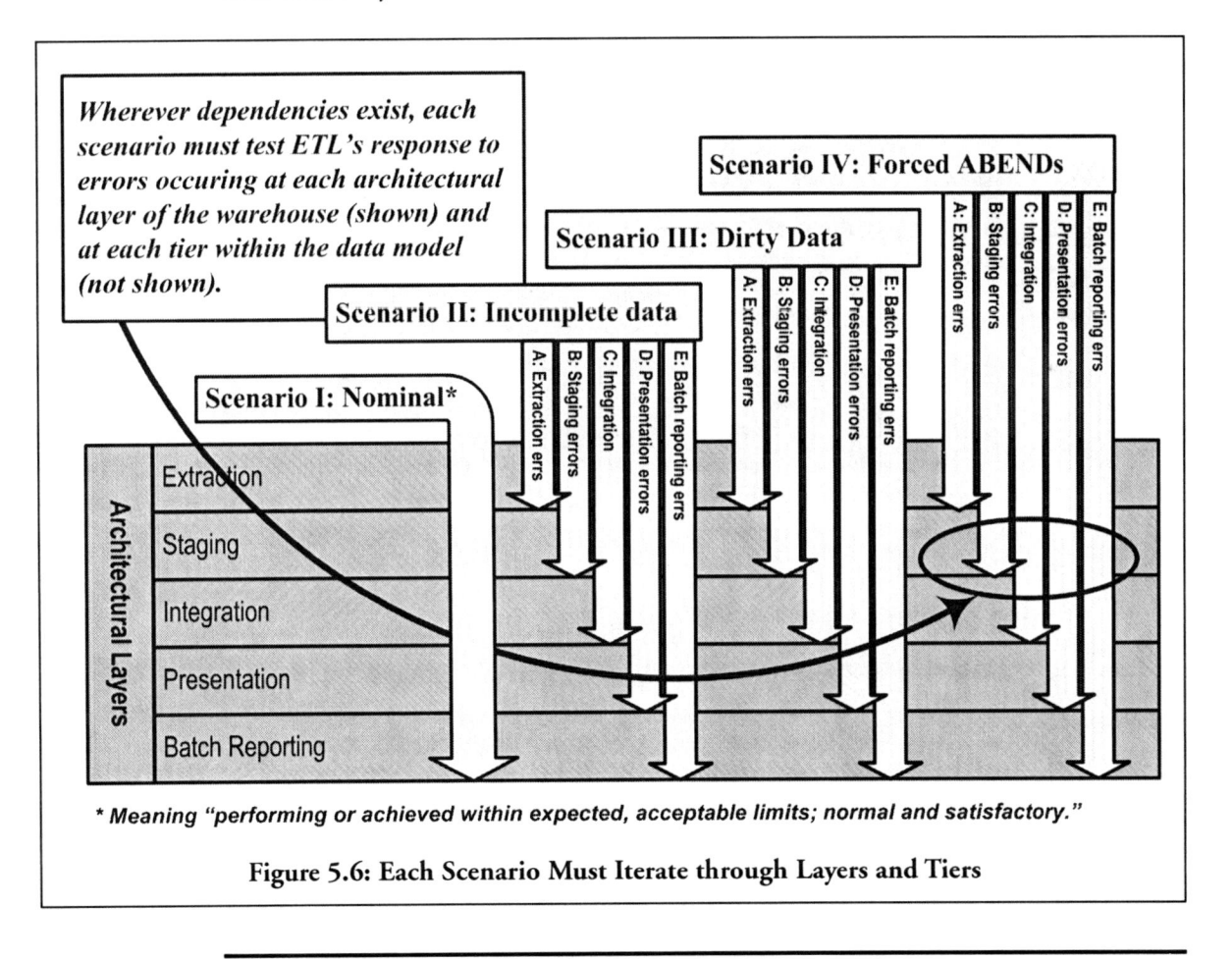

Wherever dependencies exist, each scenario must test ETL's response to errors occuring at each architectural layer of the warehouse (shown) and at each tier within the data model (not shown).

Scenario IV: Forced ABENDs
Scenario III: Dirty Data
Scenario II: Incomplete data
Scenario I: Nominal*

Architectural Layers:
- Extraction
- Staging
- Integration
- Presentation
- Batch Reporting

* Meaning "performing or achieved within expected, acceptable limits; normal and satisfactory."

Figure 5.6: Each Scenario Must Iterate through Layers and Tiers

Chapter 5–Adapting Scrum for Data Warehousing

Many of the business rules in the typical data warehouse describe how a particular entity, such as purchase orders, will be portrayed as they progress through a lengthy series of transactions. For Scenarios I and II in particular, the source test data will have to depict multiple time points in order to model the life cycle of data on the line-of-business systems that serves as a warehouse's data source. Each time a test script prepares to invoke an ETL module, it will first pull a particular "time slice" from the TDR, placing it in the appropriate starting data structures, most frequently those of the Staging layer.

Overall, each test script pursues a cycle of a) positioning the proper time slice of source data, b) running the ETL, then c) comparing actual to expected results. When the script has exhausted all its time points for its focal scenario, it is complete, and ACIT will move on to the next script which will test a different scenario, but many of the same time points. Given this pattern, we can say that the ACIT must include two types of "simulators": a "Scenario Simulator" that advances through the different *ways* we want to test the warehouse modules, and a "Time Simulator" that allows us to simulate the passing days or hours, so that we can track the evolution of data that should occur as the source systems continue to generate new transactions.

The one piece we have not yet addressed is the version of the application itself that the ACIT repeatedly runs its test suites against. In the next section we will discuss that ADW teams may wish to establish an "Integration and Testing squad." Before each run, this squad or the formal Test Managers should assemble the "current build" from all the modules checked into the team's change control repository by the developers. For a large part, moving code first from developer to change control and then from that repository to integration testing is simply a good practice because it lets teams back up a revision or two when a poorly written module gets included in the build. Moreover, it is an important notion when it comes to demonstrating ADW as a "mature" method, as will be discussed in a later chapter. The task of frequently creating the latest build for the ACIT to test can become burdensome if performed entirely by hand. To reduce the workload and to increase accuracy, teams often automate the creation of the current build and include the invocation of this process in master script that ACIT follows each time it is called.

Testing Business Rules With Row Triplets

Returning to the planning exercise we began with Figure 5.4, we have only the largest testing aspect left, business rules. A warehouse may involve thousands of business rules, so it would be impractical to use this notion at the level of naming separate ACIT driver scripts. Luckily, the rows within a test data set represent an iteration series all on their own. If we take the data set from the nominal load, where the ETL runs without error, we can duplicate the source records again and again, each time changing one column to introduce a value that will set off an error during the calculation of a particular business rule.

Before we start such an effort, we need to make one refinement to this tactic, which ADW calls the "rule of threes." Because warehouses provide a good deal of aggregation for the end user, their data transform logic often involves operations geared toward sets rather than single source rows. For example, the operation of "flagging the top ten customers by sales agent" generates a single value for the target table by aggregating all sales transactions for a given time period by customer. A single row will not be enough to test business rules involving any such aggregation because the ETL may have a programming flaw that involves only the first record of a set, or just the last record of the set, or perhaps just the records occurring in the middle. The minimum number of records required to test sets, then, is three. Because it is burdensome when creating and reviewing test data to remember which business rule involves some form of multi-record operation, we have simply adopted a policy in our practice that stipulates all errors will be tested by a set of at least three records, hence giving rise to a "rule of threes."

THE TEST DATA REPOSITORY

In planning a strategy for managing the complexity of warehouse testing, we make a clear switch in mechanism halfway down the layers of testing aspects portrayed Figure 5.5. The top half was managed by the organization of the ACIT driver scripts, but the bottom half is managed by the data set we feed the ETL. We will need many distinct data sets to span the multiple varieties of testing required. Each of these data sets will arise from careful planning and data entry, so they must be placed in a dependable storage area. With these two requirements for managing test data, every Agile data warehouse project is going to need a database built expressly to serve as a "Test Data Repository."

Given the particular pattern of testing the ACIT will conduct, the Test Data Repository (TDR) will need a data set for every combination of the testing aspects shown on the Figure 5.5. Many of these data sets will be small—for example, a warehouse might be designed to allow no ETL to proceed for a given subject area if staging is incomplete. In this case, the appropriate TDR data set for the first ACIT script iteration may only have a few source records for all staging tables except the one that will be incomplete. Other TDR data sets will be very large, such as those used to test the nominal run and those designed to stress all the business rules.

If development resources were boundless, one might attempt to save processing time by also placing intermediate ETL results in the TDR—for example, the image of integration layer tables after that stratum's loading has completed. In practice, just getting a complete set of extracts to iteratively drill down the layers is the limit of what teams can afford to invest in validation. Furthermore, intermediate results will not save enough resources to merit the effort, because many acceptance environments sit idle during the workday, waiting to run ETL overnight in parallel with the production runs. With processing time to spare, these organizations feel that running progressively longer "string tests" that all start from the extract layer as depicted in Figure 5.6 only consumes resources they were not going to use anyway.

Given the focus on extracts for the TDR, most of these repositories must provide a collection of records for all source tables required for the subject area being tested. Thus the database schema of each subject area is essentially duplicated in the TDR, so that there will be a one-for-one correspondence between the TDR tables and those the ETL will extract from source applications. Though it will have all the columns of the source tables it incorporates, the TDR tables will also need several metadata columns added. First, the ACIT must be able to pull records pertaining only to a particular scenario (error class). Secondly, developers managing the test data must be able to find what architectural layer, topic area, restart point, and/or business rule a given record is designed to test.

Aside from source data, the TDR will also hold expected testing results. On any given day, ACIT will invoke the integrated ETL code many times, iterating through subject areas, classes of errors, and the like. In order to detect flaws in the coding, each test result will have to be compared to expected results.

Sidebar: Major Requirements for the Test Data Repository

- Provide a mirror of every source table that the warehouse will draw upon.
- Provide a hierarchical metadata structure that supports all the "Testing Aspects" shown in Figure 5.5, from Subject Area down to Business Rules.
- Provide a test case table containing a foreign key to the hierarchical metadata including test script.
- Provide a "time point" metadata element, so that the test scripts can simulate the passage of time by pulling sequential time slices of data from the TDR.
- Provide long text attribute on the hierarchical metadata so that test planners can record the descriptions of each organizational element, especially test script and test case.
- Provide a data structure for storing expected results that includes an attribute where one can enter for each expected record a reference to the TDR source records from which it should have been produced.

AUTOMATED TESTING FACILITY SEEN AS A WHOLE

So far, we have taken a bottom-up approach to the ACIT, presenting components before assembling the big picture. **Figure 5.7** assembles all that we have discussed into an overview, and introduces a couple of additional concepts. There are many variations on how to combine the many aspects of testing, so the figure represents a baseline approach that has worked well for us and our customers.

Working top-down now, we see that the ACIT begins with a list of subject areas and scenarios. When invoked by a scheduler, a "dispatch" script or process automatically iterates through all the possible combinations of subject areas and scenarios, finding the appropriate test script, which will in turn kick-off the ETL and evaluate the results.

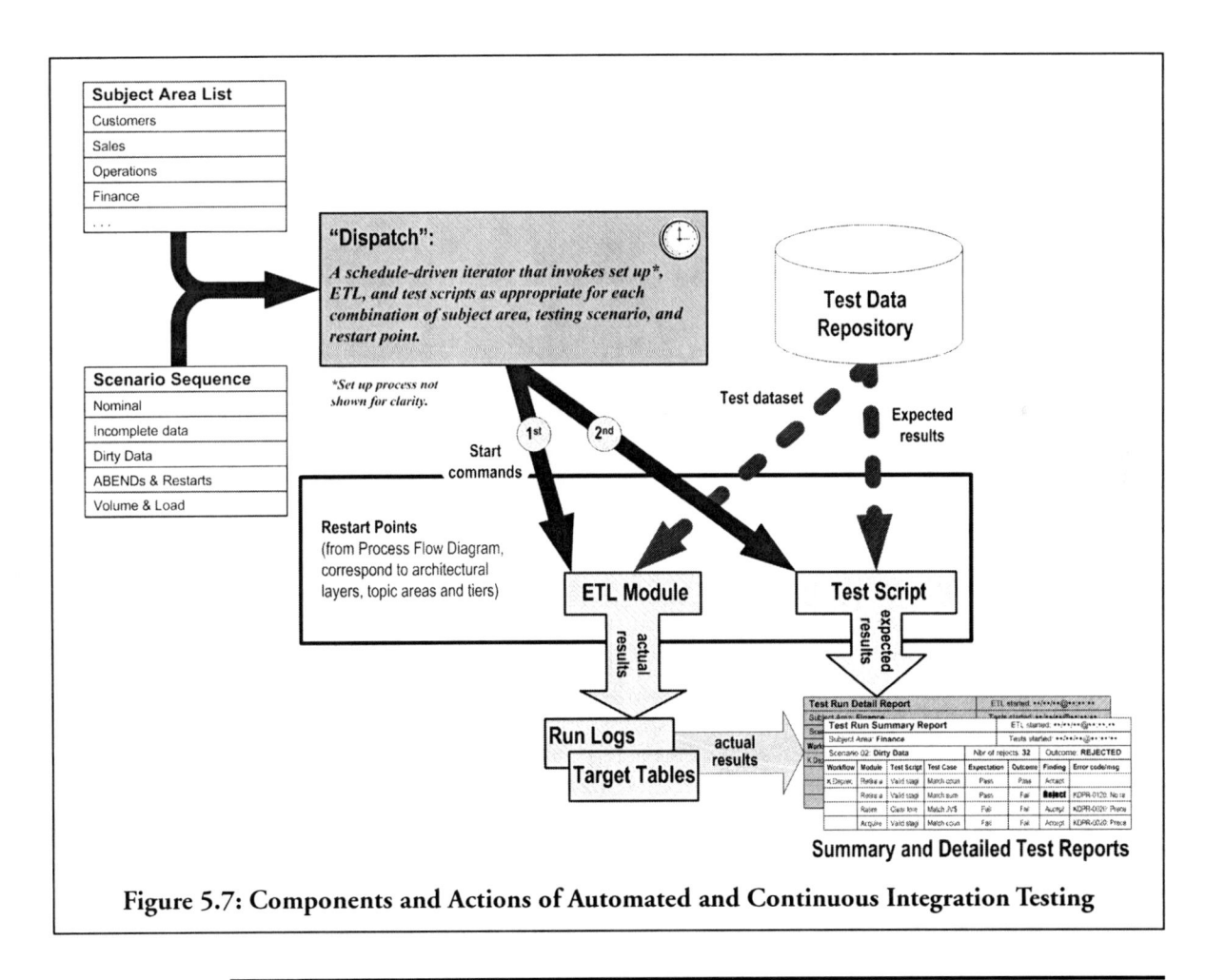

Figure 5.7: Components and Actions of Automated and Continuous Integration Testing

Chapter 5—Adapting Scrum for Data Warehousing

When called, each of these test scripts takes over the iteration and progressively drills down through all architectural layers, topic areas, and restart points programmed into the ETL code. At each point in this drill down path, the script a) runs a set-up procedure that pulls a data set from the Test Data Repository, placing it where it can be extracted or staged, b) calls the appropriate ETL modules to run against the data pulled from the TDR, and c) evaluates the actual results for that data set against the expected results (also stored in the TDR).

With the Dispatch script attending to all the possible mixtures of architectural layers, topic area, and restart points, only the bottom and most numerous layers portrayed in Figure 5.5, business rules, remains unaddressed. Here, the records of the TDR data sets submitted to ETL provide the most "inner loop" of the necessary iteration. ADW teams need to configure at least one ACIT scenario that draws upon a "Test Business Rules" slice from the TDR, that—following the "rule of threes"—contains for every branch of ETL logic a triplet of records with values deliberately chosen to cause an error if possible. Only when the ETL can successfully process such a data set can the team reasonably claim that its code is "essentially correct, and fault tolerant."

Returning to Figure 5.7, we can see that the Dispatch process follows each ETL run with a call to a test module that compares the records left in the target tables to a set of expected values. Dispatch can also compare key messages found in the ETL log to an expected collection of such messages pulled from the TDR. In preparing its error summary, Dispatch gathers the following comparisons into a *Test Run Summary Report*, where developers can see at a glance where errors occurred within large categories such as subject area and error classes. Dispatch also generates a *Test Run Detail Report*, describing points in the testing hierarchy where the faults occurred, with details such as test case identifiers.

APPLYING ACIT TO FRONT-END APPLICATIONS

Because ETL usually consumes the bulk of warehouse development efforts, it has dominated our consideration of BI application testing so far. Whereas front-end, "OLAP" applications may be comparatively less intricate than ETL, testing them is actually more difficult to discuss because most OLAP tools involve a large amount of web-based operations and output. Unfortunately, thoroughly testing web-based applications requires recording user sessions key-stroke-by-key-stroke, so that the testing tool can later pose as a living end user. Such key stroke recording is far more laborious than setting up the text-based testing scripts that suffice for validating ETL. Moreover, such testing mechanisms are very fragile to changes in the front-end screen layouts, making the testing facility very expensive to maintain.

Though the ADW development team will undoubtedly choose to build an Automated and Continuous Integration Testing facility for back-end motivations alone, the case for investing in the ACIT would be all that more compelling if we could somehow stretch its capabilities to economically cover the validation of front-end applications also, despite their web-based aspects. Luckily, most of this stretching can be achieved with a reasonable degree of effort. With a small amount of forethought, the team can design front-end modules so that the ACIT can access results and automatically test the most important portions of user access applications, namely the queries and business rules coded into the OLAP layer that generate the values users actually see.

The left half of **Figure 5.8** depicts the architectural layers that data traverse while traveling from the dimensional tables of the warehouse's presentation layer to arrive at a web-based display of the end user. The layers that belong to the front-end application begin with query definitions, stored within the OLAP tool's code or repository. These queries are invoked by a manual, on-demand event delivered to the OLAP server via an HTML connection. From there, the OLAP tool creates objects in server or workstation memory providing analytical support for the end user, starting with a result set generated by the query, a set of GUI objects such as pivot tables and graphs, all finally presented within the graphic user interface of the front-end tool running in the end user's web browser.

In order to understand how we can make front-end applications largely amendable to ACIT validation despite their web-based orientation, we must first note that most high-end OLAP tools either have a scheduling facility or can be invoked by a third party scheduler. We portray a scheduled OLAP function on the right half of Figure 5.8, where the scheduler invokes the same query as the on-demand events, but sends the results to an export file stored on disk rather than to server memory. These exports can take many formats that the ACIT can read, such as ASCII text files. With this output, the ACIT can compare actual results to expected values stored in the TDR, identical to the method used to validate ETL modules.

The value of such automated testing for front-end output will depend entirely upon the design pattern the team uses for its OLAP applications. Clearly, there are two distinct "realms" they must consider, as noted by the braces on the right side of our figure: objects on disk that ACIT can validate versus objects in OLAP server memory which it cannot access. We have labeled the divide between these realms as the "ACIT accessibility line" on

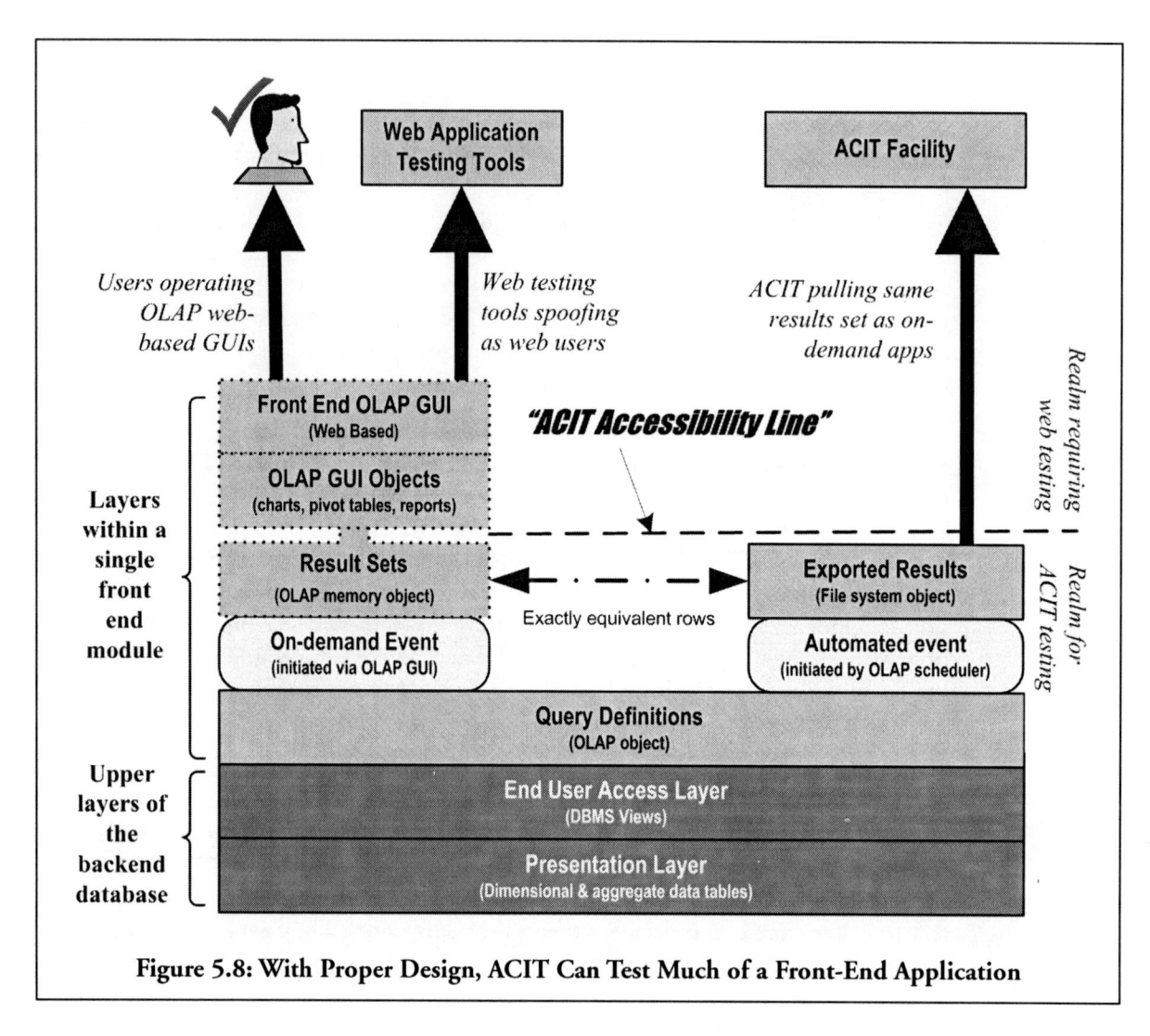

Figure 5.8: With Proper Design, ACIT Can Test Much of a Front-End Application

the diagram. With every business rule that OLAP must implement, the team chooses which side of this line to locate the supporting code—either in the ACIT-testable realm by embedding the logic in the query utilized, or in the web-testing only realm by placing it in the OLAP GUI objects.

This realization provides the key for enabling ACIT validation of the warehouse's front-end—OLAP applications that keep their business rules in their queries, rather than in their GUI objects, can rely upon the ACIT to test the bulk of their programming logic automatically. OLAP deliverables that implement business rules with server memory-based objects will have to be tested by web-based validation tools—still doable, but requiring an additional effort beyond building the ACIT. Following Agile's notion of "maximizing the work not done," an ADW team should implement the bulk of front-end business rules in the ACIT-supported realm where programming errors can be detected quickly, and regression testing occurs automatically as a matter of course.

SUMMARY OF ACIT BENEFITS

Though the discussion above is but an introduction to automated and continuous testing, we can now see that the ACIT offers crucial benefits which justify the implementation effort it requires. After reviewing the potential payoff, readers wishing the details of building the ACIT and populating its TDR can turn to Volume 2 of this series.

As long as the ADW team has faithfully compiled a TDR with the data needed to test all the functional requirements, technical requirements, business rules, error classes, and restart points, an ACIT run for a release candidate that completes without exceptions will bestow the following important benefits upon the team and the organization owning the warehouse they build:

- Developers discover almost immediately if their new code works as specified or causes errors for adjacent or downstream modules.
- Causes of errors are far easier to pinpoint because it can only be those modules updated since the last ACIT run, usually a very small number.
- The team can safely assure stakeholders that the warehouse is both essentially correct and fault-tolerant.
- Proving full coverage of functional requirements daily will greatly speed up user acceptance testing (UAT) and "production readiness reviews."
- Error-handling instructions based upon the planned restart points are accurate, greatly increasing the probability that the Production Operations team will be able to keep batches running on its own.
- Very few unanticipated errors will occur during ETL runs. Developers will not miss the late night pages from the team monitoring warehouse operations at the data center.

Additionally, if the TDR contains a data set for a nominal run of sizable volume, the ACIT can support capacity planning. Such a "performance modeling" data set would be between five and twenty percent of the size of anticipated production source extracts. Timing the load of this data into the warehouse will allow the team to extrapolate the ETL and OLAP run times the actual data volume will experience. Measuring the storage taken by the modeling data once loaded will suggest also the likely disk requirements the real load will take. If, after coding changes or the incorporation of a new topic area, the ETL or front-end run times for the performance modeling data set stretches beyond a certain threshold, the team will have an early warning that the new code may seriously impact users if promoted into production.

Because of all these benefits, Scrum Masters should encourage their teams to implement even the beginnings of an automated and continuous testing facility as early in a project as the team can manage. They should also suggest that a wide range of stakeholders—from Product Owners, future UAT participants, enterprise architects, developers, and Operations staff—be included while writing the many validations schemes that will eventually appear in the Test Data Repository's data sets.

Finally, the ACIT is an important contributor to the Agile Data Warehouse team's velocity. When a TDR is properly populated with the comprehensive range of validations scenarios described above, the team can assure stakeholders that its code is accurate and complete, despite the fact they derived the requirements working efficiently one-to-one with the Product Owner rather than compiling a massive detailed requirement specifications before development began.

Pipelined Delivery Squads

Working to the ADW's standards of reference models and automated and continuous integration testing certainly delivers robust BI applications, but as the level of quality goes up, the additional work these standards require will begin to make the team's velocity go down. Indeed, after adding these additional quality objectives, taking a half dozen user stories from concept to fully compliant and tested code in a short two to four week time box will become impossible for seven to ten developers. Whereas new teams might start out failing sprints because they commit themselves to delivering on too many stories, after a half dozen sprints or so, experienced teams may begin failing because even a few stories they take on simply require too much work.

When teams reach this point, they usually want to increase the sprint duration, which horrifies the Scrum Master because the velocity metric and indeed the team's ability to estimate are inextricably bound to the existing time box length. Luckily, there is a technique called "pipelining" that can address this time crunch problem, one that curiously gives developers two or three times the calendar days to complete their work, but does not slow down the rate at which work is delivered to the customer.

GENERIC SCRUM ONLY A PARTIAL SOLUTION

Scrum addresses the waterfall approach's weak points by slicing the software development process into many iterations, yet in one sense these iterations are "mini waterfalls" where one must finish design before starting development and development must finish before integration and testing. Any sequential linking of these distinct work types will run into difficulty because of two largely inescapable factors: developer specialization and asynchronous peak labor requirements.

Developer specialization occurs even on self-organized teams because individuals have differing interest and experience levels with the tools being employed. Whereas an OLAP developer may be interested in learning ETL, he cannot suddenly become proficient with the data transform tools, even if the team desperately needs more people writing ETL code.

Asynchronous peak labor requirements arise from the natural sequencing of analysis, design, development, integration, and testing. Scrum strives to accelerate development by focusing all these work stages upon a small amount of requirements, but cannot break their sequential dependencies within a given time box. So even within a sprint, there will be first a peak demand for architects and designers, then for developers, and finally for integration and testing specialists, as shown in **Figure 5.9**. We have placed this Agile Data Warehousing pattern beneath a similar diagram re-labeled for a waterfall project to suggest that all methods will have some "lumpiness" to their resource requirements no matter what approach they might take.

If teammates were equally talented at all skills, they could easily self-assign themselves to whatever type of work was peaking at the moment, but due to developer specialization the more likely outcome is that designers, developers, and integrators will each take a turn at being overstressed while the other specialists seem relatively untaxed.

This situation undermines ADW's approach to quality assurance. In a two-week sprint, for example, there will be only eight work days, meaning that each of these three specialties will have little more than two days each to produce a design, then write the code, and finally test the integrated system. Given the complexity of warehouse applications, none of these specialties will feel that two days is enough time to produce quality deliverables. When this realization seeps into a new team around the third or fourth sprint, tensions will run high.

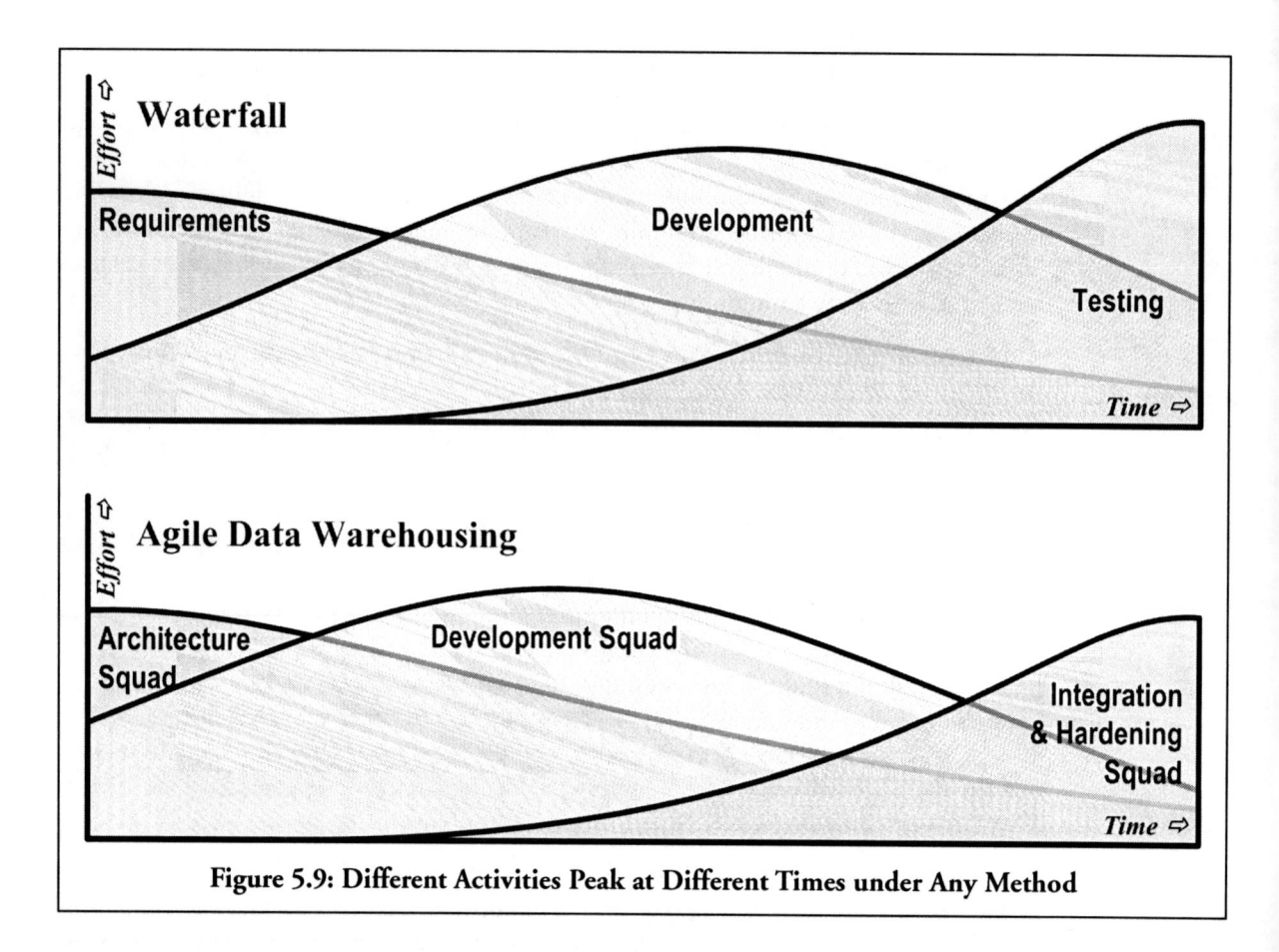

Figure 5.9: Different Activities Peak at Different Times under Any Method

THE STRUCTURE OF AN ADW PIPELINE

The "pipeline" term originates from microprocessor design, where system clocks run faster than CPUs can process instructions. If chip designers were to require the processor to complete an entire instruction within one clock tick, they would have to slow the clock down to allow enough time for all the actions required by the instruction to finish in one pass. Instead, they divide the work into a path of sequential steps such as instruction fetch, memory fetch, calculation, and register write. In this configuration, a single instruction advances one stage per clock tick. Because these component steps each take less time to execute than the full instruction, the clock can run many times faster. This approach greatly increases the microprocessor's *apparent* rate of work because, whereas it takes several cycles to load up the multistage path, once the first instruction reaches the end of the pipeline, further completed instructions begin to pour out at the accelerated pace of one per clock tick. In the Agile Data Warehousing method, the complex instruction is the customer's user story and the clock tick is the single sprint. The only component of pipelined acceleration missing, then, is an appropriate set of sequential work steps for each new module to follow.

In our Agile practice, when we attempted to move from user story to potentially shippable code in a singe time box, we noticed that the developers were frequently held up at the beginning, waiting for data structures to be defined. Thus delayed, they would then try to recoup the time by neglecting some coding of purely technical requirements that would be invisible to the Product Owner in the context of a user demo. Vexed at omitting those hidden features, they would also often try establishing "standard deadlines" for each sprint, such as "data modeling must be done by work day three, and development by day six," but this practice crystallized the fact that the sprint was just too short to program something as involved as a full ETL path.

We believed it was more than coincidence that the proposed deadlines so often aligned with the three hills portrayed for the ADW in Figure 5.9, and this correspondence suggested a good starting structure for pipelining BI development work. We also noticed that

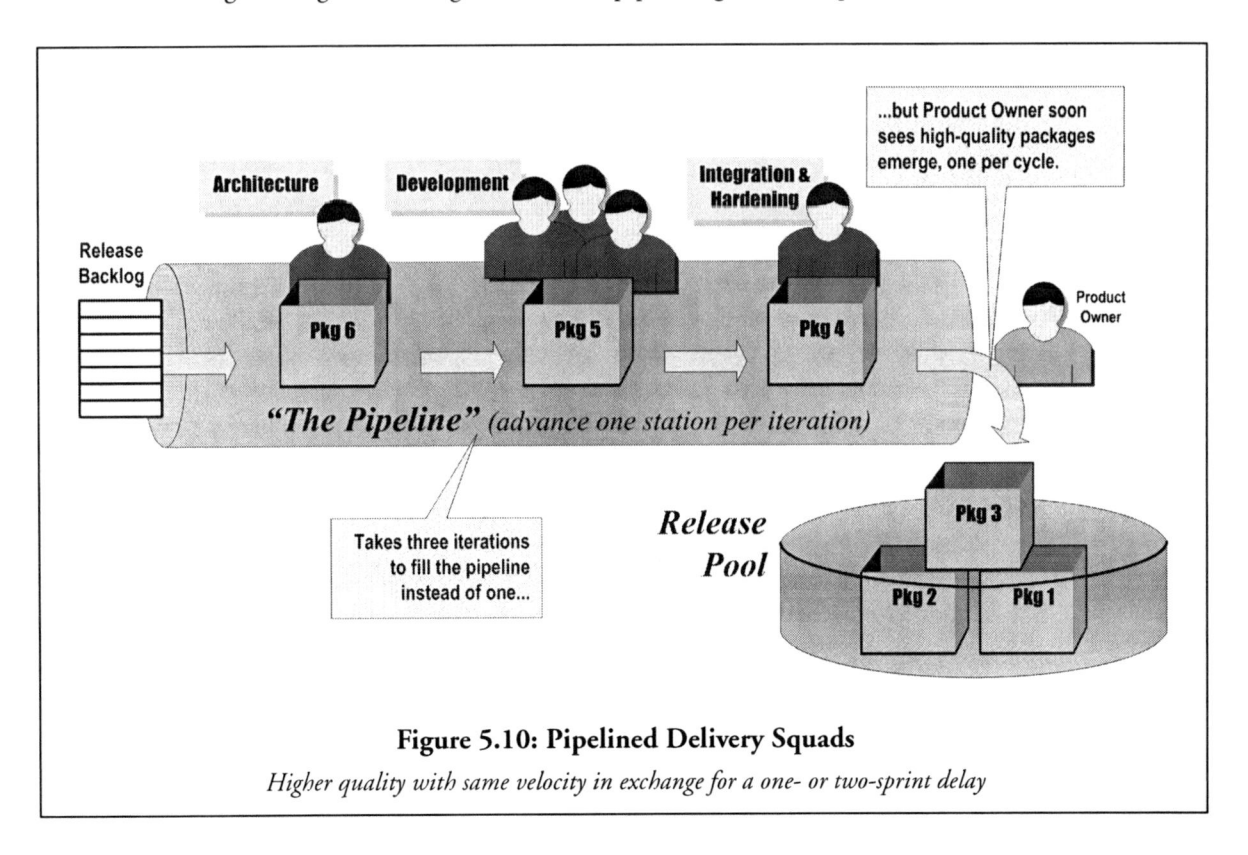

Figure 5.10: Pipelined Delivery Squads
Higher quality with same velocity in exchange for a one- or two-sprint delay

many of our teammates tended to drift toward one of three areas of interest: high-level design, cutting code, or making sure everything is "bullet proof" and fits together properly.

Rather than ignore these preferences among the team members, we used them to define a set of *pipelined development squads* (PDS), as portrayed in **Figure 5.10**. We divided the task of delivering a story into the three sequential steps of preparatory architectural work ("architecture"), "development," and "integration and hardening." We then moved the top of the release backlog through these "squads" in that order, giving each team a full iteration to finish its work. True, this arrangement required us to give the team two extra sprints at first to fill the pipeline, but starting with the third iteration, stories arrived to the Product Owner with every sprint. This was the same rate as before, but because each squad had a full time box in which to work, the deliverables turned out to be much more complete and the developers were far less stressed.

INFORMALLY-DEFINED WORK SQUADS

We deliberately chose the word "squad" when pipelining Agile Data Warehousing rather than calling the three specializations "teams," because maximum velocity requires that each developer's assignment remain *semi-formal*. Should one squad complete stories at a different pace than their comrades, labor needs to shift fluidly from the squad moving faster to those that are moving more slowly, else one squad will eventually fall idle while another has its inbox overflowing. Developers *participate* with a squad rather than being assigned to it, and they participate as needed, subject to their skill sets.

The task planning session, the daily scrum meetings, and the self-organized teams work quite well together to guide the team regarding the shifting requirements between the pipeline's work stations. Given Scrum's typical team size of seven to ten developers, squads tend to number one or two for Architecture and the same for Integration and Hardening, with the remaining teammates participating most with the Development squad.

Such freedom of movement between squads has other benefits besides keeping the team velocity up. Many developers enjoy the fact that it provides more variety to their work, and it allows members new to a particular tool to work at times with more senior developers. IT managers in particular appreciate the cross training that naturally occurs as teammates dynamically move between squads.

When the Scrum Master introduces pipelining to the team, she will need to provide at least a starter notion of when a work package is ready to move from one squad to the next. Defining the goal for the Architecture squad is straight-forward. As we will describe more fully when we explore the notion of Agile architectural methodologies in Volume 2, architecture is complete when the design has moved from requirements down to named objects. For the process side of the ETL applications, the Architecture squad is ready to handoff designs to developers when they arrive at named ETL workflows and the session objects within them.

Data structures need to be specified thoroughly, and on our projects "thorough" usually meant the Architecture squad had defined these structure in enough detail that the Development squad could start its 2-to-1 design of modules. In particular, this typically required data architects to have:

- Profiled the data contained in any new source
- Published draft Entity Diagrams for all architectural layers
- Outline test cases stressing data model notions such as relational integrity
- Generate data definition language for the desired target structures
- Apply the data definition language to the development environment

For the front-end modules of the warehouse, the Architectural squad will need to only identify named objects as was the case with the process side of ETL designs. The taxonomy of the "named objects" will include such notions as query criteria entry, master data models, results sets, and the many types of display objects. The actual roster of object types, of course, depends heavily upon the particular OLAP tool the team employs.

The target objectives for the Development squad do not change much with the introduction of pipelining from what we have been describing as team goals all along. Their focus is still the delivery of "potentially shippable code." However, they will find that the packages they receive from the Architecture squad are far less vague and much easier to estimate. In fact, the pipeline we have described here is a good solution for a new team when the reference model takes too long to establish, or the developers are having trouble making the leap to Agile estimating. By researching the technical requirements for a package in the pipeline, the Architecture squad can make key design choices that put the developers back on familiar ground where they can develop more quickly.

Even with pipelining, the developers may still feel pressured by the short time boxes of Scrum/XP. Rather than writing code that fully emulates the reference model unit they are following, they will respond to the deadline pressure by omitting some of the more technical features the Product Owner will rarely ask about during the user demo. The goal for the Integration and Hardening team, then, begins with finding the areas of incomplete coding in modules accepted by the Product Owner. Whereas the Development squad will emphasize the unit-testing qualities of test-led development, the Integration squad focuses upon incorporating each new module into the ACIT. This objective can take several attempts with every new module, each requiring the Development squad to revisit their code. The *hardening* portion of this squad's work involves verifying that the code indeed incorporates the aspects of the Reference Module units that make modules fault-tolerant. Verification will also involve the Integration squad checking that a given module creates the necessary documentation when they run it through the auto-documentation scripts.

Finally, once the module is successfully integrated and documented, the Integration team members can shave considerable time off of the promotion-to-production process if they initiate a review of new modules with the Operations group that will soon inherit the application. Agile approaches are often criticized for down playing formal reviews of deliverables, yet as we can now see, by the time code is promoted under pipelined ADW, it has been reviewed by more than one developer during coding, then by the Product Owner at the demo, by the Integration squad during hardening, and finally by the Operations group. This series of validations from a wide variety of perspectives is actually an extensive set of formal reviews, a fact that will figure prominently when we assert that ADW can be CMM-compliant in a later chapter.

The team needs to evolve its use of the task board somewhat with the advent of pipelining, and in this there are two ways to go. The simplest means is for the Scrum Master to add a column called *Under Design* between *Tasks Waiting* and *Writing Tests* to represent the Architecture squad's work station. Similarly, *Under Integration* should be added after *Ready to Demo* so the team can see the tasks that the Integration and Hardening team has in their queue. However, on some projects the architecture work is more involved, and it merits validation and demonstration steps of its own. In this case, the team can simply create "Architecture Stories" which progress across the same set of task board columns as do the "Development" stories.

Seeing a story move from Architecture to Development to Integration squads may remind the casual observer of waterfall methods, but lest readers think we are backsliding, they should realize that this is a very localized instance of the design, build, and test cycle. An isolated user story still represents a hundredth or less of the full work of implementing a given subject area, judging from the User Epic Decomposition framework we considered in Chapter 3. In pipelined ADW, we are still multiplexing "mini waterfalls" on bite-sized units of work, true to the recommendations of Scrum/XP.

IT managers might take note that the pipelined Agile approach is easier to staff than a waterfall project because it keeps all specialties busy during a project. Full employment of resources occurs because the pipeline provides all squads with packages of their own to work on each sprint, except for when the pipeline is filling at the beginning of the project. In contrast, waterfall projects need the bulk of their designs up front, greatly taxing the department's architects, but then leave them mostly idle as the wave of work moves on to development.

Should ETL and OLAP be different squads?

The pipelining we outlined above has only one Development squad with ETL and OLAP developers mixed together. OLAP tends to move faster than ETL, so there is always some tension between these two types of developers. This "impedance mismatch" can be addressed in a couple of ways, and the particulars of each team and project determines which is best.

One approach to consider is to create separate ETL and OLAP squads within one team, a technique that works especially well if the team is blessed with members that know both tool sets and can move fluidly to the squad needing the most help at any given moment. In warehouse projects, OLAP often feels it is waiting for ETL to deliver the data it needs to begin development. Rather than letting the OLAP developers fall idle, the Scrum Master can suggest that they create for themselves a robust set of "dummy data" upon which they can develop. This effort turns out to be very valuable, in fact, because the "dummy" data should be designed to expose all the OLAP errors they can anticipate. If coordinated with the Architecture squad or the ETL developers, this data can be placed in the TDR to become a very powerful set of expected values. Thus potentially idle OLAP developers can be employed in drafting better validation materials.

Alternatively, one can create a separate OLAP team with its own task board and velocity measure. This approach is more difficult to tune because it requires staffing each team with the proper number of developers, and staffing involves far more organizational constraints than having members within the team simply self-assign to work on the most pressing task at any one time. Yet this solution works well when there is little cross training between ETL and OLAP members, a situation that makes fluid self-assignment impractical. Furthermore, warehouse developers often find themselves in a particular life cycle phase for an extended period of time, such as predominantly adding new sources, versus predominantly creating new reporting on data it already has. In these situations, the relative number of ETL versus OLAP developers required will change slowly, so that the relatively static nature of formal team assignments will not undermine the team's velocity.

Maintaining a Clear Notion of Team Velocity

In exchange for all the advantages that pipelining provides, the price to pay is that it muddies somewhat the notion of "team velocity." A good measure of team velocity has been of paramount importance to us because it allows the customer to forecast when features will be available and the resources needed to complete it. When the Agile team semi-divides into three squads and developers move between them to balance out work loads, the Product Owner can become unsure of which squad's velocity should be used when estimating forward momentum.

We need to return to "first principles" to address this confusion. Regardless of why developers might prefer Agile approaches, the organization chose to try Scrum because it makes the software development process more transparent, responsive, and estimable *for the customer*. The key interaction is the eye-to-eye work between developers and Product Owner. Any other aspects of the method should be considered secondary to these customer-perceived qualities. Because the Product Owner receives tangible results delivered by the Development squad, we will maintain the highest transparency and accuracy of estimation for the customer if we base velocity upon this squad which the Product Owner can best observe.

Accordingly, the Scrum Master's role in a pipelined delivery context is to establish a consistent and usable velocity for the Development squad and then adjust participation in the Architecture and Integration squads so they match Development's input and output rate, respectively. With this balancing in place, the team will be able to advance through the stories at one Development squad velocity per iteration, and thus the velocity of this squad becomes the team's one, true metric for estimating and avoiding over commitment.

Having completed our survey of the particular techniques that Agile data warehousing will require, we have arrived at a fairly complex approach to business intelligence projects. Clearly, the entire program is too complex to drop upon a new team all at once. The Scrum Master will need to provide a step-by-step approach for those who are new to Agile to acquire the radically different mindset the methodology entails. Such a graduated approach is the topic of our next chapter, which will take the new team from plain-vanilla Scrum to a warehouse-specific method—complete with its user epic decomposition, tiered data models, automated testing, and pipelined delivery squads—in a only a half-dozen steps.

Chapter 6
Starting and Scaling Agile Warehousing Teams

What is the best way to get an Agile warehouse team started?

Is there an incremental path they can take toward full Agile data warehousing?

How do we tackle projects bigger than one team can deliver?

What adaptations can we make for geographically-distributed teammates?

The preceding chapters have provided an extensive look at how to adapt Scrum for data warehousing programs. Yet, with all the information we have provided, a Scrum Master considering the start of an important business intelligence project might view our long list of strategies and techniques with some trepidation. Though our approach will elicit over time a team that can estimate realistically and deliver value quickly, how can the Scrum Master respond to the project sponsors' impatience for results before the team attains its full level of competence? Furthermore, experienced developers are going to come to the project with years of waterfall methodology behind them, a perspective that will cause many of them to be downright hostile to a methodology that is as radically different and sometimes chaotic as Scrum. How does the Scrum Master inspire these developers to give fair consideration to the iterative approach long enough for her to introduce to them all the details involving Agile Data Warehousing?

This chapter answers these two related problems by organizing what we have examined so far into a suggested step-by-step method for the Scrum Master to employ when forming a new team. We will start by considering a successful staffing mix for an Agile Data Warehouse team, which we will present as a set of roles and responsibilities that should be established within the team. With the proper team in mind, we then describe the five stages of Agile data warehouse team maturity through which a new team can be guided. We will then turn our attention to how one would knit several such teams together in order to scale Scrum up to span large BI projects. We will conclude by addressing a vital topic in this age of globalization—coordinating developers who are geographically dispersed.

Roles & Responsibilities On ADW Teams

When faced with a newly funded warehouse project, the key stakeholders must consider what types of IT specialists that will be needed on the ADW team. Most waterfall methods provide a detailed "roles and responsibilities" (R&R) matrix that defines the skills and duties one should place on a team, and there are several for data warehousing in particular. [Kimball 1998 and Humphries 1998] Prescribing a "standard" R&R matrix for an Agile Data Warehousing team, however, is a bit too idealistic. First, Scrum keeps team sizes small, so that many of the roles found in other methods must be combined under the purview of only a few people. Secondly, Scrum deliberately declines to define roles in detail, so that teammates can freely move to whatever task needs to be completed next. Scrum's notion of a self-organization team, in fact, leads to innovative and frequently changing role definitions.

Yet there are certain themes and patterns of specialization that repeatedly emerge among the team members on most ADW projects. Some, like the Product Owner and Scrum Master, this book has been discussing all along. In order to provide a single overview in one place, however, this section sketches nine key roles for the ADW team, and does so in some detail because getting the right people involved is crucial for success. We organize our descriptions in three categories: primary leadership roles, developer roles, and methodological support.

Primary Leadership Roles

Product Owner

Scrum elevates the Product Owner to the primary leadership role within the team. She determines which modules the developers will build and in what order via her prioritized list of user stories. Naturally this position is a vital assignment to get right when building a team. A "hands-on" Product Owner is ideal, that is, one who stands at the task board during daily scrum meetings asking questions such as:

- Why aren't more task cards moving towards completion?
- Why are remaining labor estimates ballooning?
- Why is the burndown chart not trending to zero?

The Scrum Master (discussed in a moment) may be the default person to pose these questions, but it is far more "organic" for the Product Owner to do so because she owns the results of the project and cannot transfer responsibility for delivering upon its objectives to any other member of the team.

Communication is perhaps the most important role for the Product Owner, involving several considerations:

1. She will need a balance between being demanding and diplomatic. Being demanding allows her to keep the pressure on the team, so the developers will work toward peak performance. Diplomacy will allow her to elicit the team's maximum effort without jeopardizing the developers' desire to help her succeed.
2. The Product Owner must be able to express the reasoning behind the organization's conviction that the warehouse is both required and needed *now*, backing up all such assertions with detailed business reasons as to why.
3. The Product Owner must be able to express all such notions clearly, because, given the speed at which the team should be moving and the lack of time-consuming reviews of to-be documentation, ambiguity will lead to a debilitating level of mistakes and rework.

In terms of skills with tools, a senior business analyst equipped with "power user" level skills for even a simple database such as MS Access would be an ideal candidate for this posting. The BA background will help not only to make her more comfortable with the semi-technical decompositional planning approach outlined in Chapter 2, but also provide her with direct knowledge of how the data should appear when it arrives in the presentation layer of the warehouse. The experience with an OLAP tool (or even SQL) will allow her to independently examine and validate the data as it progresses sprint by sprint through staging and integration to the presentation layers. Such proactive validation is the least expensive and fastest means of error detection and positive feedback, and will bolster tremendously the team's long-term effectiveness.

Solutions Architect

By and large the most important technical position on the team, the Solutions Architect is primarily responsible for the overarching design of the warehouse—both data and process, for both the front end and back end. He guards the long-term value of the warehouse by ensuring that, rather than making the warehouse progressively incomprehensible and unwieldy, each release cycle enhances the facility's many "abilities" such as understandability, scalability, and recoverability (see Table 6.1). The previous chapter suggested that BI applications must be essentially correct and fault tolerant. The architect's role includes championing this level of quality and guiding the developers as to how it can be achieved. The strategic thinking required for long term success will involve hardware, software, and middleware, making this role the most "interdisciplinary" of the team. Furthermore, an architect who is actively monitoring the rapid progress of BI software might in fact uncover a utility or "appliance" that can substitute for months of expensive ETL development or greatly enhance data mart performance with complex queries.

Table 6.1: Desired "Abilities" for Good Architectural Designs

Also known as "Non-Functional" Requirements

EXTENSIBILITY

System is prepared for future growth in functionality, that is, it includes mechanisms for easily expanding and enhancing its capabilities without having to make major changes to its low-level code.

ADAPTABILITY

System can be re-configured for reasonable changes in operating contexts with a minimum of re-configuration or re-coding.

SCALABILITY

System is prepared for future growth in data volumes.

RELIABILITY

System performs as planned with a minimum of unscheduled downtime.

MAINTAINABILITY

Flaws found after implementation can be located quickly and corrected without excessive expense.

INTEROPERABILITY

System can exchange information and services with other applications as the need arises with a minimum of re-configuration or re-coding.

ISOLATABILITY

The boundaries of the system once implemented are well known and its actions intelligible without reference to the operations of other applications.

AFFORDABILITY

System provides intended services with reasonable development, implementation, and support costs.

UNDERSTANDABILITY

Users and IT personnel can comprehend the intended use and actions of the system without excessive training or outside support.

RECOVERABILITY

System re-establishes services after major system outage with little or no intervention by IT personnel.

AUDITABILITY

Systems actions are evident and understandable by reviewing a transaction log, even months after the actions occurred.

MANAGEABILITY

System can be kept in service without excessive monitoring or IT support, even when conditions change within reason.

SUPPORTABILITY

System services end users without prompting many calls to the IT help desk.

The Solutions Architect position has many possible names, including "Lead Designer" or "ETL Architect." Whatever the title, the need for deep skills with database and data transformation tools in this position will be clear, given that the most complex and expensive components of the warehouse are the integration layer of the database and the ETL modules that load it. This person provides decisive leadership in the first several sprints by providing exemplary modules for the reference model that will guide the work of many ETL developers for months to come. Moreover, for those warehouses with a real time data requirement, the architect will need to have mastered the highly technical subject of messaging queues and XML data exchange. [Hohpe 2004]

The Solutions Architect should also be fairly fluent with at least one standard architectural approach (such as the Object Management Group's TOGAF and MDA) [OMG 2003 and 2004] and a mainstream modeling format (such as the Unified Modeling Language) [OMG 2007]. Such a background will allow him to not only provide developers with high-level designs without delay, but also provide warehouse documentation in a manner that future teams or outside consultants can readily understand and evolve. Because the most fundamental and costly mistakes in data warehousing are made at the architectural level, Scrum Masters working with a newly promoted Solutions Architect should insist that he acquire a solid grounding in traditional architectural concepts [Mowbray 2003] and classic warehouse architecture in particular [Inmon 2001 and Kimball 1998].

Though the Solutions Architect's project title might emphasizes the back end, he will need ample expertise with the front-end tool as well, because working under Scrum, this architect must make many just-in-time design decisions that will hinge upon whether a particular BI requirement is best implemented in the ETL or left to the downstream OLAP tool to support. Furthermore, he will undoubtedly need to understand both front and back-end tool's data repositories, so that he can build the extraction facilities needed to make all project modules self-documenting.

Data Architect

The Data Architect (DA) represents another vitally important position on a warehouse team because much of the decomposition schemes we recommend for Product Owners translate directly into requirements for the warehouse's data model. As an example, say the Product Owner began a development effort asking for only "latest status" reporting for the Purchasing data, but later requested drill down to individual transactions that had occurred. This seemingly simple evolution in requirements will involve not only splitting several of the integration layer's entities original Purchasing tables along the differing time-variances found among its columns, but also adding many metadata columns to support a user's ability to request the data as of any arbitrary point in time.

Though his ultimate focus is upon defining objects in the database management system, the DA must still find a balance involving a tremendous number of broader issues. His decisions directly impact the team's velocity on the project because every table he adds to the data model can require days of ETL programming to support. As a notion of the skill level required to perform this role well, let us mention just a few of the responsibilities and concerns of the DA:

- Understand the business rules thoroughly, so that even the most detailed data elements required to implement them are identified, modeled, and implemented in the DBMS.

- For any given topic area, choose between relational and dimension paradigms, and even associative versus entity-attribute-value approaches. The proper answer often depends upon where and when not to employ non-redundant data representations given the stakeholders' current *and probable future* analytical and performance requirements.

- Select the appropriate level of granularity. Not only must the DA select how detailed the model for a particular topic area should be—choosing from third to sixth "normal form" [Date 2002 and Date 2005]—he must also must decide how many physical tables are needed to represent each business entity. We have worked upon projects where commercially available data models in only third normal form decomposed the simple notion of "customer geographic location" into two dozen small tables rather than a single entity called "address." Because the data model can be so granular that the implied ETL becomes unaffordable to build, the DA must carefully weigh theory against pragmatics in order to make the project's data model both capable and feasible.

- Choose the appropriate level of "snow flaking" in the dimensional portions of the presentation layer. Adding children entities under the standard dimension tables can not only make data loads faster to program and execute, but also supports many complex analytical requirements that would be nearly impossible to support otherwise. [Kimball 1998] However, the cost will be significantly longer query times for the OLAP users, requiring extraordinary measures to mitigate.

- Determine the degree to which the warehouse will employ standard modeling patterns to model common entities such as customers, products, sales, and work orders. Warehousing has matured to the point where the profession possesses a number of standard modeling approaches to these entities. [Silverston 2001] Whereas the DA can accelerate the Agile warehouse team by deploying such models, they often involve more tables in the warehouse than absolutely necessary and thus increase the needed ETL programming.

- Specify and support the level of metadata management. "Metadata" signifies all that the organization needs to know about a given record or column in the warehouse. At a business level, stakeholders will want to know the element's definition, the derivation of its values, the business date that each record depicts, and the individual who can authorize any erroneous values be corrected. At an ETL level, they will want to understand such notions as when each record was last updated, the quality of the values derived, and, in the case of history-oriented tables, the records holding earlier images of the data.
- Profile the data quality of source data and specify how the ETL will resolve discrepancies between similar data acquire from multiple systems. This becomes particularly analysis-intensive if the warehouse provides "master data management" such as the maintaining the organization's definitive customer database. [Berson 2007]
- Protect and enhance the performance of not only end user queries, but ETL data loads. Even if we focus upon relational databases alone, achieving high performance in the warehouse will involve complex decisions regarding partitioning, exotic table structures such as "index organized" or clustered, and many varieties of indexing, such as bit-mapped or "reverse B-trees."

Agile data warehousing places a further demand upon the Data Architect. As occurred in our example above, Scrum's quality of allowing the Product Owner to recast requirements upon any given sprint will engender the need to significantly re-design DBMS tables that are already in production. Accordingly, the DA of an ADW team must be well-versed in "refactoring" data entities, which involves careful procedures to evolve a table containing live data while breaking as few of the dependent ETL and query modules as possible. [Ambler 2006]

Clearly, Agile BI projects demand that the Data Architect be at the peak of their abilities, because on the one hand bad choices in any one of the areas sketched above can seriously impair the value of the warehouse and the velocity of the development team. Yet on the other hand, the DA must make his choices quickly because developers can design and draft very little code without having the warehouse's data model already implemented on disk.

Developer Roles

Senior OLAP Developer

Although the Solutions Architect should have some familiarity with the OLAP tool, they will need a partner who is both skilled and focused upon the front end of the warehouse and the tool with which it will be built. The team needs this person to:

- Take the early lead in working one-on-one with the Product Owner, mocking-up front-end modules

    Such mock-ups provide the Product Owner invaluable feedback on the accuracy of her requests, and thus allow her to improve early on the requirements she provides the developers.

- Provide key front-end modules given very little lead time, so that the Product Owner can test drive the sprint's deliverables for themselves during a user demo
- Author reference model "libraries" and reusable OLAP code packages such as those needed for gathering limits and executing queries

    These programming units will establish patterns for the other OLAP developers, enabling a more "cookie cutter" approach for the remaining front-end development.

- Author simple "ad hoc validation modules" that the primary leadership roles can use to inspect data as ETL pushes it step-by-step toward end user access

This last function of the Senior OLAP Developer is particularly valuable because ad hoc validation modules provide a window into the warehouse's evolving data that the team can employ to better assure design and programming quality. In staging, for example, the team can use ad hoc reporting modules to verify that source data descriptions are accurate, say by showing that there is truly a valid buyer code on every purchase order. For the integration layer, these modules enable validation of applied business rules, (e.g., "projected revenue figures for the divisions within a services company properly excludes transfer sales between its various business units"). And for the dimensional portions of the presentation layer, the team can use these modules to confirm that advanced drill-down features have been properly implemented. For example, the team might want to prove that a user can portray the company financials using either a pre- or post-merger chart of accounts. Without some ad hoc validation tools to utilize throughout the release cycle, this type of validation can be only performed during user acceptance testing, at which point the cost of fixing the errors will have grown considerably.

Integration and Testing Engineer

As we saw in the previous chapter, ADW's notion of test-led development requires someone to integrate freshly coded modules into a daily build and monitor that the Automated and Continuous Integration Testing facility properly applies the full complement of tests supplied for each module. This work falls under the purview of the Integration and Test Engineer, who must also orchestrate the iterations with the developer of each flawed module to support diagnosis and repair. Once the ADW project is underway, this role will prove very time consuming until the testing facility is online and the developers' coding practices mature.

The primary technical skill required for this engineering position must be strong knowledge of the ETL tool, not only because ETL will be the locus of most problems, but also because the test engineer must be able to inspect the transformation code. Such inspection will verify that the developers followed the breadth and depth of the appropriate reference model units, deviating only to address the exceptions noted in the automated self-documentation retrievable from each module. If the project includes scheduled OLAP services in the automated testing facility, the test engineer should also have some familiarity with the scheduling aspect of the BI front end. Furthermore, experience with web testing tools will allow this person to oversee validation of the GUI portion of the warehouse's front end. Finally, knowledge of change management tools and methods will be important, so that the test engineer can take command of promoting code out of the automated testing facility into production once the release candidate has been stabilized and receives the Product Owner's final acceptance.

ETL and OLAP Developers

Given the four technical positions described above, the remainder of an Agile Data Warehousing team's roster will consist of back-end and front-end developers, with back-end developers often outnumbering their front-end colleagues by a ratio of two to one. The team will perform best if it is staffed with developers who are "self-starters" and prefer a collaborative style of work, for these qualities will allow them to simply watch the task board and self-direct their efforts to the highest priority tasks, greatly easing the burden on the leadership roles. Of course, individuals comfortable with both front and back-end tools will have even fewer constraints on where they can contribute, adding further to team velocity.

METHODOLOGICAL SUPPORT ROLES

Scrum Master

Scrum identifies the Scrum Master as only the owner of the work process. The team is theoretically "self organizing," giving the Scrum Master a very different role than the project manager on a waterfall-based effort. First, the Scrum approach greatly reduces the paperwork required to plan and monitor the team's progress, and secondly the approach relocates the directive functions of a traditional project manager to the Product Owner role. For these reasons, generic Scrum actually suggests that the Scrum Master will be only a half-time role and that she should come from a development background so that she can spend the other half of her time writing code.

As we have seen in earlier chapters, the Scrum Master must focus upon keeping the work method as unencumbered with non-functional overhead as possible so that the developers a) have a straightforward estimation method they can commit to and master, and b) produce potentially shippable code as fast as possible. Because warehousing is a highly-scoped problem set to begin with, the Scrum Master position requires less experience than the three leadership roles described above, so that it is feasible for a senior IT professional to learn the role with a few days in the classroom plus the on-the-job experience a few sprints on another Scrum team can provide. Such a "baptism by fire" approach will undoubtedly lead to a few mistakes, but these errors will cause limited damage if the team has a highly competent Product Owner, Solutions Architect, and Data Architect. Moreover, the team will have multiple opportunities to set the new Scrum Master straight during the frequent sprint retrospectives.

That said, Scrum Master mistakes are still best to avoid. Luckily, Scrum has a well defined training and certification program, so that organizations can save themselves some heartache by either engaging a Certified Scrum Master (CSM) from the start or investing ahead of time in acquiring training for an existing IT staff member. In fact, a CSM program is both so streamlined and effective that acquiring Scrum training for not only the Scrum Master but the three leadership roles also is one of the best investments in the project's success an organization can make.

When implemented on a localized basis within a large organization, Scrum can clash with the company's waterfall-style project monitoring and reporting. In order to smooth over any consternation that this difference might cause, Scrum Masters will need to have a rock-solid understanding of why their sponsors turned to Agile in the first place, as well as the fortitude to fend off outsiders' attempts to handicap the team.

Finally, because Scrum's project tracking methods are so lightweight and because the Product Owner shoulders the responsibility for the quality and timeliness of the project's deliverables, the Scrum Master role soon requires only a half-time level-of-effort. This modest demand for time frees up another half-time person available for development or QA duties. However, the organization can also choose to deploy the Scrum Master to serve on a second team or a "scrum of scrums," enabling Scrum's to scale up for larger BI programs, something we will consider at the end of this chapter.

Project Communications Assistant

Formal presentations of generic Scrum suggest a Product Owner and a Scrum Master as the only non-developer roles on the team. While working in large corporations, however, we have found the need for a third support role, so Agile Data Warehousing adds a *Project Communications Assistant* (PCA) to the recommended team roster. Scrum may outpace waterfall-style methods in delivering newly coded modules, but traditional project management methods excel at many "collateral" aspects of managing software development, including what PMI calls a "stakeholder communication plan." A major advantage to following such a communication plan is that it re-assures the larger organization that the development project is progressing, and thus prevents the anxiety that might cause several, high-level managers to become overly involved in or critical of the Agile project. Unwilling to overlook any notion that can make BI development more effective, Agile Data Warehousing adapts the PMI communication plan by assigning it to a part-time assistant to the Scrum Master. This assistant attends to the information needs of external stakeholders, so that the Scrum Master and the remaining team members can remain focused upon meeting the stiff development deadlines of each sprint.

Not only does the Project Communication Assistant keep the wider stakeholder community generally informed regarding the ADW project, but he also deflects much interference from many parties outside the team. Commonly, this interference comes in the form of demands for the same status information that that a waterfall-based method would provide, but which an Agile effort is not designed to support—estimated completion dates by module and total project costs, for example. The parties demanding this information can be quite influential and dangerous to ignore, such as IT managers, distantly involved executives, and leaders of other business initiatives waiting (impatiently) for the services the Agile warehouse project has promised to deliver. To be constantly interpreting ADW's story points and burndown charts for outside parties could easily absorb the Product Owner or Scrum Master, so the communication assistant role was created to keep this distraction from hurting the team.

In particular, the Project Communication Assistant attends to the following exchanges:

- Preparing status reports for outside parties based upon information shared during daily scrums and top-of-iteration activities

    This communication would include the team's velocity and burndown chart, translated into terms recognizable by non-Scrum stakeholders.

- Matching waterfall-based concepts such as "requirements" and "estimates" to their Agile counterparts, so that the ADW project remains "compliant" with the organization's overarching software quality control plan

    (We explore this in detail in the next chapter.)

- Interpolating the probable release delivery dates based upon the team's velocity and the Product Owner's current release backlog

    The Project Communication Assistant must re-calculate delivery dates each time a contingency appears or the Product Owner changes the team's direction. When such interpolation does not satisfy outside stakeholders, the communication assistant will have to take the time needed to repeatedly explain why Scrum's focus on delivery speed and estimating accuracy outweighs its de-emphasis on hard and fast cost, scope, and delivery dates for a given release.

- Managing detailed information exchanges with several outside groups who must approve of the ADW team's release

    Such exchanges might include:

    - Coordinating reviews of the accumulating release candidate by Operations Support and IT security engineers
    - Orchestrating formal hand-offs, which might require large group review sessions
    - Maintaining a regular interface with downstream projects, listening for any change in their requirements and working with the Product Owner to match their needs to the ADW team's current release plans
    - Providing project time charging summaries to financial managers

- Formally gathering the team's risk management plan which includes collating the team's notion of how likely and severe the impact of uncertain events might be, and set of actions to address the most severe items on this list

- Managing' the outside communications when one of the risk events does occur, plus describing the alternative actions considered and the impacts of the recourse selected

Like the Scrum Master, the Project Communication Assistant role is usually a half-time position once the project gets established, allowing them to cover development or testing duties, or perhaps serving on more than one team at a time. However, it is important to keep the communication assistant role scoped to information exchange only. It is tempting for communication assistants, after an unpleasant program coordination meeting where important stakeholders complained about the Agile project, to insist that the Agile team start working differently. This often translates to a demand that the team provide voluminous to-be documentation such as executive-level requirements specification and a draft of the proverbial thousand-line project plan.

For this reason, ADW deliberately titles the position a communication *assistant* rather than some variation of "project manager." As we explored in earlier chapters, any modification in the team's method must provide greater velocity or estimating accuracy, otherwise it should be discarded as irrelevant. To prevent any temptation for the person in the communication assistant position to reshape the team's method, we strongly recommend avoiding individuals who are over-qualified for a communications role. For example, engage someone who has earned at most PMI's "Certified Associate in Project Management" (CAPM) status rather than the more lofty Project Management Professional (PMP) certificate, because individuals with the latter certification may be too committed to traditional project management styles to adapt happily to Scrum.

TEST-LED DEVELOPMENT AS A SHARED RESPONSIBILITY

Whereas the Integration and Testing Engineer mentioned above assembles the nightly build and monitors that the automated test runs occur, we stop short of making the test engineer *responsible* for testing. Last chapter's combination of Test-Led Development and Automated and Continuous Integration Testing evolved testing into a duty widely shared across an Agile Data Warehouse team rather than concentrated upon any one individual or special-purpose validation squad.

Figure 6.1 presents a common distribution of responsibilities among the leaders of an ADW team. The responsibilities divide into three groups: authoring tests, building support objects, and executing the tests. The three leadership roles all participate in authoring tests, but the emphasis of each is a different test category. Coming from a non-technical, business perspective, the Product Owner will be the best at drafting tests for functional requirements and business rules. These notions will be the points of service that she will insist on seeing during user demos before she accepts a module as "done." She can also create a list of service points with which the larger business community will validate the deliverables during user acceptance testing (UAT).

Integration and Testing Engineer
Executes test via queuing test cases and inspecting results

Solutions Architect (part 1)
Builds utility to automatically and continuously run test modules

Product Owner
Authors test cases for business requirements & user acceptance review

Senior OLAP Developer
1) Builds and automate test reporting modules,
2) Contributes expected results

Solutions Architect (part 2)
Authors test cases for fault tolerance & integration requirements

Data Architect
Authors test cases for domains & relational integrity

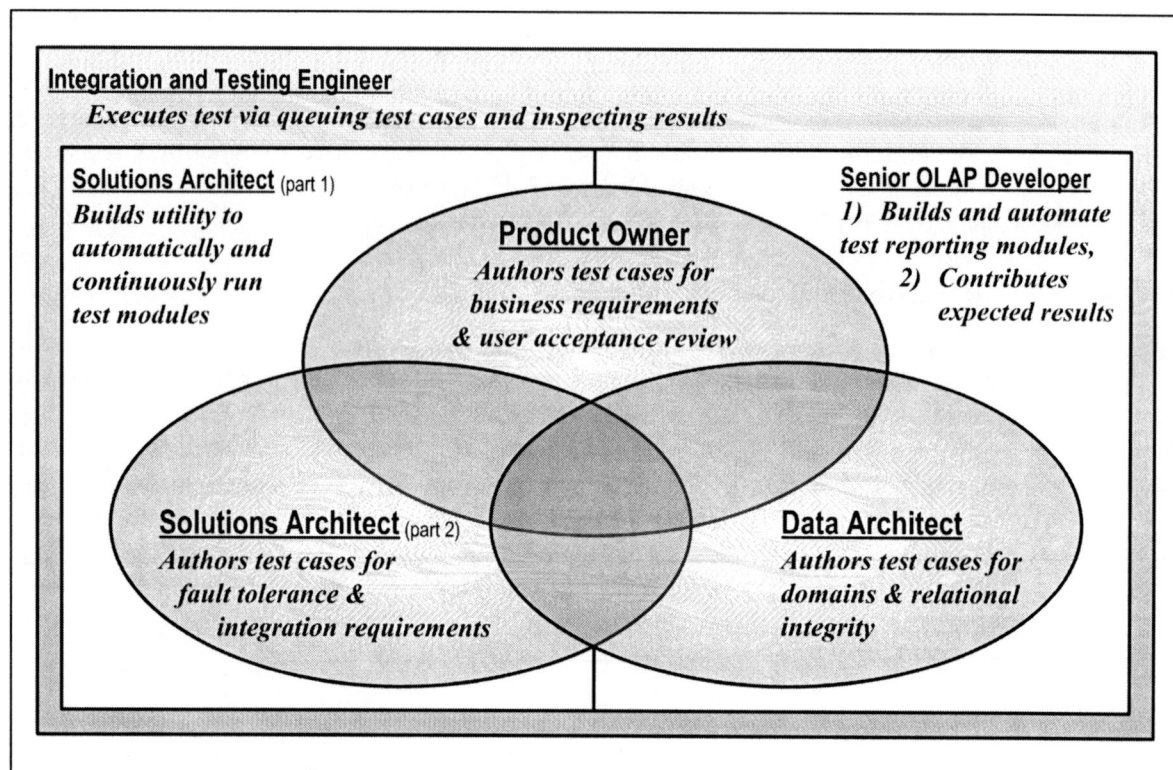

Figure 6.1: ADW Testing is a Shared Responsibility
Only together can the team roles cover the all aspects of validation

The Solutions Architect, on the other hand, will focus upon the drafting tests that prove the application's ability to recover from errors in the ETL, plus its response to unavailable data sources. Some of the architect's recommended tests will need to examine the records in source or target data tables, but a larger proportion will involve parsing ETL and OLAP logs for the occurrence of errors or other, more subtle processing flaws such as poor performance.

Lastly, having modeled every warehouse entity, column, foreign key, and domain constraint, the Data Architect's strength will be in drafting tests to ensure that the ETL transforms data with the proper patterns of non-nullability, relational integrity, and data values.

In authoring these tests, these three roles must collaborate to provide a comprehensive list of test cases, the necessary test data (loaded in one or more source tables), and the expected values one should find when ETL completes. Perhaps the team has built a Test Data Repository so user friendly that these individuals can enter this data themselves. More commonly, however, the test data repository is little more than replicas of the sources tables with extra metadata columns added to track and manage test cases. In this event, the leadership roles will need to rely on developers to maintain data in the test data repository.

Agile Data Warehouse testing will require a couple of test-specific applications, upon which several members of the team will need to collaborate. First, the Solutions Architect will need to establish the team's automated testing facility and structure it to support the desired range of testing scenarios, outfitting it with a workable user interface for configuration and control. Using this interface, the test engineer will configure the testing facility so that it runs all test scenarios across all subject areas at least once per day. Finally, the Senior OLAP developer will need to automate a front-end process that provides summary and detailed reporting on the validation that automated testing performs.

NURTURING A TOP-NOTCH ADW TEAM

When an organization's first ADW project has finally secured its funding and acquired a team approximating the mix sketched above, the Scrum Master's greatest challenge will be the traditional Information Systems mindset the newly assigned team will undoubtedly possess. One should not underestimate the staying power of the traditional waterfall paradigm in people's outlook. We regularly start Agile warehouse projects in companies whose waterfall "software development life cycle" training comprises thousands of pages of methodological documentation. Although it is never clear why IS management believes that their staff actually reads more than a fraction of such an unwieldy number of rules and regulations, the weight of the encapsulated method still finds a way to constrain the team's thinking for months to come.

In contrast, Scrum is new and iconoclastic. With its "less is more" orientation, its inclination is to exert only enough control of the development process to deliver quality results. Its lightweight approach often elicits epithets such as "chaos" from traditionally-schooled IS professionals. Given Scrum's lack of templates, procedures, specifications, and formal design reviews, the ADW Scrum Master can encounter resistance and downright hostility from all quarters of the organization, including often the newly assigned project teammates themselves.

The Agile Data Warehousing method makes the transition from waterfall an even greater stretch for the new team, given the multiple BI-specific tools and techniques we have examined in the preceding chapters. With a legacy IS mindset firmly embedded in her new teammates, how can the Scrum Master persuade them to suspend their waterfall indoctrination long enough to give Scrum an honest try or to carefully consider the remainder of ADW?

SIX STAGES OVERVIEW

We believe the answer to this conundrum is to first give the team members some time to unlearn their old ways, and then introduce the new method in bite-sized chunks. In our practice we have settled on six "stages" of ADW team maturation, which can be found by referring back to Chapter 1's Figure 1.2. A quick summary of the stages portrayed there and their motivations is as follows:

Stage 0: **Generic Scrum**—Colocate the team members and familiarize them with the central aspects of Scrum such as self-organized teams, generic user stories, and time boxed iterations.

Stage 1: **User Epic Decomposition**—Focus on the materials in Chapter 2 in order to elicit better requirements and consistent level-of-effort estimates.

Stage 2: **Formulating the Release Plan**—Utilizing the new estimation tools acquired in Stage 1 to forecast the level-of-effort for the entire release, in order to secure the continued funding for the project.

Stage 3: **Reference Models and Test-Led Development**—Begin employing the techniques presented in the first part of Chapter 5 until the team produces deliverables of the highest quality.

Stage 4: **Pipelined Delivery Squads**—Put into practice the "workstations" introduced elsewhere in Chapter 5 in order to give each specialization within the team a full sprint to complete their work.

Stage 5: **Automated and Continuous Integration Testing**—Implement the testing facility described in the previous to build error detection and rigorous testing into the work habits of the team.

Teams vary widely in the speed with which they can absorb the new ideas introduced in each of these stages. To help readers plan their ADW projects, **Table 6.2** suggests a range of durations that reflect the time new teams we have managed and coached have required to master each step listed above. In the remainder of this section, we will look at each stage individually to consider the challenges the Scrum Master will face when entering it and when she will know her teammates are ready to move on to the next phase in their learning.

Table 6.2: Realistic Timelines by ADW Stage

Stage	Number of Sprints Required to Complete	
	if Fast	if Slow
0: Generic Scrum	2	4
1: Epic Decomposition	2	4
2: Release Plan	1	3
3: Reference Model & Test-Led Development	3	5
4: Pipelined Delivery	3	5
5: Automated Testing	3	5
Total Sprints	11	26
Elapsed Time (2 week sprints)	22 weeks	52 weeks

STAGE 0: GENERIC SCRUM

The Scrum/XP community speaks of four generic phases in the development of new teams: forming, storming, norming, and performing. [Tuckman 1965] In our experience Stage 0 is the toughest for the Scrum Master to manage, for it involves both forming and storming. During forming, the Scrum Master must impart the largest amount of new ideas than at any other time. Most teammates seem willing to try the new approach at the outset, but soon begin backsliding into their old ways of building software. As the Scrum Master exhorts them to stick with Scrum, the storming begins.

The Scrum Master's primary objective for this stage is to combine the pressure of a short time box and the convenience of working eye-to-eye to scrub away the ponderous and slow work habits of the waterfall approach. The fact that the team can succeed and even perform better with little more than index cards, cork boards, and whiteboards will take them a while to accept.

Though the Scrum Master introduces Scrum/XP's lightweight notions of user stories, task boards, and burndown charts as part of Stage 0, as the first few sprints go by it will become increasingly clear that these artifacts all have one objective in mind—redirecting the team's attention to the one true metric by which they will measure their success throughout the project: team velocity. As we explored in the chapter on estimating, a team that can reliably forecast how much work it can complete with each sprint must be doing everything else right.

Stage 0 is only a partial step towards the consistent estimation required for a solid velocity number, placing the team where they can concentrate upon accurate forecasting unencumbered by waterfall habits. The actual velocity of the team will probably still be frustratingly low. The Scrum Master will know that the team is ready for the next stage when at least 60 percent of the stories points get accepted by the Product Owner for two sprints in a row. She should also wait for the team to achieve the following benchmarks:

- Team members work comfortably with the ADW's epic-theme-story vocabulary for defining requirements.
- The team progresses smoothly through all four "top of cycle" steps of the sprint—story conference, task planning, user demo, and sprint retrospective.
- Daily scrums are no longer taking more than 15 minutes.
- The project's basic infrastructure is in place (e.g., ETL and OLAP tools installed, and change management procedures have been defined and are being followed).
- Team members can estimate stories by size (story points) rather than relying solely upon labor hours.
- Team members create doable tasks cards, all with reasonable original labor estimates (OLEs).
- The OLEs for each story are generally proportionate to its story point estimate.
- The team reliably updates task RLEs each day so that the Scrum Master can update the burndown chart before the daily scrum.

STAGE 1: USER EPIC DECOMPOSITION

Once the team has internalized the rudiments of Scrum/XP, they are ready to begin honing their work habits for data warehousing in particular. ADW's Stage 1 of this process has a double agenda: increase the velocity and improve estimation accuracy to where the Product Owner is regularly accepting at least 80 percent of the story points and total Original Labor Estimates that represent the objectives of each sprint.

In our experience, the factors preventing this level of performance at the end of Stage 0 is the still unfocused nature of the user stories. Coming from a business background, the Product Owner is still giving the team large assignments, such as "add a graph of the fulfillment cycle time by week" when the required data is not yet in hand. In Stage 1, the Scrum

Master should begin to emphasize the vocabulary required by User Epic Decomposition framework of Chapter 3. As she shifts to ADW's warehouse-specific story types, the Product Owner will begin framing her user stories so that they align with the waypoints along the natural path data takes as it moves from source to warehouse to end user.

The team may not settle for the exact scheme offered in this book, but they should negotiate with the Product Owner a scheme of equivalent detail that reliably produces user stories that have the "INVEST" qualities of small, independent, testable, and estimable. Furthermore, after a few sprints in this stage, the developers should have identified a set of reference stories to which they compare other stories for relative-size estimation.

The Scrum Master will know that the team is ready for the next stage when the Product Owner accepts 80 percent or more of the story points for two or more sprints in a row. At that level the Product Owner will have sufficiently accurate information to both properly arrange the priority order of the stories, but more importantly to assure external stakeholders of delivery times and costs in order to keep the project alive.

STAGE 2: FORMULATING THE RELEASE PLAN

Stage 2 for a maturing Agile warehouse team results in a release plan solid enough that the developers are comfortable publicizing it to external stakeholders, understanding that many of them will interpret the plan as a commitment to a stated delivery date. Stage 2 is not a "stage" like the others, because, given the 80 percent estimation accuracy achieved in the previous stage, the team could conceivably draft their release plan in a single afternoon and be ready to move on to the next stage. In our experience, however, Stage 2 takes two weeks or more because the commitment the release plan represents to the project's stakeholders causes all parties to proceed cautiously.

First of all, now that the Product Owner has acquired the developer's BI lingo during Stage 1, she must revisit all the functional requirements she has for the project and translate them into INVEST-quality, warehouse-specific stories the team can reliably estimate. Secondly, the team will want to take a few passes at estimating the full list of "requirements," given that it will be held to the release date it predicts. Thirdly, and perhaps the most consuming of elapsed or calendar time, will be the negotiating process that will unfold when the team states its forecasted release date. Stakeholders seem to always push back, saying that such a long delivery time is unacceptable. Led by their Product Owner and Scrum Master, the team will need to communicate that the forecast was based upon well-defined team history—external stakeholders cannot change what has happened and what was measured, no matter how little they like the results. To a lesser degree, the team will need to revisit its estimate to "sharpen their pencils," brainstorm faster ways of tackling the largest stories, and to identify stories that can be pushed to the next release altogether. The back and forth required to negotiate a single, well-scoped release date requires more calendar time than one might guess, so we play it safe and designate this process as a stage all unto itself.

Certainly important objectives of this stage include the publication of the release date and the release plan—a list of major features to be delivered by sprint. This stage truly concludes, however, with a recommitment by the organization to the funds required for the team to continue and complete the work scoped by the release plan. This refunding is not as automatic as one might hope. Up until the publication of the release plan, the Agile warehouse team was starving the organization of crucial information, namely, whether it could deliver the BI application with sufficient features at or below an acceptable cost and time delay. The Scrum Master and Product Owner alike were sheltering the team from the external pressure to commit to a hard and fast dollar amount and delivery date, claiming the developers needed to get their feet wet first before anyone would truly know how fast they can create new code. Stage 2 changes that situation completely.

When the organization finally sees how much or how little they will receive for a given level of investment, it may legitimately decide to abandon the project and deploy the resources elsewhere. Such a decision may well take a few weeks, adding to the length of this stage. Because the re-commitment of sufficient funding determines whether the Agile warehouse project proceeds at all, we consider Stage 2 complete only when the project sponsor grants the team authority to proceed based upon the careful release plan it has provided.

STAGE 3: REFERENCE MODELS AND TEST-LED DEVELOPMENT

With the authority to proceed resulting from Stage 2, it makes sense for the Scrum Master to now focus the team's attention upon the quality of the modules they are building. Stage 3 represents the first dedicated step in this direction.

In this stage, the Scrum Master gives the developers two objectives, the first being to amass the project's reference model with units so well built and documented they can unambiguously demonstrate whether any other module is complete by comparison. The Scrum Master will know that the reference model has been sufficiently defined and communicated to the teammates when they begin using it in the following ways:

- Listing the tasks required to deliver a newly started module
- Specifying the features required to make it "bullet-proof" and restartable
- Estimating the level-of-effort required

- Design-by-exception, that is, stating that an upcoming module will behave and be coded like a unit from the reference model except for a certain list of differences
- Documentation-by-exception, that is, drafting prose that indicate that it matches the reference unit except for a particular set of differences

As the second objective of this stage, the Scrum Master can insist that the team draft tests for the intended modules before coding them. The tests should derive not only from the developers, who understand the aspects logical branches within the code that testing should validate, but also the input from Product Owner, Solutions Architect, and the Data Modeler as detailed above.

Additional objectives for this stage should include the following:

- Patterns identified for design and coding
- Complete basis-of-estimates cards for units in the reference model
- 2-to-1 design sessions for modules to be coded and later for peer reviewing the units when they are complete
- Module validation scripts written before modules are coded, that is, scripts that can automatically apply the tests defined for a module
- Self-documenting code

The Scrum Master should be prepared for some push-back from the developers when they introduce these objectives. Up until this stage, the emphasis has been upon accurate estimation, with the details of module design left largely to the developers tackling each task. Now, developers will be holding themselves to a much higher standard, and this can be discouraging for the team at first. In the previous stage, the developers achieved a respectable velocity and saw 80 percent or more of their story points accepted by the Product Owner. Because Stage 3 re-directs it to work to a much tougher notion of "done," the developers will see their velocity knocked back significantly and probably their acceptance percentage as well.

Because the next stage in ADW team maturity will focus upon rebuilding the team's velocity, the Scrum Master should emphasize in Stage 3 the quality objectives listed above. She will need also to prepare the Product Owner for the inevitable drop in velocity Stage 3's higher quality objectives will cause at first. As the team deliverables reach an acceptable level of quality, the Scrum Master can gradually focus the developers on regaining some of their velocity as well. Stage 3 is complete once the team seems comfortable with the new quality standards and the acceptance rate has reattained a 70 percent level.

STAGE 4: PIPELINED DELIVERY SQUADS

If the team is maturing as expected, at the end of Stage 3 it will be delivering modules that are far more robust than before, but at a frustratingly low pace. Whereas the developers will be no longer complaining about the corners they are cutting to meet the deadlines, they will be grumbling about how much work they must complete in such a short time box. Their stress levels will be higher at this point than during any other stage.

As these indications appear, the Scrum Master can introduce the developers to the Pipelined Delivery model described in the last chapter, and suggest that they *semi-formally* assign themselves into the Architecture, Development, and Integration squads. The team's objectives for Stage 4 will be to discover the best distribution of labor between these squads across the span of a typical sprint, understanding that teammates should move fluidly between the squads as the labor requirements imposed by the tasks change with each workday.

It will take one or more iterations to fill the pipeline, depending on how many squads the team decides to utilize, so the Scrum Master and Project Communication Assistant may find themselves explaining to external stakeholders why the team seems to have suddenly hit a lull. Once the pipeline fills, of course, the team should suddenly appear to have recovered its velocity. At first, it will be the velocity at the end of Stage 3, which was down somewhat because of the higher quality standards. A few sprints after modules begin exiting the pipeline, however, the developers should see a steady acceleration in their delivery of modules. Some of this increased speed results from the fact they are no longer working at a frantic pace and causing mistakes, miscommunications, and rework. But they also gain some speed as the reference model continues to mature and the validation scripts required by Test-Led Development fall into predictable patterns by module type and become repeatable processes.

The Scrum Master can conclude Stage 4, when she sees three conditions emerge:

- Teammates move between squads as needed so that no member falls idle waiting for an upstream squad to complete its work.

- Modules emerging from the Integration and Testing still possess all the aspects of quality achieved during Stage 3.

- The velocity of the Development squad improves to where it reaches at least 80 percent of the pace seen at the conclusion of Stage 2.

STAGE 5: IMPLEMENT THE AUTOMATED TESTING FACILITY

In commencing Stage 5, our Scrum team sets out to obtain the Holy Grail of Agile Data Warehousing: automated and continuous integration testing. As discussed in the previous chapter, a BI application cannot survive losing the goodwill of its users. It must exceed Scrum/XP's standard of "potentially shippable code" to achieve the higher objective of "essentially correct and fault tolerant" that automated and continuous testing facility makes possible.

The previous stages laid the groundwork for this last increment in ADW team maturity. Stage 3 ensured that the team writes testing scripts before coding—scripts that will run in an automated fashion when someone finds the time to write a driver program to do so. Stage 4 provides the team the opportunity to form an Integration and Hardening team who, lead by the Integration and Test Engineer discussed above, can focus upon implementing the automated testing facility and the Test Data Repository it will utilize. During Stage 5, this integration squad not only establishes the automated testing facility, but begins polishing the restart instructions that the team will send to Operations when the BI application is released.

Stage 5 is complete when the Scrum Master sees three, very obvious conditions:

- The Integration and Hardening squad displays the artifacts created by automated testing during user demos in order to prove that the code currently in the release pool is shippable.

- The integration squad also reports that they have a validated run book for Operations to use which covers restarting the warehouse after all of the abnormal endings provoked during the forced ABEND testing conducted by automated testing.

- The integration squad states that, if the Product Owner suddenly asked the team to promote to the current Release Pool to production, this wish could be achieved. Their confidence would rest on the fact that the current build passes all validation thrown at it by automated testing, where the degree of scrutiny applied is now so extensive that any code that passes its tests is "bullet proof."

SCALING UP WITH A SCRUM OF SCRUMS

Once a team completes the five stages of maturation sketched above, they should be a dynamite warehouse development group, so good that management may well wish they could propagate their work methods into multiple teams, especially if the enterprise has started an ambitious business initiative that will require many such teams coordinated under a single Business Intelligence program. While it is natural that companies would wish to scale up any successful approach to software development, the Scrum/XP approach we have studied in this book does not expand easily in its generic form. The problem is that generic Scrum provides only cursory suggestions on managing dependencies between teams, so that the challenge posed by warehousing *programs* is simply beyond its scope.

To properly coordinate multiple teams, one must wrap Scrum in an approach designed to balance the efforts of multiple parties that do not have the luxury of constant eye-to-eye communication with an embedded business representative to guide every decision with just-in-time requirements. In our practice, we have discovered that Scrum can be alloyed quite successfully with a scheduling technique recently emerging from the traditional project management profession: "Critical Chain Project Management". This new approach has, in fact, the opposite problem of Scrum—it is really too big a method for single project management. Once combined, Scrum excels at managing the details of software development in a lightweight, economical fashion, and critical chain techniques shine as a means of tracking dependencies, revealing where underperformance is about to hurt a program, and identifying the corrective action that will keep all efforts on track.

Let us first examine how one might scale with generic Scrum and where that approach might disappoint its practitioners. We can then introduce critical chain techniques, and discuss how ADW integrates the two into a more complete program management method.

RECOMMENDATIONS FROM THE AGILE COMMUNITY

Upon polling the Agile community for guidance on coordinating across large initiatives, one will receive the following suggestions:

- Staff each team with 7 to 10 members including a dedicated Product Owner.
- Eliminate dependencies between the teams as much as possible, by giving them an independent and coherent portion of the program's release backlog.
- Colocate the teams, so that they can communicate informally as much as needed and avoid the problems arising from separate time zones, cultural differences, and organizational divides (divides that technology such as email and conference phones can only partially address).
- Synchronize the teams' iterations if possible, so that a) no team is locked away in a story conference or retrospective when other teams need their input, and b) they can easily include each other's newly produced deliverables in their normal planning cycle.
- Coordinate the efforts between teams by means of a "scrum of scrums."

The Agile community envisions this scrum of scrums—which we usually label the "meta scrum"—as simply another stand-up meeting where a representative from each team who summarizes what she heard in their last stand-up meeting with her teammates. Supposedly, these meta scrums should follow the same format as the team Scrums, covering what was done, will be done, and what is blocking progress for individual teams. These team reps must speak at a more aggregate level than one does within the team Scrums, relating progress on user stories rather than for individual tasks.

If the meta scrum maintains a "task board," the cards that move across the columns will be story cards. The left-most column will be filled with cards representing the program's themes and even epics. Each representative to the meta scrum will update their story cards with the new total RLEs tallied earlier during the Scrums held by individual team. Moreover, the Program Scrum Master will have collected these story-level RLE tallies, placing them on a program-level burndown chart. Top-of-cycle planning steps, such as story conferences, will focus at this higher level as well.

Early Iterations Will Frustrate Program Sponsors

If the organization is new to Scrum, the first discontent companies will have with a program-level application of this approach will be the lack of the reliable level-of-effort estimates during the early sprints. Stakeholders throughout the company will be frustrated until someone confirms that the planned investment will achieve the desired results. The five-step maturation path presented above is the fastest means for cultivating a fully-capable Scrum warehousing team that we have found. Even so, the teams will be unable to issue solid release plans until they have mastered estimation at the end of Stage 2. Given the promises made to directors that got the effort funded, program managers will find it nerve-racking to wait the necessary ten to twenty weeks for accurate release plans to materialize.

Unfortunately, none of these alternatives for shortening this period of uncertainty will work reliably, and program managers should know this going into the effort:

- Insisting on a release plan before the new teams are ready is only to pretend that they know more about their velocity than they really do. Velocities are based upon historical data, so one must let enough history accumulate before the numbers can be trusted.
- Starting one team earlier than the rest so that it can estimate the entire project will be accurate only if every team will have identical staffing and identical story types. Such homogeneity rarely occurs, so this approach is tantamount to the dangerous practice of having one developer estimate another programmer's level-of-effort.

- Starting one team early and then spreading its members to the new teams when they are formed may help spread Agile techniques faster, but it disbands the one team that had any idea of their true velocity, placing all members in new situations where they must rediscover how fast they can actually work with their new teammates.
- Forcing teams to master one of the many software packages for coordinating Agile teams will undermine the lightweight quality of Scrum. Because accuracy requires history, such software will only give program managers a wider view of still fuzzy information rather than any greater clarity.

For these reasons, organizations deciding upon an Agile approach for an important BI initiative will have to prepare themselves for an initial "dark age" in project information, during which the team provides only the sketchiest of forecasts regarding total project duration and development costs. However, this period of uncertainty passes in a matter of weeks, replaced by a fast-moving team that provides dependable labor estimates. The key point to make here is that, despite their often elaborate pre-kickoff projections, waterfall methods provide no greater clarity than Agile teams. Early waterfall planning phases might supply program sponsors 1,000-line project plans and cost projections summed to the penny, but we should not be tempted to confuse precision with accuracy. How reliable can such plans be when the duration of their tasks were estimated in a vacuum, before the people that will actually do the work had been formed into a team and allowed to clock themselves on a single representative task? A waterfall-based project manager might employ for her forecasts durations taken from other projects, yet in all but the rarest circumstances those other projects involved very different people tackling significantly different objectives.

ADW's greatest contrast with waterfall methods can be seen most clearly at the beginning of a development effort, and can be understood as simply a matter of intellectual honesty: ADW refuses to claim greater certainty about a project's required level of effort than anyone can possibly possess, given all the unknowns involved. As the program matures, however, the ADW will grow steadily more attractive to management than waterfall methods because it yields increasingly accurate schedule forecasts, not to mention a steady stream of valuable feature enhancements for business-crucial applications.

Decoupling BI Efforts

Generic Scrum's suggestion to remove dependencies between teams when scaling is a good one—in as far as it is possible—so we should consider it in detail. At the highest levels, there are several steps we can take. First, we should remove any coupling between Agile and waterfall development teams if at all possible. The incremental delivery of the first will conflict intrinsically with the single delivery goal of the latter, leading to deep frustration on both sides over scheduling deliverables. It is quite common for waterfall teams to ask other teams for a detailed description of intended components and a planned schedule for their delivery. Agile teams, following the dictates of their Product Owners, often do not have such comprehensive plans for many months into an effort. Conversely, the Agile team might ask for the design for the interface of a small feature the Product Owner thinks is absolutely crucial to deliver next, only to be rebuffed by a waterfall team that still has three months to go on the requirements of the *entire* system.

Secondly, a BI program can achieve a good deal of decoupling between teams by moving the high-level design functions to a distinct architecture group that plays the role of the architecture squad for all teams. From this vantage point, the architecture squad can focus on providing technical specs to each team that intentionally focuses them on work that is not entwined with the deliverable of other teams in the program. Furthermore, the architects can adopt for the program a modular IT infrastructure such Service-Oriented Architecture, so that once built, the application modules can be integrated with other systems more readily due to the nature of the way they communicate with other applications.

We can also decouple teams by shrewdly aligning them along the data structures of the warehouse. **Figure 6.2** depicts just two of the architectural layers recommended by ADW, vertically partitioned to show the separate subject areas supported. Upon this sketch we draw the scope of work assigned to each team. Teams 1 and 2 have been asked to focus on one topic area each, and Team H3 has been asked to span horizontally across two topic areas of the integration layer, and Team V4 is tasked to deliver both components of a single subject area.

Though Team 1 may have little interaction with Team 2 because their topic areas do not overlap, they are both unfortunately coupled quite strongly to Team H3. The handoffs between these teams cross the architectural boundary between the integration and presentation layers, so they will have to discuss in some detail how their deliverables should integrate—which business rules, for example, were expressed in the third normal form model of the Integration Layer and which were left for the star schema of the Presentation Layer to support. Separate teams typically approach important exchanges in a risk adverse manner, that is, both sides will want to be able to prove the other is at fault should there be a crucial omission in their communication. Accordingly, they will want to interface using some degree of written documentation and reviews, greatly taxing the velocity of *both* teams. Team V4, in contrast, can focus on the transformation of one narrow set of data "from soup to nuts," thus avoiding any time-sapping need to explain integration across architectural layers. Thus to maximally decouple teams, programs should strive for a vertical division of tasks when scaling Scrum up to program-level efforts.

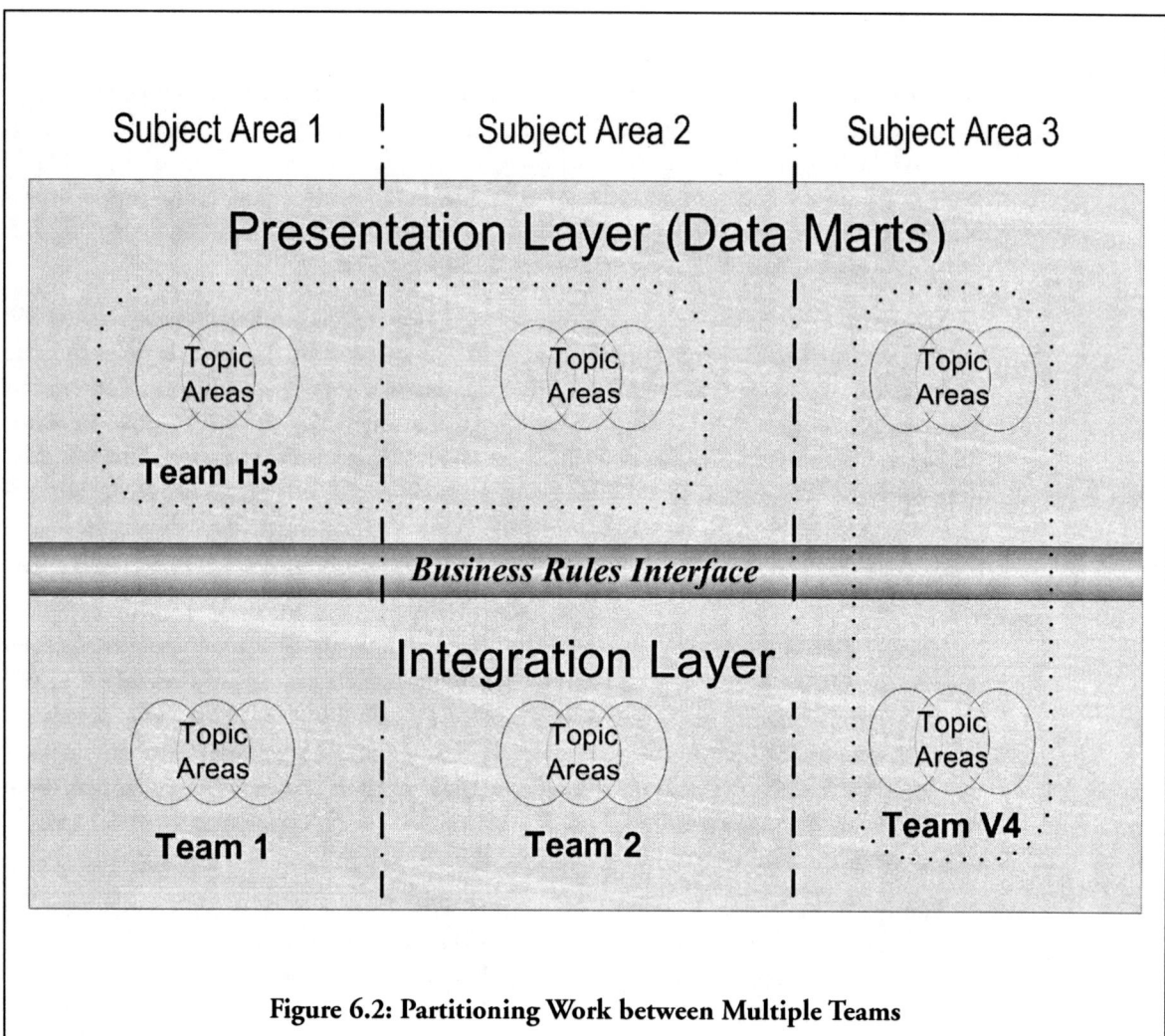

Figure 6.2: Partitioning Work between Multiple Teams
Note that vertical partitioning involves the least re-explanation of business rules

Re-Couple Teams Through ACIT For Quality Assurance

Careful decoupling may simplify development efforts, but at some point the deliverables must converge as an integrated whole. With the integration and hardening squad proposed in the last chapter, ADW provides a natural locus for merging the output of multiple teams. In the context of a program, the integration and hardening function will probably need to become a team in its own right, given the increased volumes of modules they will be responsible for testing, integrating, and inspecting. The mission statement of this integration team, then, is to collect the "potentially shippable" modules from the multiple teams into a single release pool, and guarantee to the Program Owner that assembled whole achieves the "essentially correct and fault tolerant" objective presented in the last chapter.

An integrated, automated testing facility naturally requires an integrated Test Data Repository, and here some extra effort will be needed in order to support coherent, program-level quality assurance. Whereas it would be possible for the shared test data repository to hold data sets that specifically test the units in the release pool, the integration team would provide the program far greater value if they also draft and maintain data sets that can validate the application's integration as well. Such data sets would span from extracts to the presentation and end-user access layers for all subject areas. When actual results match the test data repository's expected results in this context, all stakeholders can be confident that even those business rules have been properly applied, whether across architectural layers or entire subject areas.

Authoring and managing such a comprehensive, integrated collection of input data and expected results will require some dedication, thus BI programs should budget for a dedicated Test Engineer. Individuals in this role will need a deep understanding of the business of the enterprise, so that complicated business rules need to be explained to them only once. They will also need a high aptitude for details because if one multiplies out all the combinations needed to thoroughly test the logic of the ETL and BI applications, the required test data sets involve thousands of records. Though such a level of commitment to quality involves costs, the alternative is to leave certain aspects of the warehouse unproven—an approach appropriately termed as "deploy and pray." In our practice, we have never seen project sponsors endorse deploy and pray when the choice has been intelligibly presented by the warehouse development team.

SCRUM TOO LIGHT FOR SCALING

The discussion above notwithstanding, program managers will find a discernable limit to how independent one can actually make the multiple ADW teams required for large BI programs. This limit arises from the role that large data warehouses typically play in the enterprise. Organizations often charter the data warehouse with solving the operational nightmares that arise from decades of uncoordinated growth in information systems, either due to questionable decisions in the past or due to hurried merger and acquisition efforts. Often, BI is considered the "magic bullet" that will make feasible an essential, C-level initiative commissioned under extreme competitive stress.

One such project in which we participated for a Fortune 100 pharma/biotech firm aspired to integrate no fewer than four newly commissioned line-of-business systems (plus the still functioning legacy apps they replaced) into a near real-time repository providing current and historical transaction reporting and master data management, at a level of quality permitting data submissions to the FDA for product approval. All told, this initiative involved over 150 people for three years.

Endeavors such as this pharma repository are extremely integrated by their very nature. The data topology chart presented in **Figure 6.3** provides a schematic notion of the integration required by this project's charter between line of business systems. One can see in this diagram the central role envisioned for the warehouse by understanding that it gathers data from each "source of record" system and then delivers it to all remaining systems marked as information consumers. Given that several of the sources would be in mid-transition to new software platforms while the BI team developed the warehouse, this effort inescapably involved extensive dependencies between the many teams involved.

Programs utilizing ADW that face this level of built-in dependencies will find laughably naive generic Scrum's recommendation to simply "decouple" the Agile teams and rely upon meta scrums to coordinate the 15 to 20 development teams required by our pharma

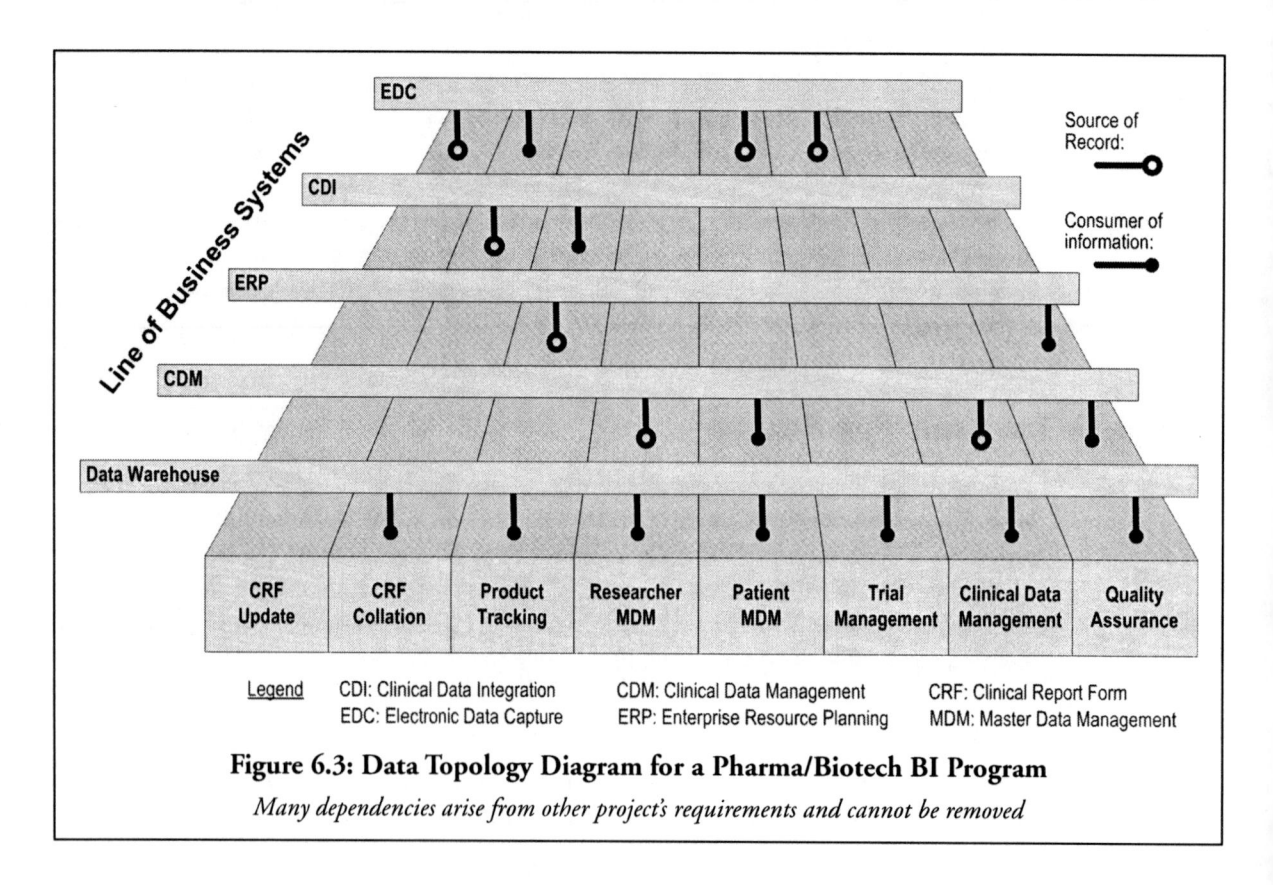

Figure 6.3: Data Topology Diagram for a Pharma/Biotech BI Program

Many dependencies arise from other project's requirements and cannot be removed

example. When many teams and vendors are involved, hidden deficiencies in knowledge and communication are guaranteed to create frequent setbacks to the master schedule. If, in our example, Team X suddenly declared that it cannot deliver everything required by the time of the next release, the Program Manager would be instantly asking questions such as:

- What will be the impact on downstream Team Y?
- Can we solve these resource conflicts by removing deliverables A, B, and C from the next release?
- Can Team Z lend Team X resources for surge programming without risking delivery of their modules to Team W?
- Where can we deploy contract labor to assure on-time deliverables without overly draining our financial resources?

The quick recitation of the short accomplishments, objectives, and hurdles comprising Scrum stand-ups at any level cannot begin to answer these types of questions. Daily scrums provide only partial visibility on progress, yet leave many long-term dynamics unverbalized and offer no methodical technique for appraising and circumventing contingencies when they arise. If we were to speak in terms of traditional project management artifacts, the obvious missing pieces at the meta scrum level is not only the cross-application dependencies shown in the data topology chart above, but also a network diagram of work tasks with which to visualize the dependencies between major program deliverables.

Scrum is a lightweight approach that excels in speeding up the work of software development within a team, and should be heartily embraced as such. When it comes to coordinating collaboration between teams to meet cost and schedule objectives, however, something more is clearly needed. We want to be careful, though, that whatever we choose to manage the dependencies between work packages at the program level leaves Scrum unencumbered to manage in its agile, semi-formal fashion the minutiae involved in writing code within the project room.

"CRITICAL CHAIN" FOR PROGRAM MANAGEMENT

Luckily another innovative attempt to improve upon classical project management called "Critical Chain Project Management" can be adapted so that it dovetails well with Scrum—as long as we constrain it to focus on program-level issues only. Critical Chain Project Management is a big topic [Leach 2007], and we have space enough only to present its most central aspects, especially those most pertinent to support Agile Data Warehousing. But even a quick introduction will demonstrate its huge potential for scaling up Agile initiatives.

Traditional project management, as defined by PMI and supported by many software tools such as MS Project, focuses upon a project's "critical path." When a project manager uses the dependencies and estimated durations of all the task of a project to build a network diagram of the work ahead, the critical path is the longest series of connected tasks. The critical path is naturally of great interest to all stakeholders because it determines the overall elapsed time required to realize the project's objectives. The critical path is also a handy planning tool for the project manager because it identifies the exact set of tasks that could be revisited in order to bring in the project's completion date.

The problem with our traditional reliance upon the critical path is two-fold. First, there is no buffer around the critical path. Any hiccup in a task on this path will instantly cause a delay in the project's forecasted delivery date. Second, because of the limits of most project management software tools, the critical path is calculated with little or no adjustment for resources that the network diagram may have scheduled to work on two or more tasks at the same time. With these two strikes against it, large programs depending upon critical path analysis alone are nearly doomed from the start to miss their target dates.

Critical chain project management provides planning insights superior to critical path management in several ways. Let us follow step by step how critical chain techniques would improve upon the traditional planning of a warehouse project before we discuss how ADW might adapt it for data warehousing programs.

Reveals Unrealistic Deadlines Through Resource Leveling

At its simplest, the critical chain is a critical path analysis performed after thorough resource leveling. Start dates for tasks are adjusted on the calendar till all resources are working at "only" 100 percent of capacity. Take for example the situation in **Figure 6.4** which shows the required sequencing for a few work packages for our pharma project that focus upon extracting and merging data from nearly a dozen different sources: Enterprise Resource Planning, Clinical Data Management, and CRF Data Integration (ERP, CDM, and CDI respectively).

In the top half of the diagram, the critical path was calculated only on the length of the tasks, and did not take into account any potential double booking of resources. Critical chain software, however, instantly identified that both the extract and the merge teams were overloaded. Repositioning the task bundles on the calendar to eliminate the overtime labor required reveals that more elapsed time will be required than the critical path analysis suggested—a very important insight for a Program Manager to have before making commitments to stakeholders.

Critical Path...
...Before resource leveling:

Required calendar time is much greater than first understood

...After resource leveling to keep Extract and Merge teams from being overloaded:

Figure 6.4: "Critical Chain" Is the Project's Critical Path after Resource Leveling
Critical Chain can reveal that a traditional plan allows too little calendar time for some resources

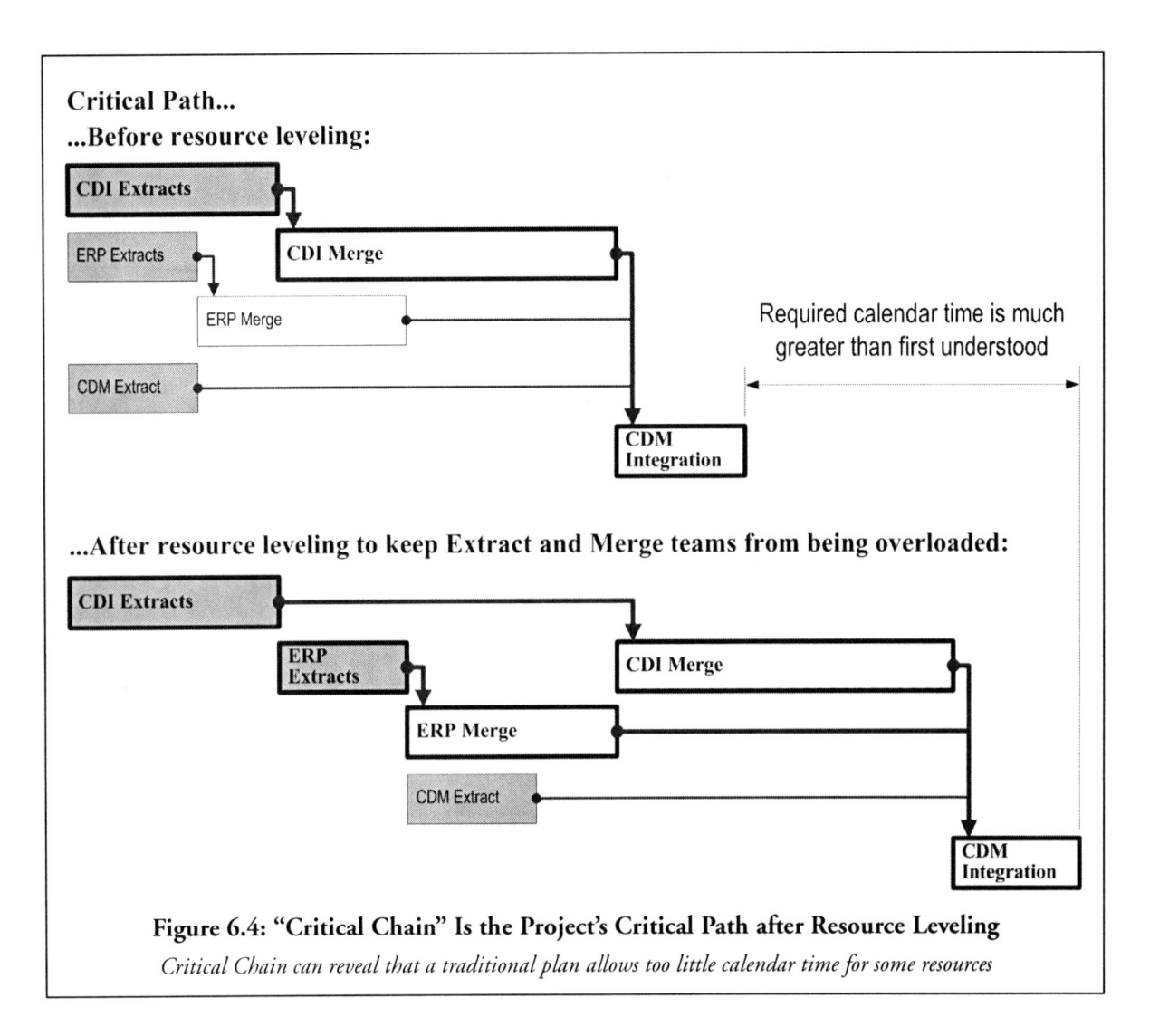

Brings Deadlines In By Pooling Task Padding

Though resource leveling appropriately increases the forecasted length of a project, critical chain project management provides two compensating mechanisms that typically shorten the project's duration. The first of these improvement arises from when Critical Chain creates a context in which developers can provide realistic estimates without risking disaster should a task run longer than expected.

Because any overrun on a "critical path" project delays the delivery and generates much gnashing of management teeth, developers typically pad their estimates to provide risk-adverse task duration estimates with 90 to 95 percent confidence intervals (PCIs). The cumulative result of such padding can be seen in the top panel of **Figure 6.5**, where each task bundle after the first one is scheduled to start much later than it needs to be.

Critical chain asks for 50 PCI estimates in addition to the risk-adverse 90 PCI forecasts, and then uses the 50 PCI estimates to schedule the tasks on the network diagram. As shown on the figure, this reduces the projected duration of the overall project. Furthermore, it utilizes the difference between the 90 and 50 PCI estimates to pad the critical path, so

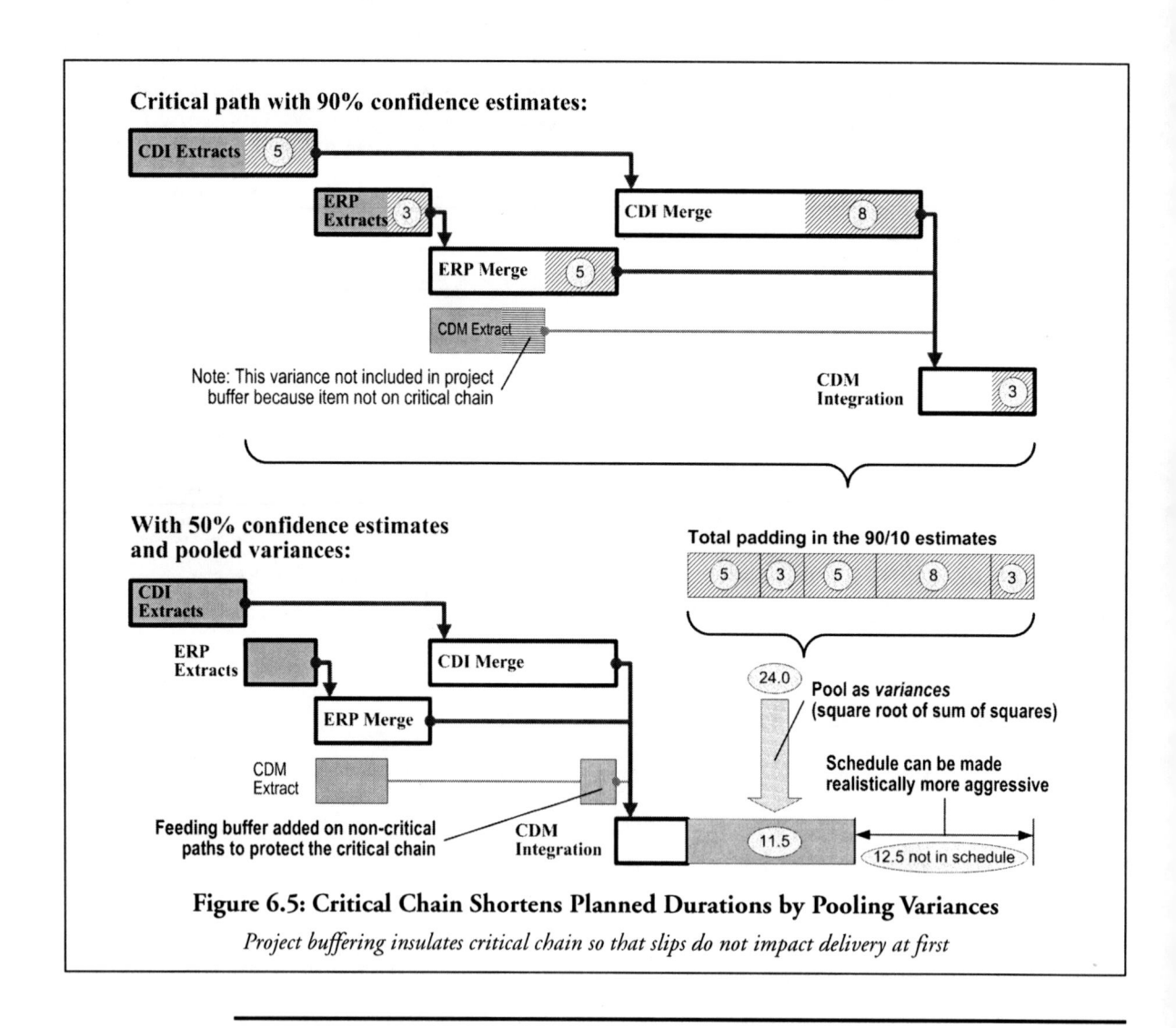

Figure 6.5: Critical Chain Shortens Planned Durations by Pooling Variances

Project buffering insulates critical chain so that slips do not impact delivery at first

Chapter 6—Starting and Scaling Agile Warehousing Teams

that many contingencies along the critical path can be absorbed without delaying the forecasted delivery date.

Careful study of the figure will reveal that the 90 PCI padding was not simply moved to the end of the critical path, but that its combined duration actually shrank. This shrinkage occurs because critical chain techniques properly pool the padding when they remove it from individual tasks. By representing the difference between 90 and 50 PCI estimates, these padding actually represent *variances* of actual versus estimated task duration. The study of statistics shows us that such variances should not be combined linearly, but instead using the square root of the sum of the squares.

This statistically correct aggregation method yields a smaller value than simply adding the padding together, as many project managers would be tempted to do. By correctly moving the padding from individual tasks to a sum of variances buffer positioned at project end, critical chain not only allows most tasks to start sooner than critical path analysis would suggest, but also reduces the project elapsed time, as shown in the bottom panel of the figure.

Protects the Critical Path With Three Types of Buffers

In addition to the properly pooled project buffer we considered above, critical chain techniques also utilize "feeding buffers" and "resource buffers" to further insulate the project's critical path from many adverse contingencies.

Feeding buffers are added to all the non-critical chain branches of the task network diagram that feed into the critical path. A feeding buffer is typically set to one-half of the overall length of the branch they pad. Feeding buffers allow project managers to monitor hiccups along non-critical paths without having to "use up" any of the overall project buffer protecting the critical chain.

Resource buffers represent the notice time that each resource needs to get ready for task work and are set to whatever amount of forewarning a particular resource requires. This type of buffering pertains more to resources such as machinery that require set-up times, and is typically used less extensively in software development projects where people manage to start tasks on time by monitoring upstream work via the project plan.

Accelerates Projects Through Changes in Work Culture

Critical chain project management reveals that once the padding on individual tasks is removed, projects are shortened considerably if teammates both jump on assigned tasks as soon as upstream dependencies are cleared and focus exclusively on completing their tasks as soon as possible. Accordingly, critical chain instructors urge their client organizations to adopt a culture of "single tasking."

Multitasking wastes time through "switching costs"—the efficiency lost by putting aside a task and then struggling to remember where one left off when returning to it later. In fact, multitasking represents an informal state of dependency between the warehouse development and everything else that the organization might possibly ask a teammate to do in the course of a business day. As we saw above, such dependencies must be eliminated to the greatest degree possible.

Critical chain's practice of removing padding from individual tasks not only yields more realistic plans but also eliminates the very costly "student syndrome" from an organization's work habits. College students taking several courses at one time frequently delay starting a demanding term paper until its deadline approaches. Furthermore, if they complete it before time has actually expired, they will continue polishing it until the deadline occurs.

For organizations competing through innovation, allowing their project teams to indulge in this student syndrome will cause projects to take longer than they need and make the enterprise far less responsive to market demands. Accordingly, critical chain recommends that organizations transform their "student" workers into "relay racers" by urging them to focus exclusively upon tasks that are on the critical chain, to start working as soon as possible, and to work their deliverables to where they are just "good enough" to handoff to the next party. This three-fold emphasis amounts to a cultural change in the organizations approach to work, but one that promises to shorten all projects undertaken and directly enhance the organization's competitiveness.

Managing Projects Focuses Upon Buffer Recovery

With critical chain's resource leveling, pooled buffers, and relay racer mentality in place, a project manager's role during a work effort is to simply watch where the project buffer and feeding buffers are being consumed. This monitoring is streamlined using a "buffer control chart" as depicted in **Figure 6.6**, which continues with our pharma example.

The buffer control chart is divided into three zones based upon what percentage of an effort's total buffering has been absorbed by tasks that finish later than planned. If little overall buffering has been consumed, then the project is in the lower, "Watch" zone. If contingencies begin to exhaust buffers, the project moves upwards on the control chart into the "Plan" zone, where the project manager begins thinking of how to adapt tasking or resources. Further buffer consumption moves the project into the "Act" zone, where the project manager begins to execute her buffer recovery plan.

Figure 6.6: Managing by Critical Chain Concentrates on Buffer Recovery
*Delay on the **Merge** epic avoided by redirecting the **Extract** team*

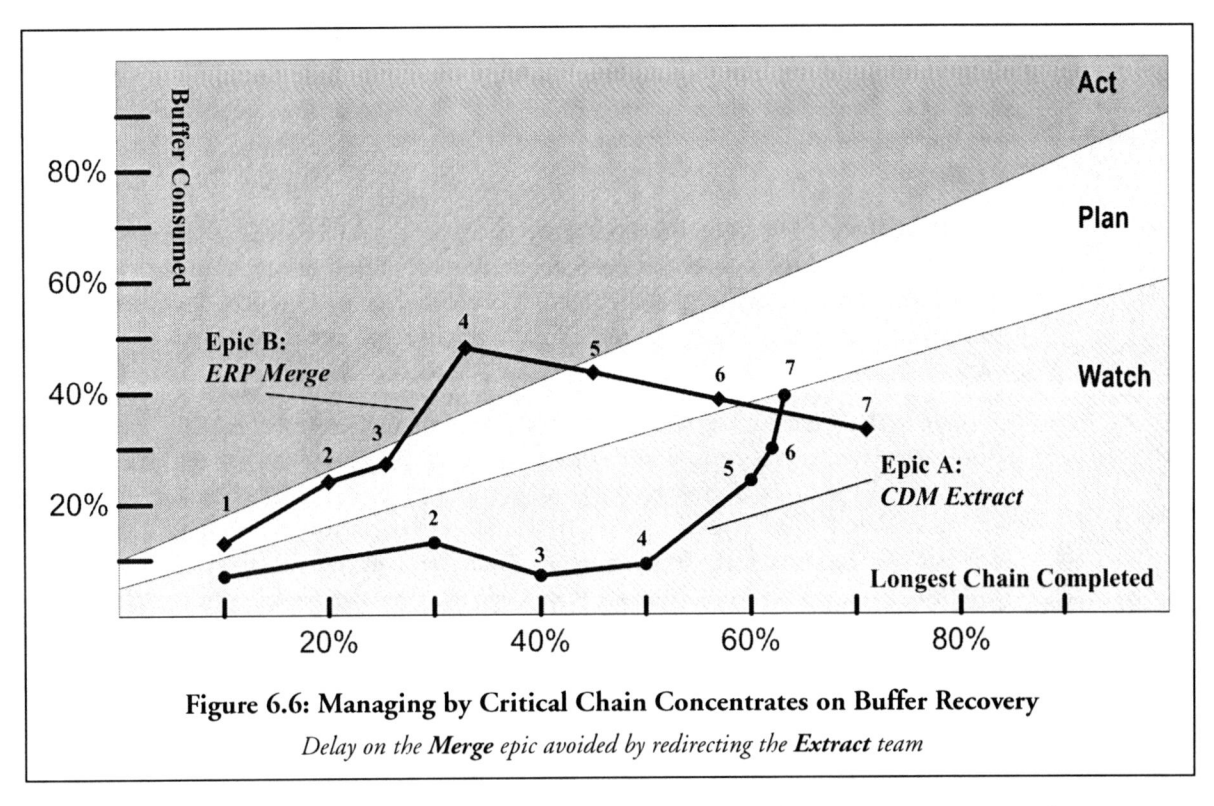

Our figure depicts a BI program tracking multiple teams. By time point four, management had realized that not only was the ERP Merge team slipping behind, but that the CDM extract team could be refocused for a while on some of the ERP Merge duties in order to bring that effort's buffer utilization back into the "Watch" zone.

ADAPTING CRITICAL CHAIN FOR SCALING SCRUM

With the above understanding of Critical Chain Project Management, we can now discuss how to adapt it to provide the program management capabilities that Scrum lacks when scaled for larger BI initiatives. Let us recap that, even before one adds an Agile approach into the mix, critical chain requires some big changes in how an organization pursues project-level work. Specifically the enterprise will need:

1. A better class of project management software that allows the project manager to easily perform resource balancing
2. Forecasts framed in terms of 50 percent and 90 percent confidence intervals
3. Single tasking teammates working as relay racers

If attempted at only the project level, the multi-tasking and student syndrome left untouched in the larger organization will quickly undermine the new thinking introduced by critical chain. Thus these techniques are best deployed at least at the program level, with implementations at a business unit or divisional level having an even greater chance for success.

Critical chain is still a top-down, plan-driven approach, and therefore subject to all the limitation of single-pass, waterfall methods we have discussed throughout this book. The key to success will be keeping the program manager balancing resources and rescheduling work at a high level, leaving Scrum/XP in charge of the detail development activities within each team.

Agile Data Warehousing as a method expands to the program level by means of a simply-expressed division of labor: critical chain for *program* management and Scrum/XP for managing work within teams. At the intra-team level, Product Owners guide their self-organizing developers using story-level work bundles organized into release and sprint backlogs. At the inter-team level, Program Managers constrain themselves to balancing work and resources at no lower than the epic- and theme-level using critical chain. When contingencies threaten to delay the project, the Program Manager can re-assign "themes to teams" in order to recover program buffers, but must treat both themes and teams as atomic, resisting the urge to meddle with the activities encapsulated inside each of them.

This division of labor immediately suggests that the meta scrums become a convocation of Product Owners where, rather than simply repeating Scrum's pro forma three questions—"what we've done, what we'll do, what's holding us up"—the Product Owners review the program buffer control charts to spot where the program is starting to "bleed time." The buffer control chart will also reveal those aspects of the program that are better off and can afford to give up some resources, at least for a while. Meta scrums thus become "horse trading" sessions between Product Owners, where they collectively work at the epic and theme level to keep the entire program on track.

As the themes get reallocated between the teams, the items comprising each team's release backlog may change considerably. Luckily, because they are using Scrum, these teams will be already quite capable of drastically changing directions—as long as a) such redirection occurs during the story conference at the top of a sprint, b) the team roster remains unchanged, and c) the time box with which their work is framed retains its standard length.

Figure 6.7 portrays how Agile Data Warehousing has married Critical Chain Program Management and Scrum/XP. In this scheme, the Product Owner serves as the communication path from meta scrum to individual teams, and each team's velocity, as measured at the end of each sprint, provides the input the meta scrum needs in order to update the program managers' buffer control charts for the current and the next program sprint. From

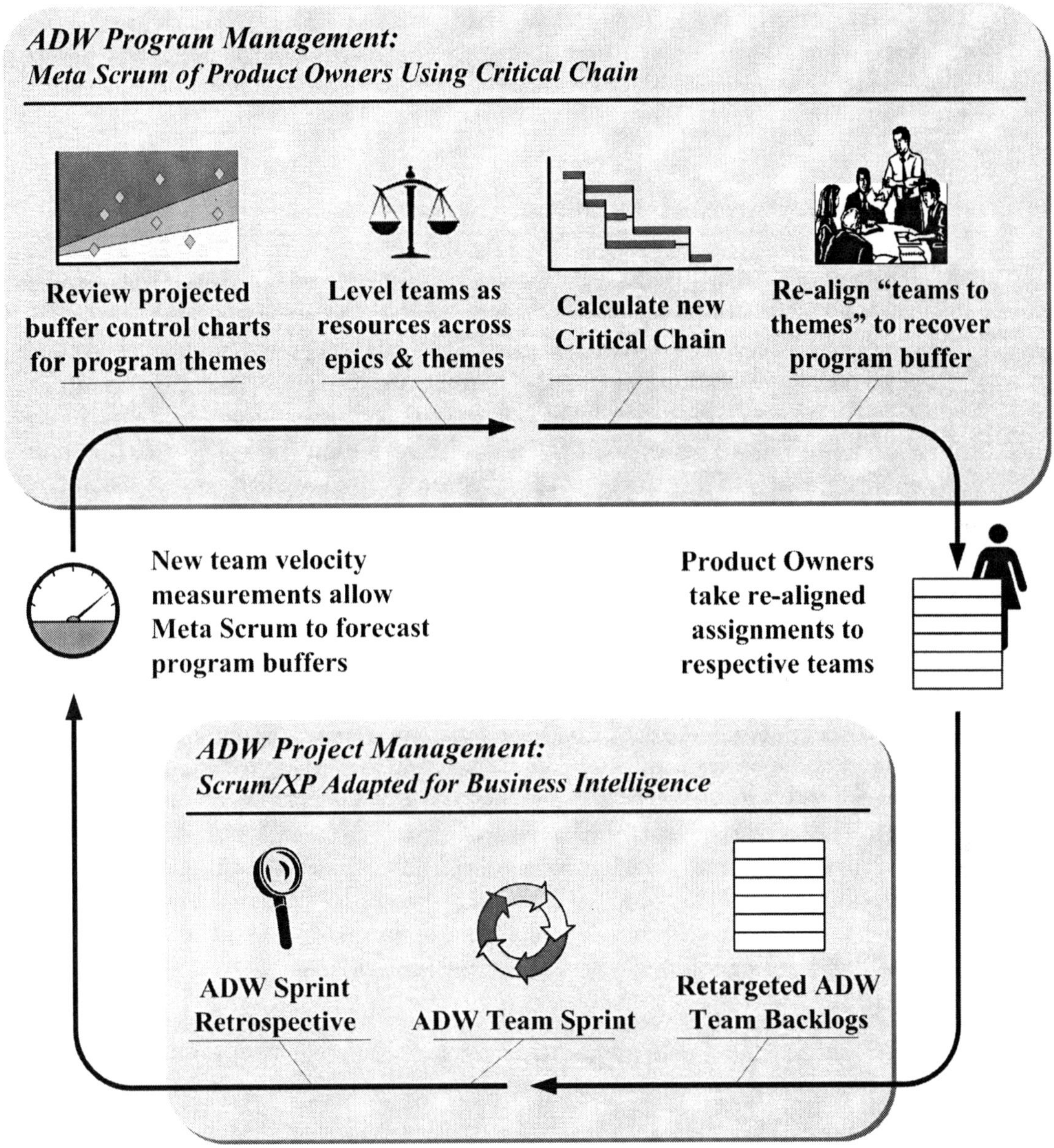

ADW Program Management:
Meta Scrum of Product Owners Using Critical Chain

Review projected buffer control charts for program themes → Level teams as resources across epics & themes → Calculate new Critical Chain → Re-align "teams to themes" to recover program buffer

New team velocity measurements allow Meta Scrum to forecast program buffers

Product Owners take re-aligned assignments to respective teams

ADW Project Management:
Scrum/XP Adapted for Business Intelligence

ADW Sprint Retrospective → ADW Team Sprint → Retargeted ADW Team Backlogs

Figure 6.7: Scaling Agile Data Warehousing for Large BI Programs
Adapted Critical Chain process guides the meta scrum of Product Owners

the individual team's perspective, they are still getting redirected only by their familiar Product Owner, and only during the story conference. Thus buffer recovery managed at the program level does not introduce any more chaos than the developers have already learned to accommodate.

OVERCOMING GEOGRAPHICAL BARRIERS

The Scrum approach, which serves as the project management heart of Agile warehousing as presented in this book, is based upon colocating a small team so they can stop wasting time on to-be documentation of short shelf life and ineffective review meetings. Yet this is an age of telecommunications and outsourcing. If colocation is so essential for Agile BI projects, then teams that include one or more staff members working remotely will naturally wonder whether Agile can work for them. In other words, does the simple fact of distributed teammates require returning to waterfall methods and abandoning all the advantages Scrum has to offer?

Scrum thrives by substituting fluid, informal communication for formal documentation. Informal communication for geographically remote teammates revolves around speaker phones and Internet-based collaborative applications such as Microsoft's Net Meeting. In practice, these are poor substitutes to actually having a coworker in the same room. Effective communication is comprised of the words employed, the tone of voice, eye contact, quickly sketched drawings, and body language. Speaker phones eliminate eye contact and make tone of voice and many of the words employed impossible to discern. Remote collaborative applications are still very clunky when it comes to sharing a quick sketch—nowhere near the efficacy of two people using a whiteboard. Email exchanges on difficult design points often involve so much back and forth that the parties involved must eventually resort to a phone call to clear up the issues. Video conferencing is expensive, vulnerable to poor sound quality, and still cannot match the ease of sharing enjoyed by two people sitting together with a document between them.

For these reasons, we encourage organizations to be realistic and colocate team members whenever possible. In our experience, colocated team members are 50 to 60 percent more productive than remote teammates, so the cost of geographic separation is very real. Two undersized teams with colocated members will be more effective than one regular-sized team struggling to span a significant geographical or time zone boundary. If colocation is impossible, then there are a few tactics for minimizing the impact of geographical barriers, which we describe below.

Choose the Geographical Division Carefully

Figure 6.8 portrays a typical BI team. The thickness of the lines connecting each pair of individuals depicts the importance of the communication between those parties. When planning a team roster, such a diagram will allow the Scrum Master to group the candidates so that the geographical separation cuts across the least important links, as shown in our figure. Furthermore, such an analysis will reveal in short order which teammates will need to travel frequently in order to keep the team cohesive.

Scrum Masters can take a second look at any proposed geographical division for the team by considering also the best vertical and horizontal partitions inherent in the project architecture, as was shown earlier with Figure 6.2 above. In general, teammates working highly coupled aspects of the project need to be colocated more than others.

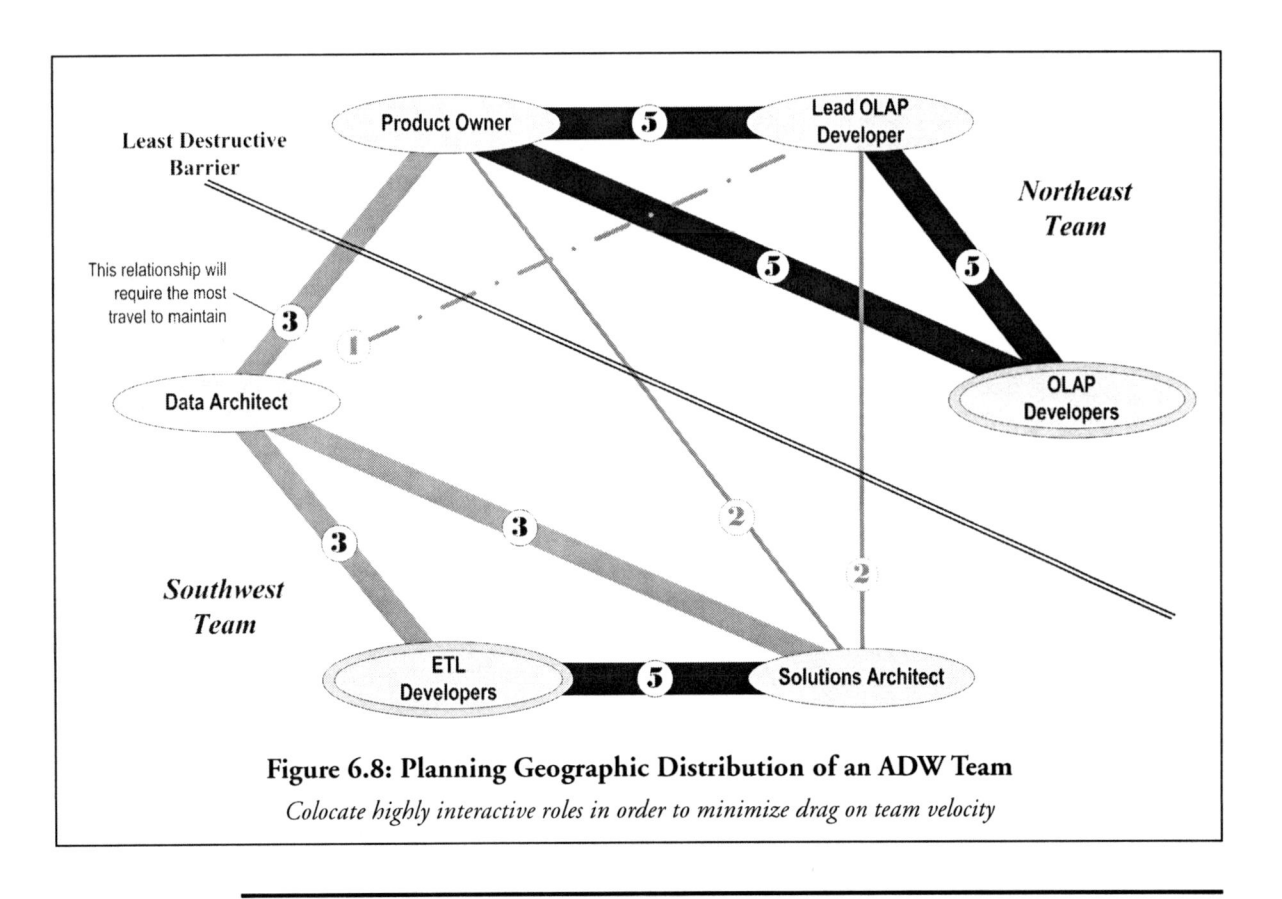

Figure 6.8: Planning Geographic Distribution of an ADW Team
Colocate highly interactive roles in order to minimize drag on team velocity

Creatively Define Roles to Mitigate Separation

The bubbles on Figure 6.8 can represent roles, which may not correspond one-for-one with team members. With some investment in cross-training, the team depicted might be able to assign a cohesive subset of data modeling duties to the northeast group's Lead OLAP Developer, eliminating much of the travel for the southwest team's Data Architect.

Budget for Top-Of-Sprint Travel

If travel expenses are not a large issue, then we encourage that the entire team be assembled for the top-of-sprint activities of the story conference and task planning. So much informal communication is required to ferret out detailed requirements and craft a consensus on estimates, that speaker phones reduce remote parties to near-total ineffectiveness. Accordingly, if some teammates must work at a distance, Scrum Masters should arrange for that isolation to occur only during the long, development phase of a sprint where developers need to work in only twos and threes.

Insist on Colocation for Two or More Sprints

Working remotely is far easier when one is on a team that he knows and trusts. The Scrum Master would be wise to insist that the remote members of the team travel and work in the team's shared "war room" for at least one or two sprints—long enough for the team to sort through the nuances of working together and the details of their preferred division of labor. In fact, the Product Owner and Scrum Master might well state that working remotely is only an option if the team maintains a particular velocity and accuracy of estimates, thus providing a tangible motivation for those who do not want to be physically present to invest the extra effort required to surmount their geographic separation.

Agile Collaboration Software

In general, we find that the many software packages introduced over the past few years to support Agile teams rarely justify the cost of purchase, implementation, training, and "fiddling" with electronic artifacts that they inevitably entail. Scrum is a minimalist approach to software development, reducing project management overhead down to the absolute essentials so more time can be devoted to development. Rarely can one drape an electronic interface around a lightweight artifact such as a task card and still have a low-cost approach to the given problem. When remote team members are involved, however, we have found two areas where software support begins to help: task boards and documenting complex business rules.

The task board can be moved to an electronic format quite easily using generic graphics or even a spreadsheet application. Whereas this makes the board a bit harder for the non-remote team to use, it can be projected onto the team room wall during each stand-up meeting without losing too much of its effectiveness. Remote teammates can follow the conversation by opening the same task board online or watching the Scrum Master's computer via NetMeeting. The advantage to this approach is that the remote teammates can reference the task board with the same effort as everyone else, removing any excuse they might have for not updating their task cards or for not knowing about the tasks they could have volunteered to work.

Complex business rules need to be documented so that the Product Owner and other subject matter experts do not need to repeatedly describe them. Chat room software can capture this information for teams with remote members far better than can be achieved with conference calls. Conference calls are less than ideal because teammates tend to "multitask," that is, they attend to other demands such as email or expense reports when it is not their turn to speak, often asking the group to repeat a segment of conversation whenever they half-hear something of interest transpire. By moving the group dialog to a chat room session, we find that people stay more focused as they read the words arriving from cyberspace and as they wait for a chance to type in their comments.

Teams will need a package that goes beyond what is available through MS NetMeeting, however—one that does not discard the chat session when parties disconnect. Dedicated chat room packages maintain a permanent record of the discussions they enable, allowing any member, whether they partook in the conversation or not, to search the transcript for the key points they need to know. For business rules, these searchable transcripts eliminate a tremendous amount of verbal rehashing and actually improve the team's velocity.

Chapter 7
ADW as a Demonstrably Mature Method

Can a "mature" method be based upon a light-weight, iterative approach?

How complete does ADW appear when appraised with a formal maturity model such as SEI's CMM?

Is there a way to ramp-in "process maturity" so that we retain "agility" as long as possible?

As can happen with any innovative approach, Agile Data Warehousing can spark strong opposition within large organizations that prefer to do things in a traditional fashion. The integrated nature of today's information systems dictates that warehousing projects will need cooperation from many individuals other than its immediate sponsor. Unfortunately this dependency provides an avenue of resistance to parties who may wish to hobble an Agile effort within the enterprise. These parties can range from executives and functional groups within IT, to business managers, vendors, and even the developers assigned to the Agile team itself. Luckily time is on the Agile project's side—if it can survive for just six to twelve months, the result will begin to speak for itself and persuade many skeptics to support this new approach for BI projects. But if left unmitigated, the resistance of these many critics can seriously impede or even defeat the Agile team before its first release sees production.

Probably the most common dismissals leveled by detractors against Agile is a single theme that comes in many flavors, such as "Agile is too tactical," "it's institutionalized scope creep," "it's excessively reactive and insufficiently planned." The common backdrop to these many claims is simply that Agile is "immature" compared to highly formalized waterfall methods. When pressed for greater precision, antagonists will typically cite an industry standard for assessing development processes, such as the Capability Maturity Model published by the Software Engineering Institute. All the condemnations we listed above can be boiled down to a single invective: "Agile methods are not CMM compliant."

Countering this single criticism of Agile Data Warehousing is difficult not only because CMM compliance itself is a large and involved concept, but also because properly repainting the picture requires drawing from several frameworks at once: approach vs. method, maturity and its discontents, thoroughness of planning vs. speed of delivery and the quality of results. Rather than pursuing a protracted arm-wrestling match with implacable critics over the relative merits of plan-driven and Agile approaches, ADW advocates sorely wish they can simply claim "Agile has been shown to be CMM-compliant," if only to silence the detractors so that the Agile warehouse project can get underway.

Luckily, this claim can be made for ADW in particular, although one has to understand the nuances of the assertion in order to make the claim stick should it be examined carefully by antagonists. This chapter provides the definitions and analyses needed to make this bold claim, leaving it to the next chapter to explore how to counter the often nonverbal resistance to Agile projects many parties will pursue once they have lost use of their favorite weapon, CMM compliance.

WHY CMM?

Since 1986, the U.S. Department of Defense has been contracting with Carnegie Melon's *Software Engineering Institute* to research and codify best practices for developing large information systems. SEI examined the achievements being made by statistical quality control in the manufacturing world, and considered how software development and system integration could be transformed into a process that can be analyzed, formalized, and tuned. Packaging the answers it found into the "Capability Maturity Model" for IT process improvement, SEI published its first CMM version into the public domain in 1991. Over the next fifteen years, SEI published numerous revisions of its CMM model that steadily merged it with other SEI and like-minded standards, until 2006, when the institute published the *CMMI model for Development* (CMMI-DEV). The *I* in CMMI stands for "integration" and signals that its many progenitors include standards for software and software-intensive computer systems, as well as products and processes. [Chrissis 2007, p 15]

There are many reasons why CMMI-DEV and its predecessors (which we will refer to somewhat loosely hereon as simply "CMM") have come to be considered the "gold standard" by which a software development method should be assessed. The steady stream of funding from the DoD for the CMM project that SEI received over the years has allowed it to attain a high level of thoroughness in both its breadth of the model's vision and the details that it contains. In many ways, CMM is the distillation of decades of lessons learned by systems developers. It provides a very complete, if rather mainstream, listing of the processes one should find in a top-rung MIS shop, and thus serves as an excellent measuring stick with which to find gaps in any newly crafted method.

Perhaps because of its thoroughness, CMM has become the "de facto standard for software-intensive system development" (at least as SEI sees it). Since its introduction, over 45,000 people have been trained in its guidelines. SEI provides a formal appraisal program by which organizations can officially document their compliance with the standard, and to date 1,500 of these appraisals have been registered with SEI. This program, plus the fact that CMM "has shown value for demonstrating process discipline against governance audits like Sarbanes-Oxley" combine to give the model a large measure of prestige among IT professionals the world over. [Chrissis 2007]

These many factors make CMM an excellent standard by which Agile Data Warehousing can assess its completeness. In fact, CMM is so ubiquitous in the IT industry today, that knowing how ADW fares within the CMM framework is probably the only such analysis the ADW advocate will need to master. If an Agile detractor were to disparagingly contrast ADW with some other standard than CMM, we can offer to analyze it using CMM. SEI's standard is so dominant that this substitution will surely be acceptable, conveniently placing the conversation back on familiar ground.

All told, examining ADW with CMM is a very positive step to take. We want our method to be "mature," not only to head off external criticism and gain IT management support, but to counter any lingering doubts within our warehousing teams. Furthermore, its good to know from many viewpoints whatever weaknesses exist in a method, so that we can evolve it to be even more valuable as a guide to crafting business intelligence applications.

CMM Overview

The Capability Maturity Model is not a method, but offers instead an ordered set of practices one might incorporate in their software development shop so as to reach progressively higher levels of overall capability or "maturity" levels. As one can see in **Figure 7.1**, which depicts the components of the CMM model in the style of an entity relationship diagram, the highest level concepts are four Process Categories—Project Management, Engineering, Engineering Support, and Process Management—which in turn decompose into a total of 22 "process areas." [SEI 2006]

Figure 7.1: Components of the SEI's Capability Maturity Model
Presented as an entity relationship diagram showing the one-to-many relationships

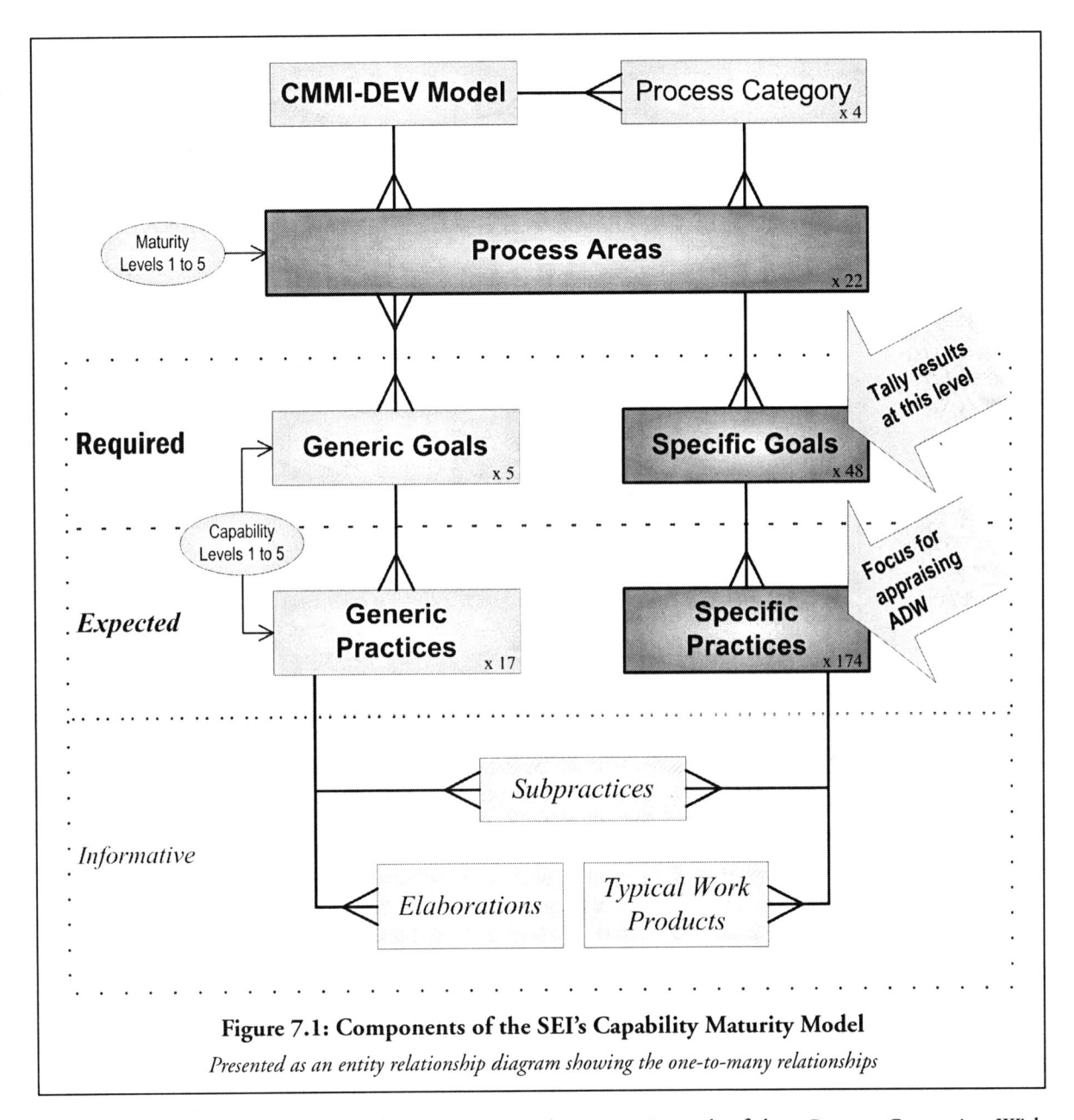

Table 7.1 lists the process areas that comprise each of these Process Categories. With just a quick glance at these process areas, much of the list makes intuitive sense to any veteran software developer, including as it does such prosaic practices as "project planning," "requirements development," "configuration management," and "quality assurance."

Table 7.1: Process Areas of CMMI-DEV v1.2 and the Level-of-Effort Required to Make ADW Compliant by Specific Goal

Process Category / Process Area	Maturity Level Supported			ADW Adjustments Needed		
				Specific Goal 1	Specific Goal 2	Specific Goal 3
Project Management						
Project Planning	2			None	Small	None
Project Monitoring and Control	2			Small	None	—
Supplier Agreement Management	2			None	None	—
Integrated Project Management		3		None	None	—
Risk Management		3		Small	Small	Small
Quantitative Project Management			4	Small	Small	—
Engineering						
Requirements Management		3		Small	—	—
Requirements Development		3		None	Small	Small
Technical Solution		3		None	None	None
Product Integration		3		None	None	None
Verification		3		Small		—
Validation		3		None	Small	Small
Engineering Support						
Configuration Management	2			None	None	None
Quality Assurance	2			None	Small	—
Measurement and Analysis	2			Small	Small	—
Decision Analysis and Resolution		3		Small	—	—
Causal Analysis and Resolution			5	None	Small	—
Process Management						
Organizational Process Focus		3		Small	Small	Small
Organizational Process Definition		3		Small	—	—
Organizational Training		3		Modest	Modest	—
Organizational Process Performance			4	Small	—	—
Organizational Innovation and Deployment			5	None	None	—

Maturity Levels: 1: Initial, 2: Managed, 3: Defined, 4: Quantitatively Managed, 5: Optimizing

However, some of the other process areas, such as "Technical Solution" and "Organizational Process Focus," will require digging a bit deeper into the SEI's write-up before they begin to make sense.

According to CMM, as an organization masters different sets of process areas, it can claim higher and higher levels of "process maturity." Our table also indicates for each process area the maturity level that it supports. All told, there are five such maturity levels an organization can attain:

ML1—Initial: An organization's processes are ad hoc and chaotic.

ML2—Managed: Projects are planned and executed in accordance to policy.

ML3—Defined: The organization has made the effort to define a standard approach to pursuing development projects, and each project tailors its particular process from this standard.

ML4—Quantitatively Managed: The organization has defined quantitative measures and goals for process quality, and uses them to manage ongoing projects.

ML5—(Continually) Optimizing: The organization continually improves upon the quality and capability of its process using the quantitative measures derived in Maturity Level 4.

For an IT organization to claim a particular maturity level, it must document that for each process area included in that maturity level it has achieved a list of "specific goals," the entity drawn below the process areas and to the right on Figure 7.1. For example, the most common maturity level goal is ML3 which, referring to our table, requires achievement of specific goals in 12 process areas, including Risk Management, Requirements Development, and Validation.

The specific goals for Requirements Development, for example, consist of "Develop Customer Requirements," "Develop Product Requirements," and "Analyze and Validate Requirements." As can be seen on Figure 7.1, each specific goal can in turn involve one or more Specific Practices. The Specific Practices for "Develop Product Requirements," for example, include "establish product requirements," "allocate product component requirements," and "identify interface requirements."

So far, we have focused upon only the right side of Figure 7.1. As one might gather by glancing at the figure, CMM with all its components can be challenging to learn. Luckily there are a couple of shortcuts that make the model understandable, at least for the purposes of judging whether a proposed methodology such as ADW is anywhere close to being a "mature" process. The first shortcut is "focus on the specific goals and ignore the Generics." Generic Goals, because they apply widely to development efforts, are very abstract—the IT version of "Mom and apple pie."

Table 7.2 lists CMM's current Generic Goals, where we see such notions as "Monitor and Control the Process" and "Stabilize Subprocess Performance." These are worthy objectives but one immediately wonders how CMM believes these common goals should be accomplished. The specific goals are the answer, for they spell out exactly how to achieve the Generic Goals within each Practice Area. As a general rule, then, when a shop implements the Specific Goals, they achieve the Generics. So, for at least the first pass, we can safely focus solely on the right side of Figure 7.1.

Table 7.2: CMMI-DEV Generic Goals and Practices
GG1 Achieve Specific Goals
GP1.1 Perform Specific Practices
GG2 Institutionalize a Managed Process
GP2.1 Establish an Organizational Policy
GP2.2 Plan the Process
GP2.3 Provide Resources
GP2.4 Assign Responsibility
GP2.5 Train People
GP2.6 Manage Configurations
GP2.7 Identify and Involve Relevant Stakeholders
GP2.8 Manage and Control the Process
GP2.9 Objectively Evaluate Adherence
GP2.10 Review Status with Higher Level Management
GG3 Institutionalize a Defined Process
GP 3.1 Establish a Defined Process
GP 3.2 Collect Improvement Information
GG4 Institutionalize a Quantitatively Managed Process
GP4.1 Establish Quantitative Objectives for the Process
GP4.2 Establish Subprocess Performance
GG5 Institutionalize an Optimizing Process
GP 5.1 Ensure Continuous Process Improvement
GP 5.2 Correct Root Cause of Problems

The second shortcut we found for our analysis is "focus on the required and the expected elements and ignore the informative ones." No doubt adapting to the innumerable ways IT organizations have devised to develop quality systems, SEI categorized only a small portion of its model components as "required," a bit more as "expected," and the overwhelming remainder as "informative." Because the specific goals and practices are still rather large concepts, CMM enumerates the subpractices and typical work products IT organizations often utilize in these areas, but these lists are informative and in no way mandatory.

Reconsidering Figure 7.1 with these two shortcuts in mind, we can see a straightforward game plan for quickly appraising whether ADW is CMM "compliant" and what maturity level an Agile BI program might achieve. For each process area we can evaluate whether ADW includes all the related Specific Practices. We can tally our results by noting at the specific goal level the degree of adjustments we would have to make to ADW for it to achieve each goal. The right three columns of Table 7.1 display the results of this analysis for the specific goals comprising all four Process Categories.

CALMLY COUNTERING THE "IMMATURITY" LABEL

Anyone urging their IT department to give Agile Data Warehousing a try will inevitably encounter some IT manager who dismisses the notion by claiming that any Agile method is "immature." Actually this summary condemnation consists of two different assertions. First, that any method based on an Agile approach cannot lead to a mature method, and secondly, any method the IT department adopts should be something like CMM-compliant. We have a six-part rebuttal to this double-barreled criticism, which we designed to create some "breathing room" for the ADW advocate by simultaneously fostering legitimate doubts as to whether standards such as CMM should be followed blindly, and demonstrating that ADW can meet the criteria CMM sets forth:

1. CMM is often too exacting or expensive for a particular IT organization.
2. CMM is not as restrictive as many people suppose, and actually allows considerable room for iterative and incremental methods.
3. Agile is only an approach. As an actual method, ADW has had many features added to it, all of which support CMM practices.
4. Multiple methods based on an Agile approach have been shown to be CMM compliant, including one by Microsoft.
5. ADW contains most of what CMM stipulates; its few omissions can be backfilled with only a small amount of effort if deemed necessary.

6. IT organizations actually achieve better economies of scale by delaying full CMM compliance till the second half of a large undertaking, and ADW offers a prudent path to such "incremental maturity."

How many of these points Agile proponents should deploy will, of course, depend on the exact criticism they are trying to counter. We have taken the time to explore these notions in the sections that follow because knowing them well will allow Agile advocates to elicit better opportunities in an IT profession that is growing progressively rigid in the face of increasing demands for "compliance."

POINT 1—CMM MAY BE OVERKILL

Just because CMM is ubiquitously accepted and very thorough does not mean that CMM Level 5 compliance is the proper goal for every IT organization developing software. Though SEI claims that some organizations have found a 15-to-1 productivity gain when CMM was employed to guide the development process improvement, one suspects that those case studies might have been "cherry picked," because the CMM model is often criticized for being too meticulous, for making programs that adopt it too bureaucratic, and for being far too expensive to implement and certify.

SEI itself has stated that the full certification process is intense, rigorous, and expensive. Accenture, for one, reported spending 8045 hours—six months' solid work for a team of eight—implementing the CMMI Product Suite. And each successive level of competence involves additional effort: the median time to move from CMM Level 1 to Level 2 is 24 months, according to Gartner. IBM's CMMI Level 5 certification required a review of 1100 developers in four cities, testing compliance with 425 distinct CMMI practices; its SCAMPI audit required five weeks' work from a team of nine auditors. As of this writing, less than 600 firms had attained certifications—remarkably low for a well-crafted reference model that has been in the public domain for nearly 20 years. [Braue 2004]

There is no escaping the fact that CMM is a complex model to implement. Version 1.2 of CMMI-DEV has grown past 550 distinct subpractices to be considered, and the model description and assessment guide total over 1,200 pages. We saw briefly above the many components contained in the model, a good deal of them intersecting in recursive patterns that are difficult to verbalize, let alone follow. Take for example, SEI's description of how just one of its Generic Practice impacts a similarly named specific goal :

Generic Practice 2.2, "Plan the Process," applied to the "Project Planning" process can be characterized as "plan to plan" and covers planning project planning activities.

With 1,200 pages of verbiage such as this excerpt, it is easy to understand why getting the organization sufficiently aligned to where it could even consider a CMM assessment is an excruciating process. In general, a CMM assessment entails a pattern common to many compliance programs:

- Formally describe what you are going to do.
- Train everyone on the procedures.
- Do it exactly how you said you would.
- Document that you did it that way.
- Audit that everyone involved was trained and has followed the procedures.
- Verify that the documentation is complete.

Such an exacting standard tends to foster IT programs that are overly concerned with properly filling out forms and seemingly obsessed with "process for process's sake." Many members of CMM-aspiring IT organizations often comment that the real goal of developing software as quickly, accurately, and inexpensively as possible is entirely forgotten. Speaking figuratively, if the objective is to get a hundred people to walk twenty miles from Point A to Point B, does it matter if we declare before hand the color of shoes they will wear, see to it that they march in lock step, or document where every step landed?

DECIDING UPON PLAN-DRIVEN OR ADAPTIVE METHODS

As we will see below, CMM is not the rigidly waterfall-based framework that many people assume, but it does share a major drawback with plan-driven paradigms: it saddles the organization with enormous opportunity costs. In the next chapter we introduce a classic device called the "Risk Exposure Analysis." As we will see when we consider that analysis, the more time a team spends on planning a process or its formalization, the more opportunities the organization will miss because the necessary software was not delivered in time. Accordingly, an enterprise must weigh the benefits of intensive planning in its process against the opportunity costs those practices incur, the optimal strategy in choosing between the extremes must be "IT organizations should go Agile except for situations where there is a compelling reason to ignore its superior economics."

We understand that companies often find themselves in a situation where a more careful, formal, or plan-driven method is necessary, such as when they are subject to external audits or they serve a customer base that demands something akin to a CMM certification. Such a situation may well be the motivation behind an IT manager who hastily judges Agile approaches as unusably immature. In that case, one will doubly value the remaining points in our "rebuttal" where we demonstrate that Agile can be CMM compliant as easily as any method.

POINT 2—CMM NOT AS RIGID AS MANY SUPPOSE

Many IT managers believe that CMM only supports a waterfall approach to systems development. Indeed, a quick glance at the model's outline strongly suggests a plan-driven, single pass approach. It takes more time than most managers can afford to find buried in the text the many ways CMM supports iterative methods. Yet latitude for time boxed methods definitely exists, and careful reflection on the model as a whole will reveal even greater degrees of freedom than that.

On first look, CMM certainly seems locked into a waterfall approach. Consider the practices included and their ordering for the important processes of project planning, requirement management, and development (the latter of which CMM calls the "Technical Solution" process area) that we have listed in **Table 7.3**: *Estimate*, then *plan*, then *gather requirements*. *High level design* precedes *detailed design*, which is followed by "make or buy" the solution. To traditionally schooled IT professionals, this is the waterfall method in its purest form. It is no wonder that most managers believe that Agile can never be CMM compliant.

Table 7.3: Sample CMM Practices for Planning, Requirements, and Development	
Establish Estimates • Estimate the Scope of the Project • Establish Estimates of Work Product and Task Attributes • Define Project Lifecycle • Determine Estimates of Effort and Cost Develop a Project Plan • Establish the Budget and Schedule • Identify Project Risks • Plan for Data Management • Plan for Project Resources • Plan for Needed Knowledge and Skills • Plan Stakeholder Involvement • Establish the Project Plan Obtain Commitment to the Plan • Review Plans That Affect the Project • Reconcile Work and Resource Levels • Obtain Plan Commitment	Obtain An Understanding Of Requirements • Develop Customer Requirements • Establish Product and Product Component Requirements • Allocate Product Component Requirements • Identify Interface Requirements • Analyze and Validate Requirements Obtain Commitment To Requirements Design The Product Or Product Component Establish A Technical Data Package Design Interfaces Using Criteria Perform Make, Buy, Or Reuse Analyses Implement The Design Develop Product Support Documentation

However, given enough time with the model, one begins to find suggestions that such rigidity is not what the model makers had in mind. In fact, in several places CMM's authors explicitly support an iterative approach and counsel against a single-pass, plan-driven approach. Consider the following passages, which we have listed by the process area in which they occur (all emphasis ours):

Project Planning

Developing a complete project plan and the project's defined process **may require an iterative effort** if a complex, multi-layered, integrated team structure is being deployed. [SEI 2006, p155]

Requirements

Requirements are identified and refined **throughout the phases of the product lifecycle**. [SEI 2006, p389]

Since stakeholder needs, expectations, constraints, and limitations should be clearly identified and understood, an iterative process is used **throughout the life of the project** to accomplish this objective. [SEI 2006, p391]

Design

Prototypes or pilots may be used as a means of gaining sufficient knowledge to develop a technical data package or a complete set of requirements. [SEI 2006, p456]

Validation and Verification

… Some questions that are raised by processes associated with the Verification and Validation process areas may be resolved by processes associated with the Requirements Development or Product Integration process area. **Recursion and iteration of these processes enable the project to ensure quality** in all components of the product before it is delivered to the customer. [SEI 2006, p62]

Product Integration

[Product integration is] more than just a one-time assembly of the product components at the conclusion of design and fabrication. [Integration] **can be conducted incrementally, using an iterative process** of assembling product components, evaluating them, and then assembling more product components.

This process may begin with analysis and simulations (e.g., ... **rapid prototypes ... and physical prototypes**) and steadily progress through increasingly more realistic incremental functionality until the final product is achieved. There is a high probability that the product, integrated in this manner, will pass product verification and validation. [SEI 2006, p293]

Clearly, CMM is not locked into the waterfall paradigm, and in fact it advocates building systems the most intelligent way possible. Why would we have thought otherwise? Because our traditional training causes us to impute to CMM a traditional intent and organization that it does not contain. First, those of us that have been classically trained in waterfall methods approach the CMM documentation with consternation when we find the chapters on process areas arranged alphabetically. Without thinking about it, we begin reading it in the order that we understand the phases of software development—first chapters on planning, then requirements, design, make and buy, and finally validation. Because the iterative comments are buried in the non-required elaborations and subpractices, we overlook them at first and thus never encounter any notion that conflicts the waterfall "baggage" we bring to the framework.

Secondly, when we first read the text of the process areas we mistake it for a sequenced list of steps. We think of CMM as a method rather than a framework for process improvement. Careful reading of the model reveals that CMM is not a list of actions to take and the order in which to execute them. Instead, it is a list of practices one should find at each stage of maturity for the organization. The higher level components CMM considers "required" and "expected." Lower level components are simply examples of what many shops do and are completely optional. Because they have to be listed in some kind of order, the authors arranged them in the sequence suggested by related inputs and outputs, which makes them read on first pass like a complete waterfall method. However, we should not misunderstand this logical sequencing of optional subpractices as somehow chaining CMM to a waterfall approach.

As a framework from which to pick and choose practices, CMM is in fact silent on the macro-organization of the work. This aspect more than any other notion allows Agile-based methods to be CMM compliant. Agile implementations can include all the practices that mature IT organizations follow, but distribute the practices across the work to be completed in the manner they see fit. If we look at ADW through CMM eyes, we see that the method still performs planning, then requirements, then design followed by coding and validation, but in a *time multiplexed* manner, as depicted in **Figure 7.2**. Time multiplexing the traditional waterfall phases locates the portion of each phase that would be applied to a given module together in time while maintaining the traditional order in which each type of work would occur. Nothing in CMM opposes this approach to organizing the development effort. In fact, judging from excerpts above, the authors would probably endorse.

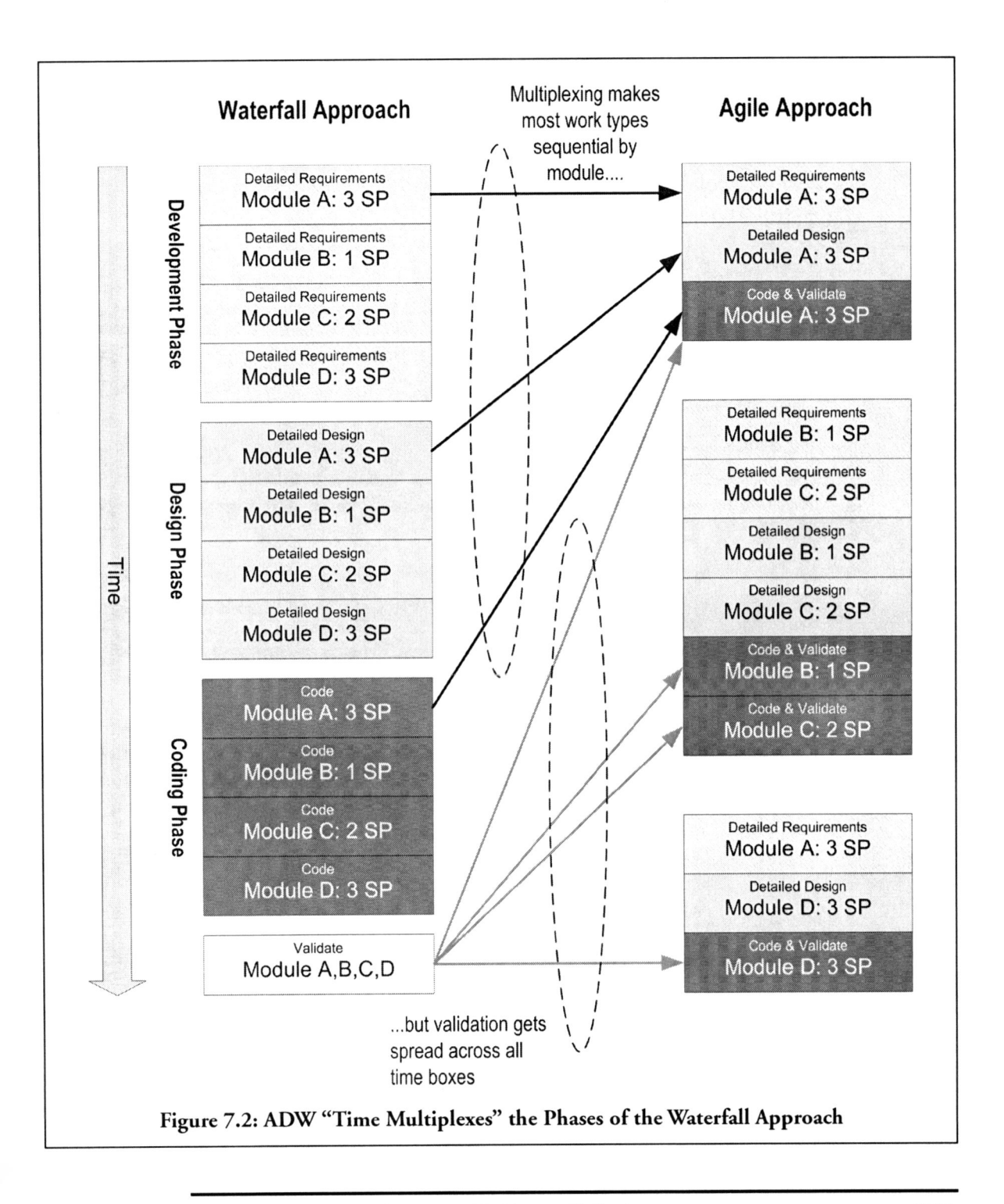

Figure 7.2: ADW "Time Multiplexes" the Phases of the Waterfall Approach

POINT 3—KEEP APPROACHES & METHODS DISTINCT

Given the discussion above, it will be no surprise that much of the "Agile is an immature method because it's not CMM compliant" criticism can be deflected by simply establishing among the parties involved a shared understanding that the accusation is mixing apples and oranges.

Agile is an *approach*—a particular understanding of the nature of a starting situation with a high-level, almost philosophical set of macro-actions that can be applied to solve a broad class of problems.

CMM is a *framework*—a set of components that are generally applicable to a large class of problems from which the practitioner selects the most efficacious items to apply to a particular challenge.

ADW is a *method*—a step by step recipe for action that can repeatedly solve a well defined class of problems. It often has reusable diagrams, templates, and training materials to guide the actions of the team to higher levels of quality and to get them started more quickly.

In order to gently rebut those who would call Agile Data Warehousing "immature," the advocate should remind them that ADW started with the Agile *approach*, added practices from the CMM *framework* in order to arrive at a *method* that will, once the teams are fully developed, deliver business intelligence applications more economically and quickly while meeting the customer's needs far more faithfully, i.e., "cheaper, faster, better."

To call Agile a method is to suggest that it is a ready-to-use recipe for building applications, whereas in truth it has enormous areas that must be filled with context-specific tasks before anyone on the team would know what to do first, and what format the results should take. To say that "Agile" is not CMM compliant is, then, to simultaneously state the obvious and miss the point. ADW is the method, and as we will see below, it has every chance of passing a CMM assessment.

POINT 4—MULTIPLE AGILE METHODS CMM COMPLIANT

With the notion of approach versus method firmly established, the ADW advocate can rebut the charge of "immaturity" by citing several methods based on Agile approaches that have been assessed to be CMM mature.

Microsoft's Solutions Framework

The best known example is the Microsoft Solutions Framework which comes in two flavors: a starter "Agile" version and an expanded "CMMI" version. Microsoft describes MSF for CMMI as "a highly iterative, agile software development process featuring adaptive planning that meets the requirements for the Software Engineering Institute's CMMI level three. It provides a smooth transition all the way to level five." [Microsoft 2007]

According to D.J. Anderson, Microsoft's Program Manager for the Solutions Framework:

> [MSF for CMMI] introduces an agile approach to CMMI and has extended the guidance from MSF for Agile Software Development with additional formality, reviews, verification and audit. In this way, MSF for CMMI Process Improvement relies on process and conformance to process rather than relying purely on trust and the ability of the individual team members. [Anderson 2005a]

AgileTek's Agile+

A similar example of building a CMM compliant method upon an Agile framework is AgileTek's "Agile+" methodology. AgileTek is a project-based software services firm with customers in insurance, chemical manufacturing, pharmaceuticals, and telecommunications. In 2003 it introduced its Agile+ methodology which combined XP with traditional software best practices, so as to be suitable for large, mission-critical applications. Conscious of large companies' interest in CMM, it added the features needed to align the method with Maturity Level 3. [Davis 2007] Since its introduction, AgileTek has employed its method on projects involving hundreds of people and resulting in more than a million lines of code.

BoldTech's BoldDelivery

Founded in 1996, BoldTech is a national U.S. software firm providing on-site and offshore development solutions to top tier telecom companies such as AT&T, T-Mobile, Verizon, and SBC. It developed a home-grown Agile method called BoldDelivery which, when deployed in its Hangzhou, China "Global Delivery Center," powered it to be one of the world's top China-based solution providers.

BoldTech has used its Agile method to deliver large applications such as customer relationship management systems and those based upon enterprise application integration (EAI) and electronic data interchange (EDI) technologies.

In 2005 its Agile method passed a rigorous SCAMPI level A assessment for CMMI-DEV Level 3 maturity. A year later, after BoldTech added to its method statistical analysis technologies for identifying and solving software development process issues, BoldDelivery passed its Maturity Level 4 certification. [SEI 2006]

Point 5—ADW Contains What CMM Requires

Our goal in this chapter is to demonstrate that ADW could be CMM compliant if the practicing organization wanted to take the time to get their implementation officially appraised. In the points made so far, we have considered CMM at a high-level, suggesting that a) airtight CMM compliance is overkill for most IT organizations and b) nothing in the model would ban ADW outright. To be thorough, we should also consider the detailed practices comprising CMM and judge whether each can be found in ADW or whether it can be added on without too much cost or disruption.

When we described the CMM model earlier with the help of Figure 7.1, we discovered two shortcuts: consider only the specific goals of the model, and focus only upon the required and expected elements. As noted in the figure, appraising ADW for CMM compliance reduces to simply examining at the Specific Practice level whether ADW contains 174 elements. For each practice, we will need to appraise whether meeting CMM's stipulations will require a large, medium, or small adjustment to ADW, or no adjustment at all. We will tally the results at the level of the specific goals, the parent containers for the specific practices.

Tables 7.1 through 7.3, which we glanced at earlier, contain the results of this assessment of specific goals, grouped by the CMM Practice Category to which each belongs. The conclusion of our analysis can be expressed quite simply: ADW is very close to supporting the CMM model completely. Of the 48 specific goals comprising CMMI-DEV 1.2 (released 2007), ADW meets 28 (58%) of them with no adjustment necessary. Of the remaining 20, only 18 (38%) require a small adjustment, most needing only that a) the team take a moment to formally define a process that they are following already, or b) the PCA scribe the decisions made during a sprint planning session and place the record in the program's document repository. Only the two remaining specific goals will need a moderate effort from the ADW team to bring itself into alignment with CMM's requirements. These goals both belong to the Organizational Training Process Area, and the adjustment will involve defining a formal training regimen for participants in the warehousing program and tracking which teammates have completed the individual training modules.

Whereas documenting the appraisal of all 174 specific practices would take far too much space, in the remainder of this section we present for each specific goal a sample of the thinking that went into our assessment of its component practices. Reviewing these individual assessments will give readers not only a feel for how little adjustment ADW will require if their IT organizations choose to invest in a formal CMM appraisal, but also a good introduction into the details of the CMMI-DEV v1.2 model.

In the remainder of this section we step through each specific goal of the model, listing (in quotes) a couple of the more interesting or challenging requirements found in the text of its Specific Practices. To these excerpts we add our conclusion (in bold) of how large an adjustment ADW will need to make to support the practice and some comments regarding that assessment.

While reading through the selected notes below, it is important to keep in mind a few characteristics of Agile Data Warehousing that we have discussed in previous chapters:

1. Though ADW is based on Scrum/XP, we have added two "wrappers" to make it more robust as a true IT program comprising multiple projects: a PMI-style project charter and critical chain program management. The former provides an opportunity to complete many of the traditional aspects of a well-run project, especially the work on a solid project charter, a concept of operations document, make vs. buy decisions, stakeholder involvement, and a risk management plan. The critical chain program wrapper provides for a meta scrum which will serve as a medium for organizational dissemination of innovations that CMM prescribes.

2. ADW, as presented in this book, is the baseline method. The Scrum Master is charged with keeping the team true to the current method. During sprint retrospectives the team identifies policies that would improve their implementation of the method, and the Scrum Master ensures that those new policies are followed in the next sprint. Thus the method is under change control because only innovations accepted during the sprint retrospectives are put into place.

3. ADW adds a Project Communication Assistant who, as we have seen already, addresses maintaining project communication with the stakeholders so that the effort does not rely entirely on the Product Owner. The PCA role can be expanded to draft the many formal statements of current practices that CMM calls for, as well as to scribe and archive the planning sessions, so that the team achieves without too much cost the high level of documentation that the CMM model requires.

Project Management Process Category

Project Planning

"Estimates of project planning parameters are established and maintained"

No Adjustment Needed

At the comprehensive planning level, ADW uses such notions as Number of Stories, Total Story Points, Team Velocity, Release Burndown Chart.

Teams take on a finer planning level within the sprints, where they add such notions as Number of Tasks, Total Original Labor Estimates (OLEs), Sprint Burndown Chart.

"A project plan is established and maintained as the basis for managing the project"

"Identify and analyze project risks"

"Plan for the management of project data"

Small Adjustments Needed

ADW needs the Product Owner and Scrum Master to probe for risks during the story conference and task planning sessions. Have teams estimate the severity of those risks that are identified before development work begins, and review the accuracy of these appraisals during sprint retrospectives.

Have the Product Owner, Scrum Master, and Project Communication Assistant collaborate on maintaining a document repository for project artifacts.

Project Management and Control

"Actual performance and progress of the project are monitored against the project plan"

"Corrective actions are managed to closure when the results deviate from the plan"

"Monitor the actual values of the project planning parameters against the project plan"

Small Adjustment Needed

ADW provides a release plan and sprint backlog which serves as the team's strategic and tactical plans. This combination must be translated to "planning parameters," however, to meet CMM's requirements. Such a list can be generated from notions already know to the team, such as number of stories, sources, targets, and major modules.

To further meet this requirements, the Solutions Architect needs to listen and record in the team's official "planning parameters" document changes in the application's overall design that would impact any of these basic project scoping counts.

Supplier Agreement Management

"Agreements with suppliers are established and maintained"

No adjustment needed.

Because ADW is a development method, its planning and execution take place after the decision of what to buy and what to develop. ADW still speaks to make vs. buy, however, in the PMI-style project chartering that it recommends. Since a charter addresses the scope, assumptions, resources, and constraints for the project, it should naturally stipulate the portion of the overall solution that is to be purchased so that the development planning is properly focused.

Integrated Project Management

"Use process assets and measurements for estimating and planning the project"

No adjustment needed.

ADW already bases its estimation on reference model and basis-of-estimate cards.

"Integrate project plan and other plans that affect it"

No adjustment needed.

ADW performs program management through meta scrums during which Product Owners from the various teams consider resource re-assignments in order to keep all projects progressing in an optimal fashion.

Risk Management

"Define parameters for analyzing, categorizing, and controlling the risk"

"Maintain the strategy to be used for risk management."

Small Adjustment Needed

As we detailed above in Point 5 of "Countering The Immaturity Label," ADW wraps the program management in a PMI-style project plan which includes a Risk Management plan.

However, as stated for Project Planning, the Product Owner and the Scrum Master should be asked to poll for risk during each sprint planning and retrospective.

As it stands, ADW allows Product Owner to re-assign stories of the release to any upcoming sprint in order to mitigate risk events. This flexibility extends to the meta scrum where the program's collected Product Owners can mitigate risk in any one project by re-assigning resources from other projects that are in a better situation.

Quantitative Project Management

"Performance of selected subprocesses are statistically managed"

"Analytic techniques are used in statistically managing the selected subprocesses"

"Record statistical and quality management data in a repository"

Small Adjustments Needed

ADW already provides team velocity, but could calculate a few more useful metrics for each sprint such as:

- Percentage of stories, story points, and OLEs completed
- Estimated vs. actual labor per task
- Story points and OLEs "burned off" per charged labor hour

With these metrics defined, the Scrum Master needs only to create a database or spreadsheet to record them.

ENGINEERING PROCESS CATEGORY

Requirements Management

"Manage changes to the requirements as they evolve during the project"

Small adjustment needed

CMM prefers extensive stakeholder involvement when it comes to changes in requirements. ADW is silent on this matter, trusting the Product Owner to communicate with other business stakeholders as needed. To meet CMM, the Product Owner's role should be formally stated to include involving and managing input from all business stakeholders, with the help of the Project Communications Assistant. To wit, she needs to a) identify stakeholders that must formally endorse requirements, and b) ensure they endorse the concept-of-operations document, initial release plan (a collection of user stories), and significant revisions to the release plan.

"Maintain bidirectional traceability among the requirements and work products"

Small adjustment needed

Developers will need to record capsule summaries and supporting details in a requirements repository as they uncover them with the Product Owner and other business experts during the sprints. This repository will need a feature where teams can record the relationships between requirements and modules on a many-to-many basis during task planning and development. This is a feature present in most contemporary requirements management packages and easily buildable with a database utility.

Requirements Development

"Stakeholder needs, expectations, constraints, and interfaces are translated into customer requirements.

"... for all phases of the product lifecycle

"... then elaborated to develop product and product component requirements.

"... which are analyzed to balance stakeholder needs and constraints

"... and validated to ensure that they are necessary and sufficient

"... then allocated across product components

"Establish and maintain operational concepts and associated scenarios"

Small Adjustments Needed

Scrum relies on the Product Owner to express all customer requirements. The story cards record operational concepts and associated scenarios, although these will probably need to be transferred to an electronic format to obtain the longevity and document management required by CMM.

ADW assists the Product Owner in deriving the product requirements by incorporating an "Architecture and Design" station along the pipeline delivery, plus the 2-to-1 design efforts for each module which uses the Product Owner as a subject matter expert.

ADW can meet CMM needs by having developers record in a requirements repository capsule the product requirement summaries for the objects they build. This prose will be later retrieved for the Product Owner to use as a Requirements Traceability Matrix during the user demos.

Technical Solution

1. "Product or product component solutions are selected from alternative solutions"
2. "Product or product component designs are developed"
3. "Product components, and associated support documentation, are implemented from their designs"
4. "Design product component interfaces using established criteria"
5. "Product components, and associated support documentation, are implemented from their designs"

No Adjustments Needed

Concerning requirement 1, alternative solutions for products and components are considered before the ADW project is even initiated as part of the effort's concept phase. The development project is defined to address the gaps not covered by a buy or reuse decision.

Considering requirements 2 through 4, ADW establishes an architecture squad that specifies interface requirements for each module before sending it to developers. These specifications are drawn using ADW's reference model which serves as a baseline design.

Regarding requirement 5, ADW precedes development with design, though a) it is multiplexed to span design and coding one module at a time, and b) design details are completed on a just-in-time basis for a given module.

Product Integration

"Prepare for product integration by determining component integration sequence"

"Maintain the environment needed to support the integration"

"Maintain procedures and criteria for integration of the product components"

"Confirm each component is properly identified, functions, and interfaces as required"

"Assemble product components and evaluate assembly"

"Package and Deliver the Product or Product Component"

"Package the assembled product and deliver it to the customer"

No Adjustments Needed

In ADW, developers submit their modules to the Automated and Continuous Integration Testing (ACIT) facility after they have finished unit testing them. As we detailed in Chapter 5, the ACIT invokes a suite of daily validation runs that demonstrates the functionality and quality of both the changed and unchanged components of the application, packaged as a whole. This continual integration of the components demonstrates the first several points required above. A run of the ACIT validation suite that finishes with no exceptions to expected results further demonstrates the proper functioning required by the next two points. The remaining requirements are covered implicitly by the ACIT's daily build and validation, because at any point the Product Owner, representing the customer, can choose to "take delivery" by instructing IT's

Operations team to promote into production the release candidate now functioning perfectly in the ACIT.

Validation

"Preparation for validation is conducted."

Small adjustment needed

Product Owner needs to generate the Requirements Traceability Matrix from the Requirements Repository before each user demo.

"Establish and maintain procedures and criteria for validation."

Small adjustment needed

Product Owner needs to record and maintain a "standard set" of criteria she checks before accepting a module during user demo reviews.

"The product or product components are validated to ensure that they are suitable for use in their intended operating environment"

No adjustment needed

This practice is inherent in ADW's use of user demos. Flaws in this process are detected and addressed in the sprint retrospectives.

Verification

"Peer reviews are performed on selected work products"

Small adjustment needed

Need only to formalize the interaction with the Operations Team which will need to be reviewed during sprint retrospective.

"Analyze data about preparation, conduct, and results of the peer reviews."

Small adjustment needed

Prepare a formal response sheet for the Operations Team to record their conclusions and discuss the contents of these once completed during a sprint retrospective.

"Selected work products are verified against their specified requirements"

Small adjustment needed

Need only to include discussion of a handoff review in a sprint retrospective.

ENGINEERING SUPPORT PRACTICE CATEGORY

Configuration Management

"Baselines of identified work products are established"

"Identify work products that will be placed under configuration management"

No Adjustment Needed

It is a rare IT department today that does not practice configuration management using a third party tool. In ADW, the "daily build" sent to the automated testing facility is pulled from the change management tool, verifying that each day's baseline is complete.

Quality Assurance

"Adherence of the performed process and associated work products and services to applicable process descriptions, standards, and procedures is objectively evaluated"

"Noncompliance issues are objectively tracked and communicated, and resolution is ensured"

No Adjustments Needed

ADW ensures quality through many mechanisms, including:
- User demos (end-user visible quality issues)
- Test led development (coding accuracy and fault tolerance issues)

- Automated and continuous integration testing (module integration quality issues)
- IT Operations Verification (coding and external system integration standards)

We stipulated for validation above that the Product Owner needs to define a standard set of acceptance criteria for use during user demo sessions. With that in place, ADW needs no further adjustment to meet CMM's requirements in this process area.

Measurement and Analysis

"Measurement objectives and activities are aligned with identified information needs and objectives"

"Measurement results, which address identified information needs and objectives, are provided"

No Adjustment Necessary

ADW provides story points and OLE estimates, velocity figures, and burndown charts. We added several additional metrics, as mentioned in Quantitative Project Management above. Any set of metrics is subject to criticism and improvement via the sprint retrospective sessions, so that the measurements provided will match the information needed.

Decision Analysis and Resolution

"Establish and maintain guidelines to determine which issues are subject to a formal evaluation process, and criteria for evaluating alternatives, and the relative ranking of these criteria"

"Identify alternative solutions to address issues"

"Evaluate alternative solutions using the established criteria and methods"

Small adjustment needed

Within the ADW project teams, the Scrum Master needs only to draft and maintain in the document control system the "official" steps for problem analysis and decision making.

Similarly, at the Program Level, the meta scrum Master needs to formalize ahead of time the steps the Product Owners will employ to analyze and resolve challenges, most of them being critical chain buffer recovery issues addressed by re-assigning product themes to the available teams.

Causal Analysis and Resolution

"Root causes of defects and other problems are systematically addressed to prevent their future occurrence"

"Causal analysis and resolution data is recorded for use across the project and organization"

Small adjustments needed

ADW includes a role for a Project Communication Assistant. The sprint retrospective is ADW's facility of identify, analyzing, and rectifying problems in the process and the work product. To meet the CMM requirement, the PCA can capture the minutes of these retrospectives and route the results to a Lessons Learned document available to project managers outside of the team or program.

PROCESS MANAGEMENT PRACTICE CATEGORY

Organizational Process Focus

1. "Strengths, weaknesses, and improvements for the process assessed periodically"
2. "Establish and maintain the description of the process needs and objectives"
3. "Deploy organizational process assets across the organization"
4. "Monitor the implementation of the standard processes and use of process assets"
5. "Incorporate ... improvement information into the organizational process assets"

Small Adjustments Required

ADW already contains the sprint retrospectives which cover points 1, 4, and 5.

Having the Project Communication Assistant scribe the retrospectives will cover point 2.

Instructing the participants in the program's meta scrum to collect process improvement ideas from individual team retrospectives and send them back out to all teams will cover point 3.

Organizational Process Definition

"Maintain organizational process assets that include:

1. "standard processes"
2. "lifecycle model"
3. "tailoring criteria and guidelines"
4. "repository of relevant process measures"
5. "work environment standards (e.g. tools, training)"

Small adjustment required

The ADW program will need to establish a library and then simply "populate" it with contents of this book to cover points 1 and 2.

Tailoring guidelines for point 3 can be derived from the "Scrum/XP as a CMM Preprocessor" discussion of Figure 7.1 later in this chapter.

Points 4 and 5 will require adding to this library some straightforward prose, mostly describing the tools and measurements the team decides it needs.

Organizational Training

"Establish an organizational training capability which supports the organization's management and technical roles"

"Provide necessary training for individuals to perform their roles effectively"

Moderate Adjustments Needed

ADW provides a staged learning path for the team as a whole which specifies roles and responsibilities at a high and medium level. At greater levels of detail, the method supports the "management and technical roles" via its notion of "self-organized teams."

ADW also provides most of the concepts needed to train for the Product Owner and Scrum Master, especially after they have attended a basic Scrum training session.

For the first requirement, an ADW program will need to formalize the training effort to meet CMM requirements. Prose describing the training needed by role and the materials used should be added to the program's Process Asset Library. A "training coordinator" role will need to be defined and staffed.

To meet the other requirement, the training coordinator will need to simply track training required by role, and evidence of each member's completion of the training steps prescribed.

Organizational Process Performance

"Maintain performance baselines and models which characterize the expected process performance of the organization's set of standard processes"

Small Adjustment Needed

To meet this requirement, an ADW program needs to:

a) pick a subset of processes that are either already tracked or easily measured and monitored (CMM's Quantitative Project Management process area lists several candidates)

b) add these measures to those that are tracked across each sprint

c) add some forecasting formulas to link those measures that can be taken early in a release with the likely values of those that can only be measured late in the process

Organizational Innovation and Deployment

"Select process and technology improvements which will contribute to meeting quality and process-performance objectives"

"Deploy improvements so that the organization's processes and technologies are continually and systematically deployed"

No Adjustments Needed

Given that the "organization" is the ADW program, and that it already promotes a meta scrum that monitors and disperses lessons learned by the individual teams, these CMM requirements are already met by the method.

POINT 6—BETTER ECONOMIES BY DELAYING ON CMM

From the analysis of Point 5 it should be clear that CMM calls for only relatively standard IT practices and that ADW can be tuned to support CMM in a straight-forward manner. In this section we wish to comment on the economics of CMM compliance, arguing that the best strategy may be to meet the model's requirements incrementally for any given project.

Incremental compliance within a single project is allowed under the CMM framework. SEI intends their model to be the baseline process for a software development shop. One of the first steps to any project is to "tailor" the baseline process to meet the needs of any particular project about to commence. Consider this excerpt from the definition of Capability Level 3: "A defined process is a managed (capability level 2) process that is tailored from the organization's set of standard processes...." Taken together, the freedom to tailor the baseline process and the support for prototyping we underlined above create the flexibility for a project to "ramp up" to CMM compliance rather than starting in full alignment with every Specific Practice on day one.

Let us set the stage for this proposition by posing the question "where in the business process of developing a new software application should the formal CMM-compliant process begin?" If one takes the extreme position of "day one," then the process is already out of compliance because there had to be plenty of informal conversations about the business problem (requirements) and how the new software could solve it (design) in the process of simply deciding to undertake the project. Many of these conversations of high-level requirements and designs probably did not get officially scribed, so that later validation efforts will not be able trace the path between them. Obviously, a project must pick a place somewhere between an application's first conception and its eventual delivery where full CMM should kick in. Scouring the CMM model will yield only the notion that the process that builds the software must include SEI's long list of recommended practices. Yes, the inputs to the process must be captured and placed under change control, but beyond that requirement, CMM says nothing about the pre-process that generates those inputs.

So, the practitioner must pick a point in an application's life cycle where the formal development process must begin. As we will see in the risk exposure analysis of Figure 8.2, this transition should occur as late as possible in order to avoid incurring ruinous opportunity costs. Drawing upon the stages of ADW team development we examined in the previous chapter, we can refine the key question to be "As the Scrum Master introduces each progressive element of the ADW method, when is the process capable of being CMM compliant?"

Figure 7.3 presents an answer to this question. Each ADW Scrum Master and meta scrum council will have to redraw this diagram for their own particular circumstance, but the approach portrayed should take a lot of the uncertainty out of doing so. In the middle stratum of the diagram we have placed the project timeline, broken into phases that will support an increasingly CMM-ready process. Above the timeline we have placed selected milestones that the team achieves in their incremental implementation of ADW. On the bottom half of the diagram we show the "compliance themes" that these ADW milestones address. The degree to which these compliance themes are supported is depicted to the right as timelines of their own, because the steady refinement of the team's process propels them to increasingly higher capabilities in terms of those themes.

As depicted in the diagram, the new project starts with a phase focused upon defining the project as a traditional PMI project manager would strive for, ending with an endorsed Project Charter. Luckily, a PMI-style project charter includes a high-level project plan and a concept of operations, two components that will be eventually required by CMM.

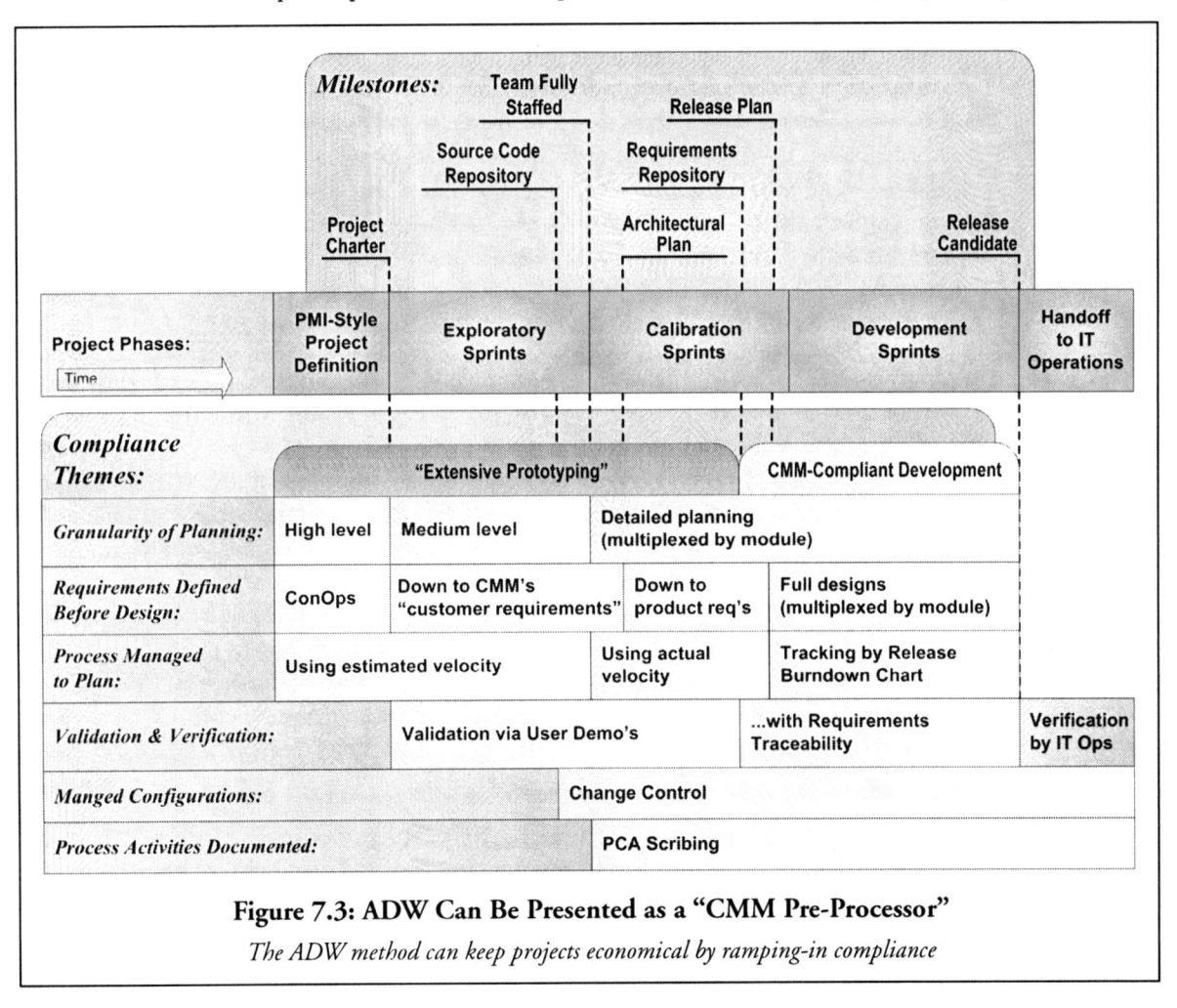

Milestones:		Team Fully Staffed		Release Plan			
		Source Code Repository		Requirements Repository			
	Project Charter			Architectural Plan			Release Candidate

Project Phases: Time →	PMI-Style Project Definition	Exploratory Sprints	Calibration Sprints	Development Sprints	Handoff to IT Operations

Compliance Themes:		"Extensive Prototyping"		CMM-Compliant Development	
Granularity of Planning:	High level	Medium level	Detailed planning (multiplexed by module)		
Requirements Defined Before Design:	ConOps	Down to CMM's "customer requirements"	Down to product req's	Full designs (multiplexed by module)	
Process Managed to Plan:		Using estimated velocity	Using actual velocity	Tracking by Release Burndown Chart	
Validation & Verification:		Validation via User Demo's		...with Requirements Traceability	Verification by IT Ops
Manged Configurations:			Change Control		
Process Activities Documented:			PCA Scribing		

Figure 7.3: ADW Can Be Presented as a "CMM Pre-Processor"
The ADW method can keep projects economical by ramping-in compliance

Once the Project Charter has been endorsed, the team begins "Exploratory Sprints," which produce system prototypes through an Scrum/XP process that generates what CMM would consider "customer requirements" and involves a medium level of planning. The team is now "working to a plan" on a sprint-to-sprint basis using the sprint backlogs and sprint burndown charts, though this in not yet CMM compliant because it covers only the current time box and not the entire project. The Product Owner is validating the team's work product, but this in not yet CMM-compliant validation because the system's features are not being traced back to detailed requirements. During the phase of Exploratory Sprints, the team gets its source code repository in place and begins putting the code for the prototypes under change control, as CMM requires.

With the addition of the Project Communication Assistant to the project, the team is fully staffed and can begin a period of "calibration sprints" in which they learn their average velocity and thus provide the metrics necessary to a) create a release plan, and b) (more importantly to CMM) work to a detailed plan that spans the entire project. With the addition of a Requirements Repository, the team can begin capturing the detailed requirements generated by their interviews with the Product Owner, in a manner that enables validators to trace the features of each model back to the requirements that call for it. Not shown on the figure in order to maintain clarity is the addition of a nightly build of release candidates in the Automated and Continuous Integration Testing facility, a practice which enables the IS Operations Team to begin verifying the internal quality of the application code. Successful ACIT runs prove that the candidate passes all required levels of internal and external integration, as stipulated by CMM.

At this point, the team has all of the practices of a fully mature development process in place, albeit one in which time multiplexes the requirements, design, development, and validate cycle so that they all occur for a given module within the same time box. It is only this latter phase that should be subject to a CMM audit. Everything leading up to this point can be legitimately labeled as "extensive prototyping," and should be understood as a "CMM pre-process" that the team needed in order to get all the CMM-required practices in place. There is no reason to think that the existence of a pre-process phase will somehow prevent the team's development process from passing a CMM assessment. Using the early months of the project's time to prepare higher quality inputs for the formal development effort, such as a requirements through prototyping, is not inherently antithetical to a disciplined development process.

By easing each project into full CMM compliance using Scrum/XP as a CMM pre-processor, ADW saves a large measure of labor costs by not getting overly formal until the project has a bundle of work sufficiently defined to enable detailed planning, requirements, and design. More importantly, with this ramped-in compliance, ADW allows the organization to avoid the bulk of the opportunity costs we will discuss in the next chapter, keeping the software development as "agile" as possible in the face of changing business requirements.

Achieving Maturity Levels 4 and 5

In our practice-by-practice examination of ADW's CMM qualities in Point 5 above, we did not distinguish between maturity levels in order to keep the primary analysis as uncluttered as possible. We should close this chapter, however, by reflecting upon which maturity level ADW might actually achieve in the eyes of SEI.

Most organizations to date have opted for formal assessments up to Maturity Level 3 ("defined") for several reasons. First, referring back to Tables 7.1 through 7.3, we can see that ML3 brings an IT organization up to the point where it is building software using all of the "Engineering" best practices and most of the recommended practices from the Project Management, Engineering Support, and Process Management categories. In practice, pressing on for formal certification for ML4 ("quantitative management") and ML5 ("continual improvement") requires enormous expense. Unless the firm has an external audit or marketing need for formal ML4 and 5 certification, codifying and documenting these practices will yield no greater business results than if they had been pursued informally.

Yet, does ADW include practices required for the business benefits of CMM's quantitative management and continual optimization? Is our method conceptually CMM Level 4 and 5 mature? For Level 4, we refer back to our notes on specific goals "Quantitative Project Management" and "Measurement and Analysis." There we indicated that ADW supports adding metrics to track sprint quality besides team Scrum's beginner set of velocity and remaining labor estimates. It can add, for example, a) percentage of story points and original labor estimates (hours) burned off by accepted stories, and b) story points and OLEs burned off per charged labor hour. Furthermore, through the sprint retrospectives, the team can add whatever additional metrics they believe will help them track and improve their effectiveness, and the Scrum Master can hold them to meeting those expanded goals during the upcoming sprints. These factors will allow ADW teams to claim they are "quantitatively managed," although they may need to distinguish between those metrics that focus upon what CMM calls "single-cause" versus "common-cause" deviations from expected values.

Maturity Level 5's notion of continual process optimization is inherently addressed by the sprint retrospectives that Scrum provides to the method, and ADW's addition of meta scrum's that can survey the lessons learned by each team and deploy the resulting process innovations to the entire ADW program once approved.

The only nuance we found while considering ML4 and 5 for ADW is how to define the "organization" that serves as the focus for Specific Practices in the Process Management category such as "Organizational Process Performance" and "Organizational Innovation and Deployment." Suggesting that the organization be defined as the entire IT department is the easiest answer and may be where a CMM appraiser will begin, however it is an inaccurate notion for the purposes that we are discussing here. The goal of this entire chapter is to assess whether the ADW method includes all the practices necessary to reach the CMM maturity levels. Therefore the proper scope for the term "organization" is the Business Intelligence program in which ADW is being applied.

To say that ADW cannot be Level 5 compliant simply because the larger IT organization has not established a mechanism to universally deploy the lessons learned from its Agile experiment would lead to rejecting the method based upon operations that are entirely outside of its control. Within its sphere of influence, ADW has mechanisms for distributing organizational learning, and therefore—despite Agile the innovations that free if from high-cost formalisms—the method can include everything that CMM requires.

Chapter 8
Managing Adversity

What types of resistance within the organization do Agile teams typically encounter and why?

How can Agile teams mitigate this opposition long enough to prove themselves and their method?

What analyses might persuade IT management in particular to accept and even protect a new Agile team from potential detractors?

Being iconoclastic in its nature, even the most modest Agile project can become a lightning rod for skepticism and opposition in an organization with well-established, traditional information technology and project management functions. These corporate "politics" can easily undermine the best of projects if not addressed and assuaged. Though most of this book focuses upon adapting Scrum/XP to the specifics of data warehousing, how the Scrum Master adapts her project to the specifics of her company will be probably more central to whether the project succeeds. We could not end our presentation of Agile Data Warehousing without alerting readers to the sometimes vehement resistance first Agile projects can foment within the company and sketching some ways to minimize the setbacks that can result.

In our experience, the greatest resistances to an Agile approach come from six directions:

- Managers in the Information Technology (IT) department
- The component IT service groups
- IT service vendors
- The Project or Program Management Office (PMO)
- Business stakeholders outside the sponsoring department
- The members of the warehouse team itself

Left unmanaged, these parties can steadily swarm and decisively cripple an Agile warehouse project long before the team can deliver its first release. In this chapter we provide some ideas on why such opposition often arises and how to avoid making it any worse once it begins. For mitigating the resistance that does take hold, we offer a compact approach that includes forging an alliance with IT management, and then leveraging that relationship. With IT managers providing some shelter, the team can invest further in their rapport with the remaining groups and buy enough time to make a few deliveries, and thus earn the goodwill of the organization. Given the important role of IT managers in this discussion, we offer three key analytical approaches to the business of delivering information systems that we have found useful in practice for cultivating among these influential players an open mind toward Agile approaches.

In developing this chapter, we found countering adversity a difficult topic to discuss for two reasons. First, it can be easy to slip into an outlook of "us versus them" and become Machiavellian in the solutions considered. Such extremism is unrealistic, however, because companies that succeed today do so largely through a high level of teamwork. Any response to internal adversity between departments and managers that strays from predominantly win-win solutions can have little chance of effectiveness in the long run. So in the presentation that follows, we use words such as "antagonists" and "detractor" to denote parties with valid business agendas that conflict with some of the Agile team's objectives. Acknowledging the possibilities of these conflicts is not inherently negative, given that our purpose is to understand why they arise and explore how the ADW team can adapt or negotiate solutions to them.

Furthermore, discussing adversity in a concise fashion requires generalizing about corporate functions across a plethora of different company sizes, products lines, competitive contexts, and executive personalities. Hopefully such generalization will not undermine our goal of merely alerting readers to the multiple parties who might feel vexed by a fast moving, lightweight development method. With even a minimum of context regarding antagonists, we can still present some basic strategies for sidestepping or minimizing the resistance that might arise. Two groups proved difficult to abstract down to a single profile, however. Variations in IT management and the Project Management Offices alter what would be the best strategy towards opposition, so we will begin our discussion of managing adversity with them.

GAINING THE SUPPORT OF IT MANAGERS

In any organization large enough to invest in business intelligence systems, the Information Technology department will have a role in the project. However, this involvement can be anywhere along a wide continuum depending upon the independence of the functional group sponsoring the project and the maturity of the IT department. At one extreme, the sponsoring group acquires project resources without involving IT, and the information department is at an early, mainly reactive stage in its development. In this situation, the ADW team will find itself "unconstrained" by IT, that is, its work methods will be free of technical, process, and governance standards imposed by this group.

At the other end of the spectrum, the sponsoring department is dependent for resources upon a mature IT organization that actively shapes how the company pursues information projects. In this situation, the project will undoubtedly find itself "constrained" by IT in many ways, such as how the application must be designed, documented, and tested before the Operations Support team will allow it to be loaded and executed on the servers in the data center. IT representatives may well sit on the governing board that approves any changes in the project's funding, delivery timeframe, or objectives. Having the ADW project constrained by IT's standards is not inherently a bad situation. Those standards undoubtedly represent many lessons learned, and a project will largely benefit by availing themselves of the guidance they represent. Unfortunately, in some organizations these IT standards become too layered or outdated, or are simply designed to slow the pace of change rather than enable innovation. When these undesirable aspects predominate, the ADW can be headed for conflict with the IT department managers.

When they begin to perceive an unconstructive web of IT standards within the company, the leaders of the ADW team need to first evaluate the relative strength of the department sponsoring the project versus that of the IT group. The weaker the sponsor, the more the ADW Scrum Master and Product Owner should invest in marketing their project to IT managers and discovering a mutually acceptable level of "compliance" with IT's expectations. Beyond gaining IT's assent for reasonable variances from those standards, the warehouse team's objective is also to receive timely and complete support from IT. Disgruntled IT managers and support teams do not always oppose Agile projects overtly. Often they thwart these efforts instead through passive-aggressive tactics such as responding slowly and incompletely when asked for technical information regarding the platforms or tools the ADW team will be using.

Even in situations where the sponsoring department can proceed largely independent of IT, the ADW team will still want to invest in some goodwill because IT managers have access to executives throughout the company. The Agile data warehouse team wants and needs them to speak kindly of the ADW project, even when the Scrum Master and Product Owner are not party to the conversations. Acquiring support from IT Managers is therefore important, and to do so effectively will first require understanding where natural conflicts of interest exist between them and the ADW team.

WHY AGILE MIGHT VEX IT MANAGERS

IT management is consumed with the struggle to deliver applications that provide crucial business services to the other departments in the enterprise. Typically, the integrated systems of present-day organizations have been assembled in a half-planned fashion by prior IT administrations, as well as through merger and acquisitions. This history often makes the infrastructure difficult for even the IT managers to understand, and also subject to sudden interruption in business services that are difficult to diagnose and repair. To make matters worse, most organizations need their IT services to expand and evolve as the business changes. IT directors thus find themselves having to make constant modifications to this infrastructure though it seems fragile in so many ways.

IT managers face further challenges. Systems are very expensive to plan, acquire, and deploy, so there is a heavy burden to deliver significant returns on these investments. Despite most CIO's best efforts, much of IT is viewed as a cost center rather than a revenue enhancer, so with each budget cycle systems groups find themselves pressured to deliver greater services with fewer resources. Taken altogether, stretching fewer resources to cover expanding demands over a complex and fragile infrastructure has lead IT managers to adopt a major strategy called "leveraging." By examining how ADW might clash with IT manager's desire to leverage every resource at their disposal, we can begin to see how Agile teams might legitimately vex IT managers.

In its essence, leveraging is solving several problems with one resource. For example, by cross-training two developers in each other's tool, they can serve as their own backups during vacations, so the department does not have to hire as many people. Also, by converting the less important applications over to the shop's predominant operating system or database, several older server boxes can be retired, saving annual licensing and support costs. As can be gleaned from these examples, leveraging requires time, making it a strategy that must be pursued relentlessly year after year. IT managers can leverage policies, too. By standardizing on a single development methodology, say, the department can lower its training and governance costs. Even if the resulting method is not perfect for efforts of all types and sizes, imposing a single method that everyone can remember upon every application built will prevent most oversights and errors. Because avoiding errors that absorb time to diagnose and rectify, a single development method allows the department to accomplish more with fewer resources, furthering the leveraging strategy.

In a leveraged IT environment, all resources are stretched as far as they can go. Agile Data Warehousing can undermine in several ways both IT's current leveraging plan and its leveraging strategy in general. ADW adherents must understand the threats they can represent before they can steer around them. Consider the following sample notions that IT managers might voice after their first exposure to Scrum/XP:

Careful requirements documents assure that an effort delivers the right services and avoids burning scarce resources on rework. Agile advocates just-in-time detailed requirements which traditional eyes will find lacking in thoroughness, inviting oversights and errors. The unplanned efforts needed to rectify such errors will draw resources from other areas, forcing the current staffing plan to be re-considered and putting the delivery of other projects at risk.

Careful project plans provide comprehensive cost and time estimates for a given level of business benefits that the new application will provide. ADW projects defer such projections for several months until the team hits its stride, making it difficult for managers to unequivocally commit to supporting the business initiatives the company has decided to pursue. When ADW finally delivers a release plan with time and cost projections, meeting the project's resource needs may suddenly require resources from other areas, again putting the delivery of other projects at risk.

Agile projects focus upon writing code to address the Product Owner's most pressing business challenges. IT managers will have difficulty seeing how an Agile method will inherently support larger concerns such as standard architectures and shared operations. They will suspect that to allow one development team to begin re-inventing how applications are built, documented, and operated will greatly complicate problem diagnosis and future application enhancements, thus increasing the staffing needed to support a given level of services.

Pursuing Agile Data Warehousing will introduce a separate development method. Training the department on a single standard procedure will no longer suffice. Staff members become more difficult to move between Agile and non-Agile projects, decreasing the current cross-supporting plan, making it difficult to provide the same level of uninterrupted service without hiring more staff.

With reservations such as these examples, gaining the support of IT managers will be difficult for the Agile warehouse team. The Scrum Master and Product Owner will need to deliberately market their Agile approach to IT managers if their project is to have a chance to prove itself. In practice, we have found advocating ADW effectively requires two presentations: first, why Agile in general improves the chances of a project's success, and second, the features of the ADW method in particular that will minimize the impact upon IT's leveraging plan. Let us consider these two components in turn.

MARKETING AGILE APPROACHES IN GENERAL

Introducing Agile methods to an organization often gets bogged down with explaining "what Agile is." Having dedicated several chapters of this book to that topic, we can say such material is too detailed for an initial presentation to skeptical IT managers. For that audience it is more effective to focus instead on "why Agile will work better," saving descriptions of ADW's components till it has sparked some interest among the IT managers. To convince these managers that Agile is worth considering, we have repeatedly employed three threads: the Standish Group's *Chaos* white papers, an adapted "risk exposure analysis," and an analysis of improved return on investment.

Agile Is Better in Terms of "Chaos"

If the Agile team desires to receive even a temporary exception to the IT department's rules for development projects, it must first establish that traditional methods might need some fixing. The Standish Group's 1995 *Chaos Report* and 1999 follow-up *Recipe for Success* white papers [Standish 1995 and 1999] that we mentioned in earlier chapters provide a quick means of illustrating the general frustration with standard IT development methods that led to Agile approaches in the first place. Based upon surveys with over 300 companies and 8,000 applications, these *Chaos* reports document that IT projects fail at an alarming rate—85 percent of projects costing between $3 million and $6 million are seriously "challenged" in terms of cost, timeliness, or features. One of the primary conclusions of these papers is that decreasing the size of a project will greatly increase the project's chance for success. The risk of failure falls 10 percentage points for efforts between $3 million and $1.5 million, another 8 points in the next tier below $1.5 million, and down to 45 percent for those efforts with costs under $750,000.

With these figures as context, the point to make to IT managers is that Agile Data Warehousing incorporates the lessons documented by the Chaos Report, especially in the way that it breaks down large projects in a disciplined manner into the smallest deliverable units of business value possible. $3 million to $6 million is a common cost range for a data warehousing project overall. ADW can transform this work into a stream of deliverables that remain under the $750K threshold, improving the project's chances for success from just 15 percent to 55 percent. When asked whether they would want to be associated with a project that offers a stream of steady deliverables with lower individual risks, or one big "crap shoot," IT managers have invariably found the former more attractive.

Agile Is Better in Terms of Opportunity Costs

The Standish Group's Chaos data makes a compelling case that IT needs a new approach to building applications, and one that involves smaller scopes. But does an organization need a particularly *faster* method, especially an Agile approach that cuts process to its bare minimum in the interest of maximum speed? The Standish studies lumped all risks together—projects were "challenged" if they were either late, over budget, or lacked requested features. We can add to our case for Agile approaches the need for speed if we highlight the higher risk of *opportunity costs* that traditional methods entail. To do so, we follow the Chaos data with an introduction of **risk exposure analysis**, as typified by first two figures of this chapter.

Risk exposure analysis powerfully presents the fundamental choice an IT department must make in choosing a development approach. A risk exposure diagram translates both cost and benefits into risks so that they can be compared directly, placing them in a graph where the optimal level of tradeoffs becomes clear. While IT management has every reason to avoid the risk of product failure, a properly drawn risk exposure diagram reveals that some product flaw risk is actually the best choice because of the price one would pay in opportunity costs to drive that risk to zero.

Figure 8.1 portrays a plain-vanilla Risk Exposure Analysis, re-cast for the question of whether IT shops should pursue a plan-intensive waterfall approach or emphasize an Agile method that entails far less up-front, detailed planning. The figure depicts how two distinct types of project risks change in response to increasing amounts of planning. At the extreme left, the project team invests in no predictive planning. Instead they start coding immediately and respond to contingencies as they arise during development. At the extreme right of the axis, they invest in extensive, pre-development planning. Such extreme planning delays the moment coding can start because the full scope of requirements is elaborated, every work task is defined and estimated, all dependencies between tasks discerned, and the entire network of actions steps scheduled on a plan that the project manager will follow line by line.

Given these two extremes in approach, should we pick one or the other, or a point in between? In advocating an extreme plan-driven waterfall method, adherents reveal the importance they place on avoiding mistakes. They took to heart the traditional IT training which warns that errors caught during requirements cost one hundred times more to repair once coded into the system. They have in mind the "Risk of Product Flaw" line as shown in the figure: one can steadily lower the risk of overlooking or misunderstanding a crucial requirement with greater and greater amounts of research and planning before starting development.

Even if we accepted this statement, the natural conclusion is not, then, that we should drive requirements and estimates down to the very last detail before coding begins. What that impulse overlooks is the fact that the organization needs new and enhanced applications such as data warehouses, and it typically needs them *now*. Whether needed for cost reduction, for compliance audits, or to respond to new competition in the marketplace, a better business intelligence system will help the enterprise succeed as a whole. Every month of delay in delivering the system beyond the absolute minimum required to build it incurs opportunity costs—either in the form of expenses resulting for lack of a good decision, or

Figure 8.1: Standard Risk Exposure Analysis

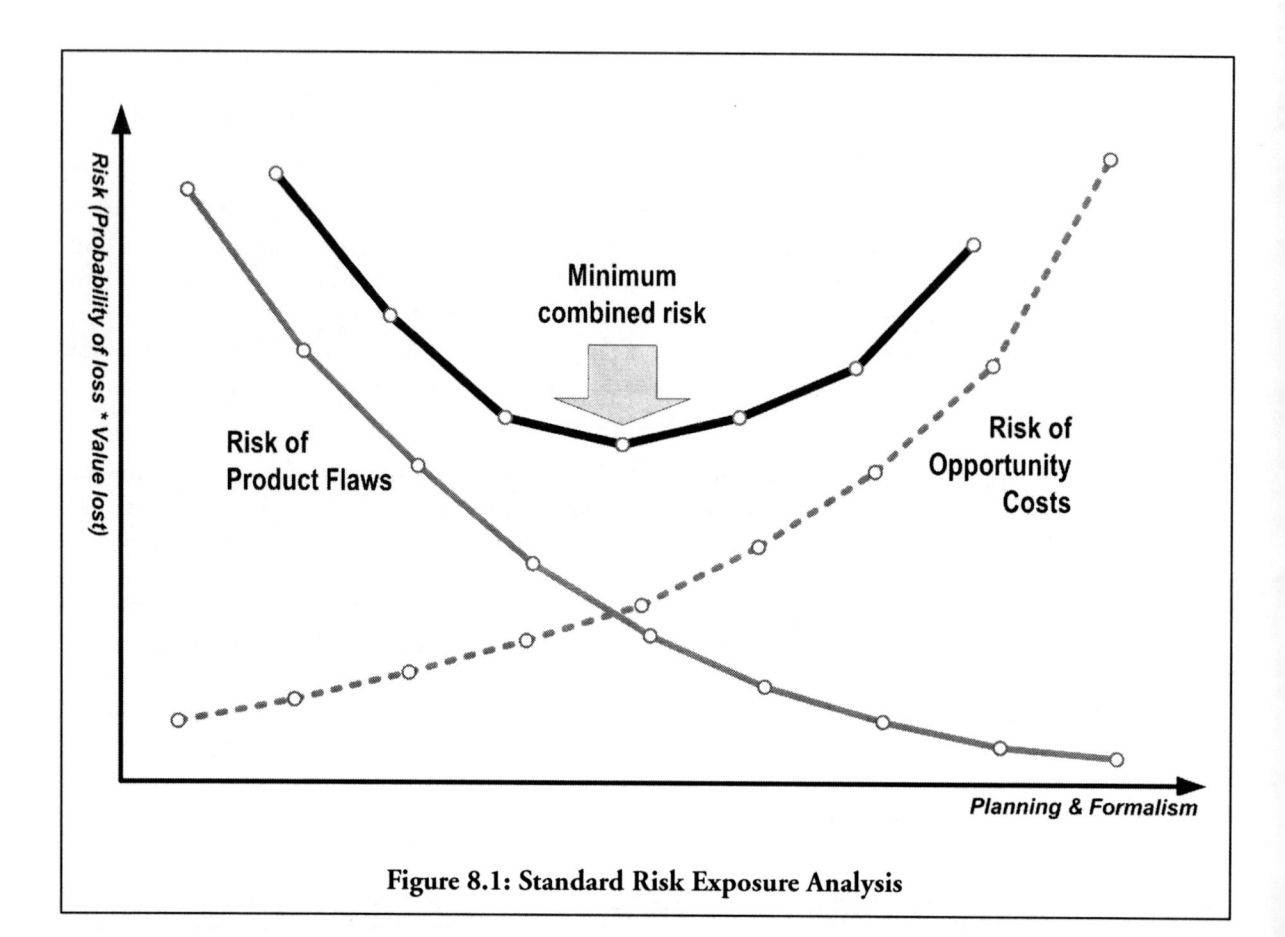

in significant revenue lost because some other enterprise got their product to marketplace first. Accordingly, the diagram includes a line for "Risk of Opportunity Costs," depicting these undesirable outcomes. This line naturally grows as greater planning pushes the delivery date increasingly outward. When one factors in such things as compounded interest and the lasting value of being first to market, it is reasonable that this curve increases exponentially rather than just linearly.

Placing the opportunity cost line against the line for product flaw risks reveals a "sweet spot" for balancing these two tradeoffs. The sweet spot is a point where the combined risks of product flaws and missed opportunities are lowest. Crucially, this optimal compromise between the two risks occurs nowhere near the right extreme of the planning axis as waterfall adherents and the typical project manager might argue. It lies instead somewhere in the middle, suggesting that in choosing a methodological approach, IT management must temper their aversion to possible product flaws. For the good of the enterprise, IT managers must consider employing methods that achieve faster time-to-market in exchange for a reasonable level of risk.

However, the plain-vanilla risk exposure graph must be updated to portray some key qualities of Agile data warehousing because the product flaw line is not yet properly drawn. Agile methods embed the customer into the development team and work on a small increments of functionality, in the order of value to the organization. With an absolute minimum of detailed planning, they avoid the mind-numbingly large requirements and design documents that consume so much time on traditional projects. With the Product Owner on the team, the Agile approach actually elicits better requirements than one can achieve with the single-pass paradigm of plan-driven approaches. Furthermore, test-led development as well as automated and continuous integration testing allow Agile teams to achieve higher coding accuracy than their waterfall brethren.

Taken together, these considerations suggest that the more upfront planning one adds to an adaptive approach, the more it will hurt the method's agility and therefore the quality of its work product. In essence, adding significant formality and planning to Agile pushes it toward the middle ground in the diagram where there will be too much process to be "agile," yet not enough to be performing a waterfall method well.

Taking this undesirable middle ground into account, **Figure 8.2** re-draws the previous diagram's product flaw line. If IT management will allow the warehousing group to decompose epic user requirements into small, well expressed work assignments, and then pursue them via a self-organized team that includes a Product Owner, the risk of product flaws actually plummets as one leaves the left edge of the axis. This graph suggests a little bit of pre-planning is good, but not too much. It must be the kind of planning that does not result in time-consuming requirement specs and to-be design documents that have fleeting shelf-life.

As one can see in the Agile-specific risk analysis diagram, the undesirable middle ground between approaches destroys the smooth continuum of the earlier graph's product flaw line. The updated line has transformed the decision into a much more binary, either-or situation. IT management cannot sit on the fence regarding the choice of development methods. There is a sweet spot for adaptive methods, and another, fully distinct optimum far to the right for plan-driven teams. The point to make with this diagram while marketing Agile to IT managers is that given the choice between any two sweet spots, one should prefer the one on the left because it entails far less opportunity costs.

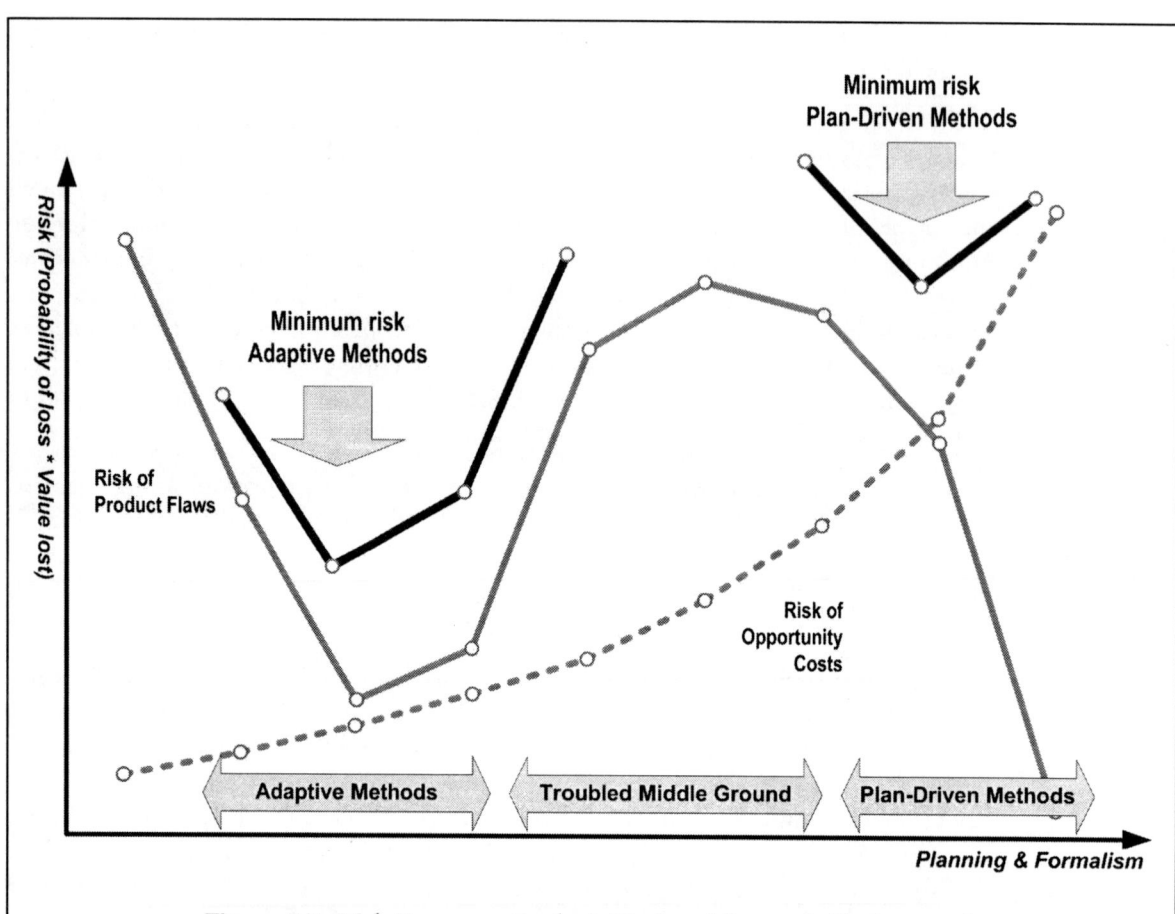

Figure 8.2: Risk Exposure Analysis Updated for an Agile Approach
Note the troubled middle ground between effective ranges for adaptive and plan-driven methods

Agile Offers Better ROI

The risk exposure analysis sketched above might cause IT managers to begin considering Agile methods more seriously, but unfortunately the argument only suggests that lightweight methods can benefit the organization as a whole. To win over these managers who often play crucial gatekeeper roles in the early days of an ADW projects, we have needed to also portray the more immediate impact Agile can have upon individual projects, namely, better results on estimated return on investment.

The more mature the IT function within an organization, the more likely projects are selected and re-funded based upon quantification of their return on investment (ROI).

Risk exposure diagrams may be intriguing to look at, but they are too conceptual to present to an IT project steering committee. Better ROI projections, however, are something IT managers can use immediately before such governance boards, and thus often prove to be the last bit of persuasion IT managers need before they give an ADW project a chance to succeed.

ROI projections do get a bit more technical, especially when one tries to choose between several, competing mathematical formulas for calculating its likely value, such as the traditional *internal rate of return* and *return on investment*. The common thread to all the formulas is that any dollar amount, whether cost or benefit, gets "discounted" by time. For example, the most common formula, net present value (NPV), uses the interest rate (and sometimes inflation, too) to convert dollars occurring in different time frames into comparable amounts by reducing them exponentially by their distance from the present. Valuing $1M today more than $1M received ten years from now makes sense, given that the funds could have been invested for a decade to create a much larger sum. In fact, $1M falls to nearly half its value if received a decade from now, if discounted at only six percent annually.

The major failing for all these traditional measures is the they do not adjust for risk nor for resource constraints. Adjusting for risk makes sense because we would all rather invest in a IT solution that is sure to come online than one of equal value that has a 50 percent chance of failing. Likewise, resource constraints are reasonable to consider because, as we saw above in the risk exposure analysis, there are opportunity costs for sinking time and money into one project when it keeps us from redeploying them elsewhere. A newer metric called the *development productivity index* (DPI) addresses these shortcomings, perhaps suggesting why it is becoming increasingly popular among IT governance boards. Before the DPI was introduced, portfolio managers had to spread projects on a scatter gram of risk versus worth to enable reviewers to consider both, leaving much ambiguity for those undertakings that lay within zones where the ratio of risk to value was approximately constant. The DPI starts with the net present value calculation and adjusts the resulting number for both risk and resources according to this formula:

$$DPI = (NPV \times \text{probability of success})/\text{development cost remaining}$$

Let us see how moving a traditional development project to an Agile approach dramatically improves its projected return on investment. We will consider the impact using both NPV and DPI, plus three other common calculations of worth: return on investment, internal rate of return, and payback period. **Table 8.1** provides the detail source data for our comparison, placing side-by-side the costs and benefits for the project when pursued using a waterfall-based method versus an Agile approach. **Table 8.2** presents the contrasting financial performance metrics based upon the previous table's cost and benefit details. All of these calculations can be performed easily upon the dollar amounts in the

Table 8.1: Financial Performance of the Same Project under Contrasting Methods

	Panel A: Waterfall Method				Panel B: Agile Warehousing			
Qtr	Event	Period Costs	Period Benefit	Cumul Net	Event	Period Costs	Period Benefit	Cumul Net
1	Analysis	-$125	$0	-$125	Dev	-$125	$0	-$125
2	Design	-125	0	-250	Rel 1	-125	0	-250
3	Code	-125	0	-375	Dev	-125	33	-342
4	Code	-125	0	-500	Rel 2	-125	33	-433
5	Code	-125	0	-625	Dev	-125	100	-458
6	Code	-125	0	-750	Rel 3	-125	100	-483
7	Test	-125	0	-875	Dev	-125	167	-442
8	Deploy	-125	0	-1000	Rel 4	-125	167	-400
9	Online	0	200	-800	Online	0	200	-200
10	Online	0	200	-600	Online	0	200	0
11	Online	0	200	-400	Online	0	200	200
12	Online	0	200	-200	Online	0	200	400
13	Online	0	200	0	Online	0	200	600
...	...		...					...
28	Retired	0	200	$3,000	Retired	0	200	$3,600
	Totals	$1,000	$4,000			$1,000	$4,600	

Table 8.2: Summary of Financial Performance of Two Approaches

		Waterfall	Agile	%Δ
Net Benefit		$3,000	$3,600	+20%
Payback Time		14 qtrs	11 qtrs	-21%
Net Present Value @ 6%		$2,112	$2,658	+26%
Return on Investment		211%	265%	+26%
Internal Rate of Return		11.7%	17.7%	+51%
P(Success)		33%	55%	+67%
Development Productivity Index	(min)	0.86	1.77	
	(max)	8.61	15.07	+75%

data table using a spreadsheet program. The difference in the two quantified valuations of this project is dramatic, and as we will see, very pertinent to the IT manager who must request or defend project funding before a steering committee or a board of directors.

The project analyzed is one that requires a $1M investment, spread evenly over the eight quarters required to build it, and providing $200K of benefits each quarter during each of the five years that it will be online. Panel A of the data table represents the waterfall approach, where the business receives zero benefits until the project is deployed at the end of the eight quarters. In contrast, Panel B depicts delivery by means of Agile data warehousing. In modeling the Agile project's performance, we took the middle road on our assumptions. We allowed that it might take the Agile team six months to get each release (increment of value) online, rather than assuming the three-month spacing between releases that we typically achieve in our projects. We also modeled the benefits to accrue slowly at first—due to cumulative synergies between the subject areas—rather than appearing evenly with each release.

Even with these constraints, the advantages to the Agile delivery method was dramatic, as the summary table reveals: 34 percent better net present value and return on investment, 51 percent improvement on internal rate of return, and six months shaved off of the payback period. The Agile approach shines even brighter when notions of risk and resource constraints are included in the calculation using the development productivity index: the same project pursued via an Agile method will score at least 75 percent better during portfolio review than it would if developed under a waterfall approach.

There are two nuances to the DPI that we should consider before moving on. First, we need to select proper probabilities reflecting the relative risks of the two development scenarios. These probabilities express the chances that the project envisioned will succeed and we will need reasonable source for the values we use. Luckily, the Standish Group's *Chaos* reports, presented to the IT managers earlier, provide some well-documented risk levels we can use. In our example, ADW transforms the $1M waterfall project into four component releases, delivered at a cost of $250K each, and each providing an independent increment of value. According to the *Chaos* data, the chance of success for projects dropping below the $750K cost level increases from 33 to 55 percent—a modest amount upon its face, but one that yields dramatic improvements for a project's estimated financial performance. Reduction in project risk appears immediately in the DPI measure used to score projects during portfolio management or any equivalent winnowing process for proposed projects.

The second nuance to the DPI is that its value naturally changes over time even if the parameters describing a project remain the same. Because it reduces a project's score by the amount of investment still to go, this divisor will be different depending whether the evaluation is performed at the time of project proposal or later once the project is underway.

Table 8.3 shows the derivations of the DPI range used in the earlier summary table. For each quarter during the project development, we have adjusted the investment-to-go and regenerated the DPI ratio. In our example, the DPI score under the Agile approach started at 107 percent higher at proposal time and fell somewhat to be only 75 percent higher than the waterfall value during the last quarter of development. As long as everyone involved understands that this variation is a natural consequence of the way the DPI figure is calculated, it should not cause any consternation during its use.

No matter which of the five ROI formulas one employs for this comparison, the bottom line should be clear—Agile projects can forecast significantly higher return on investment than projects pursued via traditional methods. This conclusion caps a three-component

Table 8.3: Comparative DPI Values While Development is Underway

		Waterfall Development				Agile Development				
		Probability of Success = 33%				Probability of Success = 55%				
Qtr	Event	Net Benefit	Forward NPV	Costs To Go	DPI	Event	Net Benefit	Forward NPV	Costs To Go	DPI	%Δ
		[1]	[2]	[3]	[4]		[5]	[6]	[7]	[8]	[9]
1	Analysis	-$125	$2,269	$875	0.86	Dev	$0	$2,823	$875	1.77	107%
2	Design	-125	2,428	750	1.07	Rel 1	0	2,990	750	2.19	105%
3	Code	-125	2,590	625	1.37	Dev	33	3,127	625	2.75	101%
4	Code	-125	2,753	500	1.82	Rel 2	33	3,266	500	3.59	98%
5	Code	-125	2,920	375	2.57	Dev	100	3,340	375	4.90	91%
6	Code	-125	3,089	250	4.08	Rel 3	100	3,415	250	7.51	84%
7	Test	-125	3,260	125	8.61	Dev	167	3,424	125	15.07	75%
8	Deploy	-125	3,434	0		Rel 4	167	3,434	0		
9	Online	200				Online	200				

Notes:
All dollar amounts in thousands.
Values for numbered columns are measured at the end of the quarter.
NPV = Net Present Value.
Forward NPV = NPV of future net benefits.
CTG = Costs to Go, P(S) = probability of success.
DPI = Development Productivity Index = NPV * P(S)/CTG.
DPI undefined when Costs To Go is zero.

case to IT managers who might be considering opposing the introduction of an Agile approach within the company. One, the Chaos data shows that traditional methods do not perform well. Two, Risk exposure analysis argues that Agile will perform better than traditional methods for the organization in general. And three, Agile methods should improve the financial performance of any project in particular. These three considerations should persuade skeptical IT managers that Agile methods have value to offer in theory. However, as we noted earlier, they will still have practical concerns about how a non-traditional method will clash with the standard procedures of their department. We need to show them characteristics of the ADW method in particular that address their natural reservations toward change.

MARKETING ADW IN PARTICULAR

We began this section by considering the leveraging strategies IT managers use to minimize the tools and methods their departments employ in order to stretch their resources across several truly difficult challenges. No matter how compelling our three-fold analysis of Agile's theoretical advantages might be, we are still asking these managers to tolerate and even support a potentially troublesome Agile project for six months or so. Before many of them will accede to this request, the ADW proponent will have to demonstrate that she understands where a non-standard method clashes with standard procedures and how she plans to minimize the static this clash will cause. As an example of the form this reassurance might take, let us consider several concerns from the IT manager's point of view, phrasing them all as "Whatever development method the department employs, it must …"

… Be more than Code-and-Fix

In Chapter 5 we detailed how Agile Data Warehousing is a method with specific deliverables and a predictable, drill-down sequencing, not just an Agile approach. It guides the Product Owner on how to divide the business intelligence objectives into "topic areas" and then direct the developers in building out these components, one architectural layer at a time. As we saw in the last chapter, this approach is far from being simply "tactical programming." It can be in fact tuned to support any level of CMMI-DEV maturity that the organization desires.

… Ensure the continuation of IT services

Agile Data Warehousing is a focused evolution of the *development* portion of a systems development life cycle. As seen in the figures of the first chapter, it involves substantial impact to only a middle pair of the nine project management disciplines that PMI has identified. Moderate changes impact another two disciplines, and the remaining five are left largely unchanged. Furthermore, through continuous integration testing ADW maintains and even enhances the verification role for IT's Operations and Support team, so that harmful changes to applications are no more likely to be deployed into production than with other methods.

... Support common architectures

Agile data warehousing maintains coordination with department architects and compliance with design standards, but does so much more efficiently through the notion of reference models rather than design specs and committee-based reviews. Furthermore, these reference models comprise working modules that can be invoked as needed, so they will actually improve the IT department's ability to perform regression testing of existing architectures in the face of platform upgrades and the addition of new applications.

... Provide budgeting and progress metrics

As seen in the burndown charts presented in Chapter 4, Agile data warehousing projects supply a core set of metrics that mesh with those that a Program Management Office might prefer. These data points include traditional system availability milestones, allowing ADW projects to coordinate with related projects as easily as plan-driven efforts. True, ADW's release burndown charts do not provide the detailed reporting of funds-spent versus spending-to-go that plan-driven efforts supply, but sponsors request these metrics largely to reassure stakeholders that a project's rising costs will someday yield tangible results. Rather than reassuring stakeholders with metrics, ADW delivers frequent, incremental releases of business-usable code. In this context, progress reporting becomes not a reassurance, but instead a summary of the benefits that will be online after the next increment of spending, making traditional variance-to-plan metrics moot.

... Offer Visibility and Correction of Underperformance

ADW does not provide a detailed work breakdown structure of projected tasks, so a typical project manager cannot fine-tune the assignment of developers as they commonly do in traditional projects. In exchange, ADW offers the high effectiveness of self-organized teams working toward tightly focused deliverables, eliminating much of the need for and the cost of traditional project management. Moreover, as we saw in Chapter 6, ADW can be deployed at a program level. The critical chain techniques that enable us to closely monitor "buffer consumption" also allow the fluid reassignment of resources on a team-to-themes basis, allowing program managers to keep the larger IT initiative optimally tuned.

... Ensure Application Quality

In this area, Agile data warehousing particularly shines. With an embedded Product Owner working with developers, the team derives dramatically better requirements than waterfall methods, and implements them far more accurately. Under a typical arrangement of two-week sprints and quarterly releases, the Product Owner has directly operated the application seven separate times, and has the assurances of the automated integrated testing facility that all modules have been designed and coded properly.

... Enhance IT Departmental Cohesion

As will be detailed below when we consider the perspectives of several important IT staff roles, Agile data warehousing teams have in mind a) the situation their non-Agile IT partners face, b) the ways that ADW could adversely impact their current working patterns, and c) many ways to mitigate those hazards.

POSSIBLE DOWNSIDES NEED TO BE CLEAR

With this level of assurance, IT management may be inclined to support Agile data warehousing, but may also astutely ask what disadvantages they must accept in order to acquire such benefits. In order to establish a durable relationship with this management group, the ADW proponent should make clear some possible inconveniences that an Agile approach might require IT managers to tolerate, such as the following.

Agile team members cannot be easily redeployed

If IT provides any of the Agile team members, it will have trouble pulling them out of the team willy-nilly for such important tasks as maintenance programming of existing applications. This rigidity arises from the fact that the accuracy of ADW's estimation and forecasting depends upon a predictable "velocity," which in turn requires a stable team composition working together via an uninterrupted process. This process is one team members crafted for themselves over the span of several sprints based upon the particulars of the people involved. Changing the team roster through the subtraction or substitution of members risks making that process no longer appropriate. The team will need to re-derive their process and team velocity, making all budgeting and planning forecasts provided to date suddenly unreliable.

Must wait a bit longer for budgeting and planning estimates

As we saw in Chapter 4, it will take Agile teams a few months on a project before they can give dependable estimates as to when particular features will be delivered and whether the project can be finished in the time and budget allowed. At first blush, this sounds ridiculous given that a PMI-compliant waterfall method provides these numbers before even the project kickoff occurs.

The difference is that Agile teams wait till they know what they are talking about before giving an estimate. In contrast, even the most skilled waterfall project manager is providing numbers from some highly problematic sources. Either they have derived an extrapolated forecast via parametric estimation, or they have collated the best guesses of likely developers. Given that this planning occurs before requirements gathering or design has transpired, how well can those developers really estimate? Are the traditional forecasts worth the paper they are printed on?

In the long run, an Agile Data Warehouse team can actually meet halfway IT management's need for pre-kickoff estimation. An existing, stable ADW team will have the facts they need to estimate the level-of-effort for a new system well enough for planning if the epics of the envisioned product decomposes in the same fashion as their past endeavors. However, new teams and new challenges will have to wait a few sprints before the estimates reach a planning-quality level.

Must keep the Product Owner embedded in the team

The Product Owner is the heart of the team, its only path toward building the right components at the right time. Situations where the Product Owner is spread too-thin across the company to focus on the project, or where business members cycle in and out of the Product Owner's chair, seriously undermine the team's ability to function accurately without resorting to voluminous to-be documentation. Often Agile projects lose the full focus of their Product Owners because they do not keep them sufficiently occupied, allowing them to get deeply embroiled in non-project related issues back in their functional departments. Fortunately, the ADW method includes several mechanisms to keep the Product Owner engaged: the user epic decomposition scheme takes concentration to complete, providing business knowledge during the drafting of ACIT tests is absorbing, and providing the business guidelines for the design decisions developers must tackle will require plenty of eye-to-eye involvement.

Hopefully the rich combination of theory and particulars we suggest above will suffice to put IT managers firmly on the side of the Agile warehouse team, at least for the project's first release or two. With this support in place, the ADW team can turn its attention to similar marketing efforts that it will need to answer opposition arising from the other groups within the organization, such as the company's Project Management Office.

Adversity From The Project Management Office

The project management profession is standardizing at an accelerating pace, to the point where one can find now project management maturity models that rival the IT Capability Maturity Model we examined in the previous chapter. [PMI 2003] In harmony with this trend, mid-size and larger companies often establish "project" or "program management office" (both "PMOs" hereon) to define and disseminate standard project management methods throughout their organizations. Agile projects, with their emphasis on lightweight processes and just-in-time requirements and design, can find themselves quickly at odds with the approved standards of the company's PMO because most of them advocate some flavor of a traditional waterfall process for software development. These PMOs will actively push ADW teams away from highly-adaptive approaches toward far more plan-intensive methods. As can be seen in the risk analysis diagram above, if the team were to yield to this pressure, they would move into the no-man's land of Figure 8.2 where projects have the highest chance of failure. To get established with their Agile process intact, the ADW team will have to find ways to hold off an aggressive PMO for several months till it can demonstrate the efficacy of an adaptive approach. We have found in our practice a few strategies for keeping peace with PMOs long enough to get a first ADW demonstration project through its crucial proof-of-concept period, strategies we might call "ducking" and "repackaging"

The degree of potential conflict with a Project Management Offices depends on the nature of the PMO group, which can vary widely from company to company. In an organization where the work is largely repeated production processes, the PMO can be almost non-existent and their input on best practices couched as advice for departments that choose to listen. As the ratio of project-to-process work grows, however, formalized Project Management Offices become more common and mature, to where a strongly-backed PMO can be chartered to entirely re-engineer the methods with which the company pursues projects.

PMOs involved with comprehensive method re-engineering often prove to be easy for an ADW team to collaborate with because they have already accepted that their organization's methods must change and that innovative approaches might have valuable insights to offer. Moreover, their focus is more on delivering benefits at program or enterprise levels, so they are less concerned with micro-managing individual projects. If faced with such a project management group, an Agile team should join the conversation, adding its concerns and solutions to the developing vision. PMOs in the middle ground, however, can be particularly difficult for an Agile team to work with. Instead of process re-engineering, the mid-sized PMO's charter revolves around implementing an existing waterfall approach (such as offered by the Project Management Institute) which usually features a traditional, plan-driven style that requires detailed task planning, as well as extensive monitoring, reporting, and control of team activities.

Unfortunately, simply ignoring these preferences of the PMO will not work. The Information Technology group may refuse to deploy a new system whose development process was not blessed by a PMO project manager. Many companies require projects as large as data warehouses to have on the team a PMO-provided manager, or at least one of its "quality engineers," who will closely monitor the team's compliance with the standard method. PMO representatives may actually sit upon the steering committee authorizing the ADW project. And, as with IT managers, PMO managers interface with executives, including moments when no one on the Agile team is present. For these reasons, an Agile warehouse effort must actively anticipate, avoid, and mitigate contention over method with the PMO.

The roots of conflict between an ADW team and a traditional PMO are easy to discern, beginning with paradigm. Whereas an Agile team revolves around self-organization and a continually improving process, PMI-schooled PMOs believes that projects fail because they were insufficiently defined, monitored, and controlled. They prefer a process-heavy approach that guarantees a standard set of artifacts and approvals, and when such a process fails, their answer is "more process" rather than re-thinking the paradigm.

Secondly, traditional project managers prefer to first have all parties negotiate up front a schedule of deliverables. They then strive to hold everyone to these promised dates, as if these estimates were actually contracts, so that the pieces of a larger program come together as senior management has been promised. With such an outlook, traditional project managers disapprove that an Agile team feels free to reshuffle its priorities whenever the Product Owner changes her preferences. They are horrified when an Agile team refuses to plan detailed milestone dates or forecast project costs upfront. Without detailed planning and extensive monitoring of performance to plan, they reason, no one can control the team, and an uncontrolled project is bound to fail.

Finally, PMOs typically demand a steady stream of detailed reporting from ongoing projects they govern, such as lists of tasks completed and hours spent on them, as well as tasks scheduled to start next and the developers assigned. In a program setting that involves several, interdependent projects, the PMO needs this detailed stream of data to a) better coordinate deliverables of one project with the needs of another, and b) redistribute resources when one project begins to slip from its schedule in a way that could delay the other, related efforts.

MITIGATING CONFLICT WITH THE PMO

Preventing and solving conflicts with the company's PMO starts with proper factual preparation by the Scrum Master. PMOs come in all sizes, with varying objectives and level of executive support. In researching the PMO's current objectives, the ADW team may discover that the PMO's expectations for IS project management are easily met. Even when faced with an ambitious and demanding PMO, understanding the process requirements will better equip the ADW team to steer around many of the potential conflicts. Moreover, by gauging the relative support from senior management for the PMO compared to the department sponsoring her project, the Scrum Master can derive a rough notion of how accommodating her team will have to be when irreconcilable conflicts arise with the PMO.

Researching the PMO also involves taking an honest look at the methods and information the PMO offers. All formalized methods are built upon a large number of lessons learned during past projects, both successes and failures. Often the Scrum Master will find much of value in the PMOs standards, such as the traditional notions of preparing for contingencies and managing stakeholder anxiety by creating project risk and communications plans. PMOs may also have a gold mine of historical data on past IT projects, such as development hours invested by module, which the ADW team could use to inform its level-of-effort forecasting during early sprints, before it has honed its own estimating skills.

Where the demands of the PMO cannot be steered around, the Agile team will need to lessen and delay their impact until the benefits of an Agile approach can be demonstrated. To this end, the Scrum Master might consider either "ducking" and "repackaging" strategies. By "ducking" we mean merely arranging the interface between the two groups so that the PMO interacts with the Product Owner rather than the Scrum Master. Without such efforts, PMO managers could easily mistake the Scrum Master for a "project manager" and request that she change the way the ADW team operates. Yet Scrum's notion of the "Product Owner" and "self-organized teams" removes many traditional Project Manager's duties from the Scrum Master role. It is the Product Owner that determines what the team will develop and when—probably the two data points the PMO will ask for most. Furthermore, it is the team that owns the development process, altering it as needed during each sprint retrospective. The Scrum Master merely ensures everyone faithfully follows the method that consensus has crafted.

Establishing the Product Owner as the ADW team's "manager" has a major advantage during conflicts with the PMO. If the Scrum Master were seen as the ADW lead, disputes with the PMO can be viewed as simply one method preference versus another when escalated to senior management to resolve. Since companies charter PMOs to be project process experts, their opinions will usually prevail in debates over the merits of competing preferences. The Product Owner, however, hails from a functional department. She can counter the PMO's demands by describing the delay a more process-heavy approach will cause and the business impact of those delays. In disagreements involving business impacts versus process preferences, the business considerations will often carry more weight. The Product Owner, therefore, has a better chance than the Scrum Master of negotiating a grace period for ADW teams to prove their approach before they must accede to the PMO's demands.

The other strategy for minimizing conflict with PMOs is "repackaging," in which the Scrum Master portrays the early sprints of an ADW project as simply "extended prototyping." Prototyping is a widely accepted approach of building a working model of an application with which to demonstrate design concepts, which in turn can catalyze detailed user feedback on both requirements and design. The advantage of introducing prototyping into the discussion with the PMO is that the concept has many, large gray areas. For example, how complete is a "working model"? The PMO might understand it to be hastily written, throw-away programming, whereas the ADW team can interpret it to be Scrum's notion of "potentially shippable code." Likewise, how extensively must requirements be gathered before the project should shift to a plan-driven method? The PMO might prefer that a requirements specification document be drafted after a couple of ADW sprints. The Product Owner, however, can insist at the conclusion of each sprint that the team needs to evolve the working model still further before the requirements will be clear. The Product Owner can continue requiring further refinements all the way up to the point where the team is ready to draft a Scrum release plan. The longer the key aspects of "prototyping" remain differently defined, the longer the ADW team will have to demonstrate the efficacy of the lightweight approach that PMO standards would have them abandon.

There may be a limit, of course, to the amount of time ducking and repackaging can buy for the ADW team. If the organization's Project Management Office is aggressive and well-supported within the company, then the Agile team may have to align with a traditional project management processes well before their first project is delivered. The ADW team leads can still mitigate the impact of this transition by seeking the "wiggle room" between what the PMO demands and the team's preferred work habits. For example, a velocity-bracketed release plan will provide the large milestones the PMO demands in order to coordinate the Agile project with other efforts the PMO managers are guiding. Moreover, knowing the number of likely sprints the release plan forecasts will allow the ADW team to provide something close to traditional cost and staffing estimates. Finally, if the user stories have been entered into a database utility as suggested in Chapter 3, it may not be too difficult to reprint their data using a template that will satisfy the PMO's notion of a requirements specification document.

Even though the ADW team may be able to bend and twist its preferred process to meet the PMO's expectations, one important problem will remain: feeding the PMO the many artifacts and data it requests will consume considerable labor hours. The Scrum Master and Product Owner need to prepare for this demand in advance by staffing the Project Communication Assistant role we suggested in Chapter 6. Much of the information needed to satisfy the PMO will entail mostly re-collating and reformatting, actions which provide little value to the ADW team. As a representative of the department funding the project, the Product Owner will not want to lose a portion of the Scrum Master nor the developers' time to the preparation of these artifacts. The solution then is to ensure a less-expensive person is in place to keep the PMO happy with a steady steam of re-hashed information when the team must begin aligning with the standard, planned-driven approach of the company.

ADVERSITY FROM IT FUNCTIONAL GROUPS

Warm rapport with IT managers and the Project Management Office may be the most important relationships for an ADW team to monitor, but the remaining groups we listed earlier will be important players, too. In most large companies, the Agile team will need dependable cooperation from the company's IT support groups. For example, the ADW team may not have its own data modeler or application database administrator. It could be therefore held to a standstill by IT's modeling and administration teams each time it needs a data model revised or some data definition language applied. While one often encounters obstinance from a few individuals in positions of informal power, if an entire systems support group tacitly decides to stonewall the Agile project, the ADW team will find itself starved of support till its project fails. To avoid and mitigate adversity among IT functional groups, we must understand the way Agile projects might pique their resentment. In our practice, the two we encounter most often are the impression that Agile teams hastily write dangerously incomplete code, and the notion that Agile teams are uninterested in supporting enterprise data models.

Tackling the issue of "sloppy code" first, the ADW team must understand that management is trying to evolve the data infrastructure quickly while stretching its IT staff as thin as possible. As the ones being stretched thin, the predominant objective of these service groups is to implement changes to specific applications carefully, without collateral damage, so that no functionality is lost in the platform as a whole. The service groups know that introducing even a small error can crash multiple systems resulting in hundreds of unhappy users. To increase the chances of implementing change under deadline pressure without introducing faults, IT groups become sticklers on standards. If they can guide developers to build all apps in the same architecture, with the same naming conventions and the same operational patterns, then code will be less likely to break, and the faults that do slip into the infrastructure will be easier to diagnose and correct.

An Agile team, on the other hand, can seem exclusively focused upon fast development in order to put envisioned business services online as soon as possible. The Product Owner hails from a business functional groups rather than IT, so she will review and reward the ADW team based upon the major functions and outward appearance of new code rather than aspects of its internal design or how robust it will be when it encounters, say, infrequent, multi-application contention once operational. If the IT service groups perceive the Agile team being exclusively concerned with the Product Owner's agenda, they will suspect that ADW code is written hastily, without regard to surrounding systems, and therefore a threat to their enterprise IT platform. With this outlook, they will be naturally reluctant to help whenever called upon to support the Agile team.

Regarding the issue of enterprise data models, many IT groups such as data architects and system architects are concerned with systems integration within the data layer. Enterprise architects invest hard work establishing standards for data normalization, data quality, and metadata definitions, so that tables between disparate applications can be joined and generate important management information for the company. An ADW team, on the other hand, might appear focused on meeting only its Product Owner's requests. If the Product Owner does not believe she needs her application to integrate or support other systems within the enterprise, then such integration will not be a priority for the ADW project. The IT service groups can easily interpret this as the Agile team members simply racing through data and application design because they are eager to code, and thus see them again as a threat to continued enterprise data integration.

In this context, the Agile team and the IT service groups can quickly develop an unspoken contest over paradigms. The Agile team might request, for example, that the DBA simply add a column to a table. The DBA, alarmed with the team's apparent disregard with fitting their BI application to the larger enterprise information system, can use the request as an opportunity to review the ADW team's entire data model. Rather than receiving a new column so that they can resume coding for next week's demo, the Agile developers get instead a myriad of detailed questions, such as which sequence generators they plan to use and how they plan to manage parallel queries. Similarly, a data architect can refuse to explain how to join the tables of an existing application the ADW team wishes to use as a data source until the Agile team promises to support a long list of coding standards and existing interfaces with other applications. As exasperating as it might be for Agile teams, IT groups quickly mount a legitimate effort to slow the ADW project down because sloppy, non-standard designs can create an unmanageable mess when deployed and even lead to repeated failures of multiple integrated applications.

MITIGATING CONFLICT WITH IT GROUPS

The ADW method presented in this book includes many aspects of careful design and development. Beside having a dedicated architectural squad and allocating twenty percent of the team's velocity to technical design issues, the team incorporates reference models, thorough testing, and automated as-built documentation into its work. Given that IT groups are legitimately concerned that every project will be built correctly, the ADW team would be wise to present these qualities of the method to them. And because they will need many services throughout the life of the project from these groups, the ADW team members will want to construct their team's appearance to their IT partners as carefully as they would the system they hope to build.

First of all, given that an Agile approach has some natural conflicts in paradigms with traditional IT training, ADW teams would do well to simply "hide the Agile." Switching adjectives and calling their approach *iterative* seems to help a great deal because "iterative" is a word IT groups already understand and indeed use in planning much of their daily work. At times, "Agile" has the misfortune of being a buzzword, and teams subscribing to it overtly can seem more interested in being trendy than building robust data processing systems.

Guarding Against Sloppy Code

The next step in building a working entente with these service groups will require a bit of marketing effort. Agile teams would acquire a large measure of goodwill from IT groups if they were to subscribe to traditional document and review cycles, yet the time lost to elaborate to-be documentation and committee walkthroughs is exactly what Agile is designed to avoid. The solution to this potential conflict is to find ways that Agile artifacts can provide the IT service groups what they really need. IT groups will say they want a gatekeeper role over the code that goes to production. What they really need is the ability to detect a dangerously flawed module before it is deployed, so they can send the code back to developers for rework. As luck would have it, the means to honor this need already exists in the ADW method:

1. Early in a project, ADW establishes reference models to control their designs. These models can be reviewed with IT groups well in advance of delivery, so that they feel they have had input on code design before code is built. To reassure the IT groups, the ADW needs only to adhere to the standards that the reference model demonstrates.

2. ADW performs 2-to-1 whiteboard designs resulting in electronic photos for documentation. These photos can be forwarded to IT architects and a mini-walkthrough scheduled requiring only one ADW team member. The extra one or two

person-hours per module that these walkthrough require will pale in comparison to the time the project would lose if the IT groups develop a consensus against the ADW project.

3. For each release, potentially shippable code pools up in the ACIT. IT's enterprise architects should be invited to perform self-guided code reviews of the modules waiting there. Furthermore, ADW's emphasis on auto-documented code will allow the Agile team to easily provide to-be design docs for the code gathering in ACIT. Whereas ADW sees these docs as "as-built", IT groups can view them as "to-be" because the code has not yet been deployed and can still be modified.

The methodological features above represent a robust process by which the ADW team can honor the need of IT support groups to review code design and construction before implementation. Presenting these considerations as a good-faith effort to avoid creating problems for the enterprise integration should go a long way to quieting the concerns of the IT support groups, especially when combined with efforts to cultivate support from IT management and to portray the early sprints as extended prototyping, as discussed above.

Supporting Enterprise Data Integration

Whereas a little marketing can address concerns regarding problematic code, quelling anxiety among data architects over data integration will require some active accommodation. Although the conversation may involve issues such as data granularity and metadata management, the data architect's will ultimately resolve to requiring that the ADW team utilize a particular set of tables and columns in their data schemas, populating them in a specific fashion. To make enterprise data universally usable, the architects frequently ask for far greater normalization than needed to meet its ADW Product Owner's needs. At first it may seem that the ADW team will have to either load dozens of extraneous tables, which will be time consuming, or suffer the wrath of the IT support groups when their requests are spurned. Fortunately, the team can buffer this request with a bit of "polymorphism" and buy enough time to get the Agile project through to its first implementation.

Usually the Agile warehouse effort can incorporate enterprise naming conventions and metadata requirements without too much disruption—the standards may actually save the team from having to reinvent some wheels—so at least the dialog with the IT architects can begin on a note of cooperation. Yet the team cannot contemplate stretching its data model to support enterprise requirements without taking on a large amount of additional, expensive ETL development. In our practice, the answer to this conundrum has been to work with the enterprise architects on defining a "translation layer" that will supply external enterprise applications with data from the Agile warehouse, formatted as they need it.

As portrayed in **Figure 8.3**, this translation layer offers data from the ADW warehouse's integration and dimensional layers for the external applications to access. At its simplest, the layer comprises simply database views that rename, combine, and aggregate warehouse data as needed. Meeting more complicated requirements may involve some additional measures such as a) materializing these view into actual tables, b) sequence generators to provide synthetic IDs when extreme normalization requires a warehouse entity be broken into two or more tables, and even c) some additional ETL.

At first it might seem that the translation layer strategy has not eliminated any work, but instead simply moved to it to another venue. However, by making this layer separate from the ADW project's base tables, the team has effectively decoupled the enterprise requirements from that of its Product Owner. The ADW team can now continue building its warehouse in a Agile fashion because it has promised to provide the necessary database objects to re-express the data as needed to support enterprise access. More often than not, the needs of the enterprise architects can be addressed later, once the Agile warehouse is

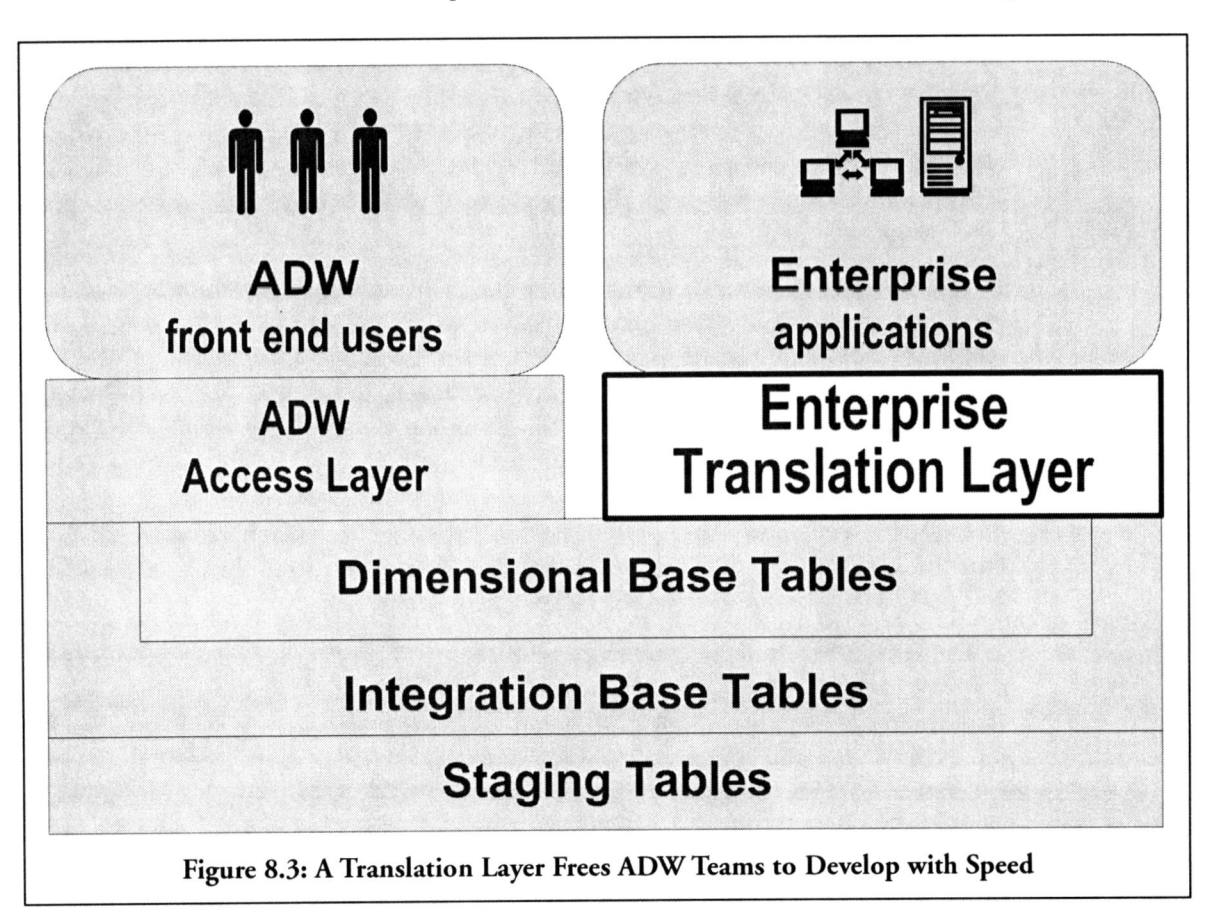

Figure 8.3: A Translation Layer Frees ADW Teams to Develop with Speed

online and meeting the needs of the Product Owner's department. Politically, getting IT approval to have a separate model for two different constituencies may take some diplomacy, but it helps to remind everyone that the goal is to allow the ADW proof-of-concept effort to demonstrate the velocity that a new method can achieve while at the same time providing a means to later connect the data to the rest of the organization. Once again, the support of IT managers as discussed earlier may play a crucial role in tipping the balance in favor of the Agile team.

ADVERSITY FROM IT SERVICE VENDORS

External vendors are quite common in large IT departments, and the ADW team will undoubtedly have several points of intersection with them. The adversity that these IT service vendors may manifest toward an ADW project might appear to be the same as presented by the internal groups we considered above, for indeed it originates from similar concerns. However, the ADW Scrum Master should realize that there is a added dimension to an external vendor's concerns regarding Agile methods that can lead it to suddenly oppose Agile projects even more strenuously than internal groups. These vendors frequently carry considerable prestige with senior management and have an important influence with IT directors, so ADW teams would be wise to maintain a good working relationship with them.

Like the project managers in the PMO, the service vendors have promised to deliver certain services or products on time, on budget, with a certain level of functionality and quality. Because they had to provide time and cost estimates when they sold their service to the company, they will undoubtedly be following a traditional waterfall approach and will therefore want to interface with the Agile warehouse project within a traditional framework. Like the technicians in the IT service groups, the IT vendors will be adding their changes to an infrastructure that, because it is not their own, can seem doubly easy to break. Naturally, they will want to proceed with a careful, disciplined approach. In as much as these considerations match the concerns discussed earlier of the IT service groups and the PMO, the solutions described above should help.

Unlike the PMO and internal IT groups, however, IT service vendors are prone toward a further conflict with Agile warehouse projects, one that comes down to money. First, if the vendors cannot deliver as they have promised, it often affects their pay. This redoubles the intensity with which the vendors will view the risks that an Agile project might pose, and can make them consequently adamant that the ADW project switch to a traditional work breakdown schedule that commit the warehouse team "by contract" to a particular delivery schedule.

Secondly, service vendors have every incentive to steadily expand the scope of their services to the organization because it results in additional statements-of-work being added to their contracts. Any party primarily interested in more and longer statements-of-work will heavily prefer a waterfall-based method because the careful, to-be documentation and review components of plan-driven efforts require considerable time and labor, all of which increases the amount of services the vendor can bill.

Unabashed Agile teams might make loud displays of how they can save their organization's funding and avoid opportunity costs by eliminating much of the to-be documentation and review cycles of traditional methods. Such overt advertising will make ADW's contrast with the service vendor's approach very apparent to people such as company executives and IT management. Making this contrast so visible to such important players can make the external vendor quite defensive and transform it instantly into an adversary of the Agile warehouse team, often one with considerable clout.

Luckily, downplaying the Agile nature of the ADW project will avoid making this contrast so evident and go a long way towards keeping the peace with IT service vendors. As far as answering their demands that an ADW project provide more traditional work plans and progress reporting, the Scrum Master should add the vendors to the list that her Project Communication Assistant supplies with progress reports, relying on the backing curried with IT managers where these tactics do not suffice.

ADVERSITY FROM BUSINESS STAKEHOLDERS

Given the integrated nature of corporate information systems today, Agile warehouse teams will undoubtedly encounter some obtrusion from business managers outside their Product Owner's departments, managers who are nonetheless stakeholders in the outcome of the project. If their concerns are rebuffed without care, these business managers can develop an understandable resentment toward the Agile team and may choose to undermine the team's Product Owner. Because the opinions of functional group managers often carries much greater weight in the organization than that of the IT department, eliciting disfavor among this group is a problem that support from IT managers cannot easily counteract. Accordingly, interference from business stakeholders must be managed deftly from the start.

When they obtrude upon the ADW project, these business stakeholders will want say-so without responsibility. That is, they want to redirect the timing and planned functionality of the warehouse without having to provide resources that can make such changes achievable. The strategy for managing this challenge when it occurs is two fold. First, Agile Scrum Masters are wise to steer these business stakeholders to the Product Owner. Because the Product Owner sets the business objectives for the team's development work, it is only appropriate that all business-level concerns be voiced to her, so that she can incorporate these concerns into the next sprint's story conference.

For those situations that exceed what the project's Product Owner can contain, the Product Owner should redirect in turn the obtrusion "upstairs" into the organization's IT steering committee or portfolio management function. The executives that sit upon these bodies might agree that a change in direction is needed—in which case the resulting consensus among all managers will make the change a priority rather than a distraction for the team developers. Or the executives will demur, in which case the Product Owner will have political cover to continue on as planned. Either way, the stakeholder will have far less reason to resent the ADW project than if the Product Owner had tried to deny the request on her own authority.

The role of the ADW Scrum Master in this strategy is essentially preparatory—she must prepare her Product Owner to field complaints from business stakeholders and refer the serious ones to the governing board. If such a body does yet exist within the company, then Scrum Master and Product Owner would be wise to quickly cobble together something like it, say a "warehouse steering committee," to provide protection when these business stakeholders wish to interfere.

Adversity From Teammates

While all the sources of opposition cited above are important to manage well, the most devastating adversity that the ADW Scrum Master can encounter on a daily basis will arise from within her own team. The resistance from team members is sometimes direct, other times passive, and often not even perceived as opposition by the person providing the challenge. Managing such adversity will require all the "soft" project management skills a Scrum Master can muster and will prompt her to frequently remind the team of the reasons the Product Owner, IT managers, and the project's sponsors decided to try an Agile approach in the first place.

Especially for new teams, members will arrive at the Agile project with traditional waterfall-based methods firmly in their backgrounds. It is only natural to expect that their old habits will not evaporate immediately at the commencement of the first sprint. The vestigial thinking that the Scrum Master will recognize from the waterfall paradigm will be multifold. Her team members will want to introduce such "innovations" as:

- **Elaborating users stories during the story conference,** steering them toward "use cases" such as the Unified Process prescribes, or even toward full-blown requirements specification documents that will take months to complete
- **Estimating stories in "ideal time" only** rather than first using the far more accurate relative-size estimation with which detailed level-of-effort estimates can be cross-checked.
- **Pre-assigning names and deadlines on tasks** so they can make teammates "accountable," rather than moving to a paradigm where everyone contributes to the most important deliverables first, and everyone assumes a shared responsibility for avoiding failure
- **Transferring the lightweight status board to electronic tools** rather than keeping the teammates as free as possible from set-up intensive, time consuming, and single threaded duties

Mitigating Adversity from Team Members

Only the Scrum Master's leadership can answer the resistance to the Agile components of ADW among the members of her team. Though she is not a traditional "project manager," the Scrum Master is defined by the approach as "the steward of the process," so it is entirely expected that she should be directly involved with any decision about *how* the team will work. In this role, she must be able to articulate quickly during any part of the sprint why shifting back to waterfall techniques and mindsets will sooner or later under mine the velocity and effectiveness of the team. To achieve this capability, she will need a solid understanding of the weaknesses of the waterfall approach, many of which we have covered in this book. She must also develop a firm appreciation of motivations that have led so many innovative software departments around the world to develop and evangelize the dozen or so incremental and iterative development methods invented to date.

Upon this basis, several of the tools described above will help the Scrum Masters make their case. When it comes to avoiding "heavyweight" processes and tools, the risk exposure analysis introduced in this chapter provides a simple and lasting rationale explaining why, if the team is going to err, it should err on the side of less detailed planning rather than more, favoring working code instead.

When it comes to deflecting attempts to return exclusively to estimation in ideal time, Scrum Masters may need to drive their teammates toward a solid velocity number in story points through repeated sessions of estimating poker until it is clear how triangulating level-of-effort with story points estimates saves them from overcommitment and pain. Developers typically hate to estimate, so this realization should not be too hard to nurture if Scrum Masters simply insist on size-based estimation during for a few sprints. As a backstop, they can request behind the scenes that the Product Owners themselves insist on fast, size-based estimation during the story conference until the reluctant teammates see the advantages that solid estimation and velocity numbers hold for them.

Other absolute priorities for ADW Scrum Masters should be to the burndown charts, test-driven development, continuous integration testing, and self-documenting code modules. If they can keep their teams reaching for these objectives, the remaining attributes of Agile data warehousing should either become self-apparent or be replaced by some other innovation even more lightweight and effective than the Agile fundamentals we have explored in this book.

The one member of the team that will require particularly constant monitoring is the one that our Agile warehousing method added to the generic Scrum and XP approaches—the Project Communication Assistant. As envisioned by the Scrum Master, this role is simply to collate the objectives and progress information regarding a current sprint, reformat them for distribution outside the team, and deliver them to stakeholders around the enterprise such as IT management, IT service groups, and PMO managers of related projects.

However, with every communication they provide, these external parties will have an opportunity to express to the PCA how much the organization is depending upon the Agile team honoring its deadlines and providing the functionality the other projects absolutely require. The PCA will also have to suffer through criticism of the Agile approach should any of these parties become vexed with the lightweight nature of the ADW project. All told, this often emphatic feedback from the enterprise may be too much for the PCA to bear, making him forget the many reasons his team went Agile in the first place. Under constant criticism, he may actually turn against the Agile approach.

ADW Scrum Masters need to watch for symptoms of this unfortunate transformation in the PCA and indeed any of their team members who interface regularly with the external parties. The symptoms typically come back expressed as notions such as: "Projects should have detailed plans.... Projects should have formal specifications.... Agile is immature.... We need to add more 'structure' to our work." The Scrum Master will know that the PCA is beginning to buckle under outside pressure when he begins voicing these demands during team meetings. If left uncheck, PCAs may well suddenly demand that the team abandon Agile and start immediately on a detailed project plan with task level estimates in ideal time—all so that he can provide artifacts in the format external parties are demanding. PCAs with PMI-type training and waterfall project management experience may even strive to displace the Scrum Master, become the Project Manager, and transform the daily, collaborative scrum meeting into a hierarchical, daily status reporting session.

Hopefully, forewarned is forearmed. Scrum Masters understanding the pressure that PCAs might encounter while interfacing with external parties can take steps to support the

PCA. Our previous chapter on method maturity and this chapter's risk exposure analysis will provide the theoretical basis for shoring up the PCA's resolve to stick with Agile in the face of widespread criticism. Scrum Masters can also dilute this exposure by accompanying the PCA to important meetings or at least providing supportive debriefings after particularly intense interactions occur.

Luckily, if the Scrum Master can hold the line against the many forms of adversity surveyed in this chapter for just one release or so, the speed of delivery, the quality of results, and the high praise from the team's business-based Product Owner will combine to quickly dampen and even remove the opposition that Agile data warehousing can initially spark within the enterprise. Introducing high-speed and high-quality development methods into an organization is always hard and sometimes lonely work, but the benefits to the company and development team alike will make all the heartache entailed seem worth it.

About the Author

Ralph Hughes earned a Masters in Quantified Economics (statistical forecasting) from Stanford University. He has formal training in both Agile and traditional project management methodologies, being both a Certified Scrum Master and a Project Management Professional, as certified by the Project Management Institute. He is a founding member of the Worldwide Institute of Software Architects.

Starting data warehousing on a IBM mainframe in 1982 as a developer for the ARAMIS project at the Stanford Medical Center, he has gone on to lead numerous business intelligence projects, defining Agile data warehousing programs for Fortune 100 companies in the aerospace manufacturing, telecommunications, pharmaceutical, and biomedical industries. He founded Ceregenics in 1988 to serve as a shared venue for data warehousing customers and contractors to meet and collaborate on cutting-edge business intelligence projects.

Fluent in French, he lives in the Denver metropolitan area and works internationally as both a Scrum Coach and a Solutions Architect. He can be reached at Ceregenics 720.951.2100 or ralph.hughes@ceregenics.com.

Acronyms And Initialisms Used

ABEND	Abnormal End (a running program crashes from an unanticipated error)
ADW	Agile Data Warehousing (method)
ASCII	American Standard Code for Information Interchange
BOE	Basis of Estimate (cards containing standard tasks for each story type)
CMM	Capability Maturity Model (www.sei.cmu.edu)
CMMI	CMM Integration
CMMI-DEV	CMMI-Development
DA	Data Architect
DBA	Database Administrator
DBMS	Database Management System
DPI	Development Productivity Index
EIS	Enterprise Information Systems
ETL	Extract, Transform, and Load
ERD	Entity Relations Diagram (showing data tables with one-to-many and other relationships between them indicated by connecting lines)
IID	Iterative and Incremental Development
IS	Information Systems (department)
IT	Information Technology (department)
LOE	Level-of-Effort (usually an estimate of labor required)
NPV	Net Present Value
OLE	Original Labor Estimate

O&M	Operations and Maintenance
PCA	Project Communications Assistant
PFD	Process Flow Diagram (especially as a re-projection of an ADW tiered data model)
PMBOK	Project Management Body of Knowledge [PMI 2004]
PCI	percent confidence intervals
PMI	Project Management Institute (www.pmi.org)
PMO	Project (or Program) Management Office
RLE	Remaining Labor Estimate
ROI	Return on Investment
RTM	Requirements Traceability Matrix
SEI	Software Engineering Institute
SME	Subject Mater Expert (especially a provider of user requirements)
SMU	(User) Story Management Utility
TDM	Tiered Data Models (an ADW coinage, see Chapter 5)
UAT	User Acceptance Testing
WBS	Work Breakdown Structure (PMI-style project task list)
XP	Extreme Programming (Agile approach)

References

Adelman, Sid. 2002. Impossible *Data Warehouse Situations: Solutions from the Experts.* Boston: Addison-Wesley.

Advanced Development Methods (ADM). 1995. *Controlled Chaos : Living on the Edge.* http://www.controlchaos.com/download/Living on the Edge.pdf (accessed February 2007).

Ambler, Scott and Pramodkumar Sadalage. 2006. *Refactoring Databases: Evolutionary Database Design.* Boston: Addison-Wesley.

Anderson, David. 2005. *Stretching Agile to fit CMMI Level 3.* http://www.agilemanagement.net/Articles/Papers/Agile_2005_Paper_DJA_v1_6.pdf, (accessed August 2007).

Anderson, David. 2005a. *MSF for CMMI.* http://www.agilemanagement.net/Articles/Weblog/MSFforCMMI.html (accessed August 2007).

Augustine, Sanjiv. 2005. *Managing Agile Projects.* Upper Saddle River, NJ: Prentice Hall.

Beck, Kent and Cynthia Andres. 2004. *Extreme Programming Explained: Embrace Change* (2nd Edition), Boston: Addison-Wesley.

Behrens, Pete. 2005. "Scrum Gathering—Enterprise Adoption." *Agile Executive Blog.* http://trailridgeconsulting.com/blog/?m=200511 (accessed Feb 2007).

Beck, Kent and Martin Fowler. 2001. *Planning Extreme Programming.* Boston: Addison-Wesley.

Berson, Alex and Larry Dubov. 2007. *Master Data Management and Customer Data Integration for a Global Enterprise.* Emeryville, CA: McGraw-Hill Osborne Media.

Boehm, Barry. 1988. Spiral Model of Software Development and Enhancement. *Computer;* 21, no. 5 (May 1988): 61-72, http://sunset.usc.edu/csse/TECHRPTS/1988/usccse1988-500/usccse1988-500.pdf (accessed Feb 2006).

Boehm, Barry and Richard Turner. 2003. *Balancing Agility and Discipline: A Guide for the Perplexed*. Boston: Addison Wesley.

Braue, David. 2004. *Certification: What's in a name?* (Part 2). http://www.zdnetasia.com/builder/manage/work/0,39045585,39198089,00.htm (accessed August 2007).

C3 Team. 1998. "Chrysler Goes To Extremes." *Distributed Computing*. http://www.xprogramming.com/publications/dc9810cs.pdf (accessed Feb 2007).

Camerer, C. F., and Johnson, E. J. 1991. "The process-performance paradox in expert judgment: How can experts know so much and predict so badly?" In K. A. Ericsson & J. Smith (Eds.), *Towards A General Theory Of Expertise: Prospects And Limits*. New York: Cambridge Press.

Chrissis, Mary Beth, Mike Konrad, and Sandy Shrum. 2006. *CMMI: Guidelines for Process Integration and Product Improvement* (2nd edition). Boston: Addison-Wesley.

Clements, Paul. 2002. *Documenting Software Architectures: Views and Beyond*. Boston: Addison-Wesley Professional.

Cockburn, Alistair. 2001. *Writing Effective Use Cases*. Boston: Addison-Wesley.

Cohn, Mike. 2005. *Agile Estimating and Planning*. Upper Saddle River, NJ: Prentice Hall.

Control Chaos. 2007. *Controlled-Chaos Software Development*. http://www.controlchaos.com/download/Controlled-Chaos Software Development.pdf (accessed February 2007).

Crispin, Lisa and Tip House. 2003. *Testing Extreme Programming*. Boston: Addision Wesley.

Date, C.J., Hugh Darwen, and Nikos Lorentzos. 2002. *Temporal Data & the Relational Model*. Burlington, MA: Morgan Kaufmann Publishers.

Date, C.J. 2005. *Database in Depth: Relational Theory for Practitioners*. Sebastopol, CA: O'Reilly Media.

DeMarco, Tom. 1986. *Controlling Software Projects* (1st edition). Upper Saddle River, NJ: Prentice Hall.

Goldratt, Eliyahu. 1990. *Theory of Constraints*. Great Barrington, MA: North River Press.

Goode, Erica. 2000 "Among the Inept, Researchers Discover, Ignorance Is Bliss," New York Times, January 18, 2000, http://www.nytimes.com/library/national/science/health/011800hth-behavior-incompetents.html, accessed Apr 2007.

Gregor Hohpe, Gregor and Bobby Woolf. 2004. Enterprise Integration Patterns: Designing, Building, and Deploying Messaging Solutions. Boston: Addison-Wesley.

Hihn, Jairus and Karen T. Lum. 2002. *Improving Software Size Estimates by Using Probabilistic Pairwise Comparison Matrices.* http://trs-new.jpl.nasa.gov/dspace/bitstream/2014/37964/1/04-0903.pdf (accessed April 2007).

Hoest, Martin and Claes Wohlin, 1998. "An Experimental Study of Individual Subjective Effort Estimations and Combinations of the Estimates." In *20th International Conference on Software Engineering (ICSE'98).* http://doi.ieeecomputersociety.org/10.1109/ICSE.1998.671386 (accessed March 2007).

Humphries, Mark. 1998. *Data Warehousing: Architecture and Implementation.* Upper Saddle River, NJ: Prentice Hall.

Imhoff, Claudia. 1999. "The Corporate Information Factory." *DM Review* (December 1999). http://www.dmreview.com (accessed May 2007).

Inmon Bill, Claudia Imhoff, and Ryan Sousa. 2001. *Corporate Information Factory* (2nd edition). New York: John Wiley & Sons.

Jacobson, Ivar. Grady Booch, and James Rumbaugh. 1999. *The Unified Software Development Process* (1st edition). Boston: Addison-Wesley.

Jørgenson, Magne. et al. 2000. Human Judgment in Effort Estimation of Software Projects, *Proceedings of the 22nd International Conference on Software Engineering.* http://www.cs.uvic.ca/icse2000/papers/2_Survey/p12.pdf (accessed March 2007).

Jørgenson, Magne. et al. 2004. "A Review of Studies on Expert Estimation of Software Development Effort." *Document Actions Journal of Systems and Software* 70, no. 1-2:37-60. http://www.simula.no/research/engineering/publications (accessed March 2007).

Jørgenson, Magne and Dag Sjøberg. 2006. *Expert Estimation of Software Development Work: Learning through Feedback.* http://www.simula.no/research/engineering/publications (accessed March 2007).

Kimball, Ralph et al. 1998. *The Data Warehouse Lifecycle Toolkit*. New York: John Wiley & Sons, Inc.

Larman, Craig. 2004. *Agile And Iterative Development : A Manager's Guide*. Upper Saddle River, NJ: Pearson Education.

Little, Todd. 2004. *Agility, Uncertainty, and Software Project Estimation*. http://www.agilealliance.org/show/1418 (accessed Mar 2007).

Lum, Karen and Jairus Hihn. 2002. *Estimation of Software Size and Effort Distributions Using Paired Ratio Comparison Matrices*. http://trs-new.jpl.nasa.gov/dspace/bitstream/2014/7276/1/03-1005.pdf (accessed Apr 2007).

Leach, Lawrence. 2000 Lawrence P. Leach, *Critical Chain Project Management*, Norwood, MA: Artech House Publishers.

McCarthy, Jim. 2006. *Dynamics of Software Development*. Redmond, WA: Microsoft Press.

Miranda, Eduardo. 2000. "Improving subjective estimations using the paired comparisons method." *International Forum on COCOMO and Software Cost Estimation*. http://sunset.usc.edu/Activities/oct24-27-00/Presentations/Miranda.pdf(accessed Mar 2007).

Mowbray, Thomas J. Mowbray and Raphael Malveau. 2003. *Software Architect Bootcamp* (2nd edition). Upper Saddle River, NJ: Prentice Hall.

Mulcahy, Rita. 2003. *Risk Management, Tricks of the Trade for Project Managers*. Minneapolis, MN: RMC Publications.

National Aeronautics and Space Administration (NASA). 2004. *Process Asset Library, ISD Wideband Delphi Estimation* (document: 580-PR-016-01). http://software.gsfc.nasa.gov/AssetsApproved/PA1.2.1.2.pdf (accessed Apr 2007).

Object Management Group (OMG). 2004. *TOGAF ADM and MDA—The Power of Synergy*. http://www.omg.org/docs/omg/04-06-01.pdf, accessed May 2007.

Object Management Group (OMG). 2003. *MDA Guide, Version 1.0*. http://www.omg.org/docs/omg/03-06-01.pdf (accessed May 2007).

Object Management Group (OMG). 2007. *Catalog of OMG Modeling and Metadata Specifications*. http://www.omg.org/technology/documents/modeling_spec_catalog.htm (accessed May 2007).

Oestereich, Bernd and Christian Weiss. 2006. *Timeboxing—Spine of agile projects*. http://www.isqi.org/isqi/deu/conf/conquest/2006/slides/B3.pdf (accessed Feb 2007).

Poole, John. 2003. *Common Warehouse Metamodel Developer's Guide*. New York: John Wiley & Sons.

Project Management Institute. 2003. *Organizational Project Management Maturity Model (OPM3®) Knowledge Foundation*. Newtown Square, PA: Project Management Institute.

Project Management Institute. 2004. *A Guide to the Project Management Body of Knowledge (PMBOK)*(3rd ed.) Newtown Square, PA: Project Management Institute.

Royce, Winston W. 1970. "Managing The Development Of Large Software Systems." *Proceedings, IEEE WESCON, August 1970*. New York: Institute of Electrical and Electronics Engineers.

Schwaber, Ken. 2004. *Agile Project Management with Scrum*. Redmond, WA:. Microsoft Press.

Software Engineering Institute (SEI). 2006. *CMMI for Development* (v1.2). http://www.sei.cmu.edu/cmmi/models (accessed August 2007).

Software Engineering Institute (SEI). 2006a. *Standard CMMI Appraisal Method for Process Improvement (SCAMPI)* (v1.2). http://www.sei.cmu.edu/cmmi/appraisals/index.html (accessed August 2007).

Software Engineering Institute (SEI). 2006b. *Published CMMI Appraisal Results, BoldTech Level 4*. http://sas.sei.cmu.edu/pars/pars_detail.aspx?a=8314 (accessed August 2007).

Takeuchi, Hirotaka and Ikujiro Nonaka. 1986. "The New New Product Development Game." *Harvard Business Review*, 137-146 (Jan.-Feb. 1986).

The Standish Group International. 1995. *The Chaos Report*. http://www.standishgroup.com (accessed February 2007).

The Standish Group International. 1999. *Chaos: A Recipe for Success*. http://www.standishgroup.com (accessed April 2006).

Thelliez, Thierry. 2006. *Scrum*. http://www.abqspin.org/PastMeetings/SPIN_SCRUM Presentation.ppt (accessed Feb 2006).

Tuckman, Bruce. 1965. "Developmental sequence in small groups." *Psychological Bulletin*, 63, 384-399.

Index

adversity to Agile approaches
    from business stakeholders, 279-280
    from IT functional groups, 273
    from IT managers, 254-255
    from IT vendors, 278-279
    from Project Communication Assistant, 282-283
    from project management offices, 269-271
    from teammates, 280-281

Agile alliance
    manifesto, 9, 24
    twelve principles, 24-25

Agile Data Warehousing (ADW)
    advantages and benefits, 14, 24, 49-54, 265-267
        see also Agile methods, advantages
    changes to normal IT practices, 2
    components, 19
    cycles within. *see* cycles
    disadvantages. *see* Agile methods, disadvantages
    evolution not revolution, 15-16
    impact upon CMMI-DEV, 17
    impact upon PMI PMBOK, 15-17
    method maturity, 232-245
    retrospective as process change board, 44
    short definition, 1, 10-13
    stages to team maturity, 14, 188-195
    tracking progress, 37, 134-135

Agile methods
    advantages, 255-265
    disadvantages, 267-269
    successful formal implementations, 230-232

architecture, achieving quality, 35

automated and continuous integration testing (ACIT). *see* testing

automation levels. *see* user epic decomposition

audits, 150, 218, 225, 231, 248

back end, definition, 20

basis-of-estimate (BOE) cards, 98, 101, 104, 109-110, 113, 115, 125, 139, 144, 193, 235

best-practices, 52, 217, 231, 249

big bang approach, Inmon-esque, 5

buffers. *see* critical chain

burndown charts, 39, 111-119
    perfect line, 112, 113
    measuring velocity, 40, 117-122
    typical patterns, 113-115

business intelligence, definition, 20

business rules
    implications for team partitioning, 199-201
    managing complex instances, 34, 49, 80-82, 86, 114, 178, 180, 185
    posing a serious challenge, 6, 76, 113-114, 153, 156
    validation of, 12, 80, 152, 156-164

business stakeholders
    managing adversity from, 279-280
    communicating with, 183-184

Chaos Reports. *see* Standish Group

Capability Maturity Model (CMM and CMMI-DEV)
    ADW as a pre-process, 246-248
    ADW providing what CCM requires, 232-245, 249-250
    as overkill, 224-225
    compliant Agile methods, 230-232
    flexible, allowing iteration, 226-229
    generic goals and practices, 222
    maturity levels defined, 221
    overview, 217-223
    process areas, 219, 220
    sample specific practices, 226

colocation of team members, 11, 25, 33, 212-213
commit line, 30-32
compliance, 44, 53, 253, 257, 270
    architectural, 35, 266
    CMM, 18, 46, 217-218, 224-225, 232, 246-248
continual improvement, 43, 73, 221, 249, 270
critical chain
    accelerates projects, 205, 207-208
    buffer recovery, 208-209
    buffers, types and properly combining, 207
    definition and overview, 203-209
    for scaling Scrum. *see* scaling ADW
critical path project management, definition and problems, 204
customers
    impatience, 5
    learning curves, 8
cycles, in ADW
    sprints. *see* sprints
    development, 28
    estimation, 102-104
    release, 27
    verbalization, 66-73
cycles, in waterfall projects
    disappointment, 4-5
    specification and review, 6

daily scrums. *see* scrums, daily
dashboards, 84
data architect, responsibilities, 177-179
data architectural layers
    end user access, 79
    enterprise translation, 276-278
    integration, 76
    presentation, 78-79
    staging, 76
data integration, supporting enterprise initiatives, 276-278
data topology chart, 202

data warehousing, definition, 20

decoupling, ADW teams, 198-201

design by exception, 193

developers, responsibilities, 181

development performance index (DPI), 261-264

development phase. *see* sprints

disappointment cycle, waterfall method, 4-5

documentation
- as-built, 140, 144, 145, 146, 148, 276
- automated, 18, 170, 181, 282
- by exception, 193
- optimal level 49, 50, 67, 74, 136, 177, 225, 233
- to-be, wasteful and short-lived, 6-7, 11-12, 29-30, 49-50, 62, 148, 185, 259, 275, 279

done, defining the word for teams, 33, 138-139, 144, 145

end user access layer. *see* data architectural layers

enterprise translation. *see* data architectural layers, enterprise translation

epics. *see* user stories

error recycling, 71, 81

essentially correct and fault tolerant. *see* quality assurance

estimation
- ADW's approach, 98-104
- ADW's size-to-hours triangulation, 92, 108, 111, 281
- causes of inaccurate forecasts, 95-98
- consistency with ADW, 108-110
- damage by inaccurate forecasts, 93
- ideal time, 105-106, 108
- developing team skills, 11
- original labor estimates (OLE), 32, 112
- proper pooling of developer padding, 207
- re-estimation after release planning, 110-111
- remaining labor estimates (RLE), 39, 112
- size-based, 31
- traditional approaches, 94-95
- twelve objectives, 101
- with reference models, 144
    - *see also* story points; basis-of-estimate cards

estimation poker, 106-108

extract, transform, and load (ETL), in general, 8, 20

extreme programming (XP)
- as standard adjunct to Scrum, 23-24
- borrowed components, 34-35

fault tolerance. *see* quality assurance

fears, addressing those of stakeholders, 54-56

front end, definition, 20-21

geographical barriers, 212-215
- choosing, 213
- overcoming, 214-215

group think, 97

ideal time. *see* estimation

immaturity, countering the label, 223-233

incompetence, invisible to incompetents, 97

incremental and iterative development (IID) methods, 23, 26

incremental loads, 71, 81

infrastructure, addressing challenges, 5

integration and test engineer, responsibilities, 181

integration layer. *see* data architectural layers

I.N.V.E.S.T criteria. *see* user stories

Information Technology (IT) departments
- adversity from its external vendors, 278-279
- adversity from its managers, 254-255
- adversity from its functional groups, 273

iterations. *see* sprints

layers, architectural. *see* data architectural layers

lessons learned, capturing, 27, 60, 94, 139, 243, 245, 249, 250, 253, 271

level-of-effort estimation. *see* estimation

maximizing the work not done, xiii, 2, 25, 106, 138, 145, 148, 163

meta scrums, 197, 202-203, 210-211, 233, 236, 242-243, 245-246, 249

methods, in general
- choosing between plan-driven and adaptive, 225
  - *see also* risk exposure analysis
- contrasted with "approach", 20
- desirable goals, 9

multiplexing, re-sequencing tasks, 170, 228-229, 239, 248

original labor estimates (OLE). *see* estimation

patterns. *see* quality assurance

perfect line. *see* burndown charts

performance, balancing against clarity, 136-137

pharmaceutical project, as an example, 201-204, 208

pipelined delivery squads, 12-13, 128, 164-172, 188, 194, 238
- impact upon measuring velocity, 171-172

PMI/PMBOK, 15
- as wrapper around ADW, 17, 233
- origin of approach, 16
- project charter, 233, 235, 247-248

potentially shippable code, 11, 15, 21, 26-28, 30, 35, 42, 53-54, 84, 124, 138, 147, 149, 167, 169, 182, 195, 201, 272, 276

presentation layer. *see* data architectural layers

prime directive, for sprint retrospectives, 36

process flow diagrams, 132-134

product integration *see* ADW, component integration

product owner, responsibilities, 174-175

program management, xiii, 1, 236
- using critical chain, 109, 209-210

progress, tracking, 37-42, 111

project communication assistant (PCA)
- adversity from, 282-283
- responsibilities, 183-185

project plans, 207, 255, 282
    and CMM, 219, 224, 234-236, 247
    traditional, problems with, 5, 7-8, 51, 55, 185, 198

project/program management office (PMO), adversity from, 269-270

promotion of code and objects, 146

provably correct. *see* quality assurance

quality assurance, 138-164
    essentially correct and fault tolerant, 150-2, 160, 163, 175, 195, 201
    overview, 138-139
    provably correct, 150
    using patterns, 139-144
    using reference models. *see* reference models

re-estimation, after release planning.
    see estimation

reference models, 3, 12, 98, 136, 138-148, 169, 177, 180, 181, 188, 192-193, 235, 239, 266, 275

refresh frequencies. *see* user epic decomposition

refresh types. *see* user epic decomposition

release cycle. *see* cycles, in ADW

release pool, 54, 74, 195, 201

release candidate. *see* release pool

release planning, 12, 41-42, 191-192
    defer for new teams, 104, 197-198

remaining labor estimates (RLE). *see* estimation

requirements
    business rules, 6
    non-functional, 175-176
    traditional, 59-61
    under ADW. *see* user stories

requirements traceability matrix (RTM), 59-60, 238, 240

retrospectives. *see* sprints

return on investment (ROI), 3, 256, 260-265

review cycles. *see* cycles, in ADW

risk exposure analysis
    adapted for Agile methods, 258-260
    standard, 257-258

risks, 6
    choosing proper level, 258
    opportunity costs v. product flaws, 257

roles and responsibilities
    data architect, 177-179
    developers, 181
    integration and test engineer, 181
    product owner, 174-175
    project communication assistant (PCA), 183-185
    scrum master, 43-44, 182
    senior OLAP developer, 180
    solutions architect, 175-177

scaling ADW, 195-198
    generic scrum too lightweight to scale, 201-203
    using critical chain, 203, 209-212
    using meta scrums, 196-197

scope, choosing boundaries for processes and modules, 130-134

scope creep, 120
    tracking, 40-41, 121-122

scrum, generic approach
    basic components, 24-29, 189
    history, 46-47
    scaling, 201-203

scrum master, responsibilities, 43-44, 182

scrums, daily 15-minute stand-up meeting, 29, 33
    standard questions, 39, 116

Software Engineering Institute (SEI). *see* CMM

self-documenting code. *see* documentation

self-organizing teams, 11, 33

senior OLAP developer, responsibilities, 180

single-pass efforts. *see* waterfall methods

snapshots. *see* user epic decomposition

solutions architect, responsibilities, 175-177
specification cycle. *see* cycles, in ADW
spikes. *see* sprints, non-standard
sprint zero. *see* sprints, non-standard
sprints, 28-37
    development phase, 32
    retrospectives, 36
    story conferences, 30-31
    time boxes, 28
    task planning sessions, 31-32
    user demos, 35-36
sprints, non-standard
    spikes, 45
    sprint zero, 44-45
staging layer. *see* data architectural layers
Standish Group, Chaos reports, 3, 47, 92, 256, 263
story cards, 30, 36-37, 42, 61-63, 67, 197, 238
story conference. *see* sprints
story points, 31, 105
    versus ideal time, 104-106
stretch goals, 31, 119

table types, defined
    fact, 79
    fundamental, 77
    historical dimensional, 78
    linking, 77
    linking history, 77
    non-historical dimensional, 78
    reference, 77
target layers. *see* user epic decomposition
task boards, 37-39, 42-43, 51, 112, 125, 134-135, 181, 197, 215
    column definitions, 37-38, 108, 147, 170
task cards, 31-32, 35
    aid to continual optimization, 104
    capturing tech debt, 35, 36

　　　　estimated RLEs, 39, 43, 103, 112-115, 125
　　　　organizing work, 37, 43, 131
　　　　tracking status, 37-38, 134, 148-149, 174
task planning. *see* sprints

teammates, adversity from, 280-281

teams, maturity levels, 13-14

team roles. *see* roles and responsibilities

tech debt, 35-36, 44-45, 89-90

testing
　　　　ADW's requirements 150-153, 155
　　　　automated and continuous integration testing (ACIT), 13, 149-150, 153, 163-164, 195
　　　　business rules, 156-157
　　　　drill down through data layers, 155-156
　　　　front ends in particular, 160-163
　　　　rule of threes, 157
　　　　scenarios, 124, 139, 153-156, 158, 160, 164, 187, 238, 263
　　　　schematic plan for ACIT facility, 159-160
　　　　shared responsibility, 185-187
　　　　strategy for overcoming complexity, 153-157
　　　　test data repository (TDR), 157-159

test-led development, 12, 147-148, 192-193
　　　　typical work pattern, 148-149

themes. *see* user stories

theory of constraints, 47

tiered data model (TDM), 128-132, 135

time boxes. *see* sprints

training, ADW teams, 146-147

two-to-one (2-to-1) design, 34

unknowns, tackling, 5

upgrades, easing testing, 146

user demos. *see* sprints

user friendliness. *see* user epic decomposition

user epic decomposition, 11, 71, 75-85, 190-191
　　　　automation types, 71
　　　　refresh frequencies, 71, 81

refresh types, 71
target layers, 71, 76-79
transformation types, 82
snapshots, 71, 80
user friendliness, 71, 83
value chains, 85-88

user requirements. *see* user stories

user stories
epics and themes, 63-65
generic, 61-63
I.N.V.E.S.T. criteria for quality, 62
management utility (SMU), 88-91
prioritization, 28, 30, 37, 191
see also user epic decomposition

validation
authoring scripts, 171, 180, 193
front ends, 160-163
requirements for, 151-152, 158
to meet CMM requirementsm 220, 221, 227-228, 239-240, 242, 248
under ADW, 12, 13, 83, 134, 148-164, 170, 171, 181, 185-187, 194
under generic scrum, 38, 43
via automated and continuous integration testing, 187, 195, 239

verbalization cycle
for product owner, 66-73
integrating with generic Scrum, 74

velocity
measuring, 116-122
setting for a new team, 119
team's "one true metric", 123-124

verification, 16, 21, 170, 220, 227, 231, 240, 242, 266

waterfall methods, 2
as a mistake from the start, 48
as a single-pass effort, 95-96
typical, lamentable outcomes, 3-8

WISCY (why isn't someone coding yet?), 60

978-0-595-47167-6
0-595-47167-6

Printed in the United Kingdom by
Lightning Source UK Ltd., Milton Keynes
137766UK00002B/150/P